Criminal Competency on Trial

Criminal Competency on Trial
The Case of Colin Ferguson

Mark C. Bardwell

Bruce A. Arrigo

CAROLINA ACADEMIC PRESS

Durham, North Carolina

Portions of Chapters 1 and 2 and the Introduction are taken from
Competency to Stand Trial: A Law, Psychology and Policy Assessment,
published in *The Journal of Psychiatry and Law*, 30(2).

ISBN: 0-89089-070-6
LCCN: 2002106613

CAROLINA ACADEMIC PRESS
700 Kent Street
Durham, North Carolina 27701
Telephone (919) 489-7486
Fax (919)493-5668
www.cap-press.com

Printed in the United States of America

For my parents, my brothers John and Matt, and for Terri:
I profess my deepest thanks to each of you
for your moral and unwavering support

For Al, Phyllis, Aaron, and Becca:
Thank you for your friendship, love, and support

Contents

Preface

.

Competency to stand trial (CST) determinations require an adherence to legal adjudication standards and psychological assessments methods. However, the forensic decision making on these matters is fraught with complex and enduring dilemmas. Thus, this book critically examines the legal and psychological pitfalls attributable to the CST determination. By revisiting the CST psycholegal dynamics in the controversial and well-publicized case of Mr. Colin Ferguson, the New York City railway gunman, *Criminal Competency on Trial* thoughtfully reviews and systematically discusses an array of policy implications on trial fitness for purposes of future criminal justice reform in the mental health arena.

To situate the overall analysis, the text skillfully explores an array of topics pertaining to competency determinations; including, the jurisprudential history of and the conceptual confusion surrounding the doctrine; the vague and ambiguous nature of the precedent-setting U.S. Supreme Court case law on mental illness and competency; the evolving CST assessment instruments and their relative strengths and limitations; and paranoid and delusional mental health disorders, impacting current and problematic CST evaluation practices. Based on this commentary, the high profile case of Colin Ferguson is thoroughly explored, focusing most especially on the defendant's pretrial competency hearing. Following the case study, the authors provide a psychological and legal analysis, demonstrating where and how unstructured CST assessment practices and problematic legal standards produced a troubling competency-to-stand-trial finding for this paranoid and delusional defendant. In the wake of the analysis, a series of (criminal justice policy) reforms are discussed. These reforms call for noteworthy changes in the judicial interpretation of CST clinical-forensic assessment practices, and recommend a series of provocative and timely legal remedies or strategies made available to the accused.

Going well beyond the isolated case of the New York City railway gunman, *Criminal Competency on Trial* demonstrates how the CST limitations in the Ferguson case are not the exception but are more often the rule, given the everyday realities of defendants whose trial fitness is called into question. To document this position, the high stakes and controversial case of Theodore Kaczynski, the unabomber, is also provisionally examined.

Suitable for students, academicians, and practitioners of mental health law and criminal justice policy, *Criminal Competency on Trial* methodically investigates one of the more complex and thorny issues impacting the mental health and justice systems today. Appropriate for upper division undergraduates and entering graduate students, the text can be used for course adoption purposes in such classes as Criminal Behavior, Criminal Justice Policy, Famous Trials of the 20th Century, Criminal Justice and the Law, Courts and the Legal System, and Psychology, Law, and Public Policy.

About the Authors

MARK C. BARDWELL, Ph.D. received his doctoral degree from the Institute of Psychology, Law and Public Policy at Alliant International University (formerly the California School of Professional Psychology), with concentrations in criminal and legal policy analysis and forensic psychology. His previously published work has appeared in *Criminal Justice Policy Review* and the *Journal of Psychiatry & Law*. Dr. Bardwell lives and works in Fresno, California, specializing in trial consultation.

BRUCE A. ARRIGO, Ph.D. is Professor and Chair of the Department of Criminal Justice at the University of North Carolina-Charlotte, with Adjunct Professor appointments in the Public Policy Program and the Psychology Department respectively. Formerly the Director of the Institute of Psychology, Law, and Public Policy at the California School of Professional Psychology-Fresno, Dr. Arrigo began his professional career as a community organizer and social activist for the homeless, the mentally ill, the working poor, the frail elderly, the decarcerated, and the chemically addicted. Dr. Arrigo received his Ph.D. from Pennsylvania State University, and he holds a master's degree in psychology and in sociology. He is the author of more than (100) journal articles, academic book chapters, and scholarly essays exploring theoretical and applied topics in critical criminology, criminal justice and mental health, and socio-legal studies. He is the author, coauthor, or editor of eight (8) books; including, *Madness, Language, and the Law* (1993), *The Contours of Psychiatric Justice* (1996), *Social Justice/Criminal Justice* (1998), *The Dictionary of Critical Social Sciences* (with T.R. Young, 1999), *Introduction to Forensic Psychology* (2000), *Law, Psychology, and Justice* (with Christopher R. Williams, 2001), *The Power Serial Rapist* (with Dawn J. Graney, 2001), and *Punishing the Mentally Ill: A Critical Analysis of Law and Psychiatry* (2002). He is presently completing a textbook titled, *Criminal Behavior: A Sys-*

tems Perspective. Dr. Arrigo is the past Editor of *Humanity & Society* and founding and acting Editor of the peer-reviewed quarterly, *Journal of Forensic Psychology Practice*. He was recently named the Critical Criminologist of the Year (2000), sponsored by the Critical Criminology Division of the American Society of Criminology. He is also a Fellow of the American Psychological Association, sponsored by the Law-Psychology Division of the APA.

Criminal Competency on Trial

Introduction

Competency to Stand Trial: An Overview

Although often a pretrial complication,[1] competency to stand trial (CST) evaluations are, quantitatively speaking, "the most significant mental health inquiry pursued in the system of criminal law."[2] The concept that an incompetent defendant can not be tried,

---

1. *See generally* B. Winick, *Restructuring Competency to Stand Trial*, 32 UCLA L. Rev. 921–985 (1985) [hereinafter Winick I].

2. A. STONE, MENTAL HEALTH AND THE LAW; A SYSTEM IN TRANSITION 200 (DHEW Pub. No. (ADM) 75-176, 1975). CST "significance" stems from the number of defendants affected by its application, the many instances and ease by which CST evaluations can be applied, and the outcome of CST evaluations. *Id.* at 200; Winick I, *supra* note 1, at 922. The number of criminal defendants who undergo CST evaluations is not clearly known, much less the outcome breakdown accurately estimated. The most recent data available concern Steadman and Hartstone's 1978 study, reporting that 6420 defendants were admitted to forensic hospitals for restoration of incompetence. Steadman and Hartstone estimated that about 1 in 4 CST evaluations result in a finding of incompetence and approximately 25,000 defendants underwent CST evaluations in 1978. Steadman & Hartstone, *Defendants Incompetent to Stand Trial*, in MENTALLY DISORDERED OFFENDERS: PERSPECTIVES FROM LAW AND SOCIAL SCIENCE 39, 41 (J. Monahan & H. Steadman eds. 1983).

The study presumed that all defendants adjudicated incompetent were admitted to mental hospitals for competency restoration. In reality, however, mentally ill defendants are often treated for incompetence in an out-patient setting. In some cases of seriously mentally ill defendants with misdemeanor charges, individuals are immediately dismissed and civilly committed. These observations suggest an underestimate regarding the 1978 survey. Indeed, in a recent 50-state survey, Grisso et al. (1994) asked forensic directors to predict the annual number of evaluations of competence to stand trial. Estimated figures ranged from 24,000 to 39,000. *See* T. Grisso, J. Cocozza, H. Steadman, W. Fisher, & A. Greer, *The Organization of Pretrial Forensic Evaluation Services: A National Profile*, 18 LAW AND HUMAN BEHAVIOR, 377 (1994).

convicted, or punished has long since been part of the American system of criminal law.[3] Indeed, it has deep roots in English common law.[4]

The modern formulation of criminal trial competency is set forth by the Supreme Court in *Dusky v. United States* (1960).[5] Broadly speaking, the *Dusky* decision requires competency or fitness to focus on two-prongs: (a) the defendant's present ability to communicate with counsel and (b) the defendant's present ability to understand the criminal proceedings.[6] Shortly after *Dusky*, the Supreme Court added detail to the competency doctrine and recognized potential due process violations with respect to competency matters and one's Fourteenth Amendment right to a fair trial.[7] In a series of decisions, the Supreme Court established procedural requirements relating to CST hearings[8] and CST evaluations.[9] These decisions require judges to carefully examine all evidence on the question of

---

3. *See* C. Foote, *A Comment on Pre-Trial Commitment of Criminal Defendants*, 108 U. PA. L. REV. 832, 834 (1960).

4. *See* GROUP FOR THE ADVANCEMENT OF PSYCHIATRY, COMMITTEE ON PSYCHIATRY, MISUSE OF PSYCHIATRY IN THE CRIMINAL COURTS: COMPETENCY TO STAND TRIAL 912–915 (1974) [hereinafter GAP].

5. *See* B. Winick, *Incompetency to Stand Trial: Developments in the Law*, in MENTALLY DISORDERED OFFENDERS: PERSPECTIVES FROM LAW AND SOCIAL SCIENCE 3, 5 (John Monahan & Henry Steadman eds. 1983) [hereinafter Winick II]. The *Dusky* decision broadened the construct from one that concentrated on the cognitive abilities to include criteria that recognized the defendant's ability to consult with counsel. *Id.* at 4. *See also* Winick I *supra* note 1, at 923.

6. *See* Dusky v. United States, 362 U.S. 402 (1960). In *Dusky* the competency doctrine received constitutional acknowledgment with respect to the Sixth Amendment and a defendant's right to a fair trial. The Court's rationale was that an incompetent defendant would be unable to assist in his or her own defense and, therefore, would be unable to receive a fair trial. *Id.* at 402. *Dusky's* landmark decision has since come to be the standard in federal court and currently every state uses some variation of the *Dusky* standard. *See* T. Grisso, *Pretrial Clinical Evaluation in Criminal Cases: Past Trends and Future Directions*, 23 Criminal Justice and Behavior, 90, 91 (1996) [hereafter Grisso I].

7. *See* Massey v. Moore, 348 U.S. 105, 108 (1954).

8. *See* Pate v. Robinson, 383 U.S. 375 (1966). Ruled that a defendant has the constitutional right to an adequate hearing when evidence raises a doubt regarding the defendant's competency. *Id.* at 375.

9. Drope v. Missouri, 420 U.S. 162 (1975). Ruled that the court must raise the competency issue itself when there is a "bona fide doubt" as to the defendant's competency. *Id.* at 162.

trial fitness and order competency hearings, when necessary, during all phases of the trial process.[10] In addition to addressing and resolving fitness inquiries in a timely manner,[11] these rules are intended to promote an accurate, fair, and dignified trial process.[12] Despite the added detail, criminal competency matters present complicated pre-trial inquiries that are sometimes not easily resolved.[13] Indeed, most jurisdictions encounter problems when issues relative to competency to stand trial are raised.[14]

Problems on the subject of competency are well documented,[15] in both social science[16] and legal commentary.[17] A central theme underlying these limitations are the legal standards that define criminal competency as well as the pretrial assessment instruments employed to arrive at the CST determination.[18] The emergence of research surrounding this psycholegal matter is of particular interest when examining the competency construct itself.[19] For example,

---

10. *See E.g., Id*; Pate v. Robinson, 383 U.S. 375 (1966). Failure to adhere to these directions will likely quash any resulting conviction. *See* AMERICAN BAR ASSOCIATION CRIMINAL JUSTICE MENTAL HEALTH STANDARDS, standard 7-4.2 c and accompanying commentary (1986)[hereinafter ABA].

11. R. Bonnie, *The Competence of Criminal Defendants: A Theoretical Reformulation*, 10 BEHAVIORAL SCI. & L. 292 (1992)[hereafter Bonnie I].

12. *See* Winick & DeMeo, *Competency to Stand Trial in Florida*, 35 U. MIAMI L. REV. 31 (1980); S. Brakel & R. Rock, THE MENTALLY DISABLED AND THE LAW 408 (rev. Ed. 1971); Note, *Incompetency to Stand Trial*, 81 HARV. L. REV. 454, 457–59 (1967)[hereinafter INCOMPETENCY].

13. Controversial competency issues are not limited to fitness to stand trial inquiries but also include, at times, whether a person with questionable mental health found competent to stand trial is also competent to waive counsel and conduct his or her own defense. These competency related areas will be discussed *infra*.

14. *See* Golding, Roesch & Schreiber, *Assessment and Conceptualization of Competency to Stand Trial*, 8 LAW & HUM. BEHAV. 321–322 (1984).

15. *See Id.* at 321–322.

16. *See generally* R. ROESCH & S. GOLDING, COMPETENCY TO STAND TRIAL (1980) [hereinafter ROESCH & GOLDING]; G. MELTON, L. WEITHORN, & C. SLOBOGIN, PSYCHOLOGICAL EVALUATIONS FOR THE COURTS (1987) [hereinafter EVALS I].

17. *See generally* M. PERLIN, MENTAL DISABILITY LAW: CASES AND MATERIALS, 713–824 (1999) [hereinafter PERLIN I].

18. *See generally* B. Arrigo & M. Bardwell, *Law, Psychology, and Competency to Stand Trial: Problems with and Implications for High-Profile Cases*, 11 CRIMINAL JUSTICE AND POLICY REVIEW. 15–38 (2000).

19. We recognize that many cases flesh out the different aspects of criminal competency. However, for purposes of this book, the (in)competency construct

some view the *Dusky* standard as a "two-edged sword," broad in scope yet lacking in content.[20] As a result, *Dusky's* standard for trial competence is low and defendants having CST issues are often, despite mental impairment, found competent to stand trial. Relatedly, a common thesis argues that the competency construct is often misunderstood.[21] Several studies corroborate this position, suggesting the criteria for trial fitness are misinterpreted by attorneys[22] and mental health professionals who confuse competency with criminal responsibility.[23] In addition to conceptual confusion, CST evaluations are often raised for strategic reasons by defense and prosecuting counsel,[24] and frequently granted by judges in fear of reversible error.[25] Accordingly, contemporary research has put forth the the-

---

refers to the definition set forth in Dusky v. United States, 362 U.S. 402 (1960). As we subsequently discuss, though, Supreme Court cases have provided detail on the meaning and use of the competency construct (e.g., *Faretta v. United States* (1975) and *Godinez v. Moran* (1993).

20. *See* ROESCH & GOLDING, *supra*, note 16, at 11.

21. *See* Winick I *supra* note 1, at 922 (noting "[c]ompetency deals with a status in the criminal mental health system that is perhaps the most frequently misunderstood by attorneys, judges, and mental health professionals, as well as the public.")

22. *See generally* A. Rosenberg & A. McGarry, *Competency for Trial: The Making of an Expert*, 128 AM. J. PSYCHIATRY, 82–86 (1972). A four year study conducted at the Bridgewater State hospital in Massachusetts indicated only 10 of 28 attorneys knew the legal criteria for determining competency to stand trial. *Id.* at 84. Moreover, 15 of the attorneys in the study's sample were able to give a partial response to the legal criteria for competency and only 3 were able to "[a]rticulate the common-law criteria for determining an accused's competency." *Id.* at 84, 85.

23. *See Id.* at 83, 84. In analyzing the psychiatric reports that Bridgewater Hospital had filed to the courts "[o]nly ten of the 48 letters correctly identified not only the issue of competency, but also the common law criteria." *Id.* at 84. Another routine problem involves mental health professionals who confuse incompetency with criminal responsibility. *See generally* E. Pfeiffer, R. Eisenstein, & E. Dabbs, *Mental Competency Evaluations for the Federal Courts,* 144 J. NERVOUS MENTAL DISEASE, 325 (1967). A study examining 89 competency evaluations revealed that in only 21 evaluations (24%) did the psychiatrists not comment on criminal responsibility at the time of the offense, whether requested by the court or not. *Id.* at 325 (table 4); ROESCH & GOLDING *supra* note 16, at 51–52; Winick I *supra* note 1, at 923–924.

24. *See* G. MELTON, J. PETRILA, N. POYTHRESS, & C. SLOBOGIN, PSYCHOLOGICAL EVALUATIONS FOR THE COURTS: A HANDBOOK FOR MENTAL HEALTH PROFESSIONALS AND LAWYERS 127–128 (2nd ed. 1997) [hereafter EVALS II].

25. *See* ROESCH & GOLDING *supra* note 16, at 192.

ory that the competency construct is conceptually flawed, intimating the operational nature of the construct is problematic because those who apply it "are not firmly anchored in a shared understanding about why (in)competence matters."[26]

Contrary to competency standards, the pretrial assessment instruments employed in CST hearings have undergone a number of significant revisions over the years.[27] Historically, pretrial assessment instruments have evolved from basic screening instruments[28] to structured measures.[29] The evolving protocols have been shown to include several notable strengths[30] and a number of obvious limitations.[31] On the one hand, the assessment instruments provide elaborate statistical methods which, in effect, help standardize the CST process by focusing examiners on the functional information relevant to the CST legal question.[32] On the other hand, practical concerns exist regarding the defendant's ability to participate during the trial and to make important decisions with his/her criminal defense.[33] Indeed, as Grisso notes,

---

26. *See* Bonnie I *supra* note 11 at 293. Bonnie argues competency is best understood as two related but separate concepts; specifically, a foundational concept and a decisional concept. *Id.* at 294. Because of the identified limitations with the competency construct as well as efforts to improve CST assessment measures, Bonnie aptly proposes a theoretical reformulation regarding the competency construct.

27. *See* Grisso I *supra* note 6, at 90–96.

28. *See* A. Robey, *Criteria for Competency to Stand Trial: A Checklist for Psychiatrists*, 122 AM. J. PSYCHIATRY, 616–23 (1965). B. Bukatman, J. Foy, & E. Degrazia *What Is Competency to Stand Trial?*, 127 AM. J. PSYCHIATRY 1225–1229 (1971).

29. *See generally* T. Grisso, *Five-Year Research Update (1986–1990): Evaluations for Competence to Stand Trial*, 10 BEHAVIORAL SCIENCES AND THE LAW, 353–369 (1992)[hereafter Grisso II]. Grisso reviews CST research and protocol used to evaluate trial competency.

30. *See generally* Grisso I *supra* note 6, at 96.

31. *See generally* R. Lanyon, *Psychological Assessment Procedures in Court-Related Settings*, 17 PROFESSIONAL PSYCHOLOGY, 260–268 (1986). Additional problems with CST evaluations relate to the correlation between CST and intelligence and a defendant's legal knowledge based on past experience with the criminal justice system. *See* A. McGarry et al., COMPETENCY TO STAND TRIAL AND MENTAL ILLNESS (1973); *See also* ROESCH & GOLDING *supra*, note 16, at 60–61.

32. *See* Grisso I *supra* note 6, at 96.

33. *See generally* T. Grisso, *Clinical Assessments for Legal Decision Making: Research Recommendations*, in S. Shah & B. Sales (Eds.), LAW AND MENTAL HEALTH: MAJOR DEVELOPMENTS AND RESEARCH NEEDS 49–80 (S. Shah & B. Sales eds.1992) [hereafter Grisso III].

"CST evaluations currently tend to be dominated by inquiry into the defendant's knowledge and appreciation of the charges, penalties, and matters pertaining to the formal trial process (e.g., roles of the [courtroom] participants, procedure in the trial). Yet, approximately 90% of these defendants, even if found competent, will never have to exercise their abilities as participants in a formal trial of their pending charges, because they will plead guilty."[34]

Consistent with Grisso's observation, several commentators argue CST evaluations should focus on general trial competence as well as decisional demands required of the defendant (e.g. comparing options in the plea bargaining process).[35] As a result, modern research concentrates on both the cognitive functions required of the defendant (i.e., understanding the nature of the trial proceedings and the role of the courtroom participants), as well as the decisional tasks that often prove determinative for the outcome (i.e., plead guilty) when conducting CST evaluations. One example of such research comes from the MacArthur Foundation Research Network on Mental Health and Law. The creation of the MacArthur Competence Assessment Tool-Criminal Adjudication (MacCAT-CA) represents an instrument used to assess the cognitive and decisional abilities of the defendant.[36]

Although many defendants plead guilty, other defendants want their proverbial "day in court." Thus, additional concerns in the CST assessment process involve defendants who opt to waive their constitutional right to counsel electing, instead, to conduct their own legal action. Decisions of trial strategy, like those requests just described, are especially troubling for defendants who meet the low competency standard and subsequently make strategic trial decisions in response to a mental health disorder from which they suffer. For example, consider the paranoid and delusional defendant who waives his or her right to counsel because of paranoid traits or suspicious propensities and, hypothetically speaking, believes defense counsel is part of a grand conspiracy designed to destroy the

---

34. *See* Grisso II *supra* note 29, at 366.
35. *See generally* R. Miller, & E. Germain, *The Specificity of Evaluations of Competency to Proceed*, 14 JOURNAL OF PSYCHIATRY AND LAW, 333–347 (1986). *See also* Bonnie I *supra* note 11, at 494, 305–311.
36. *See infra* note 361 and accompanying text.

accused. We note that current trends in CST clinical evaluations and judicial determinations do not contemplate (let alone give weight to) the misguided decision making of the paranoid delusional defendant. Indeed, these individuals are frequently found competent to stand trial and, moreover, fit to conduct their own defense.

Organization of the Book

Given the broad-based dilemmas identified above, *Criminal Competency on Trial* provides a legal, psychological, and policy analysis of competency to stand trial. In chapter 1, we offer an overview of the competency doctrine's history, including some discussion of its purposes and justifications. In addition, we describe, in some detail, the legal difference between criminal competency and criminal responsibility (not guilty by reason of insanity - NGRI). We maintain it is important to understand how these legal issues differ in terms of their development. Moreover, we contend that by presenting the evolving state of NGRI tests, other mental health law experts and criminal justice practitioners can better appreciate the nuances between competency to stand trial and criminal insanity, including the manner in which the two doctrines are confused.

In chapter 2 we offer an analytical review of the leading United States Supreme Court cases which either define trial fitness or address particular aspects of the construct (e.g., competency to stand trial, right to waive counsel and its implications with respect to trial fitness matters,[37] and competency to proceed *pro se* to trial).[38] Fur-

---

37. As will be discussed, the Supreme Court's decision concerning the right to waive counsel (i.e., *Faretta v. California*, 1975) was not based on facts involving a mentally ill defendant but instead addressed a more general constitutional issue; that is, whether all criminal defendants have a right to waive counsel under the Sixth Amendment. Although a defendant may waive his right to counsel for various reasons having nothing to do with mental disability, this book will discuss the implications of *Faretta* as it involves defendants having mental health concerns, or defendants who have undergone pre-trial competency evaluations.

38. This book investigates those cases that either define CST; *Dusky v. United States* (1960), have a direct bearing on how defendants with mental health concerns craft their defense; *Faretta v. California* (1975), or expound upon a particular aspect of the competency construct; *Godinez v. Moran* (1993). These cases are chosen because they have produced problematic holdings, thereby fueling CST controversies. In addition, these cases were chosen

ther, this chapter explores, where applicable,[39] the majority and dissenting opinions used to support the Court's logic. We review the implications of these opinions, especially in relation to the competency construct, and the problems they subsequently pose.

In chapter 3 we systematically review the pretrial evaluation instruments use to assess criminal competency. We situate this presentation in its appropriate historical context, beginning with the original protocol and moving to the most recent assessment tools (i.e., MacCAT-Ca).[40] Although clinical and social science efforts continue

---

because states typically rely only on the minimum constitutional requirement as set forth in the Supreme Court decisions listed above. Although some decisions following *Dusky* have elaborated upon the competency construct (e.g., *Pate v. Robinson,*1966; *Drope v. Missouri,* 1975) these cases primarily deal with when the issue of competency should be raised and to whom this doctrine applies. Given their relative significance on the issue of criminal competency, these decisions will receive some attention throughout this investigation.

39. In some cases, analysis is not possible given the *per curium* decisions reached by the Court (e.g., *Dusky v. United States*). In instances such as these, no concurring or dissenting opinions are expressed. Conversely, other cases (e.g., *Faretta v. California, Godinez v. Moran*) include opinions that concur with, concur in part with, or dissent from the majority's opinion. Accordingly, these cases enable a more systematic analysis concerning the opinions and rationale of the Court.

40. This investigation generally reviews and critiques the evolution of the pretrial assessment instruments, including some brief commentary on the introductory checklists and some more detailed observations on the contemporary assessment protocols. The checklists include those developed by A. Robey, and, subsequently, B. Bukatman, J. Foy, & E. Degrazia. *See generally supra* note 28. The more contemporary assessment measures include: (a) the Competency Screening Test (CT), described in Lipsitt et al., *Competency for Trial: A Screening Instrument*, 128 AM.J. PSYCHIATRY 105 (1971); (b) the Competency to Stand Trial Assessment Instrument (CAI), described in LABORATORY FOR COMMUNITY PSYCHIATRY, COMPETENCY TO STAND TRIAL AND MENTAL ILLNESS (1974) [hereinafter LAB]; (c) the Interdisciplinary Fitness Interview (IFI), described in Golding et al., *supra* note 10, at 321–324; (d) the Georgia Court Competency Test (GCCT), described in R. Wildman, E. Batchelor, E. Thompson, F. Nelson, J. Moore, M. Patterson, & M. de Laosoa, *The Georgia Court Competency Test; An Attempt to Develop a Rapid, Quantitative Measure of Fitness For Trial,* unpublished manuscript, Forensic Services Division, Central State Hospital, Milledgeville, GA (1978) and its variant the Georgia Court Competency Test, developed at the Mississippi State Hospital (GCCH-MSH); and (e) the MacArthur Competence Assessment Tool-Criminal Adjudication (MacCAT-CA), developed by the MacArthur Foundation Research Network on Mental Health and the Law. Given that the MacCAT-CA represents the most recent evaluation tool and suggests a future direction for CST assessments, considerable time is spent on its law-psychology utility. For a complete and detailed review of CST assessment protocol *see generally* EVALS

to revamp the assessment tools, problems inherent in the legal definitions and difficulties with past instruments suggest that contemporary measures will, bo logical extension, be similarly suspect.

In chapter 4 we explore the psychiatric phenomena of paranoid and delusional mental health concerns. We contend that these disorders have ubiquitous signs and symptoms that further complicate the CST assessment process. In addition to describing the diagnostic requirements of three mental health disorders having paranoid and delusional dimensions (i.e., paranoid schizophrenia, delusional disorder, and paranoid personality disorder), various and practical sub-issues are discussed in this chapter. For example, specific and detailed attention is given to the troubling connection between paranoid and delusional mental health conditions and current trends in CST evaluation practices (e.g., CST time constraints and the assessment of trial fitness for a defendant presenting with ubiquitous paranoid symptomatology, rendering a clinical opinion regarding one's trial fitness based on time constrained and questionable diagnostic findings). We maintain that carefully detailing this material helps situate subsequent chapters which either systematically chronicle or generally review noteworthy and high-profile CST cases (i.e., Colin Ferguson and Theodore Kaczynski respectively).

The balance of *Criminal Competency on Trial* pays particular attention to competency outcome difficulties, especially where delusional and paranoid traits are clearly identifiable. To address these matters, chapter 5 explores the case of the controversial and well-publicized New York City railway gunman: Mr. Colin Ferguson. Ferguson was a mental health defendant (paranoid and delusional symptomatology) whose competency evaluation was suspect and, following a competency finding, subsequently requested to conduct his own defense. In order to investigate these matters, we review the events leading up to Mr. Ferguson's criminal trial and link these events with his psychological history. This material is detailed and systematic, giving the reader a sense of who the New York City railway gunman was, what his criminal acts were, and how he found himself caught between the forces of the mental health and justice

---

II, *supra* note 24, at 139–150. We also recommend the above mentioned cites from which each of these instruments was developed for a complete understanding of their structure, scoring criteria, advantages, and limitations.

systems. Indeed, by revisiting the actual pretrial hearing transcripts and by recounting excerpts from the psychiatric report, we examine the expert testimony (via direct and cross examination), the closing arguments by the defense and by the people, and the court's decision on the issue of competency, including Ferguson's ancillary requests to waive counsel and to invoke the insanity defense.

In chapter 6 we show where and how the CST legal doctrine and the psychological fitness evaluation process produced a flawed competency to stand trial determination. Specifically, we provide both a psychological and a legal analysis regarding the courtroom events impacting Ferguson's pretrial competency hearing. The psychological or psychiatric commentary reviews the "individualized" CST examinations and the problems that ensued from psychiatry's involvement in the Ferguson matter (e.g., lack of uniformity in CST assessment practices, questionable objectivity, and the role of forensic psychological "experts" as ultimate opinion makers in the process). The legal analysis examines the logic and rationale that led the Judge to conclude that Ferguson was not only competent to stand trial but competent to waive counsel and to conduct his own legal action. Accordingly, in this section of the chapter, we present poignant examples and provocative subject matter from the trial concerning Ferguson's own defense as evidence of his lack of trial fitness (i.e., incompetent) and his inability to effectively represent himself. In addition, a review of the Ferguson pretrial competency hearing and trial outcome will also disclose why mentally disordered defendants with paranoid features illuminate problematic CST issues. Indeed, as we argue, the Ferguson case reveals problems related to CST standards, the current methods used to evaluate competency, psychiatry's role in the courts, and questionable judicial decision making on the matter of trial fitness.

In chapter 7 we link the identified CST legal and clinical limitations to criminal justice reform. Specifically, we argue that these shortcomings necessitate a reevaluation of the fitness-to-stand-trial process through alternative and untested policy considerations. Along these lines, we propose reforms related to the competency evaluation procedures, the psychological instruments, and the legal remedies and/or strategies made available to the defendant.

In chapter 8 we generalize our legal and psychological policy recommendations to other high-stakes CST cases and to trial fitness disputes more broadly. Arguing that the competency limitations identified in the Ferguson matter are not the exception but are often the rule in the everyday realities of defendants with CST concerns, we briefly review the supplemental and controversial case of Theodore Kaczynski: the unabomber. We canvass the trial fitness evaluation issues surrounding the Kaczynski case and argue that he was erroneously found competent to stand trial. Subsequently, the unabomber expressed a desire to conduct his own defense, although he was never granted a right to do so. We provisionally assess how the Court reached its decision, given the presence of ostensible paranoid and delusional mental health symptomatology. We conclude this chapter by applying our evaluation of Kaczynski to the proposed criminal justice policy remedies. Along these lines we compare the similarities and differences between Ferguson and Kaczynski, especially in relation to CST decision making. Overall, we contend that the unabomber case is another vivid example (and reminder) of the problems stemming from the legal standard for competency to stand trial and the mental health fitness evaluations pertaining to it. In this way, we argue that the courtroom dilemmas in the Ferguson and Kaczynski cases could have been meaningfully averted had our criminal justice reform measures been in place.

In chapter 9 we summarize the project. We systematically review the essential components of each chapter, and how they synthetically support the central thesis entertained throughout the text; namely, that the CST process is fundamentally flawed. In addition, we present some general observations concerning the future direction of competency to stand trial. We conclude the chapter by outlining some of the more insidious problems with the function of psychiatrists or psychologists in the courts.

Chapter 1

The Incompetency Doctrine: Historical Considerations, Conceptual Confusion, and Practical Problems

OVERVIEW

In order to canvass fully the doctrine of competency to stand trial from a legal, psychological, and policy perspective, it is necessary to review its jurisprudential evolution and its connection to related psycholegal constructs. Accordingly, in this chapter we sketch the historical dimensions of incompetency, beginning with English common law. In addition, we identify why the doctrine of competency matters, highlighting its constitutional purposes and justifications. We conclude the chapter by distinguishing between competency to stand trial and the related concept of criminal responsibility.

A. Socio-Legal History of the Incompetency Doctrine

The incompetency rule has deep roots in English common law.[41] As early as the 17th century the English courts encountered problems when defendants stood mute and failed to enter the required plea. These matters were resolved by deciding whether one was

---

41. *See* GAP *supra* note 4, at 912–15.

"mute by visitation of god" or "mute by malice."[42] The former excused the defendant and included those persons identified as "deaf
and dumb."[43] However, if one was "mute by malice" then torment-
ing rituals followed, designed to induce a plea. For example, defendants were often subjected to the medieval torture, *peine forte et
dure*. With this ordeal, weights of increasing mass were placed on
the defendant's chest to pressure the desired plea of guilt.[44]

In the 18th century, legal philosophers developed a reasonable
justification for barring trial on the grounds of mental defect as an
alternative to explanatory concepts such as "divine visitation" and,
in the extreme, "demonic possession."[45] In his *Commentaries on
the Laws of England* (1783), William Blackstone remarked that a
defendant who became "mad" after the commission of an offense
should not be tried, "[b]ecause he is not able to plead to it with that
advise and caution that he ought" [and a "mad" person should not
be tried], "[f]or how can he make his defence?"[46] Blackstone's statements on the issue of "madness"[47] and "caution" intimated a relationship between present mental status and the ability to make important trial decisions. More importantly, however, Blackstone's
comments questioned whether such individuals could receive a fair
trial.[48] Consistent with the ideas of other legal philosophers regarding the "mad" defendant,[49] Blackstone's logic helped explain the interplay between a mental defect and the law, and, ultimately, was

---

42. *See Id.*

43. Eventually, the category "mute by visitation of God" was expanded to
include "lunatics." *See* Winick I *supra* note 1, at 952; Winick II *supra* note 5, at
3–4.

44. *See Id. See also* B. Winick, *Reforming Incompetency to Stand Trial and
Plead Guilty: A Restated Proposal and a Response to Professor Bonnie*, 85 J.
CRIM. L. & CRIMINOLOGY 571, 574 [hereinafter Winick III].

45. *See E.g.,* ROESCH & GOLDING *supra* note 16, at 10.

46. *See* 4 WILLIAM. BLACKSTONE, COMMENTARIES 24 (9th ed.
1783).

47. The term "mad" as used by Blackstone suggests a general description
of mental pathology. The point is that if one is unable to understand or to assist
in one's defense because of a psychiatric illness, it is simply unfair to subject
that person to a trial.

48. *See* EVALS II *supra* note 24, at 121.

49. *See also* 1 MATTHEW HALE, THE HISTORY OF THE PLEAS OF
THE CROWN, 34,35 (1736). Hale's commentary on the issue of mental health
and trial proceedings was also used to advise early English court decisions. *See
Youtsey* discussing Hale's influence on that decision. *Id.* at 940.

used to guide English court decisions on the issue of trial competence.

In the late 18th century, the English courts set in motion the basis of an incompetency doctrine. For example, in *Frith's Case*, settled in 1790, the court stated:

> [S]uch is the humanity of the law of England, that in all stages both when the act is committed, at the time when the prisoner makes his defence, and even at the day of execution, it is important to settle what his state of mind is; and at the time he is called to plead, if there are circumstances that suggest to one's mind that he is not in the possession of his reason, we must certainly be careful that nothing is introduced into the administration of justice, but what belongs to that administration...[50]

Arguably the most influential case with respect to criminal trial competency, *Frith's Case* not only addressed general mental health status for all stages of English criminal procedure, but, moreover, commented on present mental health status in remarkable detail. Indeed, as the court concluded:

> [t]hat no man shall be called upon to make his defence at a time when his mind is in that situation as not to appear capable of so doing; for, however guilty he may be, the inquiring into his guilt must be postponed to that season, when by collecting together his intellects, and having them entire, he shall be able so to model his defence as to ward off the punishment of the law[51] ...

Following *Frith's Case*, the English common law of the 18th and 19th centuries were replete with similar examples,[52] mostly restating and refining the notion that incompetency could prevent a trial.[53]

---

50. *See* Frith's Case, 22 How. State Trials 307, 311 (1790).
51. *See Id.* at 318.
52. ROESCH & GOLDING *supra* note 16, at 11.
53. *See* HALE *supra* note 49, at 34, 35. Hale states:
    "[I]f a man in his sound memory commits a capital offense, and before his arraignment he becomes absolutely mad, he ought not by law be arraigned during such frenzy, but be remitted to prison until that incapacity be removed."
    See also Bish. Cr. Proc. §666 which states: "An insane man cannot even plead to an indictment. Therefore, if, at the arraignment, counsel have reason to suppose their client too insane to take his trial, they should then make the objection...or the court may take it on its own observations." *See generally*

In the 19th century, the American courts also recognized the rule of incompetency, persuaded by English common law.[54] For example, in *Youtsey v. United States* (1899)[55] the court explained why the common law would provide guidance[56] and why a trial violated an incompetent defendant's right to due process.[57] In an unprecedented decision, the court concluded: "[i]t is fundamental that an insane person can neither plead to an arraignment, be subjected to a trial, or, after trial, receive judgement, or after judgement, undergo punishment ... It is not 'due process of law' to subject an insane person to trial upon an indictment involving liberty or life."[58] Thus, in addition to giving the competency doctrine constitutional status,[59] *Youtsey's* central theme linking mental illness and trial decisions (e.g., [in]ability to plead to an arraignment) justified the need for an (in)competency doctrine.

Youtsey v. United States, 97 F. 937, 940 (6th Cir. 1899) for a review of common-law authorities discussing competency matters.

54. *See* EVALS II *supra* note 24, at 121; JUSTIN MILLER, HANDBOOK ON CRIMINAL LAW 28–32 (1934).

55. *See* Youtsey v. United States, 97 F. 937, 937–48 (6th Cir. 1899). In *Youtsey*, defense counsel filed a motion of appeal as a result of the Circuit Court's decision refusing a trial continuance. The appeal was based on two issues. First, the client was a confirmed epileptic, and counsel concluded that the stress of a trial would likely induce an epileptic seizure. Second, and in addition to physical problems, the motion presented an issue of present insanity as a reason to postpone any trial while that condition persisted. The Circuit Court of Appeals, Sixth Circuit, granted certiorari, based on what they characterized as a "blended issue" involving physical and mental health concerns. As a result, the court opined that "The blending of such an issue in bar of a trial with an application for a continuance upon that and another ground should not prejudice the right of the accused to have that issue considered and disposed of in some form of trial known to the law." *Id.* at 940.

56. The *Youtsey* Court clearly expressed why the common law would direct their decision and, ultimately, help resolve the matter. The *Youtsey* Court stated, "[T]he statutes of the United States present no mode for the presentation and trial of an issue of present insanity, when presented in bar of an arraignment, trial, judgement, or execution, and we must look to the common law for guidance in practice." *Id.*

57. *See Youtsey* 97 F. 937, 940–41 (6th Cir. 1899)

58. *See Id.*

59. *See* EVALS II *supra* note 24, at 121.

B. Purposes and Justifications for the (In)Competency Doctrine

Commentary concerning why the incompetency doctrine exists is well documented in historical[60] and legal contexts.[61] An investigation of these accounts indicates the presence of two interrelated, though confusing, themes. The first concerns the general purpose of the doctrine and the second involves its justification.[62] This section reviews both matters, offering a brief explanation on why it is important to distinguish between the two.

1. The Incompetency Doctrine's Purposes: What is it Designed to Do?

The incompetency doctrine assumes three principal functions in American law. Preliminarily, the incompetency doctrine's purpose is founded on the notion that every defendant is entitled to certain im-

---

60. *See generally* INCOMPETENCY *supra* note 12 ; *See also* Note, *The Identification of Incompetent Defendants: Separating Those Unfit For Adversary Combat From Those Who Are Fit*, 66 KY. L. J. 666–706 (1978)[hereinafter IDENTIFICATION].

61. *See* Winick I *supra* note 1, at 952–959; Bonnie I *supra* note 11, at 295–297.

62. A review of the historical and legal literature suggests that the terms "rationales," "purposes," and "justifications" are often used interchangeably when explaining the incompetency doctrine. *See* IDENTIFICATION *supra* note 57, at 668, stating that "The primary purpose of the incompetency rule is to safeguard the accuracy of adjudication." In concluding this section, the Note asserts that "[T]he competency doctrine has been justified as a means of insuring the integrity of the adversary method of criminal adjudication by promoting the accuracy, fairness, and dignity of the process." *Id.* at 670–671. In his discussion on why (in)competency matters, Bonnie uses the term "rationales." Bonnie I *supra* note 11, at 295. Elsewhere, in his critique of past explanations for the doctrine, Bonnie maintains that "[L]ists of purposes served by the incompetency doctrine typically include...." *See also* Winick I *supra* note 1, at 952. Notwithstanding this (somewhat confusing) nomenclature, commentators have offered valuable insight regarding the general rationale for the incompetency doctrine. In this section, however, the use of the term "purposes," in relation to incompetency, refers to the doctrine's functions. The use of the term "justifications," in relation to incompetency, refers to the doctrine's underlying jurisprudential intent. Collectively, these notions represent the incompetency standard's overall rationale.

mutable rights,[63] including a fair trial.[64] In this respect, then, the CST standard is first used as a vehicle to protect fundamental liberties provided by the constitution. Indeed, according to the Fourteenth Amendment, no state shall "deprive any person of life, liberty, or property, without due process of law; Nor deny to any person within its jurisdiction the equal protection of the laws."[65] The incompetency doctrine further supports the constellation of rights afforded by the Sixth Amendment, including the right..."[t]o be informed of the nature and cause of the accusation; to be confronted with the witnesses against [oneself]; to have compulsory process for obtaining witnesses in [one's] favor; and to have the assistance of counsel for [one's] defense."[66] These Six and Fourteenth Amendment rights provide a logical framework for protecting citizens from governmental intrusion. Thus, a second purpose of the incompetency doctrine, through these due process guarantees, is to establish practical limits for state and federal intervention when a citizen's mental state is called into question. By necessary extension, then, the CST doctrine furthers the proper administration of justice. In short, the incompetency standard's third function is to ensure the legitimacy of the criminal trial and its proceedings.[67]

2. Justifications for the Incompetency Doctrine: Underlying Jurisprudential Intent?

As several commentators note, the CST doctrine is "a means of insuring the integrity of the adversary method of criminal adjudication [because it intends to promote] the accuracy, fairness, and dignity of the process."[68] The importance of accuracy as a justification

---

63. To subject an incompetent defendant to trial "violates certain immutable principles of justice which inhere in the very idea of a free government."*See also* IDENTIFICATION *supra* note 60, at 666, 668 (1978).

64. *See* Massey v. Moore, 348 U.S. 105, 108 (1954). (Recognizing article 14 of the amendments to the constitution of the United States that all defendants are entitled to a fair trial).

65. *See* U.S. CONST. amend. XIV.

66. *See* U.S. CONST. amend. VI.

67. *See* IDENTIFICATION *supra* note 60, at 670–671.

68. *See Id.* at 670–671; INCOMPETENCY *supra* note 12, at 457–59; Winick and DeMeo *supra* note 12, at 31.

is not to be underestimated.[69] Indeed, to subject a mentally incompetent person to trial may prevent an accurate outcome because the defendant may know of events and circumstances that could prove or mitigate legal guilt but, because of mental defect, the person can not communicate such knowledge. As one court explained,

> [T]here may be circumstances in all cases of which the defendant alone has knowledge, which would prove his innocence, the advantage of which, if insane to such an extent that he did not appreciate the value of such facts, or the propriety of communicating them to his counsel, he would be deprived.[70]

In this context, an incompetent defendant may not understand how the admission of certain facts would be important when forming a defense, and, even if the significance of these facts were understood, the defendant might still be unable to convey such information to counsel. Accordingly, the suppressed information will likely contribute to an inaccurate trial decision, undermining the entire adjudicatory process.

In addition to fact suppression, it is probable that the incompetent defendant would be unable to exercise important constitutionally-protected rights. Included among these are: the right to confer with counsel; to testify; to confront witnesses; and to contest the conviction.[71] As others have observed, the underlying intent of these protections is "to safeguard the accuracy of adjudication."[72]

The concern for accuracy is but one justification for the (in)competency doctrine. In fact, accuracy is not always or exclusively a rationale governing the trial process. Indeed, there are circumstances (e.g., intoxication) wherein a defendant may be unable to recall important exonerating facts that would, if remembered, assist in the person's defense. In this instance, the defendant 's case goes to trial, notwithstanding the potential inaccuracies. However, when one is unable to "rationally"[73] understand courtroom proceedings, the in-

---

69. See IDENTIFICATION *supra* note 60, at 668; INCOMPETENCY *supra* note 12, at 457.

70. See Jordan v. State, 135 S.W. 327, 328 (Tenn.1911); See IDENTIFICATION *supra* note 60, at 668.

71. See E.g., United States v. Chisolm, 149 F. 284. 287 (5th Cir. 1906).

72. See IDENTIFICATION *supra* note 60, at 669.

73. As a matter of convenience the term "rational," draws attention to one's cognitive and mental faculties.

dividual is not required to answer to criminal charges.[74] Accordingly, it is argued that if the doctrine clearly excludes certain situations bearing on trial competence (i.e., substance abuse) but recognizes variables relating to others (i.e., mental health), then additional jurisprudential values underscore the need for the (in)competency doctrine.[75] Typically, these collateral justifications include fairness, dignity, and the philosophy of punishment.[76]

To bar a trial on the grounds of incompetence necessarily ensures that the criminal proceeding is fair. To do otherwise not only subverts certain constitutional rights (e.g., right to a fair trial — the general purpose and function of the incompetency doctrine) but defeats the state's interest in protecting its most vulnerable citizens.[77] In order to receive a fair trial a defendant must be able to form a reasonable defense. An ability crucial to forming such a defense requires that the accused compare his or her version of the facts to the testimony provided by others.[78] However, for incompetent individuals, this necessary capacity is often compromised by way of mental defect. A common expression of mental defect, resulting in an incompetency determination, involves the defendant's bizarre trial behavior. Indeed, a person "can alienate the jury if he [or she] displays such inappropriate demeanor as grinning when gruesome details are discussed, losing his [or her] temper when witnesses maintain [the person] is...violent, or acting indifferent to the proceedings."[79] In addition, the incompetent defendant's lack of basic trial knowledge (e.g., a general understanding or appreciation of the pending charges; how to plead or consult in terms of strategic decisions, or even dismiss counsel upon dissatisfaction)[80] decreases prospects for

---

74. *See* INCOMPETENCY *supra* note 12, at 457–458.

75. *Id.* at 458.

76. *See* Winick 1 *supra* note 1, at 952–959 on the *parens patriae* basis of the incompetency doctrine.

77. *See E.g.,* Winick III *supra* note 44, at 575.

78. *See* IDENTIFICATION *supra* note 60, at 669.

79. *See* IDENTIFICATION *supra* note 60, at 670–671.

80. These reasons reflect autonomous decision making abilities of the defendant. Recently, the autonomy value has been considered a reason, in of itself, to bar trial on the grounds of incompetence. Specifically, commentators argue the incompetency doctrine protects the interests of individuals who make defense strategy decisions. Thus, it is imperative that one be competent to make such important trial choices (e.g., to plea, to waive jury trial, to testify). Winick III *supra* note 44, at 576; Bonnie I *supra* note 11, at 296.

a fair trial.[81] We note that of the values used to justify the CST doctrine, fairness has a strong relationship to the general purpose of the incompetency doctrine. As described in the present section, however, the underlying jurisprudential intent of fairness, in relation to incompetency, guarantees the constitutional interests of the accused and preserves the integrity of the overall trial process.[82]

A related justification for the CST standard is the promotion of a dignified proceeding.[83] To subject to trial one designated as incompetent lacks dignity as it demonstrates the state's desire to inflict punishment not on a person but rather on an object.[84] As one commentator posits "[T]he adjudication loses its character as a reasoned interaction between an individual and [the person's] community and becomes an invective against an insensible object."[85] This invective, if endorsed, erodes the dignity and humanity of the psychiatric citizen.

Another jurisprudential value underscoring the incompetency doctrine concerns society's general philosophy of punishment.[86] To justify punitive action, the defendant must comprehend the criminal charges.[87] A prerequisite for the administration of punishment requires the defendant to understand that society considers certain behaviors morally blameworthy. Indeed, to punish in the absence of such foresight, is to endorse "a miserable spectacle, both against law, and of extreme inhumanity and cruelty, and can be no example to others."[88]

Although clearly provisional and broad in scope, the preceding review concerning the (in)competency doctrine's rationale suggests

---

81. *See* e.g., INCOMPETENCY *supra* note 60, at 458.

82. As a point of departure, fairness as a purpose/function (discussed in the previous section) centers on barring trial because of questioned competence (e.g., to ensure a fair trial), which occurs *before* the trial. As discussed in the present section, however, the term fairness as a justification/underlined jurisprudential intent—centers on the potentially incompetent defendant acting out *during* the trial (e.g, being held in contempt) which would prevent the fair trial.

83. *See* Winick I *supra* note 1, at 953.

84. *See* e.g., Bonnie I *supra* note 11, at 295.

85. *Id.*

86. *See* INCOMPETENCY *supra* note 12, at 458–59; E.G., IDENTIFICATION *supra* note 60, at 670–71; Winick I *supra* note 1, at 957–958.

87. *See* IDENTIFICATION *supra* note 60, at 670. *See also* T. Szasz, *Some Observations on the Relationship Between psychiatry and the Law*, 75 A.M.A. ARCHIVES OF NEUROLOGY & PSYCH. 297 (1956).

88. *See* IDENTIFICATION *supra* note 60, at 70, citing 3 COKE, INSTITUTES 6 (1644).

the it functions at two interrelated levels. First, the doctrine's general purpose furthers certain constitutional rights, ensuring that all defendants receive a fair trial. Second, the standard's jurisprudential basis affirms the integrity of the trial system, promoting the values of accuracy, fairness and dignity. Although (somewhat) subtle, the conceptual differences between the CST standard's design and justification highlight its manifold significance, especially for safeguarding the interests of the individual, the state, and society at large.[89]

3. Competency to Stand Trial versus Criminal Responsibility

While insanity and competency are distinct and separate legal issues, they are often confused, conflated and misapplied.[90] What makes these two legal constructs so confounding is the manner in which they interactively operate in the criminal law. To illustrate, defendants can be found competent to stand trial but excused of criminal responsibility by reason of insanity. Indeed, hypothetically,

---

89. Another possible justification with respect to the incompetency doctrine is the need to preserve "courtroom decorum," often linked to preserving the dignity of the trial process. For a review supporting this value *see* INCOMPETENCY *supra* note 12, at 458; Winick I *supra* note 1, at 953–54. In short, this notion suggests that the accused's bizarre behavior potentially could make a mockery of the proceedings. *E.g.*, INCOMPETENCY, *supra* note 12, at 458. Others have recognized the need to preserve decorum but emphasize the trial judge's responsibility to curtail such behavior and to uphold the civility of the trial proceedings. *E.g.*, Winick I *supra* note 1, at 953–54. This value of courtroom decorum has also been contested and retooled. For example, Bonnie argues that such a "purpose" should not bar trials, suggesting that "[t]he 'dignity' rationale for the incompetence doctrine refers to the inherent morality of the process carried out in the courtroom, not to its outward appearances." Bonnie I *supra* note 11, at 295. Clarifying his perspective, Winick concludes that given procedural alternatives (e.g., judicial discretion to control odd behavior, excusing the defendant for brief periods of time) preserving courtroom decorum should not be, in of itself, a "justification" to bar trial. *See* Winick III *supra* note 44, at 576. Given these differing perspectives, this section argues that preserving the decorum of the court should not be listed as a purpose or a justification necessarily. Indeed, the presence of odd behavior, at the pretrial phase of a case, *may* undermine key purposes of the doctrine including safeguarding one's constitutional right to a fair trial. However, if displays of such inappropriate conduct occur during trial, then the underlying jurisprudential basis of the incompetency doctrine is undone: trial fairness *is* compromised.

90. *See E.g.*, Winick I *supra* note 1, at 982.

an accused suffering from bipolar disorder may be deemed competent to stand trial because the person possesses the *present* ability to understand the pending charges and can, if called upon, assist in his/her own defense. Subsequently, however, the same person might be excused of criminal responsibility by reason of insanity; an inquiry that assesses one's state of mind *at the time of the offense*.[91] Given that both doctrines address the mental state of the defendant, and, further, given their potential interplay in a criminal court of law, it is useful to examine these doctrines more closely.

a. Competency

As a legal determination, a defendant found incompetent is a declaration that the person, while physically present, is mentally absent from the proceeding. As one court observed, the competency rule is a "by-product of the ban against trial *in absentia*; the mentally incompetent defendant, though physically present in the courtroom, is in reality afforded no opportunity to defend himself."[92] Consistent with the *in absentia* notion, the test for determining competence to stand trial focuses on the defendant's *present* ability to understand the charges and the *present* ability to assist in the defense.[93] According to the United States Supreme Court a defendant is presumed competent to stand trial, and the party asserting incompetency must, by a preponderance of the evidence, provide proof to the contrary.[94] Although conceptual questions persist with respect to varying aspects of the competency doctrine and recent Supreme Court decisions (e.g., competency to stand trial versus competency to waive important rights), the legal standard is considered stable and enduring when compared to the legal doctrine that excuses criminal conduct because of insanity.[95]

---

91. In regard to the hypothetical, reconstruction of events at the time the offense might reveal the defendant was in a manic phase as a result of the bipolar disorder, and did not appreciate the wrongfulness of his/her acts. However, this psychotic phase of the illness was otherwise absent during the competency evaluation. Thus, the defendant, while competent to stand trial, can be acquitted based on a finding of not guilty by reason of insanity.

92. *See* Foote *supra* note 3, at 834.

93. *See* ABA *supra* note 10, at 167–68.

94. *See* Medina v. California, 505 U.S. 437, 438 (1992).

95. *See* Grisso I *supra* note 6, at 94.

b. Criminal Responsibility

Criminal responsibility is a retrospective question focusing on the defendant's state of mind *at the time* of the alleged offense and is used as a trial defense (i.e., not guilty by reason of insanity or NGRI).[96] As one commentator points out, "the insanity defense exists as a legal compromise to a moral dilemma."[97] In contrast to those who commit crime as a product of free will,[98] the irrational offender should be excused from punishment if unable to control his/her behavior.[99] Accordingly, individuals who do not know the nature of their actions, and/or do not know that such actions are wrong, should not be held morally responsible.[100] For society to do otherwise would amount to the application of swift principles of punishment (e.g., deterrence and retribution) inflicted upon "helpless" offenders.[101]

The insanity doctrine originated from the M'Naghten standard,[102] and is often referred to as the "right wrong" test or the cognitive formula.[103] This formula excused criminal responsibility given the defendant was mentally ill and, as a result, did not know his or her conduct was wrong.[104] Since M'Naghten and the criticisms leveled

---

96. For a detailed discussion on criminal responsibility and the insanity defense, see STEADMAN ET AL., BEFORE AND AFTER HINCKLEY: EVALUATING INSANITY DEFENSE REFORM (1993)[hereinafter STEADMAN ET AL.]; PERLIN *supra* note 17, at 831–939.

97. *See* J. Footlick, *Insanity on trial.* May 8, Newsweek, 108–112 (1978), as cited in L. WRIGHTSMAN, M. NIETZEL & W. FORTUNE, PSYCHOLOGY AND THE LEGAL SYSTEM 294 (4TH ed. 1997) [hereinafter WRIGHTSMAN ET AL.].

98. *See e.g.,* PERLIN I *supra* note 17, at 825; Livermore & Meehl, *The Virtues of M'Naghten,* 51 MINN. L. REV. 789, 797 (1967).

99. *See e.g.,* EVALS II *supra* note 24, at 186–87.

100. P. LOW, J. JEFFRIES & R. BONNIE, THE TRIAL OF JOHN W. HINCKLEY, JR.: A CASE STUDY IN THE INSANITY DEFENSE 11 (1986) [hereafter INSANITY]; PERLIN I *supra* note 17, at 830.

101. *See E.g.,* EVALS II *supra* note 24, at 186–87.

102. M'Naghten variously spelled M'Naughten, McNaughten, McNaughten, and Macnaghten. *See* WRIGHTSMAN ET AL., *supra* note 97, at 295.

103. *See* STEADMAN ET AL., *supra* note 96, at 45, 46.

104. *See* M'Naghten's Case, 101 Cl. & Fin. 200 8 Eng. Rep. 718 (H.L. 1843).The M'Naghten case settled in 1843 involved Daniel M'Naghten who shot a man he believed to be the Prime Minister of England. Expert testimony suggested M'Naghten's conduct was the product of delusions bearing the theme of government persecution. Following instruction that M'Naghten would be committed to a psychiatric hospital pursuant to an insanity acquittal the jury found M'Naghten not guilty by reason of insanity. The court held a defendant

against it,[105] the insanity doctrine has undergone several revisions, including the modification of pre-existing models as well as more extreme legislative responses.[106] The various insanity doctrines have included the following: the IRI/police by the elbow test,[107] the *Durham* test,[108]

could be excused from criminal responsibility if, at the time of the offense, "the party accused was laboring under such a defect of reason, from disease of the mind, as not to know the nature and quality of the act...or, if [the defendant] did know it, did not know [that what he/she] was doing was wrong." *Id.* at 722. The term "wrong" as used in the M'Naghten standard had a meaning closer to moral condemnation not to be confused with the legal definition of wrongfulness subsequently developed. *See* People v. Skinner 39 C3d 765, 217 CR 685 (1985).

105. M'Naghten was criticized as being a unitary test, a rigid dichotomy between right and wrong, focusing on the cognitive processes of the defendant and ignoring the affective and volitional components of behavior. *See* Hermann & Sor, *Convicting or Confining? Alternative Directions in Insanity Defense Reform: Guilty but Mentally Ill Versus New Rules for Release of Insanity Acquittees*, 499 B.Y.U.L. REV 515, (1983); PERLIN I *supra* note 17, at 830–31; S. GLUECK, LAW AND PSYCHIATRY: COLD WAR OR ENTENTE CORDIALE 43–48 (Johns Hopkins 1966).

106. Modification and reform efforts have included: substantive changes/test criteria, procedural changes/burden of proof, commitment and release procedures, and, for some states, the replacement of the insanity defense with guilty but mentally ill (GBMI) laws. *See* STEADMAN ET AL., *supra* note 96, at 44. Historically, reasons for NGRI changes have varied; however, common themes involve practical (e.g., application of ambiguous tests) and political factors (e.g., public uproar over high profile cases and the identification of the insanity defense as a rich man's strategy). *See e.g.,* PERLIN I *supra* note 17, at 828–34; STEADMAN ET AL., *supra* note 96, at 1–5; WRIGHTSMAN ET AL., *supra* note 97, at 306.

107. The irresistible impulse test (IRI) asserted that a defendant could be excused from criminal responsibility if a mental illness caused an "irresistible and uncontrollable impulse to commit an act, even if he remained able to understand the nature of the offense and its wrongfulness." PERLIN I *supra* note 17, at 831, citing Dix, *Criminal Responsibility and Mental Impairment in American Law: Responses to the Hinckley Acquittal in Historical Perspective*, in 1 LAW AND MENTAL HEALTH: INTERNATIONAL PERSPECTIVES 1, 7 (Weisstub ed. 1986). Following its inception, the IRI sustained criticism with respect to theories of personality and, specifically, issues of self control. *See* Herman & Sor *supra* note 105, at 516. In response to uncertainty, the "police at the elbow test" attempted to clarify its standard by asking the following: "Would the impulse have been so overwhelming that the individual would have committed the crime even if a police officer had been standing at his or her elbow, thereby assuring that he or she would be caught?" WRIGHTSMAN ET AL., *supra* note 97, at 296–97. In addition to being impractical, the "police at the elbow test" was unable to reconcile the 'impulse' confusion of the IRI.

108. In Durham v. United States, 214 F.2d 862 (D.C. Cir. 1954), the Court rejected both the M'Naghten and IRI standard, relying on the psychological theory of the time and established a test more amenable to expert psychiatric testimony. *See* PERLIN *supra* note 17, at 832; WRIGHTSMAN ET AL., *supra* note 97, at 296–297. In short, the test excused criminal responsibility if the defen-

the ALI-MPC test,[109] the guilty but mentally ill (GBMI) laws,[110] the Insanity Defense Reform Act (IDRA),[111] and, in the extreme, the

dant's conduct was a "product" of a mental disease or defect. *See* Durham *supra,* at 874–75. In addition to creating a broader test, *Durham* shifted the burden of persuasion to the prosecution which had to prove sanity beyond a reasonable doubt, a departure from M'Naghten and the IRI where both the defense and the prosecution shared the burden. *Durham* was criticized as a vague test failing to provide a standard for the jury to judge the evidence, misidentified the issues of moral responsibility and diagnostic explanation, and relied too much on psychiatric expertise. *See E.g.,* PERLIN I *supra* note 17, at 833; A. GOLDSTEIN, THE INSANITY DEFENSE 12, (1967); A. Krash, *The Durham Rule and Judicial Administration of the Insanity Defense in the District of Columbia,* 70 Yale L.J. 905 (1961); Herman & Sor *supra* note 105, at 520.

109. The American Law Institute (ALI) doctrine was crafted in 1962. The ALI relied on its Model Penal Code (MPC) and used language which focused on both volitional and cognitive issues; thus, this test is known as the ALI-MPC. *See* PERLIN I *supra* note 17, at 833; A. GOLDSTEIN *supra* note 108, at 84. The ALI-MPC attempted to reconcile some of the more pronounced criticisms of M'Naghten, *Durham,* and the IRI. Although presented as a compilation of the previous standards, the ALI-MPC is derived from M'Naghten and, in part, modified the language used therein. With respect to the language used in M'Naghten, ALI-MPC substituted "appreciate" for the term "know," and "wrongfulness" for the term "criminality." *See* PERLIN I *supra* note 17, at 834; A. GOLDSTEIN *supra* note 108, at 87; Hermann & Sor, *supra* note 105, at 522. Additionally, where M'Naghten was premised on the "absolute" inability to appreciate right from wrong, ALI-MPC focused on "substantial" incapacity to know the difference. *See* B. ARRIGO, THE CONTOURS OF PSYCHIATRIC JUSTICE: A POSTMODERN CRITIQUE OF MENTAL ILLNESS, CRIMINAL INSANITY, AND THE LAW 36 (1996). Similar to *Durham,* the burden of persuasion was on the prosecution to prove sanity beyond a reasonable doubt. Although vested in language shifts, the modifications were applauded by critics and thought to succeed where the other tests had failed. Specifically, the ALI-MPC captured both the cognitive and affective components of human behavior. *See* Hermann & Sor *supra* note 105, at 523–524. The ALI-MPC test was adopted by over half of the states and the District of Columbia which overruled its "product test," previously championed in the *Durham* decision of 1954. *See* PERLIN I *supra* note 15, at 834; U.S. v. Brawner, 471 F.2d 969 (D.C. Cir. 1972).

110. Since the ALI-MPC, more conservative trends have been adopted, reflecting increasing public concern over the use of the insanity plea. For example, in 1976, about a quarter of the states introduced legislation allowing juries to find defendants guilty but mentally ill (GBMI) in cases where the insanity defense was raised. *See* WRIGHTSMAN ET AL *supra* note 97, at 307. Under this legislation, cases involving an insanity plea defendants can be found not guilty, not guilty by reason of insanity, guilty but mentally ill, or guilty. Although these rules vary from state to state, a GBMI determination generally results in the defendant first being committed to a psychiatric hospital for treatment purposes and then transferred to the designated prison. *Id.* at 308. GBMI laws were developed to curtail the use of the insanity plea and increase "incarcerations in secure settings." *See* STEADMAN ET AL., *supra* note 96, at 103.

111. High-stakes and controversial cases (e.g., John Hinckley Jr.) have also

abolition of the special defense of insanity.[112] The current standard emphasizes the defendant's ability to appreciate the nature and quality of the wrongfulness of the act and is known as the "appreciation test."[113] This standard combines portions of previous insanity test formulations. The current federal standard, as amended in 1984, is set out at 18 U.S.C.§17(a) and states that: "...[A]s a result of a severe mental disease or defect, [the defendant] was unable to appreciate the nature and quality or the wrongfulness of [his or her] acts."[114] Not unlike the competency statute providing for presumption of trial fitness,[115] the criminal responsibility standard does so as well. Accordingly, if the accused pleads insanity, then he or she is presumed responsible for the acts constituting the offense and must then submit evidence to the contrary; a condition known as an affirmative defense.[116] Moreover, the defendant bears the burden of proving insanity by clear and convincing evidence.

C. Confusion with Competency to Stand Trial and Criminal Responsibility

In terms of legal criteria, competency to stand trial and criminal responsibility display obvious differences; however, the two stan-

---

fueled civic unrest. President Reagan's would-be assassin sparked public concern following his acquittal by reason of insanity in 1982. In response, legislative efforts reformed the insanity defense making the prospect of NGRI acquittal more difficult. *See e.g.*, STEADMAN ET AL., *supra* note 96, at 1, 2; WRIGHTSMAN ET AL., *supra* note 97, at 293. The conservative trend culminated with the enactment of the Insanity Defense Reform Act (IDRA) of 1982. In addition to a more conservative test, the IDRA shifted the burden to the defense to prove insanity by clear and convincing evidence.

112. Some states (e.g., Montana, Idaho, and Utah) abolished the defense of insanity for alternative verdicts and guilty and mentally ill laws. *See e.g.*, STEADMAN ET AL *supra* note 96, at 38.

113. *See* ARRIGO *supra* note 109, at 36; B. McGraw, D. Farthing-Capowich & I. Keilitz. *The guilty but Mentally Ill Plea and Verdict: Current State of the Knowledge*, 21 Villanova Law Review, 18, 30 (1985).

114. *See* 18 U.S.C.§17(b).

115. *See* Medina v. California, 505 U.S. 437, 437 (1992).

116. *See* WRIGHTSMAN ET AL., *supra* note 97, at 295.

dards are often confused by mental health law professionals.[117] For example, clinicians (particularly psychiatrists) frequently misconstrue the legal criteria for competency,[118] apply the criteria for criminal responsibility to competency standards,[119] and evaluate competency and criminal responsibility together, regardless of whether the latter inquiry is requested in the court order.[120] In addition, studies reveal that both mental health experts and judges frequently equate psychosis with insanity[121] and/or incompetency,[122] even though mental illness does not resolve the legal question in either instance.[123] Notwithstanding the conceptual confusion, evaluations

---

117. See Golding et al., *supra* note 14, at 323.

118. See Winick I *supra* note 1, at 982; R. SLOVENKO, PSYCHIATRY AND LAW 93 (1973); STONE *supra* note 2, at 202–203.

119. See ROESCH & GOLDING *supra* note 16, at 16.

[1] See ROESCH & GOLDING *supra* note 16, at 51, citing a North Carolina court order which committed the defendant under a statute pending only a competency evaluation.

121. See ROESCH & GOLDING *supra* note 16, at 16.

122. For a review on the relationship between incompetency findings and psychosis see, A. McGarry, *Demonstration and Research in Competency for Trial and Mental Illness: Review and Preview*, 49 B.U.L. REV. 46, 50 (1969); Golding et al., *supra* note 14, at 323; STEADMAN & HARTSTONE *supra* note 2, at 46–47; Winick *supra* note 1, at 923; IDENTIFICATION *supra* note, 60, at 676–77. As for the judicial decision-making process, research indicates that a judge's decision is often based on the concluding statements provided in the psychiatric report. *See, e.g.*, Golding et al., *supra* note 14, at 323. Thus, it is safe to conclude that, in far too many instances, judges rely on the mental health examiner's misguided understanding of the legal standards, and the assumed, though faulty, correlation between psychosis and incompetency/insanity to guide their judgements. Judicial reliance on expert opinion is commonly discussed in reference to competency and commitment hearings. *See* ROESCH & GOLDING *supra* note 16, at 17, 140–200. *See generally* A. McGarry, *Competency for Trial and Due Process Via the State Hospital*. 122. American Journal of Psychiatry, 623–31 (1965); D. Bazelon, *Psychiatrists and the Adversary Process*, 230 Scientific American, 18–23; C. VANN & F. MORGANROTH, THE PSYCHIATRIST AS JUDGE: A SECOND LOOK AT THE COMPETENCE TO STAND TRIAL (1965); C. Vann, *Pretrial Determination and Judicial Decision-Making: An Analysis of the Use of Psychiatric Information in the Administration of Criminal Justice*, 43 University of Detroit Law Journal, 13–33 (1965).

123. For cases holding psychosis or mental disorder does not, in and of itself, equate with mental incompetency, *see, e.g.,* United States v. Adams, 297 F. Supp. 596 (S.D.N.Y. 1969) (evidence was sufficient to support a diagnosis of paranoid schizophrenia but was not sufficient to establish defendant was incompetent to stand trial) *Id.* at 596; Hall v. United States, 410 F. 2d 653 (4th Cir. 1969), *cert.* denied, 396 U.S. 970 (1969) (degrees of mental illness should not be equated with mental incompetence to be sentenced) *Id.* at 658; Swisher

are sometimes sought for fact finding purposes and, specifically, are used by attorneys to gather information relative to responsibility.[124] For example, the results of one survey exploring the legal community's interpretation and use of competency statutes and procedures indicated that 45% of the attorneys used CST evaluations to tap data relative to criminal responsibility.[125] Although this faulty and questionable practice does not occur routinely, and although changes are occurring gradually,[126] the tendency for confusion still exists, producing deleterious consequences for far too many criminal defendants.

The preceding review described, in some limited detail, the legal differences between competency to stand trial and criminal insanity. Indeed, exploring the basis of these respective legal questions demonstrates how they are often confused by various mental health law experts. We argue that the presence of conceptual confusion, and the problems inherent with court orders, demonstrate the importance of understanding the nuances of these similar, but distinct, legal standards. In the pages that follow, we consider how the modern day legal construct of competency to stand trial has been interpreted by the United States Supreme Court. The presentation of this material points to the complexities and nuances inherent in determining trial fitness; pivotal and contentious matters impacting decision making in law, psychology, and their intersection.

---

v. United States, 237 F. Supp. 921 (W.D.Mo.1965), aff'd, 354 F.2d. 472 (8th Cir. 1966) (it does not follow a defendant is incompetent to stand trial when correctly diagnosed mentally ill at the time of the trial); Feguer v. United States 302 F.2d 214 (8th Cir.), cert. denied, 371 U.S. 872 (1962) (mere presence of a mental illness does not mean an incompetency to stand trial finding). For cases holding mental illness does not, in and of itself, excuse criminal responsibility, see, e.g., U.S. v. Reed, C.A.7 (Ill.) 1993, 997 F.2d 332 (evidence suggested the accused suffered from a mental disorder, however, the defendant did not prove the illness prevented him from understanding or appreciating that his actions were wrong); U.S. v. Abou-Kassem, C.A.5 (Tex. 1996), 78 F.3d 161, cert. denied 117 S.Ct. 70 (1996) (although evidence suggested defendant suffered from paranoid schizophrenia the evidence was not enough to prove defendant was legally insane at the time of the offense); U.S. v. Cameron, C.A.11 (Fla. 1990), 907 F.2d 1051 (1990) (although defendant was previously diagnosed as schizophrenic, the diagnosis did not prove she was legally insane at those times or during the time the alleged crime took place).

124. See EVALS II supra note 24, at 127.
125. See ROESCH & GOLDING supra note 16 at 194.
126. See Golding et al., supra note 14, at 323.

Chapter 2

The Legal Standard of Competency: Case Developments

OVERVIEW

To comprehend the practical problems affiliated with CST outcomes, it is essential to examine the developments of the competency construct as formed from legal doctrines. The source of these doctrines can be traced to several United States Supreme Court decisions,[127] and these rulings appear to remain both enduring and compatible with prior holdings and certain constitutional rights.[128] The legally defined standards appear to serve dual functions when addressing competency-related issues. The relied upon standards not only define competency and varying aspects of the construct, but their language also influences how assessment instruments are configured.[129]

Social science research has focused on the limitations of the language used in the legal standards and their impact on every day competency matters.[130] For example, fitness to stand trial standards utilize broad language which is flexible in application but, nonetheless, is a source of confusion.[131] In addition, the catch-all phrase

---

127. *See generally* B. Boch, *Fourteenth Amendment-The Standard of Mental Competency to Waive Constitutional Rights Versus the Competency Standard to Stand Trial; Godinez v. Moran, 113 S. Ct. 2680 (1993),* 84 J. CRIM. L. & CRIMINOL. 883–914 (1993).

128. *See E.g.,* Grisso I *supra* note 6, at 91–92.

129. *See Id.* at 96–97; Arrigo & Bardwell *supra* note 18, at 18.

130. *See* GOLDING & ROESCH *supra* note 16, at 13–15; EVALS II *supra* note 24 at 122–124.

131. *See* ROESCH & GOLDING *supra* note 16, at 11.

"competence to stand trial" is often used to describe various contextual inquiries, even though such inquiries are unrelated to one another (e.g., competency evaluations immediately after arraignment, before defense counsel is appointed, as well as latter inquiries such as competency evaluations to understand pretrial stress and the ability to proceed to trial).[132] These and other shortcomings are attributable to the discourse on competency as linked to the prevailing case law on the matter.

Consistent with other legal critiques regarding the controlling competency standards,[133] we argue that an analysis of the relevant case materials will, in part, better explain the problematic nature of certain CST outcomes. Thus, this chapter explores the reasoning of the landmark United States Supreme Court decisions on competency to stand trial and further examines controlling Supreme Court holdings involving the right to waive counsel and the mental competence required to waive this right. The chapter suggests that these rulings not only conflate the varying competency inquiries previously mentioned, but do not adequately resolve CST matters involving certain mentally ill offenders. In what follows, we review those decisions focusing on the competency construct itself, as well as those cases that fuel the controversy surrounding the CST issue. In particular, these cases include: (a) *Dusky v. United States*, 1960; (b) *Faretta v. California*, 1975; (c) *Godinez v. Moran*, 1993.[134]

---

132. *See* Bonnie I *supra* note 11, at 293.
133. *See* ROESCH & GOLDING *supra* note 16, at 23. *See generally* Bonnie I *supra* note 11.
134. Some decisions provide more detail concerning the Court's logic (e.g., *Faretta v. California*, 1975). In addition to the majority 's opinion, *Faretta* includes opinions concurring in part, as well as those that dissent from the majority. A similar pattern exists with respect to the decision in *Godinez v. Moran* (1993). In contrast, *Dusky v. United States* (1960) provides little discussion by way of court opinion. *Dusky* resulted in a *per curium* ruling (all nine Justices reached consensus); thus, the decision, although extremely brief, reflects the opinion of the entire Court. It follows, then, that the analysis as to the Justices' reasoning is dictated by the level of detail provided in the ruling itself.

A. Competence to Stand Trial

1. The Dusky Decision

The current competency standard is derived from the U.S. Supreme Court case of *Dusky v. United States* (1960).[135] In *Dusky*, the Court held "[I]t is not enough for the district judge to find that "the defendant [is] oriented to time and place and [has] some recollection of events, but that the test must be whether [one] has sufficient present ability to consult with [one's] lawyer with a reasonable degree of rational understanding and whether [one] has a rational as well as factual understanding of the proceedings against [onself]."[136] The test established in *Dusky* has since come to be the formula used in federal court, and many state jurisdictions follow *Dusky* in substance[137] or use a variation of *Dusky's* test.[138] Although both pervasive and enduring,[139] the definition of CST provided in *Dusky* is extremely brief. Indeed, because the Court did not offer a lengthy opinion, inferential analysis is often used to understand the elements of *Dusky's* competency test. One example of such inferential analysis is provided by Melton et al.[140]

According to Melton et al., there are five relevant components embedded in the *Dusky* decision pertaining to competency to stand trial. First, *Dusky* identifies a two-prong competency test: (a) the defendant's ability to participate in the trial process, a collaborative effort between the accused and defense counsel in the construction of a defense and (b) the defendant's capacity to understand the trial process, including the role of those involved.[141] Second, these criteria make it clear that the inquiry focuses specifically on the defen-

---

135. *See* Dusky v. United States, 362 U.S. 402 (1960) (Milton Dusky helped two teenage boys rape a teenage girl, and was subsequently charged with the kidnaping of the girl). *See Id.* at 402.
136. *See Dusky,* 362 U.S. 402 (1960).
137. *See* Winick I *supra* note 1, at 923.
138. *See* Grisso I *supra* note 6, at 91.
139. *See Id.*
140. *See* EVALS II *supra* note 24, at 121.
141. *See Id.* at 122.

dant's present ability to understand and assist in the trial process.[142] Third, the accused's participation in the trial process is linked to cognitive abilities rather than a willingness to be involved. To be more precise, if 'rational factors' influence trial abilities (e.g., a sensible choice is made not to participate in the defense, the defendant does not understand trial information as a result of not being instructed by counsel), then an incompetency determination is not warranted. However, if the defendant is unable to meet the two-prong standard as a product of 'irrational factors' (e.g., mental illness as cognitive impairment), then a finding of incompetency is likely to be justified.[143] Fourth, a finding of competency requires that the accused possess a "reasonable degree of understanding."[144] According to Melton et al., this language does not require an absolute understanding and, by most researchers' accounts, this threshold is relatively low.[145] Although acknowledged as a simple burden to meet, "understanding" may vary from case to case as some offenses are more involved than others (e.g., drunk driving versus homicide). Thus, a reasonable level of understanding in one context may be sufficient as opposed to more complicated offenses.[146] From this perspective, *Dusky's* use of the term "reasonable", endorses a broad test applicable to various contexts, recognizing that levels of understanding may be governed by the alleged crime.

In relation to the second prong of *Dusky;* that is, the ability to consult with counsel, the test does not require a "meaningful relationship" between attorney and client.[147] The notion of reasonableness implies that attorney-client relations need only be sufficient in order to assist in or prepare a defense and further suggests that per-

---

142. *See Id.*
143. *See Id.*
144. *See Dusky*, 362 U.S. at 402.
145. *See Id.* at 122; INCOMPETENCY *supra* note 12, at 459; GAP *supra* note 4, at 896.
146. *See* EVALS II *supra* note 24, at 122.
147. Although based on motions relating to ineffective counsel, some commentators have suggested these rulings can be generalized to include client/attorney relations in the competency to stand trial context. *See Id.* citing Favole, *Mental Disability in the American Criminal Process: A Four Issue Survey:* PERSPECTIVE FROM LAW AND SOCIAL SCIENCE 247 (John Monahan & Henry Steadman eds. 1983).

sonality clashes do not have a direct bearing on competency to stand trial matters.[148] Fifth, *Dusky's* emphasis on cognitive functioning is related to the defendant's rational and factual comprehension.[149] Consistent with other court holdings,[150] the mere presence of a mental illness does not, in and of itself, require an incompetency finding.[151] Indeed, such concerns as mental illness and low IQ are only applicable to the legal question of competency when they bear directly on the defendant's *"rational and factual understanding"* of the trial proceedings and the individual's ability to consult with defense counsel.[152]

2. Limitations and the Dusky Decision

Consistent with Melton et al.'s analysis, an examination of the *Dusky* standard is largely achieved by inferring the standard's underlying intent. In addition to presenting the purpose of *Dusky's* two-prong test, social scientists have identified a number of shortcomings. These shortcomings address the Court's ambiguous wording, the judicial construction of the decision itself, and *Dusky's* lack of overall specifics.[153]

The two-pronged *Dusky* standard has been criticized for its range of applicability as well as its confusing and ambiguous language. For example, the extent to which mental health professionals are able to clarify what constitutes "sufficient present ability" as well as a "reasonable degree of rational understanding" presents a formidable task for forensic practitioners.[154] Although the *Dusky* requirement addresses the presence of mental illness, subsequent

---

148. *See e.g.,* EVALS II *supra* note 24, at 122.
149. *See Id.*
150. *See Id.,* citing among other court rulings, People v. Lang, 113 Ill. 2d 407, 498 N.E. 2d 1105 (1986); State v. Black, 815 S.W.2d 166 (Tenn. 1991).
151. *See* Winick I *supra* note 1, at 923; United States v. Adams, 297 F. Supp. 596 (S.D.N.Y. 1969).
152. *See* EVALS II at 122.
153. *See* ROESCH & GOLDING *supra* note 16, at 11–14; R. Nicholson & K. Kugler, *Competent and Incompetent Criminal Defendants: A Quantitative Review of Comparative Research,* 109 PSYCHOLOGY BULLETIN, 355, 356 (1991).
154. *See Dusky,* 362 U.S. at 402.

courts[155] further outlined the purpose of the construct relative to clinical evaluations.[156] These cases emphasize the effects mental impairment might have on the functional abilities of a defendant, during the course of a trial.[157] In essence, attempts to flesh out the meaning of *Dusky* suggest that although a mental illness could be present, it might not require a finding of incompetence to stand trial. However, as some critics of the *Dusky* case have observed, "while it is true that the leading and controlling Supreme Court and federal court decisions do not equate incompetency to stand trial with mental illness or mental retardation, the 'openness' of the competency construct is a source of considerable confusion among mental and legal professionals."[158] For example, if the defendant proceeds to trial and has maladaptive or otherwise ubiquitous mental health concerns (paranoid or delusional symptomatology) the *Dusky* formulation is an easy standard to meet which can often complicate trial proceedings, especially when a paranoid or delusional defendant desires to control the defense strategy.[159]

A second shortcoming in the *Dusky* decision involves the judicial construction of the standard. A review of the case discloses the Supreme Court, *per curium*, relied exclusively on the government's position and, as a result, adopted verbatim the test put forth by the Solicitor General. Although consensus was reached among the Justices, the far-reaching impact of the decision, without something more, was as considerable as it was troubling. Indeed, the Court's failure to elaborate on its holding or to explain why it concurred with the government's position offered subsequent courts a questionable form of guidance in future CST matters. As Federal Judge Oliver opined, "[n]o one quarrels with what the Supreme Court actually held in *Dusky*; unhappiness with *Dusky* is produced by the fact that the Supreme Court said so little as to why it held what it did."[160]

---

155. *See* Swisher v. U.S., 439 U.S. 1115; 99 S. Ct. 1019 (1979); United States v. Wilson, 382 U.S. 454; 86 S. Ct. 643 (1966).
156. *See* Grisso I *supra* note 6, at 91.
157. *See Id.*
158. *See* Golding et al., *supra* note 14, at 323.
159. *See* Arrigo & Bardwell *supra* note 18, at 25.
160. *See* ROESCH & GOLDING *supra* note 16, at 13, 14 citing J. W. Oliver, *Judicial Hearings to Determine Mental Competency to Stand Trial.* FEDERAL RULES DECISIONS, 39, 537–49 (1965).

On a related subject, a third limitation with *Dusky* involves the brevity of the opinion and how the two-prong standard relates to the mental and legal functioning abilities of the defendant. *Dusky's* lack of detail produces the generic phrase "competence to stand trial," categorizing and collapsing differing aspects of criminal competency (e.g., competency to stand trial v. competency to waive rights) even though these inquiries have little relationship with one another.[161] As Bonnie points out, more than 90% of trial defendants plead guilty therefore the phrase "competence to stand trial" is fundamentally misleading: it assumes all criminal cases will proceed to trial and it does not adequately calculate the relevant dimensions of a defendant's competence.[162] Indeed, in most cases, relevant inquiries regarding trial competency involve the defendant's "capacity to assist counsel, conduct an adequate investigation of the [matter], and to make whatever decisions a defendant is required or expected to make in order to defend and/or resolve the case *without* a trial."[163] In addition, collapsing various competency aspects under the catch-all phrase "competence to stand trial" can often produce flawed trial outcomes when certain mental health defendants suffer from paranoid and delusional symptoms and are subsequently found competent to stand trial. Because of the hidden symptoms such disorders entail and as a result of a general inability to trust, the paranoid/delusional defendant will often fire attorneys and make strategic legal decisions that are neither logical nor, as we argue is subsequent chapters, strategic.[164]

Relatedly, *Dusky's* lack of specificity also results in various interpretations by both lower court judges and mental health examiners.[165] These differing interpretations have had a direct impact on the instruments used to assess whether one is or is not competent to

---

161. *See* Bonnie I *supra* note 10, at 293.
162. *See Id.* at 293.
163. *See Id.*
164. *See generally* Arrigo & Bardwell *supra* note 18. The subsequent chapter discussing the connection between paranoid and delusional mental health disorders and CST evaluations further explores psycholegal limitations (i.e., CST implications with the paranoid and delusional defendant). As a matter of practical utility, the case study analysis shows what can happen when the paranoid/delusional defendant is found competent to stand trial and, then, elects to conduct his own defense.
165. *See* Arrigo & Bardwell *supra* note 18, at 19.

stand trial.[166] In the (not so recent) past, CST instruments were guided by concepts such as psychosis and IQ; variables that had no direct bearing on the legal question of competency but, in fact, focused on the mental capacity of the client. Much like the fundamental problems associated with the definition of "competence to stand trial," the clinically oriented instruments were similarly flawed. The influence of assessment and diagnostic principles (e.g., the identification of psychosis) meant that the legally relevant dimensions of a defendant's competence potentially would be ignored or neglected. Recognizing these limitations,[167] social scientists began developing clinically oriented tools and protocols that focused on the legally relevant criteria of CST inquiries.[168]

The evolution of the legally oriented CST instruments remains the most significant modern trend with respect to assessment technology.[169] This notwithstanding, some have suggested that, in an attempt to describe accurately both mental *and* legal abilities, the assessment procedures regrettably are inadequately constructed to evaluate these components thoroughly.[170] For example, in observing the *Dusky* standard in relation to legal functioning ability, ascertaining the effects a mental disorder has for causing maladaptive behavior may be compromised in order to more precisely determine the primary legal component. What this suggests is that competency outcomes will continue to be reached by way of quantifying mental illness, making it less burdensome to address legal functioning abilities.[171] As a result, examiners and trial judges may conclude some disordered defendants do not suffer from a debilitating mental illness when, in fact, they do. Limitations concerning CST assessment protocol relative to evaluating competence-related abilities, as well

---

166. *See Id.*
167. *See generally* R. Nicholson, H. Robertson, W. Johnson, & G. Jensen, *A Comparison of Instruments for Assessing Competency to Stand Trial*, 12 LAW AND HUMAN BEHAVIOR, 313–321 (1988) [hereinafter Nicholson et al. I]; Golding et al., I *supra* note 14, at 321–334.
168. *See* Grisso I *supra* note 6, at 96.
169. *See Id.* at 145; EVALS II *supra* note 24, at 145.
170. *See E.g.,* R. Nicholson, S. Briggs, & H. Robertson, *Instruments for Assessing Competency to Stand Trial: How Do They Work?*, 19 PROFESSIONAL PSYCHOLOGY, 383–394 (1988) [hereinafter Nicholson et al. II].
171. *See generally* Nicholson & Kugler *supra* note 153, at 355–370. Evaluating and discussing characteristics related to incompetency findings.

as their connection to the competency-to-stand-trial legal standards are thoroughly reviewed and systematically examined in the subsequent chapter.

B. Competence to Waive the Right to the Assistance of Counsel and Represent Oneself

1. Right to the Assistance of Counsel in Federal and State Court

The constitutional guarantee that any person brought before a state or federal court is entitled to the assistance of counsel is traceable to a series of landmark United States Supreme Court cases.[172] Indeed, under the Sixth Amendment, the Court first recognized this protection applied to all federal defendants[173] unless the right was "intelligently and competently" waived.[174] It was not until the watershed case of *Gideon v. Wainwright*[175] that the Court reviewed, and subsequently ruled, that the state had an obligation to appoint counsel to an indigent defendant who, in the absence of such protection, would experience the abrogation of his or her constitutionally ensured due process rights.[176] In fact, the *Gideon* decision was

---

172. *See* Faretta v. California, 422 U.S. 806, 807 (1975). ("The Sixth and Fourteenth Amendments of our Constitution guarantee that a person brought to trial in any state or federal court must be afforded the right to the assistance of counsel before [one] can be validly convicted and punished by imprisonment.") *See also E.g.,* Powell v. Alabama, 287 U.S. 45 (1932); Johnson v. Zerbst, 304 U.S. 458 (1938); Betts v. Brady, 316 U.S. 455 (1963); Gideon v. Wainwright, 372 U.S. 335 (1963).
173. *See* Powell v. Alabama, 287 U.S. 45 (1932); Johnson v. Zerbst, 304 U.S. 458 (1938); Argersinger v. Hamlin, 407 U.S. 25 (1972).
174. *See* Johnson v. Zerbst, 304 U.S. 458, 465 (1938). Although landmark cases such as *Powell* and *Johnson* recognized the constitutional right to counsel in federal court, this privilege was not always guaranteed in state court. Indeed, due process law did not require, in every case, an indigent's right to the assistance of counsel in state court. *See* Betts v. Brady, 316 U.S. 455, 486 (1963).
175. *See* Gideon v. Wainwright, 372 U.S. 335 (1963).
176. *See Gideon,* 372 U.S. at 335 ("The right of an indigent defendant in a criminal trial to have the assistance of counsel is a fundamental right essential to a fair trial, and petitioner's trial and conviction without the assistance of

so clear and direct on this matter[177] that the Court did not consider its alternative: the right to waive the assistance of counsel.

2. The Faretta Decision: Competency and the Right to Waive the Assistance of Counsel

One's right to the assistance of counsel is complicated when the accused's mental state is called into question. Once a defendant is found competent to stand trial, critical issues surface regarding the optimal defense strategy and the degree to which a defendant can (and should) actively participate in the trial proceedings.[178] For example, in the extreme, a situation may arise wherein the accused opts to waive counsel and proceed *pro se*, following a determination that the defendant is competent to stand trial.[179]

In 1975, the United States Supreme Court specifically addressed the question of whether a defendant in a state court was constitutionally required to accept appointed counsel, despite the accused's desire to proceed *pro se* to trial.[180] Specifically, in *Faretta v. Califor-*

---

counsel violated the Fourteenth Amendment.") The *Gideon* decision overruled the *Betts* decision. *See* Gideon, 372 U.S. at 335.

177. *See Gideon*, 372 U.S. at 344. Stating:
"That government hires lawyers to prosecute and defendants who have the money hire lawyers to defend are the strongest indications of the widespread belief that lawyers in criminal courts are necessities, not luxuries. The right of one charged with crime to counsel may not be deemed fundamental and essential to fair trial in some countries, but it is in ours." *See Id.* at 344.

178. *See generally* J. Decker, *The Sixth Amendment Right to Shoot Oneself in the Foot: An Assessment of the Guarantee of Self-Representation Twenty Years After Faretta*, 6 CONSTITUTIONAL LAW JOURNAL, 483–598 (1996)[hereinafter DECKER];Grisso II *supra* note 29, at 357.

179. See Arrigo and Bardwell *supra* note 18, at 16 (exploring the implications of this scenario in high profile cases).

180. Supreme Court decisions following *Gideon* touched on the idea of waiving counsel but did not clearly address the issue. *See* Massey v. Moore, 348 U.S. 105 108 (1954) ("[A defendant] might not be insane in the sense of being incapable of standing trial and yet lack the capacity to stand trial without benefit of counsel." *See also* Westbrook v. Arizona, 384 U.S. 150, 150 (1966) (In differentiating between a hearing into the issue of competence to stand trial and a hearing into competence to waive assistance of counsel, the Court stated there is "the serious and weighty responsibility upon the trial judge of determining whether there is an intelligent and competent waiver by the accused"). *Id.*

nia[181] the Court held that "a defendant in a state criminal trial has a constitutional right to proceed without counsel when he voluntarily and intelligently elects to do so, and that the state may not force a lawyer upon him when he insists that he wants to conduct his own defense."[182]

Although the Supreme Court's decision in *Faretta* (concerning the right to waive counsel) was not based on facts involving a mentally ill defendant but instead addressed a more general constitutional issue (that is, whether all criminal defendants have a right to waive counsel under the Sixth Amendment), its implications are discussed relative to competency matters. To be sure, while a defendant may waive his or her right to counsel for various reasons having nothing to do with mental disability, this book discusses the implications of *Faretta* for mentally disordered defendants, or for defendants who undergo pretrial competency evaluations. Thus, given the current interest in the CST legal doctrine, the following section examines the limits of the *Faretta* ruling in relation to those defendants whose mental health status, notwithstanding a competency determination, remains at issue.

(a) Limitations and the Faretta Decision

As a general proposition, the opinion in *Faretta* produced a number of (unanticipated) problems, impacting the decision's reasonable and appropriate application to psychiatrically disordered defendants. Indeed, *Faretta* created a category in which all persons subjected to criminal prosecution were held to the same standard for waiving the assistance of counsel. To illustrate, an accused who undergoes a CST inquiry and is subsequently found competent to proceed to trial, is held to the same standard as a defendant whose trial competence is not (or is never) of concern. In both instances, as long as the defendant "voluntarily and intelligently" relinquishes his or her right to counsel, waiver is constitutionally permissible. Thus, "a defendant's delusion borne of mental illness has no bearing on the knowing and intelligent choice to waive the assistance of counsel."[183] Left unanswered by the *Faretta* decision, however, is

---

181. *See* Faretta v. California, 422 U.S. 806 (1975).

182. *See Id.* at 806.

183. *See* J. Corinis, *A Reasoned Standard for Competency to Waive Counsel After Godinez v. Moran*, 80 B.U.L. REV, 265, 275 (2000) [hereinafter Corinis] citing D. Shapiro, *Ethical Dilemmas for the Mental Health Professional:*

whether an accused, found competent to stand trial *with* the assistance of counsel, is therefore competent to proceed *without* an attorney, following the mentally ill defendant's waiver of counsel.[184]

In addition, the *Faretta* decision is suspect because it attempts to promote two competing, if not conflicting, interests. As Corinis observes, "the defendant's due process right to a fair trial, which seems to require assistance of counsel, and honoring the defendant's autonomy in his decision to waive counsel, if competent, [appear incongruous]."[180] In other words, the *Faretta* decision establishes a trade-off between autonomy over reliability when defendants opt to relinquish the right to counsel and proceed *pro se* to trial.[181] Thus, a person subjected to criminal prosecution who is clinically delusional may be able to waive "competently and intelligently" the right to counsel but may be doing so based on irrational beliefs or thoughts.[182] Given these thorny and contentious matters (e.g., the Sixth's Amendment's implied intent regarding counsel, the defendant's right to a fair trial, and the privileging of autonomous decision making), the *Faretta* decision produced vastly different constitutional views by the Justices, exposing the Court's overall uncertainty.[183] In what follows, this section briefly reviews both the majority and dissenting opinions of this case.

(b) Faretta and the Majority Opinion

In delivering the opinion of the Court, Justice Stewart suggested the assistance of counsel helped preserve the right to a fair

---

Issues Raised by Recent Supreme Court Decisions, 34 CAL. W. L. REV. 177, 178 (1997) (quoting People v. Lego, 660 N.E.2d 971, 979 (Ill. 1995).

184. *See* Corinis *supra* note 183, at 275.

180. *See Id.* at 274.

181. *See* Bonnie I *supra* note 11, at 300 (discussing how "a single criterion of decisional competence is not likely to fit all decisional contexts"). *Id. See also Faretta*, 422 U.S. at 834 (discussing *autonomy* "[A]nd although he may conduct his own defense ultimately to his own detriment, his choice must be honored...," versus *reliability* "It is undeniable that in most criminal prosecutions defendants could better defend with counsel's guidance than by their own unskilled efforts").

182. *See* Arrigo and Bardwell *supra* note 18 at 22–25 exploring this problem.

183. *See Faretta*, 422 U.S. at 806. Justice Stewart delivered the opinion of the Court in which Six justices joined. Chief Justice Burger and Justice Blackmun filed separate dissenting opinions in which they, and Justice Rehnquist, collectively joined.

trial;[184] however, his opinion also stated that the imposition of such assistance might infringe on the accused's right to control the defense.[185] In articulating the logic of *Faretta*, Justice Stewart obfuscated the issues of one's right to a fair trial and the significance of one's autonomous choice making. As Justice Stewart opined,

> "[I]t is the defendant, therefore, who must be free personally to decide whether in his particular case counsel is to his advantage. And although he may conduct his own defense ultimately to his own detriment, his choice must be honored out of that respect for the individual which is the lifeblood of the law."[186]

individuality?feb [handwritten annotation]

Following this passage, trial fairness is dependent on the voluntary and intelligent judgement of the defendant, notwithstanding the presence of psychiatric disorder (e.g., paranoid and delusional thoughts), provided one is competent to stand trial.

Moreover, similar to the analysis used in *Dusky*, the judicial construction of *Faretta* reflects a questionable basis on which the Court reached its eventual conclusion. Indeed, this is most apparent in the Court's analysis of the implied structure of the Sixth Amendment.[187] For example, in support of the Court's opinion Justice Stewart observed,

> "The language and spirit of the Sixth Amendment contemplate that counsel, like other defense tools guaranteed by the Amendment, shall be an aid to a willing defendant— not an organ of the State interposed between an unwilling defendant and his right to defend himself personally. To thrust counsel upon the accused, against his considered wish, thus violates the logic of the Amendment."[188]

---

184. *See Faretta*, 422 U.S. 833–834 ("It is undeniable that in most criminal prosecutions defendants could better defend with counsel's guidance than by their own unskilled efforts").

185. *See Id.* at 834 ("To force a lawyer on a defendant can only lead him to believe that the law contrives against him").

186. *See Id.* at 834.

187. The content of the Sixth Amendment does not specifically address the right to proceed *pro se* but hints at this notion. In forming the decision, several of the Justices attempted to interpret the Amendment's implied meaning. *See Faretta* at 819. ("Although not stated in the Amendment in so many words, the right to self-representation— to make one's own defense personally— is thus necessarily implied by the structure of the Amendment").

188. *See Id.* at 820.

Following the Court's position in *Faretta*, then, (the mentally ill) defendant can exercise his or her right to waive assistance by an attorney, provided the decision is made voluntarily and intelligently.

(c) Faretta and the Dissenting Opinion

Although Justice Stewart's sentiments represent the controlling opinion of the *Faretta* Court, Justice Blackmun offered a virulent dissent on the matter of waiving counsel. As he asserted,

> "The Court believes that the silence of the Sixth Amendment as to the... right [to waive counsel] is evidence of the Framers' belief that the right was so obvious and fundamental that it did not need to be included 'in so many words' in order to be protected by the Amendment. I believe it is at least equally plausible to conclude that the Amendment's silence as to the right of self-representation indicates that the Framers simply did not have the subject in mind when they drafted the language."[189]

Justice Blackmun's statements suggest the *Faretta* Court, in one instance, reached its decision by inappropriately looking past the plain language of the Sixth Amendment. Moreover, as Blackmun intimates, the majority attempted to interpret the intent of the Framers, producing a decision fraught with vague judicial language. Although *Faretta* clearly states the constitution does not require the accused to accept counsel,[190] the Supreme Court's lack of consideration for ancillary issues (e.g., to proceed to trial *pro se* when the defendant's mental health status is at issue), left unresolved a number of important questions on the matter of competency. In addition, *Faretta's* rather narrow constitutional scope regarding the defendant's right to waive counsel[191] did not contemplate the practical repercussions of an accused's decision to relinquish this right voluntarily and intelligently, particularly in the wake of being found com-

---

189. *See Id.* at 850. *See also Id.* at 837 (Burger, C.J., dissenting) ("Its [the Court's opinion] ultimate assertion that such a right is tucked between the lines of the Sixth Amendment is contradicted by the Amendment's language and its consistent judicial interpretation").

190. *See Faretta* at 820 ("To thrust counsel upon the accused, against his considered wish, thus violates the logic of the Amendment.).

191. *See supra* notes 178–180 and accompanying text (discussing the question before the Court). *Faretta* held the waiver must be both voluntary and intelligent. *See supra* notes 181, 182 and accompanying text.

petent to stand trial and notwithstanding the presence of mental illness. These matters are the subject of the final section on the *Faretta* decision.

(d) The Relationship Between Faretta and Dusky: More Practical Problems and Conceptual Confusion on the Matter of Competency

We maintain that the Court in *Faretta* failed to affirm or advance a basic premise of the *Dusky* standard involving the defendant's ability to consult with counsel. Indeed, an accused found competent to stand trial based, in part, on the knowledge that the individual was able to consult with counsel during the CST proceeding, can, in the wake *Faretta*, dismiss his or her attorney, thereby undermining and undoing the notion that the defendant was competent in the first place.[192] As previously mentioned, the Court held that a defendant could relinquish the right to counsel but opined "when [the person] voluntarily and intelligently elect[ed] to do so."[193] Admittedly, the criteria expressed in *Faretta* (e.g., voluntary and intelligent) works effectively for most everyday citizens; however, the standard is woefully inadequate for those whose fitness for trial has already been questioned.[194]

In addition to the practical problems posed by a CST defendant who elects to waive counsel, is the conceptual confusion generated by the Court's decision. In particular, *Faretta's* efforts to promote ostensibly conflicting interests (i.e., autonomy and reliability) fueled uncertainty among several circuit courts attempting to interpret and

---

192. In a subsequent Supreme Court case revisiting issues of competence to waive rights and represent oneself, Justice Blackmun clarified this point ("A finding that a defendant is competent to stand trial establishes only that he is capable of aiding his attorney in making the critical decisions required at trial or in plea negotiations. The reliability or even relevance of such a finding vanishes when its basic premise— that counsel will be present— ceases to exist"). *See* Godinez v. Moran, 509 U.S. 413.

193. *See Faretta*, 422 U.S. at 806.

194. The facts of the *Faretta* case reveal that the defendant did not have mental health problems nor was he subjected to a competency evaluation. *See Faretta* at 835 ("The record affirmatively shows that Faretta was literate, competent, and understanding, and that he was voluntarily exercising his informed free will"). *See also Godinez*, 509 U.S. at 416 ("But *Faretta* does not confer upon an *incompetent* defendant a constitutional right to conduct his own defense").

apply the decision accurately. Indeed, some state courts believed that *Faretta* overruled previous holdings impacting a person's constitutional rights, including the right to waive the assistance of counsel.[195] Conversely, other state courts did not recognize *Faretta* as abrogating the constitutional right of assistance from counsel.[196] In addition, Federal Courts of Appeal and state courts produced a number of inconsistent opinions on whether the competency standard for relinquishing the right to an attorney was higher than the competency standard for standing trial.[197]

Regrettably, the *Faretta* Court did not elaborate further upon its meaning or intent and, consequently, it is here that another considerable forensic dilemma becomes appreciably evident. Relying on the expertise of mental health professionals to inform courts about the elective and knowing decisions of disordered defendants for *pro se* purposes, is fraught with as many assessment difficulties as are the psychological evaluations themselves that determine competency.[198] Indeed, the *Faretta* Court's use of ambiguous language, will, by necessity, lead others to seek out interpretations for the implied meaning of "voluntary" and "intelligent." Thus, rather than offering greater conceptual and practical clarity on the psycholegal

---

195. *See* e.g., People v. Sharpe, 499 P.2d 489, 493–96 (Cal. 1972). In *Sharpe* the court held a criminal defendant had no right to waive counsel and to represent oneself under the state or federal constitution.

196. *See* Commonwealth v. Cavanaugh, 353 N.E.2d 732, 737–39 (Mass. 1976)). In *Cavanaugh* the court required a separate "probing" inquiry to waive counsel in order to protect the defendant's right to counsel). *See* Corinis *supra* note 183, at 275 n. 58.

197. *See generally,* Godinez v. Moran, 509 U.S. 387 (1993) *infra* note 191, at 395 n. 5, 6. For Federal Court of Appeals holdings that the competency standard to waive counsel is "vaguely higher" than that to stand trial, *see* United States ex rel. Konigsberg v. Vincent, 526 F.2d 131, 133 (2d Cir.1975); United States v. McDowell, 814 F.2d 245, 250 (6th Cir. 1987); Blackmon v. Armontrout, 875 F.2d 164, 166 (8th Cir. 1989). *See also* Seiling v. Eyman, 478 F.2d 211, 214 (9th Cir. 1973) (recognizing heightened standard for competency to waive counsel). *See* United States v. Clark, 943 F.2d 775, 782 (7th Cir.1991) (holding that competency to waive counsel is identical to competency standard for standing trial).

For state court holdings, *see generally* Godinez, 509 U.S. at 396 n. 6 citing among others Pickens v. State, 96 Wis. 2d 549, 567–568 (1980) (requiring a "heightened standard for waiver of counsel); People v. Reason, 37 N.Y. 2d 351, 353–354 (1975) (recognizing identical standard for competency to waive counsel and competency to stand trial).

198. *See generally* Grisso I *supra* note 6.

matter of competency to stand trial in relation to the accused's right to waive counsel, the *Faretta* Court's use of imprecise language only served to obfuscate the CST issue further.[199]

3. The Godinez Decision

In an attempt to reconcile nearly two decades of confusion among circuit courts in the wake of *Faretta*, the Supreme Court addressed the issue of competency and the right to waive counsel in *Godinez v. Moran* (1993).[200] Specifically, the question before the Court was whether the competency standard for pleading guilty or relinquishing the right to counsel was higher than the standard used to determine trial competence.[201] Before reviewing the Court's opinion, the factual and procedural history of the case is reviewed. These matters are significant as they draw practical attention to the dilemma of waiving counsel when one's mental health status is questioned in a criminal court of law.[202] In addition, however, recounting the factual and procedural sequencing of events in

---

199. *See* Decker *supra* note 178, at 488–498.

200. *See* Godinez v. Moran, 509 U.S. 389 (1993).

201. *See Godinez,* 509 U.S. at 391. Aside from addressing the specific question before the Court, *Godinez* sought to clarify the standard put forth in *Faretta* (i.e., competency to plead guilty and waive the right to counsel) and to resolve the confusion among the state and federal circuit courts on the matter. In addition, *Godinez* addressed the web of competency decisions (i.e., piecemeal rulings) expanding on specific aspects of the CST construct. *See infra* note 215 and accompanying text (discussing some of the relied upon cases refining the competency construct). The term "piecemeal" is uses as short-hand for the various cases elaborating on the competency construct and the partial clarification they added to it. The Ninth Circuit Court of Appeals relied heavily on such cases (e.g., *Westbrook v. Arizona* and *Rees v. Peyton*) to support their decision in *Moran v. Godinez,* 972 F.2d 263 (9th Cir. 1992). These piecemeal decisions were also reiterated by Justice Blackmun in his response to the majority's opinion in *Godinez v. Moran,* 589 U.S. 389 (1993). Generally speaking, the majority concluded the Ninth Circuit "read too much" into these decisions. *See E.g.,* Godinez, 509 U.S. at 397.

202. In contrast to the facts surrounding the *Faretta* case, the defendant Richard Moran showed marked signs that he was mentally impaired and, specifically, that he suffered from depression. *See infra* note 214 and accompanying text (discussing the psychiatrists' observations regarding Moran's depression). Furthermore, as the dissenters implied, Moran's depression had a direct bearing on his decision to relinquish his right to counsel and to plead guilty. *See Godinez,* 509 U.S. at 416, 417 (Blackmun, J., dissenting).

Godinez demonstrates the judicial uncertainty regarding the application of long-standing case law in the area of criminal competency matters.[203]

(a) Factual and Procedural History

On August 2, 1984, the defendant, Richard Moran entered a saloon and shot a bartender and a customer, each four times before removing money from the cash register.[204] Nine days after this initial incident, Moran went to his former wife's apartment, opened fire on her, and connected with five of the seven bullets.[205] Following the fusillade against his wife, Moran tried to commit suicide. First, Moran shot himself in the abdomen and then sliced his wrists.[206] He was unsuccessful in both attempts.[207] All three of Moran's victims died from the gunshot wounds.[208] On August 13, 1984 while in his hospital bed, Moran contacted the authorities and confessed to the murders.[209] Later, however, Moran would retract the confession and protest his innocence.

After pleading not guilty to three counts of first degree murder, Moran was evaluated and found competent to stand trial by two psychiatrists.[210] Following the CST evaluation, Moran discharged his counsel and changed his pleas to guilty, endeavoring "to prevent the presentation of mitigating evidence at his sentencing."[211] The court record also revealed that Moran was taking multiple medica-

---

203. The procedural history of the case involving Richard Moran is especially revealing. Although the state and federal courts rely on various landmark competency decisions, including the key decisions set forth in *Dusky* and *Faretta,* review of the *Godinez* matter shows the problems associated with fusing together piecemeal decisions addressing various aspects of the competency construct. Indeed, as this section will show both the Justices joining the Court's decision and the dissenters in *Godinez,* 509 U.S. 389 (1993) reach opposite conclusions with respect to interpreting longstanding case law.

204. *See Godinez,* 509 U.S. at 391.

205. *See Id.*

206. *See Id.*

207. See *Id.*

208. *See Id.*

209. *See Id.*

210. *See Id.*

211. *See Id.* at 392. As Justice Blackmun explained in the dissent, Moran's decision to plead guilty was a transparent attempt to suppress any mitigating evidence that might save his life and by doing so "essentially volunteered himself for execution." *See Id.* at 416.

tions[212] and was clinically depressed, according to both evaluating psychiatrists.[213] However, the trial court made no further inquiries into Moran's depression or the possible side effects of the prescription drugs. The trial court concluded that Moran had "knowingly and intelligently" waived his right to counsel and had "freely and voluntarily" pled guilty to the pending counts.[214] Moran was subsequently sentenced to death.

The Ninth Circuit Court of Appeals reversed the decision and used longstanding case law to support its holding.[215] The Ninth Circuit concluded that the facts in *Godinez* should have revealed a "good faith doubt" as to the defendant's competence to make a

---

212. During an interview, the trial judge asked whether defendant was under the influence of drugs or alcohol. Moran divulged he was under the influence of several prescribed medications. The medications were prescribed to control seizures stemming from his cocaine use. *See Id.* at 393 n. 2.

213. *See Id.* at 410. During the CST evaluation two psychiatrists observed Moran's depression yet both minimized its importance in relation to his trial competence. "Dr. Jurasky felt that Moran's depressed state of mind was not necessarily a major consideration. [And] Dr. William D. O'Gorman also characterized Moran as very depressed, remarking that he showed much tearing in talking about the episodes that led up to his present incarceration, particularly in talking about his ex-wife." *See Id.* at 410 (Blackmun, J., dissenting) (internal quotation marks omitted). However, with respect to whether Moran was competent to stand trial "[O]ne of the psychiatrists stated that there was not the slightest doubt that respondent was in full control of his faculties... [T]he other psychiatrist believed that respondent was knowledgeable of the charges being made against him." *See Godinez*, 509 U.S. at 391 n. 2 (1993) (internal quotation marks omitted).

214. *See Id.* at 393.

215. *See* Moran v. Godinez, 972 F.2d 263 (9th Cir. 1992). The Ninth Circuit relied heavily upon *Westbrook v. Arizona*, 384 U.S. 150 (1966). In *Westbrook*, the Court vacated the lower court's judgement confirming conviction because the trial court failed to provide separate competency inquiries. Although the court conducted a competency inquiry requiring fitness for trial, the court failed to conduct a hearing or inquiry into the defendant's competence to waive the right to counsel. *See E.g., Id.* at 150; *See also* Seiling v. Eyman, 478 F.2d 211, 215 (1973) (holding that a defendant must be able to "make a reasoned choice among the alternatives presented to him and to understand the nature of the consequences of his plea"). In addition, the Ninth Circuit inferentially drew from the following cases: Massey v. Moore, 348 U.S. 105 (1954) (holding that a person found CST with the assistance of counsel should be given a hearing as to his competence to represent himself); Pate v. Robinson, 383 U.S. 375 (1966) (discussing the criteria for doubting a defendant's competence); Drope v. Missouri, 420 U.S. 162, 181 (1975) (holding "a trial judge must always be alert to circumstances suggesting a change that would render the accused unable to meet the standards of competency to stand trial").

"voluntary, knowing, and intelligent waiver of constitutional rights," and, ultimately, should have resulted in a follow-up competency hearing before accepting the accused's decision to relinquish the right to counsel and to change his plea.[216] The Ninth Circuit further argued that the CST standard to waive important constitutional rights "requires a higher level of mental functioning than that required to stand trial...and a defendant is competent to waive counsel or plead guilty only if he has the capacity for 'reasoned choice' among the alternatives available to him."[217] The Ninth Circuit concluded that the District court "erroneously applied the competency to stand trial standard, instead of the correct 'reasoned choice' standard."[218]

It is clear that the case of Richard Moran produced conflicting findings among the state and federal courts reviewing the matter. Moreover, the factual and procedural history of this case reveal the complex interplay between a defendant with questionable mental health and the application of relevant case law in which various circuit courts recognize different standards.[219] Given that lower courts were in conflict over which standard to apply with respect to an adjudicated competent defendant's ability to plead guilty or waive counsel, and given that this very question divided the Federal Court of Appeals and the state courts of last resort, the Supreme Court granted certiorari to resolve the matter.[220]

(b) Godinez and the Majority Opinion

In the Supreme Court decision of *Godinez v. Moran*, seven of the nine Justices concurred in judgement.[221] The Court held that "the

---

216. *See* Moran v. Godinez, 972 F.2d 263, 266 (9th Cir. 1992). According to the Ninth Circuit Court of Appeals "the state court's postconviction ruling was premised on the wrong legal standard of competency."
217. *See* Moran v. Godinez, 972 F. 2d 263, 266 (9th Cir. 1992).
218. *See Id.* at 266–267.
219. *See infra* note 225 (discussing the varying standards adopted by state and federal circuit courts).
220. *See* Godinez v. Moran, 509 U.S. at 395 (1993).
221. Justice Thomas delivered the opinion of the Court, in which Justices Rehnquist, White, O'Conner, and Souter joined, and in Parts I, II-B, and III of which Justices Scalia and Kennedy joined. Specifically, Justice Kennedy filed an opinion concurring in part and concurring in the judgement, in which Justice Scalia joined. Justice Blackmun filed a dissenting opinion, in which Justice Stevens joined.

standard of competency for pleading guilty or waiving the right to counsel is the same as the competency standard for standing trial."[222] The decision hinged on a discussion of the CST doctrine, and the competency required to make important trial decisions (e.g, competency to plead guilty or waive the right to counsel), without drawing a distinction between the two. In support of its holding, the Court criticized the Ninth Circuit for reading too much into the *Westbrook* decision,[223] and argued that the Ninth Circuit was in error for "applying two different competency standards."[224] Specifically, the Court did not recognize the distinction between the Ninth Circuit's "reasoned choice"[225] standard regarding a defendant's ca-

---

222. *See Godinez*, 509 U.S. at 387.

223. *See Id.* at 397; *See also supra* note 215 (discussing the *Westbrook* decision).

224. *See Godinez*, 509 U.S. at 397. As the Court explained "[A] finding that a defendant is competent to stand trial, however, is not all that is necessary before he may be permitted to plead guilty or waive his right to counsel." *See Id.* at 400. The *Godinez* Court relied on the 'knowing and voluntary' standard required of all defendants seeking to waive the right to counsel as an explanation for why there should not be two different competency standards. *See Id.* at 400 citing Parke v. Raley, 506 U.S. 20, 28–29 (1992) (guilty plea); Faretta, 422 U.S. at 835 (1975) (waiver of counsel). According to the *Godinez* Court, there was a heightened standard with respect to waiving counsel but not a heightened standard for competency. *See Id.* at 401. The Court also opined that "[W]hen we distinguished between "competence to stand trial" and "competence to waive [the] constitutional right to the assistance of counsel, we were using "competence to waive" as a short-hand for the "intelligent and competent waiver" requirement of *Johnson v. Zerbst.*" *See Id.* at 401 citing *Westbrook*, 384 U.S., at 150 (1966).

225. The *Godinez* Court criticized the Ninth Circuit's reliance on Seiling v. Eyman, 478 F.2d 211 (1973), and the adopted "reasoned choice" standard. *Seiling* was the first Ninth Court decision to apply a higher standard than *Dusky* with respect to waiving constitutional rights. *See Godinez*, 509 U.S. at 396–397. *Seiling* found its support in the *Westbrook* decision and held the criteria associated with a CST inquiry "does not measure the defendant's capacity by a high enough standard. *See Seiling* at 214. The *Seiling* Court also relied on the dissenting opinion expressed in Schoeller v. Dunbar, 423 F.2d 1183 (9th Cir. 1970). In dissent, Judge Hufstedler stated "A defendant is not competent to plead guilty if a mental illness has substantially impaired his ability to make a reasoned choice among the alternatives presented to him and to understand the nature of the consequences of his plea." *Schoeller* at 1194 as cited in Seiling v. Eyman, 478 F.2d. 211, 215, n.1 (9th Cir. 1973). *Seiling* subsequently adopted the "reasoned choice" formulation articulated by Judge Hufstedler stating, "this formulation is the appropriate one, for it requires a court to assess a defendant's competency with specific reference to the gravity of the decisions with which the defendant is faced." *See Seiling* at 215.

pacity to plead guilty or waive the right to counsel, and the "rational understanding" formula as outlined in *Dusky* for fitness evaluations.[226] Indeed, as the Court indicated, if such a difference existed it was "merely one of terminology"[227] and largely irrelevant given that "we [the Court] reject the notion that competence to plead guilty or to waive the right to counsel must be measured by a standard that is higher than (or even different from) the *Dusky* standard."[228]

The majority's opinion is replete with examples supporting the idea that the *Dusky* formulation is sufficient to evaluate the capacity to plead guilty or relinquish constitutional rights. For example, as the Court explained, "while the decision to plead guilty is undeniably a profound one, it is no more complicated than the sum total of decisions that a defendant may be called upon to make during the course of a trial."[229] And elsewhere, as the Court commented regarding one's right to relinquish assistance by an attorney, "there is no reason to believe that the decision to waive counsel requires an appreciably higher level of mental functioning than the decision to waive other constitutional rights."[230] In addition, the majority in *Godinez* drew support for its position from the decision in *Faretta*. As the *Godinez* Court remarked, "we made it clear that the defendant's technical legal knowledge is not relevant to the determination [of] whether he is competent to waive the right to counsel."[231] Admittedly, the *Godinez* Court acknowledged that states were free to adopt competency standards more detailed than the *Dusky* formu-

---

226. *See Godinez*, 509 U.S. at 397 ("How this standard [i.e., reasoned choice] is different from[,] much less higher than[,] the *Dusky* standard— whether the defendant has a "rational understanding" of the proceedings— is not readily apparent to us").

227. *See Id.* at 397.

228. *See Id.* at 398.

229. *See Id.* at 398.

230. *See Id.* at 399. The Court then states "the competence that is required of a defendant seeking to waive his right to counsel is the competence to waive the right, not the competence to represent himself." *See Id.*

231. *See Id.* at 400 citing *Faretta* at 836 (internal quotation marks omitted). Regrettably, the *Godinez* Court applied a decision in which mental health concerns were not at issue— unlike the case involving Richard Moran whose mental health was a constant issue. Indeed, Justice Blackmun states " . . . *Faretta* does not confer upon an *incompetent* defendant a constitutional right to conduct his own defense." *See Id.* at 416.

lation; however, as the majority concluded, the "Due Process Clause does not impose these additional requirements."[232]

(c) Godinez and the Dissenting Opinion

Justice Blackmun, joined by Justice Stevens, criticized the majority's analysis, arguing that it was "contrary to both common sense and longstanding case law."[233] From the outset, Blackmun concentrated on the practical limitations surrounding the Court's ruling. In a passionate dissent, he wrote that the majority's decision, in effect, "upholds the death sentence for a person whose decision to discharge counsel, plead guilty, and present no defense may well have been the product of medication or mental illness."[234] To illustrate his point, Blackmun fleshed out the factual history regarding Moran's mental health[235] and discussed how the possible side effects[236] of the medications influenced the "dramatic change in his chosen course of action."[237] Blackmun further criticized the trial judge who failed to question Moran in regard to "the type, dosage, or effect of the medications to which he referred."[238] The dissent concluded that the trial court disregarded mounting evidence which suggested that Moran was mentally ill.[239] Further, Justice Blackmun

---

232. See Godinez, 509 U.S. at 402.
233. See Godinez, 509 U.S. at 409 (Blackmun, J., dissenting).
234. See Id. at 409.
235. Blackmun relied on the expert testimony provided by the evaluating psychiatrists, who documented Moran's depression. See Id. at 410 (Blackmun, J., dissenting) noting Dr. Jurasky observed Moran was in a "depressed state of mind" and Dr. William O'Gorman characterized Moran as "very depressed."
236. For the effect of the medications, see Id. at 410 (Blackmun, J., dissenting) ("Moran later testified to the numbing effect of these drugs, stating: "I guess I really didn't care about anything.... I wasn't very concerned about anything that was going on... as far as the proceedings and everything were going").
237. See Id. at 410.
238. See Id. at 410 (Blackmun, J., dissenting) (internal quotation marks omitted). For the type, dosage and potential side-effects of Moran's medication, see Id. ("defendant was presently being administered simultaneously-phenobarbital, dilantin, endaural, and viosterol). Blackmun notes "the records show that Moran was administered dilantin, an antiepileptic medication that may cause confusion; endaural, a beta-blocker antiarrhythmic that may cause light-headedness, mental depression, hallucinations, disorientation, and short-term memory loss; and viosterol, a depressant that may cause drowsiness, tremors, and convulsions." See Id. at 411 n. 1.
239. See Id. at 411.

noted that the trial court accepted the defendant's waiver of counsel and subsequent guilty plea based largely on his monosyllabic responses to questions regarding the accused's understanding of his legal rights and pending charges.[240]

Blackmun's critique also focused on the majority's universal application of the *Dusky* standard. Whereas the majority reasoned there was no need to elevate the *Dusky* formulation for queries involving the ability to relinquish counsel and proceed to trial *pro se*, Blackmun explained why different standards were necessary. Indeed, Blackmun's analysis centered on the first prong of the *Dusky* criteria requiring "sufficient present ability to consult with [one's] lawyer with a reasonable degree of rational understanding."[241] Thus, the dissent argued that the criterion was not applicable to queries involving a defendant inclined to represent himself, without counsel, and the application of *Dusky* in such instances therefore was not controlling.[242] As Justice Blackmun noted, "[t]he reliability or even relevance of such a finding [competent based on the ability to assist counsel] vanishes when its basic premise—that counsel will be present—ceases to exist. The question is no longer whether the defendant can proceed with an attorney, but whether he can proceed alone and uncounseled."[243] Relatedly, the dissent admonished the *Godinez* Court's "monolithic approach to competency,"[244] and argued that "[c]ompetency for one purpose does not necessarily translate to competency for another purpose."[245] Consistent with

---

240. *See Id.* "In a string of affirmative responses Moran purported to acknowledge that he knew the import of waiving his constitutional rights, that he understood the charges against him, and that he was, in fact, guilty of those charges." *See Id.* In a poignant example Blackmun considers the following exchange between the trial judge and Moran: "When the trial judge asked whether he killed his ex-wife deliberately, with premeditation and malice aforethought, Moran unexpectedly responded: No. I didn't do it—I mean, I wasn't looking to kill her, but she ended up dead. *See Id.* at 411 (Blackmun, J., dissenting) (internal quotation marks omitted). Instead of probing further as to Moran's true intent, the trial judge simply redefined the meaning of deliberate and premeditated and again asked Moran if he was guilty of the charges, to which Moran responded yes. *See E.g., Id.* at 411.
241. *See Dusky*, 362 U.S. 402 (1960).
242. *See E.g., Godinez*, 509 U.S. at 412–413.
243. *See Id.* at 413 (Blackmun, J., dissenting).
244. *Id.*
245. *Id.*

leading accounts in the forensic literature to view the specific circumstances wherein a fitness-to-stand-trial evaluation is ordered,[246] Blackmun asserted that "the majority cannot isolate the term competent and apply it in a vacuum, divorced from its specific context. A person who is competent to play basketball is not thereby competent to play the violin."[247]

Finally, the dissent in *Godinez* relied on longstanding case law to substantiate its position[248] and sanctioned the very case law the majority accused the Ninth Circuit of "reading too much into."[249] Defending the Ninth Circuit's use of *Massey vs. Moore*[250] and *Westbrook vs. Arizona*,[251] Justice Blackmun intimated that the majority disregarded the plain language of *Massey* and *Westbrook*, and that the Court in *Godinez* "overrule[d] those cases *sub silentio*."[252] Further, Justice Blackmun endorsed the Ninth Circuit Court's "reasoned choice" formulation opining that it "closely approximates the rational choice standard set forth in *Rees*."[253] In short, Blackmun distinguished competence to consult or assist counsel from the

---

246. *See generally* Bonnie I *supra* note 11; Winick *supra* note 1.

247. *See Godinez*, 509 U.S. at 413 (Blackmun, J., dissenting) (internal quotation marks omitted); *See also Id.* at 416 (Blackmun, J., dissenting) ("The majority's attempt to extricate the competence to waive the right to counsel from the competence to represent oneself is unavailing, because the former decision necessarily entails the latter").

248. Specifically Blackmun relied on Reese v. Peyton, 384 U.S. 312, (1966). In reference to Reese v. Peyton (1966), Blackmun states "[A]lthough the Court never has articulated explicitly the standard for determining competency to represent oneself, it has hinted at its contours." *See Godinez*, 509 U.S. at 414.

In *Reese* the Court required an inquiry as to whether the defendant "possessed the capacity to appreciate the position and make a *rational choice* with respect to continuing or abandoning further litigation or...whether [t]he defendant...suffer[ed] from a mental disease, disorder, or defect which...substantially affect[ed] his capacity in the premises" as cited in *Godinez*, 509 U.S. at 415.

249. *See Id.* at 397.

250. *See Massey*, 348 U.S. at 105, 108 ("[O]ne might not be insane in the sense of being incapable of standing trial and yet lack the capacity to stand trial without the benefit of counsel") as cited in *Godinez* at 414.

251. *See supra* note 215 (noting that Westbrook overturned a conviction because a separate hearing or inquiry was not conducted to assess the defendant's competency to waive right to counsel and proceed pro se).

252. *See Godinez* at 415. *Sub silentio* meaning under silence or without any notice being taken.

253. *See Godinez*, 509 U.S. at 415 (Blackmun, J., dissenting) (internal quotation marks omitted). *See supra* note 248 (discussing the *Reese* decision).

competence required of a defendant inclined to relinquish counsel and present his or her own defense. Indeed, as Blackmun concluded, competency evaluations should be "specifically tailored to the context and purpose of a proceeding."[254]

(d) Ambiguity, Conceptual Confusion, and the Godinez Decision

The majority in *Godinez* explicitly held that the *Dusky* standard was sufficient for purposes of ascertaining one's competence to plead guilty or waive counsel.[255] However, Justice Thomas also made clear that states were free to adopt more elaborate competency standards, indicating that "the Due Process Clause d[id] not impose these additional requirements."[256] Given the uncertainty expressed in this latter passage, *Godinez* will most likely have minimal impact on how states define the competency required to plead guilty or relinquish the right to counsel. Indeed, jurisdictions requiring higher formulations presumably will continue to do so; jurisdictions not insisting on higher standards presumably will not be so inclined to change.[257]

Although *Godinez* established a rule regarding fitness requirements for pleading guilty or waiving counsel, it did so at the expense of competency in the context of self representation.[258] Despite references to other procedural requirements,[259] the Court's use of

---

254. *See Id.* at 413.

255. *See Id.* at 389.

256. *See Id.* at 402.

257. *See* Grisso I *supra* note 6, at 94.

258. As the dissent observed "[t]he majority concludes that there is no need for [a competency hearing for defendants seeking to waive counsel and proceed pro se] because a defendant who is found competent to stand trial with the assistance of counsel, *ipso facto*, is competent to discharge counsel and represent himself." *See Id.* at 413 (Blackmun, J., dissenting). Simply stated, *Godinez* held the level of competence required to assist counsel is no different from the level of competence required to represent oneself. As a result of the *Godinez* decision, a defendant whose mental illness has already been called into question can be found CST, can later waive counsel, and can conduct one's own defense, regardless of whether the mental illness influenced any of those decisions. In this context, then, the Court's position neglected (or minimized) fundamental factors of cognition and volition essential to one's choice to proceed to trial *pro se* and, further, did not consider the potential impact of accepting such a waiver from defendants with a history of mental illness.

259. The majority asserted that relinquishing counsel must be "voluntary and intelligent" in accord with *Faretta* and, further, that the waiver must be "intelligent and competent" as provided in *Johnson v. Zerbst*, *See Godinez* at

precedent was suspect as it clarified inconsistencies in past decisions but failed to distinguish anomalies in the *Godinez* matter that had obvious significance.[260] Relatedly, the majority opinion supported a unitary standard for fitness, upholding *Dusky* as sufficient for waiving one's right to counsel and for conducting one's own defense, while conflating the various mental and legal abilities required of a defendant under the generic notion of "competence."[261] On a practical level, *Godinez* did not consider the demands necessary of a defendant to conduct competently his or her own defense, nor did it contemplate mental illness as a contributing factor informing the trial decisions that some defendants make (e.g., decisions that follow as a product of paranoid or delusional beliefs). In addition, while the Court explicitly stated that "a defendant's ability to represent himself [or herself] has no bearing upon [the accused's] competence to choose self-representation,"[262] the distinction is meaningless as the former demands the latter.[263] Simply put, competence to

---

400–401. As the Court opined, while this creates a "heightened standard for pleading guilty and for waiving the right to counsel, [it does not create] a heightened standard of competence." *Id.* From this language, the *Godinez* Court implied that the defendant's ability to plead guilty or waive counsel was more demanding and weighty than the ability of a defendant to conduct his or her own defense.

260. The Court's reasoning appears to be confounded as it articulates different standards in past holdings (e.g., *Faretta/Westbrook*; abilities to plead guilty or waive counsel different from *Dusky*; competence required to stand trial) but declines to do so in the *Godinez* matter (e.g., there is no difference between the competence formulation to stand trial and the competence standard required to conduct one's own defense). Obviously, the abilities required of a defendant to proceed *pro se* are more demanding than the abilities required to stand trial.

261. *See* Corinis *supra* note 183, at 283. The term competence includes the mental capacities required of a defendant to stand trial (e.g., ability to assist the attorney with a "reasonable degree of rational understanding" and a "rational and factual understanding" of the courtroom proceedings), as well as the legal capacity required to defend oneself during the trial (e.g., legal abilities associated with waiver to plead guilty or relinquish counsel, the legal abilities required to conduct one's own defense). *Godinez* helps promote the "one size fits all" approach to competency. *See Id.* at 283.

262. *See Godinez,* 509 U.S. at 400 (Thomas, J., referring to the holding in *Faretta*). *See also Faretta,* 422 U.S. at 836 ("For his technical legal knowledge, as such, was not relevant to an assessment of his knowing exercise of the right to defend himself").

263. *See E.g., Godinez,* 509 U.S. at 416 (Blackmun, J., dissenting). Blackmun refuted the majority's contention that *Faretta* supported a comparison between "the competency required to represent oneself and the competency re-

proceed in one capacity does not address necessarily the defendant's capacity to proceed in another. As Justice Blackmun poignantly explained, "a defendant who is utterly incapable of conducting his own defense cannot be considered competent to make such a decision, any more than a person who chooses to leap out of a window in the belief that he can fly can be considered competent to make such a choice."[264]

(e) Godinez: Defining Competency and Unanswered Questions

Others have challenged the *Godinez* decision for creating ambiguity[265] and for promoting a unitary competency standard.[266] On a related subject, critics have speculated upon *Godinez's* association with *Dusky*, pondering whether the former case changed the definition of competency as developed in the latter ruling.[267] Echoing Jus-

---

quired to choose self-representation. Blackmun explained "[*Faretta*] does not confer upon an incompetent defendant a constitutional right to conduct his own defense. Indeed, *Faretta* himself was literate, competent, and understanding, and the record showed that he was voluntarily exercising his informed free will." *See Id.* at 416 citing *Faretta,* 422 U.S., at 835. Simply, Blackmun noted that *Faretta's* competence had never been in question as compared to *Moran* who underwent a CST evaluation, and was clinically depressed. Despite these differences, both successfully waived their right to counsel.

264. *See Id.* at 416 (Blackmun, J., dissenting) (internal quotation marks omitted).

265. The contention that the majority's decision is ambiguous finds support in Justice Thomas's closing remarks, stating "[a]nd while States are free to adopt competency standards that are more elaborate than the *Dusky* formulation the Due Process Clause does not impose these additional requirements." *See Godinez,* 509 U.S. at 402. *See also* WINICK III *supra* note 40, at 619 (explaining how the *Godinez* standard "is still quite broad, open-textured, and vague, permitting clinical evaluators substantial latitude in interpreting and applying the test"); WINICK I *supra* note 1 at 982–983; BONNIE I *supra* note 11, at 549–50.

266. *See* Corinis *supra* note 183, at 283 (commenting on how the *Godinez* decision advances a unitary competency standard and noting that "[t]he problem with a unitary competency standard is that the mental abilities a defendant needs vary according to context; not all competencies are the same").

267. *See,* for example, Grisso I *supra* note 6, at 94, in which Grisso remarked:

"clinical examiners face an important conceptual question: Did *Godinez* change the meaning of *Dusky?* Does the *Godinez* decision mean that it is sufficient for defendants to be able to participate in the trial process if they might be deficient in the ability to process information (that is, to engage in reasoning) related to the decision to

tice Blackmun's virulent dissent, these observations draw attention to the decision's shortcomings in which the Court seemingly (and regrettably) chose to ignore the context and purpose of competency proceedings.

In the wake of *Godinez*, legal and psychological experts must address a host of questions left unanswered by the majority opinion. Of the more thorny and troublesome matters, two stand out warranting systematic attention. In short, these include the following: how, if at all, does *Godinez* alter *Dusky's* first prong which centers on the defendant's ability to assist counsel?; and, more generally, why did the *Godinez* Court selectively apply certain competency standards over others (e.g., *Dusky's* "rational understanding" model instead of *Seiling's* "rational choice" standard for waiving the right to counsel)?[268]

On a more practical level, the conflicting opinions expressed by way of the majority and dissenting opinions in *Godinez* raise another concern: Is it possible for lower courts to adjudicate adequately matters concerning mentally ill defendants (found competent) who later elect to waive counsel, given the degree of uncertainty voiced by the United States Supreme Court on such matters? This is precisely the kind of competency issue examined in the case study analysis of Colin Ferguson, entertained in chapter 5. Preliminarily, however, when inspecting the Justices' statements more closely, their opinions were not based so much on weighty differences in constitutional logic, but were, instead, the result of reaching opposite conclusions, informed by different judicial frames

---

waive important rights? Or did the court mean that reasoning abilities were (or should have been) an important part of the *Dusky* standard all along?"

268. The logic of the Court is indeed curious as the majority held there was no difference between the more demanding requirements related to the competency required to plead guilty or to waive counsel versus the competence required of defendants to stand trial. The court simply stated that the *Dusky* formulation was a sufficient standard, despite the fact that it was partially derived from the defendant's ability to assist counsel. *See supra* note 261. Curiously, to support the Court's decision, Justice Thomas later drew a distinction between two issues that obviously had a direct bearing on each other. As he stated, "the competence that is required of a defendant seeking to waive his right to counsel is the competence to *waive the right*, not the competence to represent himself." *See Godinez* at 399. In the dissent, Justice Blackmun admonished such logic. *See Godinez*, at 415.

of reference. How could this be? As previously mentioned, one explanation is found in *Godinez's* support of a unitary competency standard (i.e., the *Dusky* formulation), applicable to all contexts. While the majority believed this standard to be a sufficient test of competency throughout one's trial, the dissent vigorously argued to the contrary; that is, competency standards should "be specifically tailored to the context and purpose of a proceeding."[269] Again, this matter is revisited elsewhere in this book, particularly in the policy recommendations calling for legal reform on the matter of competency to stand trial.

In sum, the preceding review and analysis of the relevant United States Supreme Court cases and the pitfalls associated with the controlling decisions, allow one to better appreciate and evaluate the problems associated with those clinical instruments employed for purposes of ongoing CST determinations. Indeed, the next chapter demonstrates how the evolving (and existing) assessment technology is firmly anchored in the (questionable) logic of the Supreme Court. In particular, as we demonstrate, assessment difficulties are traceable to the legal standard as set forth in *Dusky* and its progeny (i.e., *Godinez*).

---

269. *See Godinez*, 509 U.S. at 413.

Chapter 3

The Psychological Standard of Competency: Assessment Developments

OVERVIEW

Debate concerning CST outcomes centers on the legal standard for competency and the various clinical procedures assessing the same.[270] Historically, research has recognized that standardized procedures evolved from earlier methods.[271] Notwithstanding the wholesale support for valid and reliable testing protocols, more recent revisions attempt to curtail CST evaluation controversies stemming from clinical judgements. In some instances, commentators have even offered to reformulate conceptually criminal competency and specifically restructure the way the law should define and evaluate trial fitness.[272] Indeed, these proposed initiatives have had a significant influence in the production of modern day competency assessment procedures.[273]

This chapter reviews the development of those assessment tools used to evaluate a criminal defendant's trial competency and discusses the limitations of these instruments. Particular attention is accorded the relationship between the psychological tests and the

---

270. *See generally* Grisso III *supra* note 33; EVALS II *supra* note 24.
271. *See* Grisso I *supra* note 6, at 95.
272. *See generally* Bonnie I *supra* note 11; Winick III *supra* note 33.
273. *See E.g.,* EVALS II *supra* note 24, at 145 (discussing how Bonnie's proposed theoretical reformulation of competency influenced modern day assessment procedures).

legal construct of competency.[274] In this context, the more conventional measures of CST assessment are examined; including: [a] the Competency Screening Test (CST),[275] [b] the Competency to Stand Trial Assessment Instrument (CAI),[276] [c] the Interdisciplinary Fitness Interview (IFI),[277] and [d] the Georgia Court Competency Test (GCCT).[278] This chapter concludes by providing a detailed review of the MacArthur Competence Assessment Tool-Criminal Adjudication (MacCAT-CA). Although clinical and social science efforts continue to revamp the assessment tools, problems inherent in the legal definitions and difficulties with past instruments suggest contemporary measures will, by logical extension, be similarly suspect. From this perspective, an argument is made that although contemporary assessment utility (e.g., Mac-CAT-CA) is sound in theory, the instruments remain largely deficient in application.

A. The Evolution of the CST Clinical Protocol

Contrary to the legal formulation of competency, the pretrial assessment instruments employed in CST hearings have undergone a number of significant revisions over the years.[279] Historically, these instruments have evolved from less structured checklists to more involved protocol.[280] In 1965, Robey was the first to develop a checklist which centered on the court process and specifically took a func-

---

274. To be sure, this chapter briefly examines how clinical assessment instruments compound problems associated with the open-textured competency legal standard. *See* T. GRISSO, EVALUATING COMPETENCIES: FORENSIC ASSESSMENTS AND INSTRUMENTS. (1986) [hereinafter GRISSO I]. For instance, these instruments often list several relevant capacities a defendant might need throughout the criminal trial process without indicating which ones are most important. As some suggest, such ambiguity is a product of the open-textured competency standard. *See* Winick III *supra* note 44, at 619; Bonnie I *supra* note 11, at 549–550.

275. *See* Lipsitt et al., *supra* note 40.

276. *See* LAB *supra* note 40.

277. *See* Golding et al., *supra* note 14.

278. *See* Wildman et al., *supra* note 40.

279. *See* Grisso I *supra* note 6, at 90–96.

280. *See Id.* at 95.

tional approach to the evaluation of trial competence.[281] Whereas former models focused on a diagnostic approach, Robey's checklist concentrated on the defendant's ability to communicate with counsel and his or her understanding of the legal process.[282] Shortly thereafter, other checklists and interview formats were developed, arguing that "medical questions, such as absence of psychosis, depression, etc., seemed irrelevant unless they cast useful light on legal questions."[283] To their credit, these checklists translated legal criteria into psychological indices of competency, improved the relevance of written and oral expert testimony, and provided a useful guide for interviewers.[284] Regrettably, these measures were not structured instruments and the field quickly moved in the direction of developing more standardized tests.[285] In the early 1970s, A. Louis McGarry and his colleagues produced two quantified tests to assist mental health professionals in the assessment of competency: the Competency Screening Test (CT);[286] and the Competency to Stand Trial Assessment Instrument (CAI).[287]

1. The Competency Screening Test

Developed by Lipsitt, Lelos, and McGarry, the CT is a 22 item sentence completion test used to expedite the initial screening process of defendants for whom the issue of competency is raised.[288] In developing the CT, McGarry's team considered relevant data regarding referrals for competency and outcomes. At the time, research indicated that 80% to 90% of defendants who raised competency concerns were later found competent to stand trial.[289] For

●

---

281. *See* Robey *supra* note 28.
282. *See* ROESCH & GOLDING *supra* note 16, at 58–59; EVALS II *supra* note 24, at 139.
283. *See* Bukatman et al., *supra* note 28.
284. *See* Nicholson et al., I *supra* note 167, at 313–321.
285. *See* EVALS II *supra* note 24, at 139.
286. *See* Lipsitt et al., *supra* note 40. The Competency Screening Test is more commonly called the CST; however, the acronym CT is used because the shorthand CST, in this investigation, refers to competency to stand trial.
287. *See* Wildman et al., *supra* note 40.
288. *See* Golding et al., *supra* note 14, at 324.
289. *See Id.*

this reason, the CT was designed to identify incompetent defendants from those clearly fit, and ultimately reduced the many unnecessary competency evaluations that were both time consuming and costly.[290]

In designing the CT, McGarry's team not only sought to quantify a competency measure but endeavored to further align competency evaluations with the legal criteria set forth in *Dusky*.[291] Accordingly, each of the 22 sentence stems describes a hypothetical legal situation in which the defendant must respond.[292] Typical questions include: "The lawyer told Bill that___," "Jack felt that the judge___," "Each time the DA asked me a question, I___," "If the jury finds me guilty, I___."[293] Each of the responses is scored either 2 (competent response), 1 (a questionable response), or 0 (an incompetent response). Test scores range from 0 to 66 and McGarry and his colleagues designated a cut-off score of 20. Those defendants scoring below 20 were "screened in" and underwent a more extensive competency evaluation.[294]

The results of several studies support CT's use as a screening device,[295] capable of identifying defendants with apparent mental health problems.[296] Other investigators consider the CT a worthy addition to the more comprehensive competency evaluations.[297] Finally, empirical studies indicate that the CT has high interscorer re-

---

290. *See* ROESCH & GOLDING *supra* note 16, at 59.

291. *See* Golding et al., *supra* note 14, at 323.

292. Although the CT was drafted as a written test, examiners also used an oral administration of the test. *See* R. Nicholson, S. Briggs, & H. Robertson, *Instruments for Assessing Competency to Stand Trial: How Do They Work?*, 19 Professional Psychology: PROF. PSYCHOL.: RES & PRAC. 384, 385 (1988) [hereinafter Nicholson et al. III].

293. *See* Lipsitt et al., *supra* note 40.

294. *See Id.* at 107. The scoring manual is described in LAB *supra* note 40, at 75–88.

295. *See generally* J. Randolph, T. Hicks, & D. Mason, *The Competency Screening Test: A Replication and Extension,* 8 CRIM. JUST. BEHAV. 471–481 (1981) [hereinafter Randolph et al. I]; J. Randolph, T. Hicks, D. Mason, & D. Cuneo. *The Competency Screening Test: A Validation Study in Cook County, Illinois,* 9 CRIM. JUST. BEHAV. 495–500 (1982) [hereinafter Randolph et al. II].

296. *See* EVALS II *supra* note 24, at 141 (noting CT accurately identifies a high percentage of defendants with mental health concerns, usually over 50%).

297. *See* Nicholson et al., I *supra* note 167, at 314; *See also* Grisso III *supra* note 33, chap 5 for a more complete review.

liability with coefficients ranging from .88 to .95,[298] in which it accurately predicts forensic staff decisions[299] and judicial decisions regarding competency.[300]

Despite its widespread use and the ease of its application, follow-up studies concerning the competency screening test have offered results contrary to the instrument's original validation work.[301] First, several studies indicate the CT has the lowest mean predictive validity of all the competency instruments, resulting in a high level of false positives, otherwise labeling competent persons as incompetent.[302] However, as Melton et al. note, if errors on screening measures are to occur, false positives are better than labeling an incompetent person competent; a potentially devastating determination in which the accused is subjected to a trial where one's understanding may be compromised or otherwise jeopardized.[303]

Another concern regarding the CT is whether it adequately samples competence-related abilities.[304] Nicholson and his colleagues conducted a study using internal consistency analyses, item analyses, and factor analyses to determine how the CT and another standardized scale predicted the competency criteria. Their investigations indicated that the CT could not provide a clear basis of its predictive power,[305] and their study was unable to replicate the factor structure reported by CT's developers.[306] Additionally, Nichol-

---

298. See Lipsitt et al., *supra* note 40; Randolph et al., I *supra* note 286; Randolph et al., II *supra* note 286.

299. See Nicholson et al., II *supra* note 170, at 384; L. Shatin, & S. Brodsky, *Competency for Trial: The Competency Screening Test in an Urban Hospital Forensic Unit*, 46 The Mount Sinai Journal of Medicine. 131–134 (1979).

300. See Nicholson et al., I *supra* note 167, at 314.

301. See generally LAB *supra* note 40.

302. See EVALS II *supra* note 24, at 139–140 (noting the CT's false-positive rate is rather high, ranging from 14.3% to 28.6%).

303. See *Id. citing* S. Brakel, *Presumption, Bias, and Incompetency in the Criminal Process*, 1974 WIS. l. Rev. 1105, 1118–1119 (the reason for so many false positives on this exam are the biases against a defendant who has a negative perception of the legal system). For example, "Jack felt that the judge____" "was fair" is a 2 point (competent) response, while, "was unjust" is a 0 point (incompetent) response. See EVALS II *supra* note 24, at 140.

304. See EVALS II *supra* note 24, at 40. See also Nicholson et al., II *supra* note 170, at 383.

305. See Nicholson et al., II *supra* note 170, at 383.

306. See *Id.* at 390. Although unable to summarize factors predicting the competency criterion, Nicholson et al. note however that "they did not correspond in any straightforward manner to the three components set forth by the

son and his team suggested the CT may predict competency criteria based on abilities (e.g., intelligence) largely irrelevant to the concept of fitness to stand trial.[307] Given that research has been unable to establish a stable factor structure for the CT,[308] this instrument continues to quantify levels of competence. Rather than offering a descriptive appraisal of different psycholegal abilities, the CT simply supplies a number from which to determine competency. For this reason, the competency screening test may also raise concerns about its face validity in the legal community.[309]

2. The Competency Assessment Instrument

McGarry and his colleagues also developed the competency screening instrument or the CAI.[310] The CAI is a semi-structured interview and rating scale, offering a more comprehensive evaluation for those defendants "screened in" following the administration of the CT. In developing the CAI, McGarry et al. considered both courtroom and clinical experience and the scale "was designed to include all possible bases for a determination of incompetency."[311] Specifically, however, the scale centered on 13 items relevant to the accused's ability to function at trial. Some of these abilities include: "Appraisal of available legal defenses," "Unmanageable behavior," "Quality of relating to attorney," and "Planning of legal strategy including guilty pleas to lesser charges where pertinent."[312] The defendant is rated on each of the 13 items and scored on a 5 point Likert scale ranging from 1 (total incapacity) to 5 (no incapacity). Al-

---

developers of the test: potential for a constructive relationship between the client and lawyer, understanding of the court process, and ability to deal emotionally with the criminal process." *Id.*; *See also* LAB *supra* note 35, at 27 (discussing original validation work and relevant components of the CT set forth by McGarry and his colleagues).

307. *See* Nicholson et al., II *supra* note 170, at 390.

308. *See* EVALS II *supra* note 24, at 140; *See also* K. Ustad et al., *Restoration of Competency to Stand Trial: Assessment with the Georgia Court Competency Test and the Competency Screening Test*, 20 LAW & HUM. BEHAV. 131 (1996).

309. *See Id.*

310. *See generally* LAB *supra* note 40.

311. *See* ROESCH & GOLDING *supra* note 16, at 65.

312. Adapted from LAB *supra* note 40.

though the CAI does not designate a specific cut-off score, the scoring manual suggests a substantial number of scores of 3 or less should be cause for in-patient observation.[313]

Although few empirical studies of the CAI exist, this measure has been recognized as a useful interview-structuring devise.[314] In addition, its large number of sample interview questions and case examples provide a beneficial tool to assist mental health examiners in learning how to administer competency evaluations.[315] Finally, research indicates that the 13 items of the CAI have high face validity, thereby facilitating acceptance among attorneys and judges.[316]

As compared to earlier competency measures, the CAI puts a clear emphasis on the legally relevant question of competency;[317] however, this focus has been targeted as a limitation. Although the CAI was reportedly developed with "clinical experience" in mind, this measure "is primarily designed to assess legal, rather than mental health, dimensions of competency."[318] Another concern for the CAI involves the lack of scientific research conducted in the area with respect to reliability, validity, and clinical utility.[319] Perhaps most problematic is the fact that the CAI is not standardized nor does it provide clinicians any norms for interpreting scores and assigning value to its 13 items.[320] Moreover, although clinical case examples are provided for certain scores of each of the items, "[no] specific scoring criteria are provided," and the 13 scores "are neither summed nor weighted. "[321] Thus, as Melton et al. conclude,

---

313. See Id. at 100.

314. See T. GRISSO, COMPETENCY TO STAND TRIAL EVALUATIONS: A MANUAL FOR PRACTICE. 80 (1988) [hereinafter cited as GRISSO II].

315. See MELTON ET AL II supra note 22, at 141.

316. See Id.

317. The 13 items of the CAI are "related to an accused's ability to cope with the trial process in an adequately self-protective fashion." See ROESCH & GOLDING supra note 14, at 64 citing A. MCGARRY ET AL, COMPETENCY TO STAND TRIAL AMD MENTAL ILLNESS. 99 (1973).

318. See ROESCH & GOLDING supra note 16, at 65.

319. See Golding et al., supra note 14, at 324. See ROESCH & GOLDING supra note 14, at 65. (Noting that studies on CAI's reliability and validity have been sparse at best— studies conducted by the developers of the scale— and with small sample sizes, including one study on the reliability of the CAI based on a sample size of 18).

320. See ROESCH & GOLDING supra note 16, at 141.

321. See GRISSO II supra note 314, at 84.

"whether the CAI scoring system is helpful is essentially un-known."[322]

3. The Interdisciplinary Fitness Interview

Developed by Golding and Roesch in the early 1980s,[323] the Interdisciplinary Fitness Interview or IFI was largely a response to the CAI and its identified shortcomings. According to Golding et al., because the CAI centered too much on the legal issues of the competency construct, "[i]t is our position that it would be more appropriate to develop a balanced assessment procedure, one which would take both legal and psychological issues into account."[324] Accordingly, the IFI was designed to cover issues involving both psychopathology and the law, addressing these domains from a functional perspective.[325] In addition, their procedure utilized an interdisciplinary approach, relying jointly on a legal and mental health professional for the administration of the interview.

The IFI is a semi-structured interview and rating scale designed to assess 5 aspects of specific legal functioning (e.g., questions regarding the *Dusky* criteria), 11 items pertaining to psychopathological symptoms (e.g., questions about disturbance of thought, delusional processes, and general impairment of judgement/insight), and 4 items on overall evaluation of competency (e.g., questions regarding overall fitness, comments on the basis for one's decision, and comments on other factors used to reach a decision).[326] Each of the items is rated in terms of the level of capacity a defendant demonstrates during the course of the interview, and the scores can range from 0 ("no or minimal incapacity") to 2 ("substantial incapac-

---

322. *See* EVALS II *supra* note 24, at 141.

323. The IFI was developed by S. Golding & R. Roesch, *Interdisciplinary Fitness Interview Training Manual* (1980) (unpublished manuscript), and evaluated in Golding et al., *supra* note 14.

324. *See* Golding et al., *supra* note 14, at 324 (Golding and Roesch felt psychopathology concerns were relevant to overall (in)competency determinations even though such issues did not, in and of themselves, automatically result in an incompetency determination. *See Id.*

325. *See Id.* at 324 n. 2. A functional perspective would consider the defendant's behavioral, emotional, communicative, and cognitive capacities.

326. *See Id.* at 326, Table 1, For a complete review of the Interdisciplinary Fitness Interview Items.

ity"). The examiner is also required to assign, again on a scale of 0–2, a weight to each of the items in terms of its influence on the overall decision.[327] Golding and Roesch devised a follow-up scale assuming certain dimensions would vary given the particulars of a case.[328] For instance, while delusions may impact an accused's ability to assist in his or her own defense in some cases (e.g., distorting testimony important to defense efforts), these delusions may have little to no bearing on other cases (e.g., defendant's testimony is not crucial to defense efforts). Thus, the second scale of the IFI considers such items according to the context of a given case.

Although the empirical research concerning the IFI is practically non-existent, one published study indicated positive results. Golding et al. evaluated the IFI to provide preliminary reliability and validity data on its use in state mental hospitals in the Boston, Massachusetts area.[329] Utilizing the interdisciplinary approach, one clinician in concert with one attorney administered the IFI to 77 pretrial defendants referred by the courts for competency evaluations. The study revealed the panelists concurred in final judgements of competence in 75 of 77 cases evaluated (97%). Agreement between IFI panelists and hospital examiners conducting follow-up competency evaluations was also high overall (75.7%).[330] Consistent with the orientation of the IFI, interrater reliability between clinician and attorney was greatest for legal items most related to functional aspects of fitness ("capacity to appreciate," item 1 and "appreciating legal options," item 5).[331] Moreover, attorneys were

---

327. See Id. at 325.
328. See EVALS II supra note 24, at 141. For instance, Golding and Roesch state "a defendant might have a seriously distorted view of the consequences of various legal options available, but this does not necessarily influence his or her ability to stand trial on the given charge." See Golding et al., supra note 14, at 325.
329. See Id. at 327.
330. See EVALS II supra note 24, at 331. Notwithstanding the high agreement level, Golding and his colleagues note problems persist in the area of what constitutes "unfitness rather than fitness." The study indicated that IFI panelists and hospital examiners concurred 83% of the time with respect to competency determinations but only agreed 58% of the time on incompetency determinations. See Id. at 331.
331. According to Golding et al., (1984) "the legal and psychopathological items most closely related to functional aspects of competency would be of most importance in competency decisions." See Golding et al., supra note 14, at 327.

able to achieve respectable levels of agreement with clinicians on items concerning psychopathology (e.g., concurring 91% of the time for items involving delusional processes), despite their limited clinical training.[332]

The IFI covers more completely than past clinical protocols domains believed to be most important when making (in)competency determinations (both legal and mental health issues). Further, however, the procedure's second scale provides additional information regarding those items that influence the overall decision, specifically allowing trial judges to better understand the rationale used in competency determinations.[333] Thus, preliminary findings of the IFI suggest it is reliable and rich in terms of the qualitative data it supplies to judges who make the final judgement regarding trial competence.[334]

In addition to limited empirical review, the IFI has been criticized for its structural orientation and its emphasis on decisional influences. Indeed, although the second scale can provide useful data to judges, some critics note the subjective nature of this process as jurists have discretion in ascertaining what factors are important in making competency determinations.[335] Melton et al. argue competency centers on the fairness of trial, and "the law may require defendants to be capable of performing any (or all) psycholegal functions at some minimal level" even though those factors may have no bearing on the defense strategy.[336]

Expounding upon this latter criticism, the IFI's ability to consider certain factors in the context of a given case (e.g., the presence and impact of the accused's delusions for purposes of a defense strategy) is potentially problematic for certain mentally disordered defendants. While the IFI minimizes the need for certain psycholegal abilities if not applicable in a particular instance (e.g., a delusion may not affect defendant's ability to assist his attorney), difficulties may arise if (and when) a mentally impaired defendant chooses to take a more active role in the case. Unfortunately, the IFI does not consider potential changes in defense strategy which may include, in

---

332. *See Id.* at 328.
333. *See* EVALS II., *supra* note 24, at 142.
334. *See Id.*
335. *See Id.*
336. *See Id.*

the extreme, a paranoid schizophrenic waiving the right to counsel and conducting his or her own defense. Although the IFI's second scale weighs certain psychiatric symptoms according to a forecasted defense strategy (thereby clearly emphasizing how CST is a legal question), the instrument creates (unintended) problems involving the discretion of judges, presumes a consistent defense strategy, and underestimates the sometimes unpredictable nature of a criminal trial, especially when the defendant is mentally impaired (the paranoid/delusional who waives counsel and conducts his own defense).

A final limitation concerning the IFI involves its practical utility; specifically, its contemplated interdisciplinary approach. Theoretically speaking, while this participatory model is laudable, commentators have challenged its everyday usefulness.[337] For example, based on their own personal experiences, Melton and his colleagues note that most attorneys generally lack the necessary time to observe competency evaluations let alone engage in the process, ostensibly neutralizing the routine feasibility of the proposed cross-disciplinary fitness strategy.[338] To be clear, if these critics are correct about the implausible collaboration between mental health and legal professionals, the very basis for administering the IFI instrument would be significantly compromised if not altogether undone.

4. The Georgia Court Competency Test and Georgia Court Competency Test-Mississippi Hospital

The original version of the Georgia Court Competency Test or GCCT was developed at the Central State hospital in Georgia by Wildman et al.[339] The instrument was devised as a quick, quantitative measure to assess competency.[340] The test consists of 17 questions designed to assess a defendant's knowledge in four areas; including: [a] understanding of courtroom procedure; [b] knowledge of the charge; [c] knowledge of possible penalties; and [d] ability to

---

337. *See* EVALS II *supra* note 24, at 142.
338. *See Id.*
339. *See* Wildman et al., *supra* note 40.
340. *See* R. Nicholson, & K. Kugler, *supra* note 153, at 361.

communicate rationally with an attorney.[341] The 17 questions are then grouped into six categories; including: (1) *Picture of Court*, with 7 questions regarding a picture of an empty court room; (2) *Functions*, with 5 questions about the roles and functions of the court room participants; (3) *Charges*, with two questions pertaining to the type of indictment(s); (4) *Helping the Lawyer*, with one question about assisting the attorney; (5) *Alleged Crime*, with one question about the circumstances of the pending charge(s); and (6) *Consequences*, with one question concerning the possible penalty of a guilty verdict.[342] Examiners use explicit scoring criteria to assign a weight to each of the 17 test questions (e.g., "what do the witnesses do?", "How can you help your lawyer defend you?") and these can range in score from 0 to 10 points. Scores on individual items are then summed and multiplied by 2 producing a score between 0 and 100.[343] Higher scores reflect higher degrees of competence and, as Wildman et al. advised, defendants scoring a 69 or below should undergo further clinical observation.[344]

The revised GCCT model was developed at the Mississippi State Hospital (GCCT-MSH). Four questions were added to the original 17 to further investigate a defendant's knowledge about courtroom procedure (e.g., "What will you do during the trial?"), and the accused's ability to assist counsel (e.g., "What is your attorney's name?", How can you contact him/her?").[345] In addition, item weights given to some of the original questions were changed and the scoring criteria for certain questions were modified to preserve the original 0–100 scoring range and the recommended cutoff score of 69 (e.g., questions regarding the charge and possible penalty were made more explicit).[346]

Empirical research on the GCCT reflects promising results. Data from studies on both models indicate that interscorer reliability is high. For example, Mullett and Johnson[347] reported an interscorer

---

341. Description adapted from Nicholson et al., II *supra* note 170, at 385.
342. Description adapted from EVALS II *supra* note 24, at 142.
343. *See* Nicholson et al., I *supra* note 167, at 314.
344. *See* Wildman et al., *supra* note 40.
345. *See* Nicholson et al., I *supra* note 167, at 315.
346. *See* Nicholson et al., II *supra* note 170, at 385.
347. *See* N. Mullett & W. Johnson, *The Assessment of Competency to Stand Trial* (March, 1984) (paper presented at the 30th annual convention of the Southeastern Psychological Association, New Orleans).

reliability of 96% for the GCCT and Nicholson et al. reported an interscorer reliability of 95% for the GCCT-MSH. Similarly, other studies demonstrate high scores on criterion-related validity, including the GCCT's ability to predict staff competency decisions.[348] In contrast to the CST, research indicates that the GCCT-MSH has a stable internal factor structure consisting of a three-factor solution; including: "General Legal Knowledge", "Courtroom Layout", and "Specific Legal Knowledge."[349] The finding of a stable internal factor structure has also been replicated across samples.[350] Generally speaking, both versions of the GCCT exhibit notable advantages (simplicity, interscorer reliability, and predictive validity). Moreover, not only do the explicit scoring criteria allow investigators to assess where and how the GCCT works but they enable social scientists to understand how this instrument predicts competency to stand trial.[351]

Similar to its predecessors, the structure of the GCCT has been criticized. Of noteworthy importance (given that models of the GCCT endorse a designed cutoff score) is the fact that these instruments encourage practicing clinicians to make ultimate decisions about competence. Indeed, as others have observed, mental health clinicians offer conclusory opinions and their use of "a recommended cutoff score on either of the tests in order to classify a defendant as competent or incompetent and then testifying solely on that basis...perpetuate[s] the misguided involvement of mental health professionals in the criminal justice system."[352]

The GCCT has also been criticized for its item content and for placing too much of an emphasis on "cosmetic and superficial issues."[353] For example, GCCT's first category, *Picture of the Court,* consists of 7 questions (approximately one third of all test items) which arguably have no bearing on a defendant's understanding of,

---

348. *See* Nicholson et al., I *supra* note 167, at 315 (citing Wildman et al., (1978) study which revealed the GCCT was able to correctly predict 78% of the staff decisions as well as Mullett & Johnson's (1984) study reporting an impressive 81% validity rate in terms of the GCCT predicting staff decisions.
349. *See* Nicholson et al., II *supra* note 170, at 388 (Table 5).
350. *See* EVALS II *supra* note 24, at 143. *See also* Ustad et al., *supra* note 308, at 143.
351. *See* Nicholson et al., II *supra* note 170, at 392.
352. *See Id.* at 392.
353. *See* EVALS II., *supra* note 22, at 143.

or participation in, the trial process.[354] Thus, legitimate concerns have been raised about the content validity of the GCCT and the GCCT-MSH, and whether either version adequately samples one's abilities relative to the competency construct.[355]

B. Reviewing the Instruments and a Call for Greater Attention to Trial Abilities

The development of psychological assessment technology on the matter of competency to stand trial reflects vast changes over the years leading to several significant improvements (e.g., simplification of instruments, interscorer reliability and predictive validity). However, the most notable development has been the evolution of standardized procedures. The establishment of explicit scoring criteria has allowed researchers to investigate (empirically) the efficacy of various instruments and to understand more systematically how these tools measure fitness to stand trial.

Notwithstanding these advantages, empirical research has also identified problems, especially in regard to how these assessment tools correctly measure competency. Indeed, representatives from both the legal and psychological communities have raised concerns, questioning the extent to which the instruments' scores and ratings actually relate to trial participation abilities.[356] Moreover, non-empirically animated criticisms have drawn attention to the range of psycholegal abilities required of defendants during the trial process, linking the (mostly) inaccurate assessment of such skills to the vagueness of the CST concept.[357] For example, Bonnie has argued that the criminal trial process involves a host of decisions for the defendant (e.g., waiving important rights, deciding about a plea bar-

---

354. *See Id.*
355. *See Id. See also* R. Nicholson, *Defining and Assessing Competency to Stand Trial* (1992) (paper presented at the meeting of the American Psychological Association, Washington, D.C.).
356. *See* EVALS II *supra* note 24. *See also* Grisso I *supra* note 6, at 96.
357. *See* R. Bonnie, *Competency in the Criminal Process.* (Unpublished paper presented at the meeting of the MacArthur Network for Research on Mental Health and the Law, New York, NY. (1989) [hereinafter Bonnie II]. *See also* Winick I *supra* note 1.

gain, or pleading guilty), requiring certain cognitive abilities not necessarily related to the *Dusky* criteria.[358] Given these shortcomings, researchers eventually called "for the development of a more theory-based model of criminal competency, which in turn would guide both the clinical evaluation and the legal determination of competency."[359] Highlighting both advantages and limits, the next section of this book examines one such "theory-based" model used to assess competence related abilities.

C. The Macarthur Competence Assessment Tool-Criminal Adjudication

1. The MacArthur Research Network and the Competency Project

In the late 1980s, the MacArthur Foundation Research Network on Mental Health and the Law initiated an extensive development project in response to concerns involving the assessment of competency. Although a number of fitness-related considerations influenced the project,[360] working members stated that "[t]he primary

---

358. *See* Grisso II *supra* note 29, at 357.

359. *See* R. Roesch, S. Hart, & P. Zapf, *Conceptualizing and Assessing Competency to Stand Trial: Implications and Applications of the MacArthur Treatment Competence Model*, 2 PSYCH. PUB. POL. & LAW 96, 100 (1996). *See generally* Bonnie I *supra* note 10; R. Bonnie, *The Competence of Criminal Defendants: Beyond Dusky and Drope*, 47 MIAMI LAW REVIEW. 539–601 (1993) [hereinafter Bonnie III]; R. Miller, & E. Germain, *Evaluation of Competency to Stand Trial in Defendants Who Do Not Want to Be Defended Against the Crimes Charged*, 15 BULL. AM. ACAD. PSYCHIATRY LAW. 371–379 (1987) [hereinafter Miller & Germain II].

360. *See* S. Hoge, R. Bonnie, N. Poythress, J. Monahan, M, Eisenberg, & T. Feucht-Haviar, *The MacArthur Adjudicative Competence Study: Development and Validation of a Research Instrument*, 21 LAW & HUM. BEH. 141 (1997) [hereinafter Hoge et al., I]. The working group identified a number of concerns relating to both competency assessment and the competency construct itself. One identified reason involved the frequency with which courts referred competency inquiries to mental health professionals. According to more recent surveys, the annual number of evaluations of competence to stand trial ranged between 24,000 to 39,000. *See Id.* at 142; *see generally* T. Grisso, J. Cocozza. H. Steadman, H. Fisher, W. Fisher, & A. Greer, *The Organization of Pretrial Forensic Evaluation Services: A National Profile*, 18 LAW AND

obstacle to progress in this area [i.e., improving assessment technology] is the absence of adequate measures of competence-related abilities,"[361] and, in particular, those psycholegal abilities related to decisional competence.[362] Thus, the MacArthur competency network set out to develop an instrument unlike its predecessors, focusing on the *competence to proceed to adjudication* rather than *competence to stand trial.*[363] The MacArthur project attempted to fill the existing void with respect to discrete competence-related abilities. As Melton et al. explain, the change in terminology reflected a broader test[364] as the MacArthur measures included specific inquiry into capacities related to fitness to assist counsel and capacities associated with decisional competence. Stated another way, the MacArthur measures evaluated cognitive understanding related to anticipated trial proceedings (i.e., the focus of current assessment measures) and, additionally, posed questions relative to decisional competence (e.g., defendant's ability to compare alternative courses of action).[365] Ultimately, the MacArthur Adjudicative Competence Study would produce structured and standardized research measures used to inform clinicians and instruct policy makers on matters of adjudicative competence for criminal defendants.

HUMAN BEHAVIOR. 377–394 (1994).

With respect to the theory of competence, the working members argue the term "competence to stand to trial" is misleading in a fundamental way as trial participation is hypothetical in most cases. *See* Hoge et al., I *supra* at 145. To support this contention, the group notes 90% of all criminal cases in the US are resolved by way of guilty pleas. Accordingly, the members suggest "adjudicative competence" is a more appropriate term than "competence to stand trial." *See* Bonnie I *supra* note 10, at 293; Hoge et al., I *supra* at 145.

361. *See* Hoge et al., I *supra* note 360, at 141.The group emphasized the need to evaluate abilities related to decisions or what they coined "adjudicative competence."*See Id.* at 141.The group also noted empirical research had failed to establish a stable foundation for the clinical assessment of competency stating "none of the measures currently available yields quantitative indices of discrete competence related abilities." *See* Hoge et al., I *supra* at 144. On this point, the members argued that existing measures centered on defendants' current cognitive abilities as they related to anticipated trial decisions and that such measures did not pose decisional problems defendants might encounter (e.g., considering alternative courses of action, or defendants' perceptions about how they would be treated by various authorities in the criminal system of law.) *See Id.*

362. *See Id.* at 144.

363. *See* EVALS. II *supra* note 24, at 145.

364. *See Id.*

365. *See* Hoge et al., I *supra* note 360, at 144.

2. The MacArthur Treatment Competency Study

In 1997, the working members of the competency research network detailed the results of the full-scale adjudicative competency study.[366] They presented "the legal framework, assessment strategy, instrument description, psychometric properties, and construct validation of the MacArthur Structured Assessment of Competencies of Criminal Defendants (MacSAC-CD)."[367] This comprehensive research instrument would later serve as the prototype from which the MacCAT-CA would be developed.[368]

The MacSAC-CD was based on Bonnie's legal theory of competence,[369] and the instrument relied on the assessment strategy for treatment competence to measure those capacities identified by the legal theory as important to adjudicative competence.[370] The Mac-

---

366. *See* Hoge et al., I *supra* note 361.

367. *See* Otto et al., *Psychometric Properties of the MacArthur Competence Assessment Tool-Criminal Adjudication*, 10 PSYCHOLOGICAL ASSESSMENT. 435 (1998).

368. *See Id. See also* EVALS. II *supra* note 24, at 145.

369. *See generally* Bonnie III *supra* note 359. Briefly, Bonnie's model provides a theoretical framework for a more structured approach to assess competency, arguing "adjudicative competence" is best understood as two related but separate constructs: competency to assist; and competency to make decisions. *See* Bonnie I *supra* note 11, at 294; Roesch, Hart, & Zapf *supra* note 359, at 103.

Competency to assist has three components including: [a] able to understand the charges, criminal trial process, adversary system, and the job of the defense counsel; [b] defendant must have the ability to appreciate one's situation as a criminal defendant; and [c] defendant must have the ability to recognize and express relevant information regarding the facts of the case. *See* Bonnie III *supra* note 359, at 554.

Competency to make decisions is modeled after Appelbaum & Grisso's (1988) formulation regarding treatment competence. Decisional competence involves the defendant's ability to "understand and choose among alternative courses of action." *See Id.* at 556. Although presented as a general outline for decisional competence, the psycholegal abilities include: [a] communicate a preference; [b] understand relevant information; [c] appreciate the significance of information in one's case; and [d] rationally manipulate information. *See* Bonnie I *supra* note 11, at 305, 306. In summary, Bonnie argues defendants may be competent to assist their attorneys but incompetent to make important legal decisions such as the right to plea guilty, waive constitutional rights, or to raise an insanity defense. *See E.g.,* Roesch, Hart, & Zapf *supra* note 360, at 104.

370. Specifically, the items were modeled after those created by T. Grisso, P. Appelbaum, E. Mulvey, & K. Fletcher, *The MacArthur Treatment Compe-*

SAC-CD contains seven scales, consisting of items measuring psycholegal abilities relative to two primary legal domains: competence to assist counsel (CAC); and decisional competence (DC). The two domains measure three psycholegal abilities (i.e., understanding, appreciation, and reasoning and, with respect to decisional competence, the ability to make a choice is also included).[371]

Consistent with Bonnie's theory of competence, competence to assist counsel describes three minimum abilities required of a defendant to participate in his or her own defense: "(1) the capacity to understand the charges, the nature and purpose of criminal prosecution, and the basic elements of the adversary system; (2) the capacity to relate pertinent information to counsel concerning the facts of the case; [and] (3) the capacity to appreciate one's situation as a defendant in a criminal prosecution."[372] The second legal domain, decisional competence, refers to defendants' abilities to make specific decisions that may arise during the trial process.[373] Modeled after Appelbaum & Grisso's[374] assessment strategy for treatment competence, these abilities include: "(1) the capacity to understand information relevant to the specific decision at issue, (2) the capacity to weigh and consider information to reach a decision, (3) the capacity to appreciate one's situation as a defendant confronted with a specific legal decision, and (4) the capacity to express a choice among alternatives."[375]

---

tence Study. II: Measures of Abilities Related to Competence to Consent to Treatment, 19 LAW AND HUMAN BEHAVIOR. 127–148 (1995). For a review of more comprehensive discussions on the development of assessment measures regarding competence-related abilities for treatment competence, *see generally*, P. Appelbaum & T. Grisso, *Assessing Patients' Capacities to Consent to Treatment*, 319 NEW ENGLAND JOURNAL OF MEDICINE. 1635–1638 (1988) [hereinafter Appelbaum & Grisso I]; P. Appelbaum & T. Grisso, *The MacArthur Treatment Competence Study. I: Mental Illness and Competence to Consent to Treatment*, 19 LAW AND HUMAN BEHAVIOR. 105–126 [hereinafter Appelbaum & Grisso II]. *See* Hoge et al., I *supra* note 360, at 148 (noting "the Grisso-Appelbaum work offered a model for disaggregating the capacities necessary to make a legally effective decision and provided measures of these capacities that could easily be adapted from treatment decision making to the context of criminal adjudication"). *See Id.*

371. *See* Hoge et al., I *supra* note 360, at 149; *See also* Otto et al., *supra* note 367, at 436.

372. *See* Hoge et al., I *supra* note 360, at 149 (relying on Bonnie's model).

373. *See Id.* at 153.

374. Appelbaum & Grisso I, *supra* note 370, at 1635.

375. *See* Hoge et al., I *supra* note 360, at 153.

The first three scales measure understanding relative to various legal issues. First, understanding is evaluated in relation to a defendant's competence to assist counsel, termed *Competence to Assist Counsel: Understanding* (CAC-U). This measure consists of seven items about trial issues and the role of the participants.[376] The Mac-SAC-CD employs a four-step sequence designed to measure both current knowledge and the capacity to learn new knowledge.[377] To measure the items, the examiner scores each producing an item score of 0–4 with a total CAC:U score ranging from 0–28.[378]

The next two scales measure understanding as it relates to decisional competence (DC). Specifically, the second scale measures the defendant's capacity to understand information specific to making

---

376. *See Id.* at 149 (specifically, the CAC:U measures the defendant's understanding about: "(1) the basic characteristics of criminal prosecution and defense; (2) the role of the judge and the jury; (3) the nature of criminal charges; (4) the nature of a guilty plea; and (5) the consequences of a conviction").

377. This process relies on a vignette involving a legal situation. For a review of the specific content of the vignette, *see* Hoge et al., I *supra* note 360, at 150. The four steps involved in the sequence include: (1) "The defendant is asked an open-ended question designed to elicit his or her existing understanding (i.e., 'actual understanding') of an area of relevant information; (2) Correct information, embedded in a vignette, is disclosed to the defendant; (3) The defendant is asked to demonstrate understanding of the information by paraphrasing the disclosure; and (4) Finally, the defendant is asked a set of true-false questions based on the disclosure"). *See Id.* at 150. This process is best understood as a response to some of the more outstanding criticisms involving the existing assessment instruments (e.g., the instruments concentration on current knowledge, rather than a defendant's capacity to acquire new information). *See Id.* at 149.

378. *See Id.* at 150, 151. The first step "predisclosure" provides information pertaining to a hypothetical situation (e.g., describing a fight between Fred and Reggie and the chain of events which result in an accident). This step is designed to measure the defendant's current knowledge. In the second step the examiner discloses information concerning how the legal system works (e.g., there are two sides, Fred's lawyer will attempt to show no crime, and the prosecutor will endeavor to show Fred did commit a crime). In the third step the defendant paraphrases what he or she just learned about the legal system (e.g. tapping into capacity to learn new knowledge). In the final step the defendant is asked a series of true-false questions based on information provided in the disclosure (e.g., Fred's lawyer is called the prosecutor). This step also taps the defendant's capacity to learn new information. A similar sequence is followed to measure understanding "the role of the judge and the jury, the nature of [the] criminal charges, the nature of [a] guilty plea, and the consequences of a conviction." *See Id.* at 151.

the decision of whether or not to waive the right to trial by pleading guilty, termed *Decisional Competence: Understanding-Pleading Guilty* (DC:U-PG). This measure consists of five items about understanding as it relates to waiving rights and the reasoning used to make such decisions.[379] The third scale involves the decision to choose between a trial by jury and a bench trial, termed *Decisional Competence: Understanding-Waiving Jury* (DC:U-WJ). This measure focuses on six topics involving a defendant's understanding about differences and the reasons for choosing one over the other.[380] The same four-step sequence used in the (CAC:U) is used to measure the items contained in the DC:U-PG (five items generating a score between 0–20) and the DC:U-WJ (six items generating a score between 0–24).[381]

The forth scale, termed the *Competence to Assist Counsel: Reasoning* (CAC:R), requires defendants to consider and apply relevant facts to a hypothetical criminal case and focuses on six topics.[382] The accused is asked to choose among two items of information, disclosed or implied in the vignette, and to explain why that item, rather than the other, should be conveyed to the attorney.[383] This

---

379. *See* S. Hoge, N. Poythress, R. Bonnie, J. Monahan, M. Eisenberg, & T. Feucht-Havier, *The MacArthur Adjudicative Competence Study: Diagnosis, Psychopathology, and Competence-Related Abilities*, 15 BEHAV. SCIENCES AND THE LAW. 329 (1997) [hereinafter Hoge et al., II]. The DC:U-PG focuses on the defendant's understanding about: "(1) the admission of criminal conduct, (2) the waiver of legal rights, (3) plausible reasons for pleading guilty rather than going to trial, (4) plausible reasons for going to trial rather than pleading guilty, and (5) the prerogative to decide how to plead." *Id* at 335.

380. *See Id* (specifically, the DC:U-WJ focuses on the defendant's understanding about: "(1) the distinction between a trial by judge and a trial by jury, (2) the constitutional right to a jury trial and prerogative to waive this right, (3) the participation by the defense in jury selection, (4) plausible reasons for choosing a trial by judge, and (5) plausible reasons for choosing a trial by jury").

381. *See Id.*

382. Expanding on the vignette provided earlier, the examiner provides additional information about Fred and Reggie's situation with specific emphasis on facts that might or might not be relevant in forming a defense. For a review of the specific content in this version of the vignette, *see* Hoge et al., I *supra* note 356, at 151.

383. Specifically, the defendant is asked "[i]f Fred's lawyer asks Fred about the his reason for fighting with Reggie and for hitting him with a pool stick, which of these two pieces of information would be more important to tell the lawyer..." *See Id.* at 152. The defendant can choose either card 1, "[a]fter Reggie pushed him, Fred thought he saw Reggie reaching for a knife" or card 2

scale contains six items generating scores of 0–2 each and, thus, the CAC-R produces a total score ranging from 0 to 12.[384]

The fifth scale of the instrument measures the defendant's capacity to think rationally about alternative courses of action with respect to making decisions concerning the defense, termed *Decisional Competence: Reasoning* (DC:R).[385] This measure entails 7 topics involving a defendant's rational thinking capacity, including his or her ability to reason and solve problems in a logical manner.[386] The DC:R contains 13 items, each of which is scored from 0–2 producing an aggregate score ranging from 0–26.[387]

The final two scales center on the defendant's beliefs, perceptions, and abilities to reason about the same type of issues contained in the other scales but as applied to their own legal situation, rather than the hypothetical case vignette.[388] Accordingly the sixth scale, termed *Competence to Assist Counsel: Appreciation* (CAC:A), focuses on six beliefs relating to the person's ability to ap-

---

"Fred picked up a paycheck at work before he picked up Julie to go to a baseball game." Once selecting a card, the defendant is asked to explain why the section was made. *See Id.* at 152.

384. *See* Hoge et al., II *supra* note 379, at 334.

385. *See* Hoge et al., I *supra* note 360, at 154.

386. *See E.g.,* EVALS. II *supra* note 24, at 145. *See also See* Hoge et al., I *supra* note 360, at 154, 155. Specifically, the items contained in this scale address the defendant's capacity to: "(1) request information needed to make a decision; (2) to conceive the primary legal effects of alternatives; (3) to conceive the personal consequences of the alternative outcomes; (4) to compare alternative choices; (5) to assign relative values to alternatives in a consistent way; (6) to think transitively (i.e., if A > B and B > C, then A > C); and (7) to think using probabilities."

Perhaps the most involved measure, assessment of the capacities vary as 1–4, listed above, require defendant to respond to questions based on added information added to the vignette emphasizing potential outcomes (e.g., two ways to plead, advantages and disadvantages about both, and making a decision). For a review of this version of the vignette as it relates to the DC:R, *see* Hoge et al., I *supra* note 360, at 155. The remaining items contained in topics 5–7 of the DC:R do not relate to the vignette. Specifically, items associated with topic 5 are measured by the defendant choosing a preference involving a series of activities such as reading a book or seeing a movie. The activities are presented in multiple different pairings, and scores are contingent on the defendant's ability to consistently rank their preferences across different pairings. Items contained in topics 6 and 7 are measured by presenting short questions to the defendant whereby they respond via multiple choice. *See Id.* at 155.

387. *See* Hoge et al., II *supra* note 379, at 336.

388. *See* EVALS. II *supra* note 24, at 145.

preciate specific circumstances surrounding his or her case.[389] A primary goal regarding this measure is whether or not the defendant is influenced by delusional traits or other symptoms that may affect the accused's ability to appreciate the nature of the proceedings or the individual's role as a defendant during the criminal trial process.[390] Similar to the CAC:A, the seventh scale, termed *Decisional Competence: Appreciation* (DC:A), measures the defendant's ability to appreciate his or her own situation; however, in this case, appreciation relates to decision making abilities. The DC:A focuses on two items: the decision to plead guilty; and the decision to relinquish counsel.[391] The DC:A is designed to measure whether delusions or other symptoms relating to a mental illness have any bearing on the defendant's ability to make decisions relevant to defense efforts.[392]

The adjudicative competency study (MacSAC-CD) involved three groups of criminal defendants in Virginia and Florida.[393]

---

389. *See* Hoge et al., I *supra* note 360, at 152. The six items include "(1) the criminal charges; (2) the likelihood of conviction; (3) the impartiality of the adjudication process; (4) the possible helpfulness of the defense attorney; (5) the possible benefits of disclosing information to the defense attorney; and (6) the severity of punishment."

The defendant is asked to consider questions relative to each of six items and choose between five response options, explaining the reasoning for one's response. Each item can be assigned 2 points (clearly plausible), 1 point (of questionable plausibility), or 0 points (clearly implausible). For responses yielding a plausibility score of 1, the defendant is asked an additional question challenging the reasoning behind that response and the second response and its reason is used as the item score. *See also* R. Bonnie, S. Hoge, J. Monahan, N. Poythress, M. Eisenberg, & T. Feucht-Haviar, *The MacArthur Adjudicative Competence Study: A Comparison of Criteria for Assessing the Competence of Criminal Defendants*, 24, J. AM. ACAD. PSYCHIATRY LAW. 249–259 (1997). Bonnie et al. note the index score that is reported for the CAC:A is whether the defendant registered a score of 0 for any of the six items, indicating the defendant's reasoning for the responses was facially implausible and possibly the product of a mental disorder. *See Id.* at 254, 255.

390. *See* Hoge et al., I *supra* note 360, at 152.

391. The structure of the DC:A items is similar to the model used for the CAC:A; that is, the defendant is asked to make a probabilistic judgement for each of the items (e.g., whether to plead guilty, whether to waive counsel) and then asked to explain the reasoning behind his or her decision. The responses are scored in the same manner used in the DC:A. *See supra* text accompanying note 379.

392. *See* Hoge et al., I *supra* note 360, at 155.

393. *See Id.* at 158.

Specifically, the sample included pre-trial jail detainees, defendants receiving mental health treatment in jail facilities, and defendants admitted to hospitals for the restoration of competence.[394] The methodology and results of the study are described in detail by Hoge et. al.[395] For our purposes, we briefly summarize the findings, drawing attention to the most noteworthy outcomes of the research. The study produced rich observations and successfully addressed many areas regarding adjudicative competence. Generally, the research indicated the MacSAC-CD had satisfactory psychometric properties (i.e., internal consistency and interscorer agreement) and, moreover, demonstrated potential for distinguishing groups of competent and incompetent defendants.[396]

Hoge et al. identified several advantages the MacSAC-CD produced, otherwise absent in the existing measures. First, the Mac-SAC-CD indicates superior content validity as it covered both a foundational requirement concerning "competence to assist counsel" and a separate requirement of "decisional competence."[397] Second, the MacArthur measures examine competence-related abilities involving appreciation, reasoning, and choice as opposed to most existing measures which center on understanding in relation to the trial process.[398] Third, the MacSAC-CD uniquely measures understanding as it applies to new knowledge. Indeed, the "first-disclose-and-then-test" format of the MacSAC-CD allows the examiner to assess the defendant's capacity to learn new information that may be disclosed during the course of the trial (e.g., information arising during the course of preparing the defense).[399] Fourth, as the working group noted, the MacSAC-CD "offers standardized administration and criterion based, objective scoring,"[400] consistent with the call for more objective competence assessment measures.[401] Follow-

---

394. See Id. at 158, 159.
395. See generally Id. at 158–174.
396. See Id. at 141 (noting the MacSAC-CD was able to reflect changes in competency status, revealed a positive correlation with clinical judgements, and a negative correlation with psychopathology and impaired cognitive functioning.)
397. See Id. at 172.
398. See Id.
399. See Id.
400. See Id. at 172.
401. See Id. at 144; See also Grisso II supra note 29, at 367 (noting "that without an objective measure of the legally-relevant abilities, development of a

ing the successful completion of the full-scale study, an adaptation of the lengthy research instrument was developed resulting in the MacCAT-CA.

3. Development of the MacArthur Competence Assessment Tool-Criminal Adjudication (MacCAT-CA)

Having successfully completed the field study, the project set out to develop a clinically portable version of its lengthy research instrument.[402] Although producing many positive findings, the field study revealed that the MacSAC-CD took approximately two hours to administer, and exceeded considerably the 30 to 45 minute administration time required by existing measures.[403] Further review suggested a need to streamline the instrument as suggested by duplication in scoring techniques and redundancy across specific measures.[404] Moreover, Hoge et al. note that some of the measures (DC:U-WJ) were needless in many evaluations as jury waiver decisions were not at issue,[405] and empirical analysis indicated that some of the items were weak with respect to face validity.[406] In addition to these observations, members of the network employed standard item-reduction techniques and considered legal face and content validity to form the MacArthur Competence Assessment Tool-Criminal Adjudication (MacCAT-CA).[407]

---

research foundation for the field of CST assessment will continue to be limited.)

402. *See* Otto et al., *supra* note 367, at 436. The description of the MacArthur Adjudication Competence Assessment Tool-Criminal Adjudication (MacCAT-CA) is adapted from Otto et al., *supra* note 367; Hoge et al., I *supra* note 360 and EVALS II *supra* note 24.

403. *See* Otto et al., *supra* note 367, at 436; *See also* Hoge et al., I *supra* note 360, at 176.

404. *See* Otto et al., *supra* note 367, at 436.

405. *See* Hoge et al., I *supra* note 360, at 176.

406. *See* EVALS. II *supra* note 24, at 148.

407. *See* Hoge et al., I *supra* note 360, at 176. *See also* Otto et al., *supra* note 367, at 436 (noting "decisions about item retention were informed by an examination of (a) the item-total correlations for each item with its original MacSAC-CD measure, and (b) the impact of coefficient alpha for the MacSAC-CD measure if the item was removed.")

The MacCAT-CA is a 22-item clinical instrument using a vignette format which produces quantitative indices of three discrete competence-related abilities: *understanding* (capacity for factual understanding of general information about the legal system and the adjudication process), *reasoning* (ability to grasp the potential relevance of certain legal information and the ability to reason about options that confront a defendant during the course of adjudication; pleading or not guilty), and *appreciation* (capacity to appreciate the legal situation surrounding the defendant's own case).[408]

As previously mentioned, the MacCAT-CA utilizes a vignette format and begins by presenting a hypothetical legal situation involving an accused charged with aggravated assault upon which eight items concerning *understanding* and eight items concerning *reasoning* are measured.[409] Specifically, the 16 items involve questions about the prosecution of the hypothetical defendant. Six additional items contained in the appreciation component of the test involve questions about the accused's own legal situation (resulting in a total of 22 questions).[410] The examiner assigns item scores on a 0–2 scale, and the score ranges are provided for three levels of impairment (e.g., none or minimal, mild, or clinically significant).[411]

Follow-up field studies suggest the MacCAT-CA sub-scales demonstrate satisfactory internal consistency ranging from .75 to .77,[412] and a comprehensive study conducted on the instrument indicates that the MacCAT-CA possesses psychometric integrity.[413] Specifically, Otto et al. conducted a multi-state study sampling three groups of criminal defendants: (1) randomly selected jail inmates whose competence was not in doubt (n=197), (2) jail inmates whose competence was not in doubt but were receiving treatment for a variety of disorders (n= 249), and (3) defendants found incompetent to proceed as a result of a mental illness (n=283).[414] The results of

---

408. *See* Otto et al., *supra* note 367, at 436.
409. *See Id.*
410. *See Id.* For a review of the specific legal content of all three measures, *see* Otto et al., *supra* note 367, at 443.
411. *See Id.* at 436.
412. *See* EVALS II *supra* note 24, at 148.
413. *See generally* Otto et al., *supra* note 367.
414. *See Id.* at 437, 438.

the study revealed some positive findings, suggesting the psychometric properties met or exceeded the accepted indices regarding internal consistency and interrater reliability. To be sure, the study indicated strong internal consistency (*understanding*, α = .86; *reasoning*, α = .81, *appreciation*, α = .85), and the mean inter-item correlations suggested appropriate homogeneity for all three measures (*understanding*, r= .42; *reasoning*, r= .36; *appreciation*, r= .54).[415] Interrater reliability was also moderate to excellent with interclass R= .90 for understanding, R= .85 for reasoning, and R= .75 for appreciation.[416] Consistent with findings from the MacSAC-CD research, correlations between the MacCAT-CA measures and clinical measures showed the MacCAT-CA correlated negatively with impaired cognitive functioning and psychopathology, and positively with present cognitive ability.[417]

In summary, the study conducted by Hoge et al. demonstrated the utility of the MacCAT-CA in clinical evaluations of adjudicative competence and reiterated many of the benefits revealed in the field study. For example, with its three-prong component (i.e., understanding, reasoning, and appreciation capacities) the MacCAT-CA is able to assess competence-related areas relevant to adjudicative competency that do not exist in other areas. Moreover, consistent with results from the initial prototype, the MacCAT-CA offers "standardized administration and criterion-based scoring" which fills the much needed void relative to other protocol used in the field of CST assessment.

4. Structural Limitations and the MacCAT-CA

Although the MacCAT-CA addresses many shortcomings that plague existing assessment protocol, it has inherent problems with its structure.[418] As the developers of the instrument observe, the

---

415. *See Id.* at 438, 439.
416. *See Id.*
417. *See Id.* at 439.
418. Similar to their description concerning the structural and practical limitations involving other assessment instruments, the members of the MacArthur Network and those assisting with the project outlined some of the more outstanding limitations of the MacSAC-CD and the MacCAT-CA. *See* Hoge et al., I *supra* note 360, at 174–176 and Otto et al., *supra* note 367, at 439. Accordingly, the pursuing discussion will rely on these sources.

MacArthur measures do not attempt to assess all dimensions believed to be relevant for "competence to stand trial,"[419] since this aim was neither feasible nor desired.[420] In addition, the basic premise of the instrument is to assess adjudicative competence and "it is not offered as a measure of legal competence per se."[421] Relatedly, no plan to develop a cutoff score for the empirical classification of a defendant as either competent or incompetent is contemplated by the network's model.[422]

The project members also note several concerns for their instrument, especially in relation to fitness to stand trial. Some of these concerns include the following: (1) the model does not consider certain psycholegal abilities relevant to the ultimate competency decision (e.g., memory of specific events surrounding a defendant's case; speech issues); (2) the model does not consider non-psychological factors (e.g., unusual factual or legal complexity of a given case) that may influence the court's decision, and (3) the model does not include scales designed to measure a defendant's test-taking set, particularly as it relates to malingering.[423] Moreover, the MacCAT-CA, was created by eliminating items and measures from the more comprehensive prototype (MacSAC-CD).[424] Unfortunately, the stream-

---

419. *See* Hoge et al., I *supra* note 360, at 174 (Hoge et al (1997) state "as a predominantly cognitive assessment devise, the MacSAC-CD does not attempt to assess a defendant's behavioral ability to conform his or her demeanor to standards appropriate for a courtroom, and it does not attempt to assess a defendant's interpersonal ability to cooperate with a specific defense attorney." Although explaining limitations relative to the MacCAT-SD the above mentioned observations relate to the MacCAT-CA as well.

420. *See* Otto et al., *supra* note 367, at 439. The working members aptly point out "no instrument, no matter how nuanced, can encompass all the variables relevant to a competence determination."

421. *See* Otto et al., *supra* note 367, at 439.

422. *See Id.*

423. *See Id. See also* Hoge et al., I *supra* note 360, at 175 (1997). Stating "incompetence, like insanity or dangerousness, is a conclusion that involves social policy and value judgements that stand outside scientific measurement."(internal quotation marks omitted). Accordingly they do not attempt to measure "competence" but rather provide quantitative measures of discrete competence-related abilities embedded within their legal theory of competence. *See also* S. Morse, *Law and Mental Health Professionals: The Limits of Expertise*, 9 PROF. PSYCHOLOGY. 389–399 (1978) (discussing social policy and value judgements with respect to incompetency, insanity and dangerousness).

424. *See* EVALS. II *supra* note 24, at 148.

lined version was unable to preserve the decisional component, a key construct of Bonnie's model, and inquiry into this psycholegal ability was embedded in the MacCAT-CA's *reasoning* measure.[425] Accordingly, in a very meaningful sense, the development of the MacCAT-CA, compromised a key aspect (i.e., decisional competence) that not only inspired the adjudicative competency measure but served as a basis for the legal theory from which the MacSAC-CD was originally formed. These limitations notwithstanding, the MacCAT-CA provides a model that is sound in theory, representing the "next wave" of instruments furthering the thoroughness and quality of clinical evaluations on matters of competency.[426]

5. Summary of CST Protocol: Psychological Tests and Competency Constructs

The purpose of this section was to provide an overview of the existing competency assessment instruments, highlighting their evolution and exploring the most recent protocol. Clearly, the psychological tests for competency have significantly developed over the years, culminating in a new generation of instruments such as the MacCAT-CA. Recognizing the significance of the assessment protocol for clinical and psychometric purposes, it is axiomatic that these developments are contingent on legal formulations and constructs (e.g., *Dusky)* from which they are conceived. It follows then that advances in the clinical evaluation area are constrained by legal cases, and, thus, the psychological measures are limited in what they can achieve.

Given this critical juncture, this section describes how limitations with the CST assessment protocol go beyond mere structural problems to include dilemmas with the controlling legal standards, judicial ideology, and certain forms of mental illness, thereby raising several (additional) concerns about fitness for trial matters. This additional (and provisional) analysis makes possible the subsequent discussion on the CST finding for defendants with mental health is-

---

425. Unpublished data, personal communication from Richard Bonnie.
426. *See Id.*

sues (e.g., paranoid traits/delusional themes) who then *pro se* their legal action, and the competency screening process in high profile cases.

Although competency constructs vary from state to state, the legal CST standard is typically drafted so that its language is compatible with *Dusky*.[427] The fact that most jurisdictions rely upon this case to construct fitness standards supports the proposition that judges are constrained decision makers who adhere to precedent.[428] According to this model, precedent influences judicial decisions and those decisions determine the controlling competency standards within a given jurisdiction.[429] It follows, then, that psychometricians must also adhere to those controlling doctrines, incorporating and transforming their respective key points of law into measurement scales.[430] The legal theory from which adjudicative compe-

---

427. *See* Grisso I *supra* note 6, at 91.

428. *See generally* T. George, & L. Epstein, *On the Nature of Supreme Court Decision Making*, 86 AMERICAN POLITICAL SCIENCE REVIEW. 323–337 (1992) (discussing the differences between the legal model (adhering to *stare decisis*) and the extra-legal model (e.g, sociological, psychological, and political factors influencing judicial outcomes among the Justices of the Supreme Court).

Another school of legal jurisprudence suggests Supreme Court Justices are influenced by their own attitudes or ideals. This is termed the attitudinal model. According to this model, Justices manipulate precedent to meet their ideological preferences. Although worthy of exploration in its own right, discussion concerning the attitudinal model is beyond the scope of this investigation. For a detailed legal analysis of this matter, *see generally* S. Segal, H. Spaeth, THE SUPREME COURT AND THE ATTITUDINAL MODEL (1993) (New York).

429. *See* L. Epstein, V. Hoekstra, J. Segal, & H. Spaeth, *Do Political Preferences Change? A Longitudinal Study of U.S. Supreme Court Justices*, 60 THE JOURNAL OF POLITICS. 801–818 (1998). Epstein et al. note that, the occasional anomaly notwithstanding, most jurists evince consistent voting behavior over the course of their careers. *See Id.* at 801. This contention seems to obtain when reviewing important Supreme Court cases involving competency matters. Indeed, both *Faretta* and *Godinez* produced conservative decisions and, more specifically, many of the Justices representing the majority in *Faretta* also joined the majority in the *Godinez* case. The dissenting opinions in these decisions also reflected a similar pattern.

430. *See* Arrigo, and Bardwell *supra* note 16, at 23, 24. *See also* Nicholson et al., I *supra* note 162, at 314 (noting "[t]o improve the quality of forensic assessments, investigators have developed instruments that are designed to translate legal guidelines into psychological indices of competency." In other words, for example, the meaning of *Dusky* (i.e., ability to understand and assist) is extracted from the case and transformed into psychological measures of compe-

tence and the MacCAT-CA was developed (i.e., Bonnie's legal theory of competence) illustrates this point.[431] Although Bonnie's reconceptualization of adjudicative competence posits many advantages,[432] the application of sound theory to assessment technology is frustrated by the inconsistent case law.[433] Indeed, efforts to revamp older evaluation methods are bound and confined as they must comport not only with *Dusky* but also with cases like *Godinez*. As we previously argued, the latter decision promotes conflicting and seemingly incompatible interests (e.g., a defendant can *pro se* the defense even though that person may lack the ability to conduct it competently).[434]

Although measures such as the IFI and the MacCAT-CA are configured to better assess an accused's functional abilities as they apply to the trial complexities (e.g., IFI's interdisciplinary approach, the MacCAT-CA's ability to measure discrete psycholegal abilities), confounding variables do exist, undermining the accuracy of CST evaluations. For example, traits associated with certain mental disorders (e.g., paranoid schizophrenia/delusions) and their influence on behavior are minimized in order to evaluate legal knowledge

---

tency. Review of the MacCAT-Ca's development demonstrates this was a primary goal of this measure from its inception. *See* Hoge et al., *supra* note 360, at 145.

431. For an overview of Bonnie's model, *see supra* text accompanying note 369. *See generally* Bonnie I *supra* note 11; Bonnie III *supra* note 359.

432. *See* Hoge et al., II *supra* note 379, at 177 (discussing how Bonnie's model addresses the many shortcomings produced by the inconsistent case law and ultimately creates a sound theory for legal competence identifying the two dimensions of the competency construct (i.e., competency to assist and decisional competence).

433. Again, in *Godinez* the Supreme Court held the tests for competence to stand trial and competence to make important decisions (e.g., plead guilty, or waive counsel) were the same. Not only does this decision promote a one size fits all standard for criminal competency issues but it is inconsistent with past precedent. Specifically, *Godinez* overruled Seiling v. Eyman, 478 F.2d 211, 214 (9th Cir. 1973) (applying a heightened formulation for competency required to relinquish counsel).

434. *See* Decker *supra* note 178, at 522 (Decker notes how *Godinez* promotes countervailing concerns and further questions "the validity of a doctrine that allows defendants to proceed *pro se*, yet fails to specifically address the defendants' ability, or lack thereof, to competently conduct their own defense, or to take account of mental disorders that could jeopardize the defendants' legal capacity."

consistent with *Dusky.*[435] Thus, assessing dual functioning abilities (i.e., various psycholegal abilities contained in existing measures) suggests an accused could meet some of these requirements consistent with *Dusky* but not others and still be found competent to stand trial.[436]

While clinical and scholarly efforts continue to revamp assessment measures, problems inherent in the controlling and enduring standards (i.e., *Dusky,* and *Godinez*) logically suggest the instruments themselves will also be similarly flawed.[437] On a related note, although academicians and researchers continue to retool assessment protocol (MacCAT-CA), contemporary instruments are not used in everyday practice and are largely absent in application.[438] Simply put, because the courts are not informed about or conversant in various CST assessment technology (that is, certain instruments can tap competence related abilities), mental health professionals often do not employ uniform CST assessment protocol but instead have discretion in the way they elect to evaluate trial competency. Consequently, examiners who work for the courts continue (freely) to conduct highly individualized CST assessments and proffer clinical conclusions that can be crafted to fit attorney beliefs or courtroom inclinations. In other words, these opinions can be used,

---

435. The implications of CST findings and defendants diagnosed with paranoid features (e.g., paranoid schizophrenia or Paranoid Personality Disorder) will be discussed *infra.*

436. *See* Arrigo & Bardwell *supra* note 18, at 24. *See* Golding et al., *supra* note 14, at 327. In their discussion about the competency construct, Golding et al., (1984) recognize the functional nature of competency evaluations and state the defendant must "be able to reasonably comprehend, understand, and assist just like the "average" defendant in the criminal justice system." Right or wrong the law is clear on the point that a person can be mentally ill and still be found competent to stand trial. *See* Winick I *supra* note 1, at 923 (stating "a psychiatric diagnosis of psychosis or the existence of particular descriptive symptoms is not dispositive of the legal question of competency to stand trial."

437. As described earlier, *Faretta* further complicates matters. Again, according to *Faretta,* the right to self representation is a right belonging to the accused which he or she can either accept or reject. Thus, once a defendant is found competent to stand trial, he or she is considered competent to accept or reject the constellation of rights guaranteed by the Constitution such as the right to be present at all material proceedings, confront witnesses, and testify if one so chooses.

438. *See* M. Bardwell & B. Arrigo, *Competency to Stand Trial: A Law, Psychology, and Policy Assessment,* J. PSYCHIATRY & L. (in press).

somewhat manipulatively, to lend credibility to a particular legal theory (e.g., supporting a litigator's desire for either a competency or incompetency finding). From this perspective, the lack of uniformity with the CST assessment process and the wholesale presence of individualized forensic evaluations raise other troubling questions about the role of psychiatry in the courts; specifically, concerns about objective evaluations.[439]

We contend that the combinatory effect of ambiguous CST legal standards coupled with individualized and faulty CST evaluation practices often produce flawed (or suspect) CST outcomes, especially when defendants suffer from a paranoid or delusional mental health condition. On this latter point, we argue that problems in assessment utility are compounded further when persons experience psychiatric disorders having ubiquitous signs and conditions (i.e., paranoid and delusional mental health traits). Hypothetically speaking, some mentally disordered defendants (e.g., those suffering from paranoid personality disorder or delusional disorder) may not evince maladaptive symptoms during the CST exam and, thus, may be found competent to stand trial, notwithstanding hidden paranoid and delusional beliefs. Given their symptomatology, these individuals may elect to waive counsel and conduct their own legal action. As we demonstrate in the instance of Colin Ferguson, these situations do occur even when high profile and controversial cases receive careful judicial and clinical attention, thereby producing disturbing trial outcomes. However, before proceeding with this analysis, it is necessary to review several noteworthy psychiatric disorders that all too frequently present themselves in competency to stand trial determinations. Indeed, by detailing the signs and symptoms of paranoid and delusional disorders in chapter 4, we will then be equipped to explain more fully how these conditions impact and confound the clinical forensic assessment of trial fitness in cases like Colin Ferguson and with competency to stand trial more generally.

---

439. Issues about individualized CST assessment are explored in the next chapter on mental health disorders and further fleshed out in the case study analysis and the discussion pertaining to it.

Chapter 4

Mental Health Disorders: The Case of Paranoid and Delusional Features

OVERVIEW

Critics of assessment measures derived from faulty legal standards contend their use in CST cases is problematic, especially in relation to defendants having psychotic and paranoid mental health conditions.[440] For instance, certain mental health disabilities present problems in fitness to stand trial evaluations because of the hidden and often complicated symptoms these disabilities entail.[441] What follows is a somewhat extensive treatment of the signs and conditions of three mental health disorders and three subtypes linked to these disorders. The selected subtypes entail both psychotic and paranoid features and include: schizophrenia, paranoid type; delusional disorder, persecutory type; and paranoid personality disorder. To avoid excess elaboration on the clinical nomenclature, conventional features and diagnostic requirements are chosen to describe the selected disorders. The following diagnostic summary largely relies on the American Psychiatric Association's Diagnostic and Statistical Manual, Fourth Edition (*DSM-IV*).[442] This summary does

---

440. *See generally* Arrigo & Bardwell *supra* note 18.
441. *See Id.* at 24.
442. *See* American Psychiatric Association. THE DIAGNOSTIC AND STATISTICAL MANUAL OF MENTAL DISORDERS (4th ed.1994) (hereinafter DSM-IV). This nomenclature is considered the standard for achieving a clinical diagnosis. The *DSM-IV* is a categorical classification of mental disorders used for clinical, diagnostic, educational, forensic and research purposes. When the issue of competency is raised the evaluation is conducted by a li-

not cover all paranoid mental health disorders, nor does it describe other mental conditions having a potential impact on competency evaluations and findings.[443] Only a narrative of much greater detail and scope could accomplish this task.[444]

On a more theoretical level, the presentation and treatment of these diagnostic matters will provide the necessary backdrop against which a discussion concerning the interplay between psychotic and paranoid mental health conditions and potential competency-to-stand-trial pitfalls can be meaningfully undertaken. Stated differently, expounding upon these disorders will help explain the troubling connection between CST proceedings, diagnostic (un)certainty, and judicial decision making. Moreover, reviewing the general mental health features and diagnostic criteria will also illustrate the subtle workings of symptoms associated with these disorders and their impact on CST issues (i.e., waxing and waning effects of

---

censed psychiatrist or psychologist who adheres to the *DSM-IV* for diagnostic purposes. Moreover, the *DSM-IV* is a compendium of mental health disorders recognized by the courts. *See Id.* at xxvi.

443. Various mental health disabilities can have a direct bearing on competency matters. However, there is a historical connection between psychotic disorders and mental disability law. *See* ROESCH & GOLDING *supra* note 16, at 148–149 (indicating that of their 130 incompetent defendants 77 (55%) were diagnosed with schizophrenia, and another 13 (10%) with other diagnoses of psychosis). *See also* M. Slodov, *Criminal Responsibility and the Noncompliant Psychiatric Offender: Risking Madness*, 40 CASE WESTERN RESERVE LAW REVIEW, 296 n. 152 (1989–90) (noting the relationship between schizophrenia and the insanity defense). Indeed, a study conducted in the late 1980's indicated that as many as 80.5 percent of cases implicating the insanity defense were diagnosed as schizophrenic). *See* Steadman, Rosenstein, MacAskill, & Manderscheid, *A Profile of Mentally Disordered Offenders Admitted to Inpatient Psychiatric Services in the United States*, 12 LAW & HUMAN BEHAV. 91, 97 (1988). Additional psychotic disorders include psychotic mood disorder, brief reactive psychosis, atypical psychosis, schizophreniform disorder, schizoaffective disorder, organic hallucinations, and organic delusional disorder. *See* Slodov *supra* at 296 n.152 (recounting the types psychotic disorders as reported in the Diagnostic and Statistical Manual of Mental Disorders (3rd ed. Rev. 1987).

444. It is beyond the scope of this project to comment on mental health conditions different from those with psychotic and paranoid features. As will be discussed, the case study reveals that Colin Ferguson was clearly guided by delusional themes consistent with delusional disorder— persecutory type, paranoid schizophrenia, and paranoid personality disorder. Neither the historical behavioral patterns nor the psychiatric information on Mr. Ferguson indicate that he suffered from disorders to the contrary.

psychotic and paranoid disorders and the issue of competency, and judicial decision making related to the CST determination).

On a more practical level, exploring the general features of these disorders will enable us to appreciate more completely the courtroom reality defendants confront, especially those experiencing psychotic and paranoid mental health disorders who are called to answer a criminal indictment(s). Indeed, the focus on diagnostic matters and selected disorders lays the necessary foundation for the ensuing case study analysis. As we subsequently argue, Mr. Ferguson (a criminal litigant) demonstrated behavior consistent with delusional disorder, persecutory type; paranoid personality disorder; and schizophrenia, paranoid type. As such, the criminal matter of the New York City railway gunman was fraught with delusional themes and paranoid ideology.

Accordingly, we begin this chapter with an overview of schizophrenia and then discuss the subtype of paranoid schizophrenia.[445] We then briefly outline the general features of delusional disorder, including the persecutory subtype. The final mental disorder canvassed in this chapter addresses the general features of personality disorders, especially the paranoid personality type. Materials drawn from the *DSM-IV* are cited in the text. Following the sections on general characteristics and diagnostic requirements, we discuss the interplay between psychotic and paranoid mental health concerns, diagnostic (un)certainty, and judicial decision making relative to those psycholegal constraints as embedded in CST evaluations and legal proceedings.

---

445. Schizophrenia, paranoid type is included in the present section for several necessary reasons. First, although Colin Ferguson was not diagnosed as suffering from schizophrenia, paranoid type by the three evaluating psychiatrists, this disorder was not ruled out given the difficulties related to the evaluation methods used to determine Mr. Ferguson's competence (i.e., Ferguson did not cooperate (fully) with the CST examination process thus the psychiatric conclusions were based on interviews ranging from 1.5 to 3 hours). Second, schizophrenia, paranoid type, is included in the analysis because of its close relationship to delusional disorder as both involve the positive symptom of delusions. Third, a description of schizophrenia and its paranoid subtype is provided because the standard for diagnosis (DSM-IV, *see generally supra* note 442) compares delusional disorder, persecutory type, schizophrenia, paranoid type and paranoid personality disorder for clinical decision making and, specifically, for differential diagnosis (i.e., comparing and contrasting related but different disorders to identify and assign the most appropriate diagnosis.)

A. Schizophrenia: General Features and Diagnostic Requirements

When describing schizophrenia, paranoid type it is essential to examine the principal disorder from which it is derived. Statistically speaking, the Axis I disorder,[446] schizophrenia "accounts for approximately two-thirds of mental hospital inmates in the United States."[447] Schizophrenia, a psychotic disorder, manifests symptoms by virtue of thought, speech, perception and desire with onset occurring in late adolescence.[448] The general features of schizophrenia are a mixture of characteristic symptoms that may include delusions; hallucinations; disorganized speech; grossly disorganized or catatonic behavior; and negative symptoms (Criterion A).[449] The "prodromal phase," the first stage of the disorder, encompasses conditions such as unusual perceptual experiences, bizarre and odd beliefs, speech that is understandable but digressive, poor personal uptake, and general lack of volition or drive.[450] These characteris-

---

446. The *DSM-IV* is a multi-axial classification system with each covering a special domain of information. See DSM-IV *supra* note 442, at 25. The five axes are included to classify specific conditions to facilitate clinical treatment planning and predictive outcome. See *Id.* Axis I classifies all the various clinical disorders and is considered the principal diagnosis unless otherwise specified; Axis II covers Personality Disorders and Mental Retardation; Axis III involves General Medical Conditions; Axis IV details Psychosocial and Environmental Problems; and Axis V includes Global Assessment of Functioning (GAF) which describes psychological, social, and occupational functioning on a continuum of mental health impairment. GAF scores range from 100 to 0 with high scores indicating superior functioning and low scores suggesting impairment in the psychological, social and occupational domains. See *Id.* at 25, 32.

447. See S. Munger, *Bill Clinton Bugged My Brain!: Delusional Claims in Federal Courts*, 72 Tulane L, Rev. 1809, 1818 (1998). See also G. SHEAN, SCHIZOPHRENIA vii (University Press of Am. Ed. 1987) (1978). Moreover, a comprehensive study conducted by Hoge et al., looked at the characteristics of incompetent defendants. In addition to other important findings, the study indicated that of the 159 inmates admitted to a mental hospitals in Florida and Virginia for restoration of competence 65% were diagnosed with schizophrenia. See Hoge et al., I *supra* note 361, at 162.

448. See DSM-IV *supra* note 442, at 274–285.

449. See *Id.* at 285.

450. See *Id.* at 278. The presence of such symptoms usually suggests to family members that something is wrong and they often report from their interactions the individual as "gradually slipping away."

tics eventually desist, and the individual enters the "active phase" such that delusions and hallucinations, and formal thought disorders are present.[451] In what follows, we provide a more specific overview of the hallmark features of schizophrenia.

According to the *DSM-IV*, there are six diagnostic criteria for schizophrenia.[452] However, schizophrenia is best understood by its first prong (Criterion A; Characteristic symptoms), which is a detailed network discussing the positive and negative symptoms of this disorder.[453] In regard to Criterion A, the *DSM-IV* states:

> [C]riterion A for schizophrenia requires that at least two of the five items [delusions, hallucinations, disorganized speech or catatonic behavior, and negative symptoms] be present concurrently for much of at least 1 month... if delusions are bizarre or hallucinations involve voices commenting or voices conversing, then the presence of only one item is required.[454]

The first general category encompasses the positive symptoms that involve a system of delusions and hallucinations, disorganized speech, and grossly disorganized or catatonic behavior.[455] To capture the divergence of the positive symptoms, the *DSM-IV* fashions two distinct dimensions including the "psychotic dimension" and the "disorganized dimension."[456] Delusions (Criterion A1), a segment of the psychotic dimension, "[a]re erroneous beliefs that usually involve a misinterpretation of perceptions or experiences. Their content may include a variety of themes (e.g., prosecutory, referen-

---

451. *See Id.*

452. *See Id.* at 285. These criteria include: Characteristic symptoms (Criterion A); Social and occupational dysfunction (Criterion B); Duration (Criterion C); Schizoaffective and Mood Disorder exclusion (Criterion D); Substance/general medical condition exclusion (Criterion E); and Relationship to a Pervasive Developmental Disorder (Criterion F). *See Id.* at 285–286.

453. *See E.g., Id.* at 274. The remaining criteria center on psychosocial impairment (Criterion B), duration (Criterion C) or conditions excluding a diagnosis of schizophrenia (Criterion D, E) and the presence of schizophrenia relative to a pervasive developmental disorder (Criterion F). These diagnostic requirements are largely explained by way of definition (schizoaffective and mood disorder exclusion), however, for a review of the diagnostic requirements for Criterion B-F, *see generally Id.* at 285–286.

454. *See* DSM-IV *supra* note 442, at 277.

455. *See Id.* at 275. *See also* B. SADOCK, & V. SADOCK, KAPLAN & SADOCK'S COMPREHENSIVE TEXTBOOK OF PSYCHIATRY 1741 (7th ed. 2000).

456. *See* DSM-IV *supra* note 442, at 275.

tial, somatic, religious, or grandiose)."[457] Hallucinations (Criterion A2), the other component of the psychotic dimension, are sensory distortions (e.g., auditory, visual, olfactory, gustatory, and tactile).[458] The most common hallucinations are auditory hallucinations in which the person hears voices separate from one's own thoughts and very often indicate a diagnosis of schizophrenia.[459] According to one recent study of psychiatrists in the United States "delusions ranked second [among] the top 10 symptoms indicating schizophrenia and hallucinations ranked fifth."[460]

Disorganized speech (Criterion A3) and grossly disorganized or catatonic behavior (Criterion A4), the remaining positive symptoms, comprise the disorganization dimension. Disorganized thinking and behavior have been considered by some as the single most important feature of schizophrenia.[461] The individual with disorganized speech will often "slip off track"[462] —such that responses are either inapplicable to the questions asked or tangential to the topic

---

457. *See Id.* at 275. *See also* SADOCK & SADOCK *supra* note 455, at 1195 (emphasizing the grey area concerning delusions and overvalued ideas or beliefs). For example, Sadock and Sadock state "A person who is convinced that he is deliberately discriminated against by his foreman at the factory, that his wife is running around with other men, or that his wife is trying to poison him may have paranoid delusions, but they are not necessarily due to schizophrenia. On the other hand, a man who is convinced that he is the victim of a Pentagon-directed plot to destroy his brain by special death rays beamed at him from space satellites or that he is the Virgin Mary expresses delusions that, by their very bizarre character, point definitely in the direction of schizophrenia." *See Id.* at 1195.

458. *See* DSM-IV *supra* note 442, at 275. *See also* SADOCK & SADOCK *supra* note 455, at 1195. Although sensory or perceptual symptoms such as hallucinations are key diagnostic clues indicating schizophrenia, important qualifications exist relating to sensation, time, and the content of the hallucinations. For example, "Experiences of being controlled by outside forces or having strange, continuous, somatic (cenesthetic) hallucinations [change in normal quality of feeling in sections of the body] or auditory, verbal hallucinations (particularly if the voices are coming from God or the devil or address the patient in the second person or talk about him) may support a diagnosis of schizophrenia." In addition, such symptoms should occur over a period of time (e.g., as least several days) *See Id.* at 1195.

459. *See Id.*

460. However, Sadock and Sadock were quick to note that the presence of delusions and hallucinations only imply psychosis. Indeed, such symptomatology does not, in of itself, confirm schizophrenia. *See* SADOCK & SADOCK *supra* note 455, at 1194.

461. *See* DSM-IV *supra* note 442, at 276.

462. *See Id.*

at hand. In addition, persons with grossly disorganized behavior (Criteria A4) exhibit a range of erratic emotions. For example, this person may, in one instance, act childlike then suddenly become angry or agitated.[463] These individuals also demonstrate problems in goal-directed behavior, compromising their ability to perform daily tasks (e.g., can not prepare meals, or lack personal hygiene). These individuals may also engage in clearly inappropriate behavior (e.g., public masturbation) or may display uncertain agitation (e.g., shouting and swearing).[464] By the same token, signs associated with catatonic behavior (Criteria A4), also include a range of bizarre behaviors but center on a "marked decrease in reactivity to the environment."[465] For example, this person may become completely unaware of how he or she is reacting to a situation (catatonic stupor), sit or stand in a rigid position without moving (catatonic rigidity), ignore instruction to move (catatonic negativism), exhibit a bizarre pose (catatonic posturing), or engage in unstimulated excessive motor activity (catatonic excitement).[466]

The second general category of Criterion A describes negative symptoms (Criterion A5) and includes affective flattening, alogia, and avolition.[467] According to the *DSM-IV*, "[N]egative symptoms include restrictions in the range and intensity of emotional expression (affective flattening), in the fluency and productivity of thought and speech (alogia), and in the initiation of goal-directed behavior (avolition)."[468]

Individuals with these conditions simply demonstrate behavior that is either disconnected or absent. For example, during a conversation, individuals with affective flattening often do not change facial expression, have reduced body language with poor eye contact.[469] The hallmarks of alogia are poverty of speech, poverty of content of speech, and blocking.[470] Here, the individual will often have a diminution of thoughts evinced by empty replies, and lack-

463. *See E.g., Id.*
464. *See Id.*
465. *See Id.*
466. *See Id.* Although historically associated with schizophrenia, catatonic behaviors are also symptoms of other disorders (e.g., Mood Disorders with catatonic features, a product of a general medical condition and Medication-Induced Movement Disorders. *See Id.*
467. *See Id.* at 275.
468. *See Id.*
469. *See* SADOCK & SADOCK *supra* note 455, at 1194.
470. *See Id.*

ing in significant content. Much of what is said is perhaps vague, impressionistic, hollow, or muddled. This person may appear unable to express a sustained flow of thought that focuses on a single notion or a single line of inquiry. Avolition, the third mainstay negative symptom, may manifest itself via goal directed behavior, where individuals simply lack an interest in occupational goals or education.[471] The *DSM-IV* regards these three negative symptoms as strong indications of schizophrenia "account[ing] for a substantial degree of morbidity associated with the disorder"[472] and also showing a relationship with the associated features of schizophrenia.[473]

Determining what is or is not a negative symptom often presents problems for the observing clinician. In other words, the presentation of negative symptoms is often ubiquitous in schizophrenia "because they occur on a continuum with normality."[474] The *DSM-IV* suggests other factors may explain negative-like symptoms. For example, they could be a result of positive symptoms,[475] side effects from medication, a mood disorder, environmental understimulation, or even demoralization.[476] What's more, the socially withdrawn individual could evince signs similar to negative symptoms. In terms of sifting through this grey area, the *DSM-IV* advises such conditions should be both pervasive and the best test is the persistence of such signs for a considerable period of time.[477] We note that the emphasis on time and clinical evaluation is clear, especially when deciding whether a negative symptom is sufficiently persistent to meet the criteria.[478] Thus, the general features of schizophrenia (Criterion A)

---

471. *See Id.*

472. *See* DSM-IV *supra* note 442, at 277.

473. *See Id.* Associated features show how the general symptoms (e.g., negative symptoms) influence everyday experiences. For example, the individual with schizophrenia may display inappropriate affect (e.g., smiling, laughing in absence of an appropriate stimulus). *See Id.* at 276–277 for a discussion on the associated features of schizophrenia.

474. *See Id.* at 277.

475. *See Id.* at 277 (noting "the behavior of an individual who has the delusional belief that he will be in danger if he leaves his room or talks to anyone may mimic alogia and avolition.")

476. *See Id.* at 277.

477. *See Id.*

478. As discussed *infra*, time is often a precious but, nonetheless, absent commodity when clinicians attempt to diagnosis a defendant in the context of a CST evaluation.

suggest a diverse range of distortions, both positive and negative. No single trait warrants a diagnosis of schizophrenia but several of the symptoms must be present in a given month and persist for at least six months.[479] Overall, a diagnosis of schizophrenia suggests a marginal level of social and occupational functioning.[480]

In addition to the general definition of schizophrenia, subtypes of the disorder exist. According to the *DSM-IV* there are five different subtypes of schizophrenia including the paranoid type, disorganized type, catatonic type, undifferentiated type, and the residual type.[481] Generally speaking, the prevalence of specific symptoms distinguish the different subtypes. For example, the characteristic symptoms of schizophrenia include (1) delusions; (2) hallucinations; (3) disorganized speech; (4) grossly disorganized or catatonic behavior; (5) negative symptoms. Thus, a catatonic subtype is assigned when catatonic behavior is the prominent feature; the disorganized type is assigned when disorganized speech and flat or inappropriate affect are the prominent features, and so forth. As is evident from the previous comments, the subtypes of schizophrenia are contingent on the "predominant symptomatology at the time of evaluation."[482] Because this chapter centers on psychotic and paranoid disorders, the specific features and diagnostic requirements of schizophrenia, paranoid type are discussed in the following pages. Included in this section is a brief discussion on paranoid schizophrenia and CST evaluations; that is, how this disorder can complicate competency to stand trial testing via assessment protocol and ultimately the judicial CST determination.

B. Schizophrenia, Paranoid Type: General Features and Diagnostic Requirements

Diagnostic criteria for the paranoid type of schizophrenia include a "preoccupation with one or more delusions or frequent auditory hallucinations [Criterion A] and none of the following are promi-

---

479. *See Id.* at 285.
480. *See Id.*
481. *See Id.* at 278.
482. *See Id.* at 286.

nent: disorganized speech, disorganized or catatonic behavior, or flat or inappropriate affect [Criterion B]."[483] Clearly, the paranoid subtype concentrates on the positive symptoms of schizophrenia (e.g., delusions and hallucinations). Delusions associated with the paranoid type are often prosecutory and grandiose,[484] and the hallucinations are usually related to the content of the delusional theme.[485] For example, a person with a delusional theme involving religion may believe he or she is the messiah and have auditory hallucinations relating to the religious theme (e.g., hears voices about religion). In addition, "the combination of persecutory and grandiose delusions with anger may predispose the individual to violence."[486] The *DSM-IV* provides the following definition with respect to schizophrenia, paranoid type, "[T]he essential feature of the Paranoid Type of Schizophrenia is the presence of prominent delusions or auditory hallucinations in the context of a relative preservation of cognitive functioning and affect."[487] In other words, individuals who are diagnosed with this disorder have a preoccupation with one or more delusions or have frequent auditory hallucinations but these symptoms do not markedly impair cognitive faculties. These criteria differentiate the paranoid type from a general

---

483. *See Id.* at 287. Criterion B is provided to differentiate the paranoid subtype from the other subtypes. In addition, the *DSM-IV* notes the onset of this disorder tends to occur later in life.

484. *See* Munger *supra* note 447, at 1818. Munger notes many delusions associated with paranoid schizophrenia have common themes. Specifically, "[o]ne man believed that he was Jesus Christ who communicated with God via a radio inside his brain, waiting for a holy cataclysm from space to kill off everyone on Earth who defiled themselves by ingesting human semen; a woman accused her family of reading her thoughts from a radio-transmitted code fed into her brain and maintained that the President of the United States was in love with her but the First Lady would not let them marry;...a man claimed to hear telephone conversations in his head from the Pope, Jesus Christ, and various movie stars; another person jumped out of a moving car in response to personal messages from God." (citing SHEAN *supra* note 447, at 53–90).

485. *See Id.*

486. *See Id. See also* W. Pincus, *Civil Commitment and the "Great Confinement" Revisited: Straightjacketing Individual Rights, Stifling Culture*, 36 Wm and Mary L. Rev. 1769 (1995) (although there is conflicting data whether schizophrenics are more likely to commit violent acts as compared to the general population, *see* DSM IV *supra* note 442, at 280, Pincus notes the *DSM IV* "warns of violence as a feature associated with *only* paranoid schizophrenia." (italics added for emphasis). *See* Pincus *supra* note, at 1771 n. 10.

487. *See* DSM-IV *supra* note 442, at 287.

diagnosis of schizophrenia emphasizing the absence of disorganized speech, disorganized or catatonic behavior, or flat, inappropriate affect.[488]

Criteria indicating the preservation of cognitive functioning, specified in the above definition, can present problems when paranoid schizophrenics undergo CST evaluations. We note that other commentators have also considered the relationship between schizophrenia and competency evaluations.[489] For example, as a practical matter, defendants with schizophrenic and paranoid features can harbor symptoms essential in cooperating with counsel in the preparation of the defense; however, if they lack other indicators of psychopathology these individuals will be found competent to stand trial.[490] Put another way, certain defendants can be floridly delusional, however, if the chosen evaluation technique does not specifically flesh out the symptomatology that would impair client/attorney cooperation, the defendant will easily meet the *Dusky* standard.[491]

---

488. *See Id.* (italics added for emphasis).

489. *See also* Golding et al., *supra* note 14, at 322. The fallout with respect to paranoid schizophrenia is not only logically apparent but also confirmed in the literature. Golding et al. stress that defendants need not be experts in the area of law and state, "a defendant may be suffering from a reliably diagnosed mental disorder within the psychotic spectrum (e.g., paranoid schizophrenia)...and still may be found competent to stand trial." *See Id.*

490. A recent study demonstrated the effect schizophrenia has on criminal defendants and their ability to perform on certain psycholegal measures. *See* Hoge et al., II *supra* note 379, at 329. Specifically, researchers administered the MacSAC-CD to mentally disordered criminal defendants with a diagnosis of schizophrenia, affective disorder, other psychiatric disorders, and to defendants without a diagnosed mental disorder. The following findings were among the study's results: over half of the defendants with a diagnosis of schizophrenia were deficient on measures concerning competence-related abilities relative to adjudicative competence (i.e., understanding, reasoning and appreciation), more so than the other groups. Moreover, conceptual disorganization was associated with poor performance on all measures for defendants with schizophrenia and defendants with affective disorders. Based on these findings, the investigators suggested a schizophrenic might manifest symptoms of psychosis (i.e., hallucinations), but would likely be unimpaired [competent to stand trial] absent other psychopathology. *See Id.* at 343.

491. This, however, is not the fault of forensic researchers. Indeed, as observers conclude, a "diagnosis of schizophrenia should alert defense and prosecution attorneys, judges, and mental health professionals that a significant impairment in competence-related abilities may be present." *See* Hoge et al., II *supra* note 379, at 343.

As previously mentioned, we contend that certain traits related to mental disorders are minimized, especially delusions associated with paranoid schizophrenics. Once again we note that such symptomatology is problematic for CST evaluations and the trial process at large. Indeed, as Hoge et al. indicated "[o]ther symptoms of psychosis— hallucinations and delusions— were not associated with impairments in understanding or reasoning in defendants with schizophrenia..."[492] rather delusions stemming from schizophrenia were only associated with impaired appreciation.[493] Although a defendant may manifest certain traits, this symptomatology does not preclude adjudication or even require further observation. Moreover, CST assessment measures typically do not consider how hallucinations or delusions may materialize during the course of the trial.[494] As is often the case, these defendants will adamantly resist the idea of an insanity defense and instead will represent themselves so that "the facts of the case set them free" or will represent themselves to escape the perceived miscarriage of justice brought about by the criminal justice system itself.[495] Indeed, the fear and terror some defendants engender when labeled mentally disordered may in fact be a symptom of their very psychiatric illness.[496] Regrettably, the present system of CST evaluation does not adequately or fully account for this very real and disturbing courtroom situation.

C. Delusional Disorder: General Features and Diagnostic Requirements

Similar to schizophrenia, delusional disorder is also reported as an Axis I clinical disorder.[497] As indicated in the title, a clinical diag-

---

492. See Id. at 343.
493. See Id.
494. See generally Arrigo & Bardwell supra note 18.
495. See E.g., Decker supra note 178, at 485–486 (noting reason why some defendants conduct their own legal action.) Paranoid logic and other bizarre reasons used to strike an insanity defense (interposed by defense counsel) are further explored and actualized in the case study on Ferguson.
496. See generally Arrigo & Bardwell supra 18, at 25–30.
497. See DSM-IV supra note 442, at 25–26 (specifically considered a psychotic disorder).

nosis of delusional disorder is determined by the presence of delusions and, more accurately, the occurrence of nonbizarre delusions.[498] The *DSM-IV* reports a five-pronged criterion based formula defining delusional disorder.[499]

The essential feature of delusional disorder is the presence of one or more nonbizarre delusions lasting, at the minimum, one month's time (Criterion A).[500] The next benchmark feature entails a search for the absence of specific diagnostic criteria ensuring that the presenting symptoms are not otherwise attributed to another Axis I psychotic disorder. In other words, the second criterion gives special attention to the symptom presentation mindful that some psychotic disorders have similar symptomatology (e.g., delusional disorder as compared to schizophrenia, paranoid type).[501] Since the distinction is often murky and time consuming, the *DSM-IV* offers specific detail with respect to comparing delusional disorder with particular features of schizophrenia. Accounting for other symptom presentations, Criterion B eliminates a diagnosis of delusional disorder if the individual evinces symptoms consistent with Criterion A of Schizophrenia.[502] With respect to differential diagnoses between schizophrenia and delusional disorder, the clinical decision must be based on the presence or absence of the essential features of schizophrenia

---

498. A nonbizarre delusion refers to situations that can conceivably occur (e.g., being followed, poisoned, or deceived by person's of trust.) *See* DSM-IV *supra* note 444, at 297. In contrast, a bizarre delusion involves a situation that is not possible (e.g., an ongoing exchange between an individual and aliens from outer space). *See E.g., Id.* at 296. Distinguishing between delusional disorder and schizophrenia is often difficult especially when deciding whether a delusion is bizarre or nonbizarre. Consequently, making this distinction is (ostensibly) a source of considerable confusion given the subjective nature in deciding what is or is not bizarre. This notwithstanding, bizarre delusions will often indicate schizophrenia where nonbizarre delusions are more consistent with delusional disorder. *See E.g., Id.* at 296.

499. *See Id.* at 301.

500. *See* Id. at 296.

501. *See* SADOCK & SADOCK *supra* note 455, at 1195. (Noting a differential diagnoses between delusional disorder and schizophrenia, paranoid type requires careful consideration given "delusions of persecution or grandeur are essential symptoms in both the paranoid type of schizophrenia and in the paranoid type of delusional disorders...") *See Id.*

502. *See* DSM-IV *supra* note 442, at 296. *See infra* notes 452–469 (discussing the various positive symptoms and negative symptoms of schizophrenia).

and (most often) its paranoid subtype.[503] In some cases, however, certain positive features of schizophrenia (e.g., tactile and olfactory hallucinations) can occur but only under specific conditions. The *DSM-IV* speaks to this very issue:

> "Auditory or visual hallucinations, if present, are not prominent. Tactile or olfactory hallucinations may be present (and prominent) if they are related to the delusional theme (e.g., the sensation of being infested with insects associated with delusions of infestation, or the perception that one emits a foul odor from a body orifice associated with delusions of reference)."[504]

Clarifying the interplay between hallucinations and delusional disorder indicates that hallucinations, if present, should center on the delusional theme (e.g., tactile; bugs crawling on skin relating to the delusion that insects have infested the individual's body), otherwise if hallucinations are present and unrelated to the delusion the disorder is perhaps best understood as the workings of another clinical disorder such as schizophrenia or its paranoid subtype.[505]

Similar to the paranoid schizophrenic, symptoms stemming from delusional disorder do not markedly impair cognitive faculties.[506] The *DSM-IV* reports that aside from the direct influence of the delusion, "psychosocial functioning is not markedly impaired, and behavior is neither obviously odd or bizarre (Criterion C)."[507] On a related note, studies indicate that delusional disorder is not a severe impairment nor does it result in a change in personality; rather, the condition leads to a gradual and progressive involvement with the delusional belief.[508] Consistent with schizophrenia and its paranoid subtype, the remaining criterion accounts for symptoms that may be the product of other disorders or medical explanations (Criterion D; mood episodes concurrent with delusions are brief compared to the duration of the delusional periods;

503. *See* SADOCK & SADOCK *supra* note 455, at 1195.
504. *See* DSM-IV *supra* note 442, at 296.
505. The Axis II paranoid personality disorder is automatically ruled out since there are no delusional beliefs. *See Id.* at 301; *See also infra* (discussing paranoid personality disorder.)
506. *See Id.* at 296.
507. *See Id.*
508. *See* SADOCK & SADOCK *supra* note 455, at 1261.

and Criterion E; delusions are not caused by the physiological effects of a substance (e.g., cocaine) or a general medical condition (e.g., Alzheimer's disease).[509]

Associated features of delusional disorder often involve problems stemming from the content of the delusional theme.[510] A most common feature involves ideas of reference (e.g., placing special significance on random events) which can result in difficulties with social, occupational, and interpersonal relations. The *DSM-IV* notes that although cognitive abilities are relatively preserved, psychosocial functioning can be variable: "[s]ome individuals may appear to be relatively unimpaired in their interpersonal and occupational roles. In others, the impairment may be substantial and include low or absent occupational functioning and social isolation."[511] In other words, delusional disorder does not impair cognitive ability but its resulting dysfunctions, in reaction to the delusion, can affect social, occupational, and interpersonal relations.[512]

Another noteworthy associated feature suggests individuals suffering from delusional disorder are litigious and invoke mechanisms to resolve grievances which often leads "to hundreds of letters of protest to government and judicial officials and many court appearances."[513] Changes in mood are also common. For example, individuals suffering from delusional disorder will develop irritable feelings or dysphoric mood as a way to reconcile their own beliefs or in reaction to individuals who do not agree with the delusional theme.[514] Onset for this disorder can begin in adolescence but generally occurs in middle to late adult life.[515]

Similar to schizophrenia, delusional disorder has a variety of subtypes. The subtype attached to the delusional disorder is directly related to the predominant delusional theme.[516] The *DSM-IV* describes six subtypes including the erotomanic type, grandiose type, jealous type, persecutory type, somatic type, mixed type, unspeci-

---

509. *See* DSM-IV *supra* note 442, at 296.
510. *See Id.* at 298.
511. *See Id.* at 297.
512. *See Id.*
513. *See Id.* at 298.
514. *See Id.*
515. *See Id.* at 299.
516. *See Id.* at 297.

fied type.[517] Once again, because mental health disorders with paranoid features are the focus of this chapter, the next section explores the specific criteria and diagnostic requirements associated with the persecutory subtype. Moreover, in the ensuing case study the defendant, Colin Ferguson, not only evinced signs consistent with the persecutory subtype but was diagnosed by one of the evaluating psychiatrists as suffering from this very disorder.

D. Delusional Disorder, Persecutory Subtype: General Features and Diagnostic Requirements

As previously stated, delusional disorder retains a variety of subtypes and of its various forms the persecutory type is the most common.[518] This subtype applies when the general theme of the delusion involves beliefs that the individual "is being conspired against, cheated, spied on, followed, poisoned or drugged, maliciously maligned, harassed, or obstructed in the pursuit of long-term goals."[519]

Consistent with Criterion B for delusional disorder, functioning is variable for the persecutory subtype and behavioral difficulties that may occur are in direct response to the delusion.[520] Although the disorder may be chronic, a waxing and waning effect often occurs regarding preoccupation with the delusional ideals.[521] Thus, the persecutory subtype is best understood as an encapsulated disorder. In other words, aside from the workings of the delusional belief itself, psychosocial functioning is largely preserved and the person does not engage in strange or bizarre behavior.[522] Practically speaking, intellectual pursuits are not impaired and an individual can be articulate and lucid but nonetheless suffer from the persecutory subtype.

---

517. See Id. at 297–298 (describing the various subtypes and their application and definition relative to delusional disorder).
518. See Id. at 299.
519. See Id. at 298.
520. See Id. at 298.
521. See Id. at 299.
522. See Id. at 296.

Given that the delusional themes relating to the persecutory sub-type involve a general distrust towards others, small slights are often exaggerated and eventually incorporated into the delusional belief. As we noted above, individuals suffering from delusional disorder often pursue legal outlets in order to correct perceived wrongs. This associated feature is clear with individuals suffering from the persecutory subtype. Indeed, these individuals often seek redress (through the court system) to deal with disputes and those people they believe are responsible.[523] As the *DSM-IV* states, "the affected person may engage in repeated attempts to obtain satisfaction by appeal to the courts and other government agencies."[524] On a related topic, an associated feature recognized by the *DSM-IV* also indicates individuals with persecutory delusions are frequently angry, resentful, and can ultimately resort to violence as a means of expressing their frustration.[525]

The associated features relating to the persecutory subtype can have troubling implications in the context of CST evaluations. Although guided by delusional themes, if a defendant is able to preserve cognitive abilities, organize delusions around a coherent theme,[526] and demonstrate appropriate affect (e.g., not engage in disorganized behavior), some examiners and trial judges may conclude these disordered individuals are not suffering from a debilitating mental illness, when in fact they are.[527] From this perspective, the defendant who is paranoid can be evasive and guarded with information key to preparing a defense. Indeed, an accused may withhold information because of a belief that defense counsel is part of the conspiracy designed to destroy the defendant. As a result, the delusional preoccupation with one's own paranoia can complicate the ability to cooperate with counsel such that this disordered defendant may even fire his or her attorney and conduct his or her own (misguided) legal action.[528]

As is axiomatic by now, the root of the problem is quite simply the controlling competency cases themselves (i.e., *Dusky*) which

---

523. *See Id.* at 298.
524. *See Id.*
525. *See Id.*
526. *See* DSM-IV *supra* note 442, at 287.
527. *See* Arrigo & Bardwell *supra* note 18, at 25.
528. *Id.*

continue to insist that a defendant need only be able to reasonably assist counsel and understand the proceedings. Moreover, the problem is complicated by *Dusky's* progeny (*Godinez*). *Godinez* allows potentially mentally impaired defendants to waive their right to counsel and conduct their own defense, despite being competent (or not) to do either. Unfortunately, as we discussed in chapter 3 on CST assessment practices, the instruments are lacking in their ability to measure accurately or adequately the impact of psychotic and paranoid conditions on CST abilities. Moreover, even when comprehensive tests are developed (MacCAT-CA) these measures are not employed on a regular basis. In the next section we turn to personality disorders with an emphasis on the paranoid subtype. Although psychotic elements are absent in this mental health condition (i.e., paranoid personality disorder), the paranoid beliefs can be quite sophisticated and problematic, especially when this defendant is called upon to assist in the direction of his or her criminal case.

E. Personality Disorders: General Features and Diagnostic Requirements

Unlike schizophrenia and its paranoid subtype and unlike delusional disorder and its persecutory type, personality disorders are reported as Axis II conditions.[529] According to the *DSM-IV*, "a personality disorder is an enduring pattern of inner experience and behavior that deviates markedly from the expectations of the individual culture, is pervasive and inflexible, has an onset in adolescence or early adulthood, is stable over time, and leads to distress or impairment."[530]

---

529. Specifically, "Axis II is for reporting Personality Disorders and Mental Retardation." *See* DSM-IV *supra* note 442, at 26.

530. *See Id.* at 629. The various personality disorders include the Paranoid, Schizoid, Schizotypal, Antisocial, Borderline, Histrionic, Narcissistic, Avoidant, Dependent, Obsessive-Compulsive and the Personality Disorder Not Otherwise Specified-meets general criteria for more than one of the identified personality disorders, or criteria for personality disorder not included in the classification such as passive-aggressive personality disorder.) *See Id.*

Personality disorders are grouped into one of three clusters (e.g., Clusters A, B, C) based on common qualities.[531] Generally, when reaching a diagnosis of a personality disorder an examiner must conclude that an individual's personality traits are inflexible and maladaptive to such a degree that they cause marked signs of functional impairment or subjective distress.[532] The diagnosis of a personality disorder should be based on an individual's long-term functioning and maladaptive personality features should appear by early adulthood.[533] The *DSM-IV* accounts for maladaptive personality traits relative to social and personal functioning, duration, onset and elimination criteria in terms of other causal factors. As the *DSM-IV* reports:

> The essential feature of a Personality Disorder is an enduring pattern of inner experience and behavior that deviates markedly from the expectations of the individual's culture and is manifested in at least two of the following areas: cognition, affectivity, interpersonal functioning, or impulse control (Criterion A). This enduring pattern is inflexible and pervasive across a broad range of personal and social situations (Criterion B) and leads to clinically significant distress or impairment in social, occupational, or other important areas of functioning (Criterion C). The pattern is stable and of long duration, and its onset can be traced back at least to adolescence or early adulthood (Criterion D). The pattern is not better accounted for as a manifestation or consequence of another mental disorder (Criterion E) and is not due to the direct physiological effects of a substance ... or a general medical condition ... (Criterion F).[534]

The criteria outlined above, focus on the duration of a specific pattern and, by doing so, distinguish personality disorders from

---

531. *See Id.* Cluster A comprises the Paranoid, Schizoid, and Schizotypal Personality Disorders— the common features include odd or eccentric behavior. Cluster B represents the Antisocial, Borderline, Histrionic, and Narcissistic Personality Disorders, demonstrating dramatic, emotional, or erratic behavior. Cluster C signifies the Avoidant, Dependent, and Obsessive-Compulsive Personality Disorders and notable behavior includes anxiety and fearfulness. *See Id.* at 629–630.

532. *See Id.* at 630.

533. *See Id.*

534. *See Id.*

other clinical and medical explanations.[535] Indeed, the *DSM-IV* indicates that a personality disorder should be diagnosed under specific conditions such that the characteristic features are formed before early adulthood, represent an individual's long-term pattern of behavior, and do not solely occur during an episode of an Axis I disorder.[536] Once again, because this chapter is centering on paranoid and delusional mental health disorders, the next section addresses the paranoid personality disorder. More importantly, as we will see with the preceding analysis of the Colin Ferguson case, two of the psychiatrists considered this diagnosis in their clinical opinions and conclusions concerning Ferguson's mental state. For now, however, we draw attention to the specific criteria and diagnostic requirements for paranoid personality disorder. In addition, we assess the implications or, more accurately, the limitations paranoid personality disorder imposes on the defendant's ability to make important and strategic trial decisions.

F. Paranoid Personality Disorder: General Features and Diagnostic Requirements

The trademark of the paranoid personality disorder is systematized paranoia resulting in significant functional impairment or subjective stress.[537] As outlined in the *DSM-IV*, the diagnostic criteria for paranoid personality disorder are excessive distrust and suspiciousness of others expressed as a pervasive tendency to interpret the motives of others as malevolent.[538] The onset of this pattern of

---

535. However, frequently multiple disorders are present and explain an individual's maladaptive behavior thus requiring special recording procedures. The *DSM-IV* demonstrates the relationship and recording measures when both Axis I and Axis II disorders are evident. For example, "[W]hen an individual has a chronic Axis I Psychotic Disorder (e.g., Schizophrenia) that was preceded by a preexisting Personality Disorder (e.g., Schizotypal, Schizoid, Paranoid), the Personality Disorder should be recorded on Axis II, followed by "Premorbid" in parentheses. For example: Axis I: 295.30 Schizophrenia, Paranoid Type; Axis II: 301.20 Schizoid Personality Disorder (Premorbid). *See Id.* at 631.

536. *See Id.* at 632.

537. *See E.g.,* SADOCK & SADOCK *supra* note 455, at 1741.

538. *See* DSM-IV *supra* note 442, at 637. *See also* SADOCK & SADOCK *supra* note 455, at 1741.

behavior begins by early adulthood and is expressed in a variety of contexts, both social and occupational (Criterion A).[539] In addition to harboring general suspiciousness and distrust, the *DSM-IV* indicates an individual must meet four or more of the following criteria:

> "suspects, without sufficient basis, that others are exploiting, harming, or deceiving him or her [Criterion A1]; is preoccupied with unjustified doubts about the loyalty or trustworthiness of friends or associates [Criterion A2]; is reluctant to confide in others because of unwarranted fear that the information will be used maliciously against him or her [Criterion A3]; reads hidden demeaning or threatening meanings into benign remarks or events [Criterion A4]; persistently bears grudges, i.e., is unforgiving or insults, injures, or slights [Criterion A5]; perceives attacks on his or her character or reputation that are not apparent to others and is quick to react angrily or to counterattack [Criterion A6]; and has recurrent suspicions, without justification, regarding fidelity of spouse or sexual partner [Criterion A7]."[540]

For Criterion B, the *DSM-IV* indicates that this behavior does not occur exclusively during the course of schizophrenia or another mood disorder, and it is not the product of physiological effects stemming from a general medical condition.[541]

The associated features of paranoid personality disorder are often a reflection of the deep and intense beliefs harbored by a person with this condition.[542] For instance, given the level of excessive distrust and suspicion, individuals with paranoid personality disorder often have difficulty with close relationships.[543] Other noteworthy features suggest these individuals are argumentative, resentful, ready to take the defensive, and critical,[544] especially when defending their beliefs. On this latter point, the *DSM-IV* stipulates that, "individuals with [paranoid personality disorder] seek to confirm

differential diagnosis aspect

---

539. *See Id.* at 634, 637.
540. *See Id.* at 634–635, 637–638.
541. *See Id.* at 635, 638.
542. *See Id.* at 635–636 for a detailed account of the associated features of paranoid personality disorder.
543. *See Id.* at 635.
544. *See Id.* at 635; SADOCK & SADOCK *supra* note 455, at 1261.

their preconceived negative notions regarding people or situations they encounter, attributing malevolent motivations to others that are projections of their own fears."[545] Because individuals suffering from paranoid personality disorder lack trust in others, these persons often display an excessive need to be self-sufficient and independent.[546] Moreover, given the guarded features and patterns of behavior exhibited by these individuals, it is not surprising that persons with paranoid personality disorder complicate CST evaluations and the trial proceedings.

For example, problems surface when paranoid features are measured against *Dusky's* two-prong standard. Hypothetically speaking, while a paranoid defendant may be able to understand the nature and purpose of the courtroom proceedings (PRONG 1), those same elements of paranoia may prohibit the defendant from cooperating with counsel (PRONG 2). Stated differently, the person suffering from paranoid personality disorder may be lucid, articulate and intelligent (presently knowing and understanding the proceedings) but, nonetheless, may be guided by paranoid beliefs suggesting, for example, that defense counsel is part of an elaborate legal process designed to undermine the accused. As this example clearly implies, a general lack of trust would prevent genuine dialogue; dialogue essential to cooperating with counsel especially in the preparation of one's own defense. Understandably, then, individuals who harbor such strong feelings and intense beliefs, anchored as they undoubtedly are in the paranoid personality's imagination, may be inclined to pursue the path of self representation at all costs, even if such efforts result in their own courtroom demise.[547]

---

545. *See Id.* In terms of stress, the *DSM-IV* also notes individuals with paranoid personality disorder may experience *brief* psychotic episodes. *See Id.* at 635 (italics added for emphasis). This notwithstanding, the person with paranoid personality disorder is considered to harbor overvalued ideas (not delusions), a feature of particular importance in relation to differential diagnosis (e.g., paranoid personality disorder vs. schizophrenia, paranoid type).

546. *See Id.* Individuals with paranoid personality disorder also appear guarded, secretive, unable to collaborate, blame others for their shortcomings, often pursue legal disputes, and are unable to accept criticism although critical themselves. Moreover, these individuals tend to foster negative stereotypes, especially in terms of population groups unlike their own.

547. *See E.g.,* Decker *supra* note 178, at 487.

Thus far, this chapter has described three general and three specific subtypes of mental health conditions with paranoid and delusional features. In addition, this chapter has briefly touched upon the implications of these psychiatric disorders in the context of CST proceedings. In the next section, we address, in more detail, the troubling intersection between CST examinations, psychotic and paranoid symptoms, mental health expert opinions, and judicial decision making. In short, the final section of chapter 4 examines the (un)certainty surrounding CST opinions and determinations.[548] We maintain that this analysis makes possible the subsequent discussion on the competency screening process in high-profile cases (e.g., Colin Ferguson). As we explain in chapter 5, by virtue of a questionable competency determination and the defendant's paranoid and delusional mental health condition, the New York City railway gunman fired his defense counsel and conducted his own legal action.

G. CST Complications: The Intersection of Psychology and the Law

With respect to CST examinations, psychological/psychiatric input is both required by law[549] and an influential component in the court's decision on criminal competency matters.[550] Indeed, expert testimony concerning the CST examination process and subsequent CST judicial findings are profound opinions that have monumental effect for both the defendant and how the case will proceed (e.g., competent/proceed to trial, or incompetent/suspend prosecution until defendant is competent). Generally speaking, the trial court can either use this information to inform their decision about the issue of competency (the intent of such testimony) or the judge can shift responsibility for disposition to the experts (even though CST

---

548. *See* Arrigo Bardwell *supra* note 18, at 31.
549. *See* People v. Pulecio, 237 N.Y.S. 2d. 633 (1997), also discussed *infra*.
550. *See* J. Reich & L. Tookey, *Disagreements Between Court and Psychiatrist on Competency to Stand Trial*, 47 J. CLINICAL. PSYCH. 29–30 (1986).

is a legal decision and not a clinical one).[551] Although the use of such information falls to the discretion of the court,[552] the weight and meaning assigned to expert opinions is variable.[553] This notwithstanding, judges defer to the wisdom of clinical forensic experts (expressed via written reports or witness testimony), and these findings on competence can present the court with competing CST opinions.[554] Moreover, mental health experts can present various "provisional" or "absolute" diagnostic conclusions to support their CST determinations which, as we will see, can lead to controversial courtroom outcomes.[555]

At the outset, we note that many states have concluded, following *Dusky*, that deficits linked to competence related abilities must be a *product* of a "mental disorder,"[or a] "mental disease or defect."[556] Although mental illness alone is not dispositive for the legal question of competency,[557] examiners often times base CST findings on the presence or absence of a mental disease or defect.[558] For example, mental health experts may reach a competency-to-stand-trial finding and still conclude a defendant suffers from a mental disease or defect.[559] Indeed, some studies indicate 10% to 25% of defen-

---

551. *See* Miller & Germain II *supra* note 359, at 376–377. The process of shifting responsibility to the clinician ultimately fuels critics who believe mental health experts "usurp judicial authority by preempting decision making [in CST hearings]." *See Id.* at 378.

552. *See* People v. Orama, 150 N.Y.S. 2d. 505, 506 (1989), also discussed *infra*. Even when presented with conflicting psychiatric testimony, great deference is accorded the court's findings.

553. *See* Nicholson & Johnson, *Prediction of Competency to Stand Trial: Contribution of Demographics, Type of Offense, Clinical Characteristics, and Psycholegal Ability*, 14 INT'L J.L.& PSYCHIATRY 287 (1991) (indicating that in over 90% of the cases, courts agree with psychiatric conclusions and, generally, expert testimony is dispositive at competency hearings.)

554. *See* Brock v. United States, 387 F.2d 254 (5th Cir. 1967). Discussing how the court must compare the relevance and strength of contrary expert testimony. *Id.* at 258.

555. *See infra* discussing the case of Colin Ferguson. Indeed, provisional and absolute diagnostic opinions dominated the direct and cross examinations of the three experts who evaluated Ferguson.

556. *See* GRISSO II *supra* note 314, at 5.

557. *See* Winick *supra* note 1, at 923; Steadman & Hartstone, *supra* note 2, at 46–47.

558. *See E.g.,* GRISSO II *supra* note 314, at 15–16.

559. *See E.g.,* Winick *supra* note 1, at 923 n.4.

dants found competent to stand trial have psychotic diagnoses.[560] Nevertheless, if a defendant is deemed incompetent to stand trial, a mental disorder is likely to be the only explanation "contribut[ing] to a legal decision that the defendant's deficits in competency abilities constitute incompetency."[561] In either case, the presence or absence of a mental disorder is a common issue in competency to stand trial evaluations and legal proceedings.

In light of these considerations, many questions exist as to how experts reach diagnostic conclusions relative to the CST examination process. For example, when is a personality trait considered maladaptive, otherwise understood to be abnormal? If designated abnormal, when is the manifestation of certain behaviors better understood to constitute a specific disease? Furthermore, how is a differential diagnosis achieved? A practical answer to many of these questions is time and testing. However, as this section will explain, time is often a precious, yet scarce, commodity in the CST examination process. Before delving into the many issues concerning diagnostic (un)certainty and, specifically, the latitude afforded the examiner with respect to diagnostic opinions, this section addresses some of the more critical variables regarding competing psychological and legal objectives in forensic settings, diagnostic procedures, CST examination practices, and the judicial decision making process. The format for an assessment of these matters is discussed below.

The preceding issues are presented in five parts: first, a brief discussion about clinical objectives in forensic settings; second, time constraints, the CST examination process and paranoid mental health disorders, and a legal and psychiatric analysis; third, normal and abnormal traits, degrees of impairment and clinical diagnoses; fourth, confusing the issue of competency with diagnostic conclusions; and fifth, a sum and substance review, theoretical groundwork, and practical meaning of competency to stand trial. Once again, we assert that this section provides the necessary foundation by which to engage in the subsequent case study analysis of the Colin Ferguson matter. Moreover, as we demonstrate, this material specifically highlights the various clinical forensic problems surrounding the contentious area of trial fitness and other competency

---

560. *See Id.* at 9.
561. *See* at 16.

related abilities (e.g., competency to waive counsel and proceed *pro se* to trial).

1. Clinical Objectives in Forensic Settings

The American Counseling Association Code of Ethics and Standards of Practice[562] states that, "counselors take special care to provide proper diagnosis of mental disorders."[563] To achieve an accurate diagnosis, an examiner must collect information on the individual's presenting problem as well as information relative to the client's background.[564] In discussing guidelines for making accurate and useful diagnoses, Seligman states the following:

> "Be aware that the symptoms people present may change rapidly, depending on the time of the day, their immediate stressors, the progression of the disorder, or the characteristics of and questions posed by the interviewer. Diagnosis is not an exact science and often takes considerable time and many samples of behavior as well as information from records and other people before an accurate diagnosis can be made."[565]

In addition to the careful process of reaching a diagnosis, other problems surface regarding the law-psychology interface. For example, competing goals in clinical psychology and criminal law often present problems in CST assessment and the way the examiner interacts with the defendant. Indeed, on the one hand, clinical studies of human behavior largely entail therapeutic intervention.[566] For the clinician, the goal is to establish a treatment plan in order to help those who suffer from a mental illness. On the other hand, the criminal law is concerned with moral accountability thereby determining responsibility (i.e., blameworthiness).[567] From a legal per-

---

562. *See American Counseling Association Code of Ethics and Standards of Practice*, COUNSELING TODAY 33–40 (1995).
563. *See Id.* at 36, *as cited in* L. SELIGMAN, DIAGNOSIS AND TREATMENT PLANNING IN COUNSELING 55 (rev. 2nd ed. 1996).
564. *See* SELIGMAN *supra* note at 57.
565. *See Id.* at 58 guideline number 2 of 4.
566. *See* R. BONNIE, J. JEFFRIES, Jr., & P. LOW, A CASE STUDY IN THE INSANITY DEFENSE: THE TRIAL OF JOHN W. HINCKLEY, JR 6 (2000)[hereinafter BONNIE ET AL].
567. *See E.g.,* DSM-IV *supra* note 444, at xxiii.

spective, the criminal law seeks clear and unequivocal answers concerning the relationship between a clinical diagnosis and ultimate questions of law (e.g., what is the effect of a *DSM-IV* diagnosis on a specified legal standard). In other words, clinical objectives (e.g., treatment and planning) are quite different from forensic courtroom objectives (e.g., impairment relative to legal abilities; competency or establishing responsibility; insanity). Given these competing goals embodied by psychology and law respectively, problems often surface regarding the use of the *DSM* in forensic settings. As the *DSM-IV* warns in this setting,

> "there are significant risks that diagnostic information will be misused or misunderstood...[and] [i]n determining whether an individual meets a specified legal standard (e.g., for competence, criminal responsibility, or disability), additional information is usually required beyond that contained in the DSM-IV diagnosis. This might include information about the individual's functional impairments and how these impairments affect the particular abilities in question."[568]

In the context of CST (ability to understand the charges and assist in the defense), this legal question requires tapping information not otherwise necessary for therapeutic objectives; that is, trial fitness information is not necessary to establish a plan for treatment, but it is necessary to address the legal question of competency. Requiring additional information implicitly underscores the value of time for the CST exam. From this perspective, commentators argue evaluations conducted in an inpatient setting potentially violate the defendant's civil rights (e.g., confining for evaluation without the defendant's consent);[569] however, court statutes require explicit time for forensic assessment.[570] The next section of this chapter addresses this very matter; that is, the interplay between time constraints and CST evaluations.

---

568. *See Id.*
569. *See* K.Yates, *Therapeutic Issues Associated With Confidentiality and Informed Consent in Forensic Evaluations,* 20 N.E. J. CRIM & CIV. CON. 345, 361–362 (1994) [hereinafter Yates]. *See* also Winick *supra* note 1, at 930–931.
570. *See* 18 U.S.C. § 4247 (b) discussed *infra.*

2. CST Evaluation Time Constraints and Paranoid/Delusional Disorders: The Interplay Between Assessment, Time, and Other Confounding Subissues

Most court orders for CST examinations are constrained by time. As such, the expert, if fortunate, will conduct an initial interview (acquiring background information) and a follow-up examination(s) (administering various tests)[571] to determine if the defendant is fit for trial.[572] Typically, however, assessments run a rather short period[573] creating complications for subsequent examinations and, ultimately, jeopardizing the defendant/client's right to a fair and thorough review.[574] In one sense, this is not the fault of forensic examiners. Although courts will order a formal competency evaluation in basically all cases where doubt about trial fitness is raised,[575] the courts have specific expectations about competency evaluations.

First, as previously mentioned, is the matter of explicit time considerations. For example, under federal statute where CST examinations are conducted (usually jails), defendants are held for a period not to exceed thirty days.[576] Second (and related), many courts maintain strict expectations relative to attorney requests for a con-

---

571. *See* Yates *supra* note 569, at 352–353. Research suggests, however, that "[d]espite the availability of formal and reliable competency to stand trial measures...practioners create and utilize their own assessment tools." *See Id.*

572. *See E.g.,* Golding et al., *supra* note 14, at 323; Otto et al., *supra* note 367, at 435.

573. *See* M. PERLIN, MENTAL DISABILITY LAW: CIVIL AND CRIMINAL sections 14.04 at 226 (1989)[hereinafter PERLIN II].

574. The issue of competency should be considered at a "suitable hearing." *See* United States v. Masthers, 539 F.2d 721, 725 (D.C. Cir. 1976). *See also* Hill v. State, 473 So. 2d 1253 (Fla. 1985).

575. *See* Winick *supra* note 1, at 925. *See also* Drope v. Missouri, 420 U.S. 162 (1975); Pate v. Robinson, 383 U.S. 375 (1966). Under federal statute, a motion to determine competence can be denied "only if the trial judge correctly determines that the motion is frivolous, is not in good faith, or does not set forth the grounds for believing that the accused may be incompetent." *See* United States v. Bradshaw, 690 F.2d 704, 712 (9th Cir. 1982); United States v. Irwin, 450 F.2d 968, 970 (9th Cir. 1971).

576. *See* 18 U.S.C. § 4247 (b) (stating a *reasonable period* for examination is not to exceed thirty days). (emphasis added).

tinuance on the matter of trial fitness.[577] Continuances of this sort typically entail the litigator's request to develop collateral evidence relevant to a defendant's competency by way of independent or additional CST examinations. However, because "the trial court is accorded deference with respect to decisions denying motions for continuance,"[578] CST requests for continuance are often dismissed and frequently considered to be an empty appellate issue.[579] However, when motions for continuance are granted, the extension period is slight (under federal statute not to exceed fifteen days).[580]

Based on these collective considerations, we note that the time allotted for competency evaluations (and the court's discretion to deny CST continuances), necessarily expedites the fitness-for-trial

---

577. Not unlike any other motion for a continuance, the courts consider such motions with a specific parameters in mind. Specifically, courts will consider (1) diligence in preparing the defense; (2) the likely utility of the continuance if granted; (3) the inconvenience to the court and the opposing party, such as the witnesses; (4) the extent to which the moving party will suffer prejudice if the request for continuance is denied. See United States v. Soldevila-Lopez, 17 F.3d 480, 488 (1st Cir. 1994); United States v. Flynt, 756 F.2d 1352, 1359 (9th Cir. 1985); United States v. Barrett, 703 F.2d 1076, 1081 (9th Cir. 1983); United States v. Pope, 841 F.2d 954, 956 (9th Cir. 1988).

578. See United States v. Bruck, 152 F.3d 40, 46 (1st Cir. 1998); See also United States v. Soldevila-Lopez, 17 F.3d 480, 487 (1st Cir. 1994).

579. For an example of the court denying a request for independent counsel see Mackey v. Dutton, 217 F.2d 399 (6th Cir. 2000) (ruling the trial court's denial of motion for independent psychiatric examination and refusal to grant continuance did not violate due process.) In Mackey, the Appeals Court also states "The matter of continuance is traditionally within the discretion of the trial judge... [t]he answer must be found in the circumstances present in every case, particularly in the reasons presented to the trial judge at the time the request is denied," See Id. at 408 citing, in part, from Ungar v. Sarafite, 376 U.S. 575, 589 (1964).

For an example of the court denying an additional CST examination see United States v. Rothschild, 956 F.ed 1163 (4th Cir. 1992) (affirming conviction (per curiam) where, after the defendant found competent to stand trial following a court ordered psychiatric evaluation under 18 U.S.C. § 4241, 4244 (1988), the trial court denied a motion of continuance for an additional evaluation on the grounds that the original examiners were biased and further affirmed the district court's opinion that the defendant failed, at a hearing one week prior to trial, to show evidence contradicting the original CST finding.)

See ROESCH & GOLDING supra note 16, at 192. There is also an implicit assumption behind the request for continuance—that the goal is a delay tactic cooked up by the defense counsel. See E.g., Winick supra note 1, at 933.

580. See 18 U.S.C. § 4247 (b) (According to the Federal Criminal Code and Rules a "reasonable extension" should not exceed fifteen days.)

process.[581] Indeed, case precedent also indicates how courts routinely minimize the importance of time and CST review as compared with other psycholegal issues. For example, in *United States v. Taylor*[582] the Federal Court of Appeals for the Fourth Circuit upheld the trial court's finding that a 10 minute competency evaluation was sufficient to establish the defendant's competency.[583] In support of the decision, the Appeals Court argued that the issue of insanity was a more searching inquiry than the assessment of trial fitness. As the Appellate Court noted, "[u]nlike a determination of competence to stand trial, which focuses on a limited aspect of a defendant's present mental condition..., [an assessment to develop a

---

581. This position is consistent with other holdings regarding the need for additional competency examinations. Generally speaking, courts are not obligated to require additional CST hearings or evaluations if evidence does not bring into question the defendant's already established trial fitness, *see* United States v. Lebron, 76 F.3d 29, 32 (1st Cir. 1996) (holding that once a qualified mental health professional has determined that a defendant is competent to stand trial "a court is not required to hold a further evidentiary hearing absent extenuating circumstances." *See Id.* at 32. *See also* PERLIN II *supra* note 570 § 14.04 at 217 (noting it is not necessary to require "a full-blown competency hearing everytime there is the slimmest evidence of competency." *quoting, in part, from* Curry v. Estelle, 531 F2d 766, 768 (5th Cir. 1976). *See also* United States v. Horovitz, 584 F.2d 682, 683 n.3 (5th Cir. 1978).

582. *See* United States v. Taylor, 437 F.2d 371, 373 (4th Cir. 1971).

583. *See Id.* The competency evaluation ended because Taylor, the defendant, threatened to "choke the life out of" the psychiatrist. Notwithstanding the 10 minute interview the psychiatrist concluded "though the interview was quite brief and we do not pretend to offer a complete evaluation it is clear that Mr. Taylor fully understands the nature of his charges." *See Id.* at 375. Based on these findings, Taylor was deemed competent to stand trial. During the trial, however, Taylor attacked a guard on the witness stand, resulting in a mistrial. In the subsequent hearing, Taylor entered a plea of not guilty by reason of insanity, and was eventually found guilty. On appeal from his conviction the defendant raised numerous questions relating to procedures for evaluation concerning his competency and defense of insanity.

Although the Federal Court of Appeals remanded with instructions, their reasoning centered on the issue of insanity not competency. The Court of Appeals for the Fourth Circuit argued "the ten-minute interview was insufficient for an [NGRI determination]" and further did not provide the needed evidence to support the defendant's NGRI defense. *See Id.* at 378.

The Court of Appeals agreed with the trial court, concluding the 10 minute evaluation was sufficient to establish competence. The court held because the examination provided a basis for a determination of present competence there was no reason to order another [CST] evaluation, *citing* Hall v. United States, 410 F.2d. 653 (4th Cir. 1969).

possible insanity defense] requires that the expert have a substantial opportunity to observe the defendant and his mental processes."[584] Moreover, recent accounts in the forensic literature also recognize time constrained CST reviews. According to several empirical studies, "evaluators usually base their decision on a single interview, often lasting less than an hour, and usually completed within a few days of the individual's admission to [a] maximum security inpatient facility..."[585] Thus, from the judicial, case law, and social science perspectives, the limited emphasis placed on time and CST review seems quite clear.

On a more pragmatic level, the intersection between CST evaluations and time constraints is further complicated by the practical issues facing the mental health expert. The busy schedule of the examiner and the unpredictable nature of CST evaluations[586] raise other troubling concerns which, nonetheless, again beg the pivotal question: are time-constrained competency-to-stand-trial exams reliable given the importance of the inquiry? Put another way, do time constraints on the practitioner influence or, more accurately, jeopardize the defendant's right to a fair CST review? We assert that time-limited CST evaluations negatively impact the trial fitness review process, especially when the paranoid/delusional defendant undergoes a competency evaluation.

In support of our contention that time is important and that quick CST reviews preclude a defendant's right to a fair trial, are

---

584. See Taylor, 437 F.2d at 378.

585. See PERLIN II supra note 573, §14.06 at 226. See also ROESCH & GOLDING supra note 16, at 204 (noting how practioners reach conclusions about competency very rapidly and "an increase in the information available to them rarely results in changes in their decisions) Id. at 218–219 citing Williams & Miller, The Processing and Disposition of Incompetent Mentally Ill Offenders, 5 LAW & HUM. BEHAV. 245 (1981).

586. See Yates supra note 569, at 360 (noting "disciplinary differences and personal preferences tend to guide the professional in selecting data sources considered useful for obtaining information, despite the availability of published research which identifies measures which are reliable predictors of competency from those which are not." See also R. Roesch & S. Golding, Treatment and Disposition of Defendants Found Incompetent to Stand Trial: A Review and a Proposal, 2 INT'L J.L. & Psychiatry 349 (1979) [hereinafter Roesch & Golding, Treatment]. Moreover, the examiner may be confronted with the non-compliant defendant who rejects the CST examination process completely.

several historical accounts regarding the competency of defendants experiencing paranoid and delusional mental health problems. On this point, Menninger observes the following on the importance of conducting a thorough review:

> "[M]ore than three or four hours are necessary to assemble a picture of a man. A person sometimes refuses for the first several interviews to reveal his delusional thinking, or other evidence about mental illness...[P]aranoid patients particularly may be able to guard against their disorder with extraordinary skill...[F]rom hours of interviewing, and from the tests and other materials, a skilled psychiatrist can construct an explanation of personality and inferences about how such a personality would react in certain situations."[587]

Contrary to Menninger's recommendations, psychiatric evaluations are variable[588] and are based on the *reasonable* time allotted by the courts for the CST evaluation.[589] Thus, it follows that forensic exams contingent on time are hard pressed to account (adequately) for the personality dynamics of paranoid mental health disorders let alone the nuances involved in such psychiatric conditions (e.g., a defendant who is intelligent and articulate but extremely paranoid or delusional).

In addition to these practitioner limitations are the broader law and policy implications which suggest that CST reviews contingent on time are problematic when defendants present with certain mental health conditions. Indeed, rapid fitness-to-stand-trial exams fall short in their ability to understand the relationship between paranoid or delusional traits and the criteria set forth in *Dusky*. Thus, the interaction between CST time constraints, consistent with *Dusky* criteria, and paranoid/delusional disorders poses a series of troubling questions in competence exams. Some of these questions may include: how does paranoid behavior affect a defendant's abil-

---

587. *See* Rollerson v. United States, 343 F.2d 269, 274 (D.C. Cir. 1964) *citing* K. MENNINGER, A MANUAL FOR PSYCHIATRIC CASE STUDY, 64–65 (2nd ed. 1962)[hereinafter MENNINGER].

588. *See* Roesch & Golding, Treatment *supra* note 586, at 11. "The [CST] examination may take several forms and last anywhere from about one half-hour to many hours..."

589. *See* 18 U.S.C. § 4247 (b) (discussing federal statue and guidelines reasonable time periods for CST evaluation and extension.) (emphasis added).

ity to understand the charges? Moreover, will paranoid and delusional defendants fail to understand the proceedings because they believe, for instance, that the judge is out to destroy them?

Perhaps most troubling, however, is the interplay between paranoid and delusional symptomatology and *Dusky's* first prong related to the defendant's ability to consult with counsel. In other words, for example, how will paranoid delusional themes affect the defendant's ability to assist the defense? Similarly, will delusional or paranoid behavior influence important trial decisions (e.g., the decision to waive counsel and proceed *pro se* to trial)? And finally, if a defendant elects to waive his or her counsel opting, instead, to conduct his or her own defense, is this trial strategy a direct product of a paranoid delusion or of clear and level-headed thinking/judgement?[590] In sum, given the ubiquitous signs and symptoms surrounding paranoid and delusional disorders (whether an individual is paranoid or just suspicious), rapid and unitary CST reviews raise a number of serious questions about the interplay between paranoid traits and one's competency abilities as set forth in the *Dusky* standard. Thus, we contend that CST evaluations are (clearly) inadequate when tapping adjudicative competence (i.e., ability to make important trial decisions), especially when a defendant suffers from a paranoid and delusional mental health condition.

Another problem with time and CST assessment pertains to the liberty interests of and the screening measures for the defendant.[591] Understandably, some critics have asserted that conducting multiple fitness-to-stand-trial exams by way of involuntary hospitalization[592]

---

590. As we have indicated, even when adequate time is applied to the examination process, mental health experts rarely use instruments adequately assessing abilities related to trial competence. *See E.g.,* Yates *supra* note 566, at 360. ("many evaluation centers and private practioners create and utilize their own assessment tools.") *See Id.* at 353.

591. *See* Yates *supra* note 569, at 361.

592. *See* Winick *supra* note 1, at 930–931. Winick states "[m]ost competency evaluations continue to occur in an inpatient setting, such as a state hospital, even though inpatient evaluation is rarely necessary, is often unduly stigmatizing to the defendant, and takes considerably longer than evaluation in a jail or a court mental health clinic." *See Id. citing* Roesch & Golding, Treatment *supra* note 586, at 364–365; Janis, *Incompetency Commitment: The Need for Procedural Safeguards and a Proposed Statutory Scheme*, 23 CATH. U.L. REV. 720, 728 (1974); R. Roesch, *Determining Competency to Stand Trial: An Examination of Evaluation Procedures in an Institutional Setting*, 47 J. CONSULTING & CLINICAL PSYCHOLOGY 542, 548–49 (1979).

violates important civil rights,[593] especially when such defendants are confined without consent.[594] On the matter of involuntary hospitalization, some argue convincingly that social and political forces are at play.[595] Indeed, according to Perlin, a third of the states compel competency examinations to be conducted on an inpatient basis and are used "as a means of insuring the defendant's longer-term removal from the community."[596]

In cases not involving social and political goals, some researchers note that repeated CST exams are unnecessary. For example, Golding and Roesch report "that a prediction of competency status made on the basis of the intake interview alone (the Mental Status Exam) was about as accurate as predictions based on information contained in later reports [e.g., psychological tests and additional interviews]."[597] In response to this problem, commentators suggest

---

593. For a (general) discussion on how CST examinations infringe on liberty interests of defendants committing minor crimes *see* Winick *supra* note 1, at 930–931. Winick points out, CST evaluations are often used as an alternative method of providing treatment for defendants committing minor crimes. *See Id.* at 930.

594. *See* Yates *supra* note 569, at 361–362.

595. *See* PERLIN II *supra* note 573, § 14.06, at 226–227.

596. *See Id. See also* Winick *supra* note 1, at 933 (noting some defendants are committed for evaluation in inpatient settings "to effect hospitalization that might not otherwise be possible under the state's civil commitment stature.")

A similar and troubling psycholegal matter concerns defendants found incompetent and the well known cycle of transcarceration. *See generally,* B. Arrigo, *Transcarceration: A Constitutive Ethnography of Mentally Ill Offenders.* THE PRISON JOURNAL, 81(2): 162–186 (2001) [hereinafter Arrigo, Transcarceration]. *See also* Winick *supra* note 1, at 934. Typically, when defendants are found incompetent to stand trial they are hospitalized, treated with psychotropic drugs, stablized and returned to court. Upon return, the courts often have the defendants reevaluated which frequently results in a new finding of incompetence and, once again, the defendants are re-hospitalized. Shuffling the defendant from court to the hospital can range in time from months to years. *See Id.* For a further review on how the high court addressed this matter *see,* Jackson v. Indiana, 406 U.S. 715 (1972) and moreover the states failure to implement *Jackson's* findings (e.g., can not indefinitely confine the incompetent defendant) *see generally,* M. Perlin, *Symposium: The American With Disabilities Act: A Ten-Year Retrospective: "For the Misdemeanor Outlaw": The Impact of the ADA on the Institutionalization of Criminal Defendants with Mental Disabilities,* 52 ALA. L. REV. 193 (2000)[hereinafter Perlin, Outlaw]. *See also* Winick *supra* note 1, at 940.

597. *See* ROESCH & GOLDING *supra* note 16, at 204. From this perspective an interview alone can provide sufficient information for CST referrals.

using a comprehensive screening instrument (e.g., ABA's "first level of competence") to curtail repeated and unnecessary CST reviews.[598] Additional research supports this alternative. One study found that a single, *comprehensive* evaluation resulted in a reliable CST decision in the majority of the cases observed[599] and, moreover, suggested that hospitalization is rarely necessary for a determination of competency.[600]

We note, however, that employing a single comprehensive competency evaluation or the implementation of screening instruments (e.g., ABA's screening recommendation[601]) "to avoid or minimize the formal evaluation process,"[602] is not without its own disadvantages. Although cognizant of possible civil rights violations (i.e., sustained civil confinement), the implementation of a unitary screening measure raises a significant question for purposes of our

---

598. In her discussion on the CST evaluations, Yates suggests that adopting the American Bar Association's recommendation for a "first level of competence" may curtail many unnecessary inpatient CST evaluations and ultimately help preserve defendant's rights. According to the ABA the criteria for a first level of competency includes "(a) understanding of the nature of the trial process, without undue perceptual distortion; (b) capacity to maintain the attorney-client relationship; (c) ability to recall and relate factual information; (d) capacity to testify relevantly; and (e) the above abilities in light of the particular charge, extent of the defendant's participation, and complexity of the case." *See* Yates *supra* note 569, at 361 n.81. *citing* ABA *supra* note 10, at 7-4.1 at 173–175; ABA Standards for Criminal Justice xv (1989) section 7-4.1, at 7-173 to 7-174.

599. *See* J. Schreiber, R. Roesch & S. Golding, *An Evaluation of Procedures for Assessing Competency to Stand Trial*, 15 Bull. Am. Acad. Psychiatry & L. 187 (1987) (emphasis added). As discussed *infra*, what a comprehensive CST exam exactly entails is in question, especially on the issue of adjudicative competence.

600. *See* J. Schreiber et al., *An Evaluation for Assessing Competency to Stand Trial*, 15 BULL. AM. ACAD. PSYCHIATRY & L. 187 (1987); Yates *supra* note 569, at 361; Winick *supra* note 1, at 931 n.931.

601. *See* Yates *supra* note 569, at 361 discussing the ABA's "first level of competence" (According to the ABA, defendants who meet the first level of competency do not have to be examined further while defendants deficient in one or more of these domains should undergo additional CST inquiry.) *See supra* note 598 for specific criteria regarding the first level of competence.

602. Proponents of screening instruments argue laborious CST exams are not necessary considering "[a] large percentage of defendants evaluated for competency are found competent— ninety-six percent or more in some jurisdictions, and probably no less than seventy-five percent in most." *See* Winick *supra* note 1, at 932 *citing* LAB *supra* note 40, at 65; Lipsett et al., *supra* note 40, at 105.

study. In short, can a single screening instrument adequately and accurately assess the intelligent yet paranoid and delusional defendant? Moreover, even when defendants are "screened in" for further assessment via a single evaluation, the question remains the same: what is a comprehensive CST review?

Although a single CST evaluation can save time and money, as well as champion the cause of therapeutic jurisprudence[603] (e.g., protect the liberty interests of the CST defendant), the quality of the exam— especially on the issue of adjudicative competence— is likely to be less than probative. Additionally, unitary and rapid CST reviews are alarming when a defendant has paranoid and delusional mental health concerns. As previously discussed in this chapter, the subtle symptoms associated with paranoid and delusional disorders (the preservation of cognitive functioning despite delusions and paranoid beliefs) can present CST complications. Accordingly, the time needed to identify (adequately) paranoid and delusional traits once again suggests that single reviews will remain a less than compelling mechanism by which to effectuate this outcome.

We suggest that lawyers and clinical practitioners are best equipped to resolve the dilemmas posed by courtroom time constraints and the clinical forensic review of trial fitness. Indeed, they must toil over how best to safeguard the liberty interests of the defendant while safeguarding the need for a fair CST examination by mandating both thorough and detailed competency evaluations. Although ostensibly a psycholegal conundrum, our position suggests

---

603. Although a subject of relevance on the issue of competency to stand trial, a discussion of therapeutic jurisprudence is beyond the scope of this project. Coined and developed by Bruce Winick and David Wexler, therapeutic jurisprudence involves an interdisciplinary approach which endeavors to assess the therapeutic and anti-therapeutic consequences of the law. Briefly, therapeutic jurisprudence applies a mental health model to issues involving the law and ultimately attempts to give new form to law and policy in ways that improve the psychological functioning and well-being of individuals who interact with the criminal justice system.

For a review of the seminal work of Wexler and Winick see D. WEXLER, THERAPEUTIC JURISPRUDENCE: THE LAW AS A THERAPEUTIC AGENT (1990); D. WEXLER & B. WINICK, ESSAYS IN THERAPEUTIC JURISPRUDENCE (1991); D. WEXLER & B. WINICK, LAW IN A THERAPEUTIC KEY: DEVELOPMENTS IN THERAPEUTIC JURISPRUDENCE (1996); B. WINICK, THERAPEUTIC JURISPRUDENCE APPLIED: ESSAYS ON MENTAL HEALTH LAW (1997).

that a comprehensive evaluation will, by necessity, require follow-up exams. This contention finds support in the fact that evaluators do not use (and are not required to use) uniform measures which address practical issues of competency (adjudicative or decisional competence). More importantly, however, because certain defendants with paranoid/delusional features may pass a less formal screening mechanism ("screened out" as competent) and proceed to trial, notwithstanding paranoid delusions that may ultimately influence the outcome, the decision for complete and detailed CST review here is clear.[604]

Another important component to the problem of time constraints and CST evaluations is money.[605] In other words, examiners could spend more time conducting assessments but they are only compensated up to a certain dollar amount.[606] Thus, for example, if the court or hiring party is prepared to pay no more than $200.00 for the full evaluation, then the psychologist/psychiatrist is confronted with a dilemma, especially if a thorough assessment would require 10–15 hours over a two or three day period. From this hypothetical, payment of $20.00 per hour is not what psychologists/psychiatrists are accustomed to receiving. Thus, given these very real financial considerations, practitioners may form a CST opinion based (potentially) on the initial meeting (i.e., screening interview), and on otherwise limited information.[607] It follows,

---

604. Another practical problem involves noncompliant CST defendants. These individuals purposefully sabotage CST reviews or refuse the tests in fear of being labeled mentally ill. Again, this occurrence calls into question the practical utility of instruments used to screen defendants for further CST review.

605. For an opinion discussing monetary implications regarding competency evaluations, *see generally* Winick *supra* note 1, at 928–938.

606. Although funds vary regarding what mental health experts are paid for CST evaluation. Federal statutes dealing with funds for indigent defendants in need of services additional to those provided by defense counsel are found at 18 U.S.C. §§ 3006A(e) which provides "[S]ervices other than counsel. Counsel for defendant who is financially unable to obtain investigative, expert, or other services necessary to an adequate defense in [his or her] case may request for services [and if deemed necessary] the court shall authorize counsel to obtain the services on behalf of the defendant... [T]he compensation to be paid to a person for such [services] shall not exceed $300." *See also* Winick *supra* note 1, at 932 for a detailed discussion about variable rates with respect to competency evaluations.

607. As the subsequent case study analysis demonstrates this was the exact procedure followed by the three psychiatrists who examined Colin Ferguson.

then, that a possible correlation exists between the amount of compensation received (e.g., $20.00 per hour) and the quality of expert service tendered (e.g., willingness to provide a thorough review). Although untested, we maintain that this not so inconceivable correlation would significantly affect the quality of the examination and, ultimately, the fitness-to-stand-trial outcome.[608]

Although issues involving financial remuneration and psychiatry's role in the courts are discussed in the conclusion section of this investigation, we preliminarily assert that this problem has clear and unfortunate implications on the matter of competency and the entire adjudicatory process. In short, until fees are removed from the courtroom (i.e., compensation for psychologists representing either side in the legal dispute), the scales of justice will be tilted toward an unfair CST review. We maintain that each and every one in the system should (and must) coordinate their efforts and strive toward this agenda of change and reform. Indeed, personal financial gains and loses are of no consequence, especially when the fate of another human being rests firmly in the hands of a clinical forensic expert, whose evaluation, diagnosis, and testimony helps resolve the matter of one's competence. Conclusions reached by practitioners, limited and lacking in substance, are nothing more than the misguided opinions of well-paid "hired hands." In sum, then, time

---

608. For a poignant example of how monetary issues complicate psychiatric evaluations (e.g., competency and NGRI issues), see Kordenbrock v. Scroggy, 919 F.2d 1091 (6th Cir. 1990).

In *Kordenbrock* the state refused to fund an independent psychiatric expert for the defense. The facts of the case indicate that the county in which the defendant was tried felt the state should pay for the defense expert; however, the state refused to pay for a psychiatric expert. Although responsibility for payment was in dispute, the defense hired an expert who evaluated the defendant but refused to file the report until compensated. The defense counsel, without an expert, requested a motion for continuance. The trial court, however, refused the continuance and refused to enter an order for payment until the expert filed the report. In the face of evidence indicating that the defendant desired to use psychiatric testimony to establish a defense of diminished responsibility and for sentencing, the trial proceeded without a defense expert and the defendant was found guilty of murder and attempted murder and the jury sentenced the defendant to death. *See* Kordenbrock v. Commonwealth, 700 S.W.2d 384 (Ky. 1985), cert. denied, 476 U.S. 1153, 106 S. Ct. 2260, 90 L. Ed. 2d 704 (1986). The Court of Appeals for the Sixth Circuit granted a rehearing *en banc* and later reversed judgement of the District Court (based on several issues not all related to the psychiatric evaluation).

constraints and financial incentives are formidable obstacles to the effective and thorough clinical forensic evaluation of competency to stand trial. Indeed, these are matters that seriously and irreparably jeopardize the defendant's right to a fair and thorough review.

In the face of potential problems about time and evaluation of trial fitness (albeit a product of court deadlines or issues such as money and questionable screening measures), court appointed mental health professionals and independent experts are expected to reach opinions about a defendant's competence to stand trial.[609] Moreover, experts often support their findings with provisional, if not absolute, diagnostic conclusions. This brings us to the process by which such experts form these clinical opinions. The following section describes the diagnostic process in the context of time constrained CST evaluations and questionable screening measures. Again, these processes are considered against disorders having paranoid and delusional symptomatology.

3. Normal and Abnormal Traits: Degrees of Impairment and Clinical Diagnosis

Earlier the suggestion was made that delusional disorder, paranoid personality disorder, and schizophrenia, paranoid type are good examples of mental health conditions harboring "tricky" symptoms and traits.[610] In what follows, we describe how limitations in CST assessment regarding the paranoid/delusional defendant go beyond mere CST time constraints to include problems in the way examiners understand and define maladaptive traits and, more importantly, achieve a clinical diagnosis. Along these lines, this section discusses the degree (or more accurately the persistence) to which a symptom must occur before it is considered abnormal.

According to most mental health experts, clinical decisions about traits are identified as either normal or abnormal depending on,

---

609. *See* M. Perlin, *Pretexts and Mental Disability Law: The Case of Competency*, 47 U. Miami L. Rev. 625, 643 (1993) [hereinafter Perlin, Pretexts]. (noting how expert testimony is the key to incompetency to stand trial inquiries.)

610. As already mentioned, these conditions entail symptoms that oftentimes do not impair cognitive abilities unless directly influenced by the delusion or maladaptive belief.

among other things,[611] degrees of impairment. One way to view and compare individual behavior is to place individuals along different dimensions and quantify degrees of personality to understand how individuals are more or less likely to react in certain situations.[612] In other words, "mental health professionals view individuals as varying from one another along a number of different dimensions, usually characterized as personality traits or behavioral propensities."[613] However, this process is somewhat arbitrary. For example, deciding whether an individual is cautious/suspicious rather than paranoid is a somewhat subjective, idiosyncratic decision, otherwise left to the discretion of the examiner.

The effects of this psycholegal matter are the serious and contentious questions raised for the law,[614] including the imperfect fit regarding the criminal law's "either/or" choice, (i.e., whether an individual meets a legal standard) and the clinician's "more or less" conclusions (i.e., about a defendant's personality). Low et al.[615] address this very issue:

> Psychological tests and clinical criteria seeking to measure personality traits or behavioral tendencies place all individuals along a continuum, just as intelligence testing does. Of course, designating the point on the continuum at which the trait should be characterized as "abnormal" (and at which the person should be characterized as "retarded," "dependent," or "paranoid") is necessarily somewhat arbitrary. People can be described as "more" or "less" suspicious of others, but it is not possible to say that a particular individual is *categorically* different from other people. It is this latter point that poses special difficulties for courts and lawyers. In an important sense the criminal law is faced with an either/or choice. Questions of degree can be taken into account in determining the seriousness of an offense and in sentencing, but determining whether to impose criminal liability in the first instance presents a categorical choice; the defendant is either guilty or not guilty. And

---

611. As will be discussed *infra*, expert decisions concerning what is or is not abnormal or what does or does not warrant a clinical diagnosis is left to the discretion of the examiner. *See E.g.,* INSANITY, *supra* note 100, at 6.

612. *See Id. See also* MENNINGER *supra* note 587, at 94.

613. *See* INSANITY *supra* note 100, at 6.

614. *See* DSM-IV *supra* note 442, at xxiii.

615. *See E.g.,* INSANITY *supra* note 100, at 6–7.

momentous consequences—both for the individual and the public—turn on which determination is made.[616]

Since certain symptoms and traits are difficult to evaluate because they occur within a continuum of normality, psychological/psychiatric experts often share different opinions on what *is* or *is not* abnormal. For instance, do paranoid features indicate abnormal traits or do paranoid features indicate general suspiciousness? Delineating a distinction is a fine line and arguably a case could be made for either conclusion. In regard to psychiatric opinions and CST findings, a trial judge must sift through conflicting expert opinions about degrees of personality that inform the expert's CST findings. In other words, when the court is presented with conflicting evidence (i.e., differing expert opinions regarding what *is or is not* abnormal) the court must reconcile the conflict and understand how particular traits are likely to contribute to deficits in competency related abilities.[617] This is something the judge is not trained to do and, thus, it is here that a considerable forensic dilemma becomes evident.

To take the position surrounding diagnostic (un)certainty one step further we might ask the following: when is an abnormal trait considered a product of a mental health condition? Again, mental health experts are often not of the same opinion about what constitutes a disease. As a result, different experts examining the same individual may arrive at conflicting opinions about what, if any, disorder a person is suffering from. In their example regarding the concept of disease, Low et al. aptly illustrate this very point. As they state: "[T]he experts are not of the same mind, for example, about whether it is sensible to think of compulsive behavior, such as gambling or alcohol abuse, as a disease."[618] With this observation in mind, consider the trait of paranoia as linked to a particular individual. Is the person so paranoid or delusional as to indicate a mental health condition (perhaps paranoid personality disorder or delusional disorder), or, once again, is the paranoid behavior better understood as general suspiciousness toward others? Thus, the problems stemming from what is or is not an abnormal trait necessarily extends to what is or is not a mental disorder.

---

616. *See Id.*
617. *See E.g.,* GRISSO II *supra* note 314, at 16.
618. *See Id.* at 6. (internal quotation marks omitted).

4. Confusing the Issue of Competency with Diagnostic Conclusions

Even presuming that a diagnostic conclusion can contribute to a CST finding, achieving a (valid) diagnosis in a time constrained competency evaluation is, to say the least, an optimistic goal. Experts will frequently form and use diagnostic conclusions— "magical" opinions often gleamed from a single evaluation[619]— to buttress their CST findings. In other words, rather than concentrating on the issue at hand, mental health experts seemingly conflate the issue of CST with a diagnostic opinion. This is precisely the issue examined in the subsequent section. Preliminarily, however, we assert that too much emphasis is placed on achieving a diagnostic opinion while the specific criteria attached to a legal question remain largely ignored.[620] Not unlike the time constraints surrounding the CST evaluation, clinicians (if supporting their findings with a diagnosis) must also form such clinical judgements under the same conditions. Assuming for a moment that practitioners agree on the existence of a disorder, the diagnostic process is complicated further when making the differential diagnosis. Ultimately, issues such as diagnostic disagreements and differential diagnoses create a situation ripe for clinical confusion.[621] These complicated issues

---

619. As previously mentioned clinicians reach a CST conclusion very quickly not often supplemented by more developed assessment instruments. *See* GOLDING & ROESCH *supra* note 16, at 218–219 *citing among others* J. WIGGINS, PERSONALITY AND PREDICTION: PRINCIPLES OF PERSONALITY ASSESSMENT (1973).

620. *See* Perlin, Pretexts *supra* note 609, at 643.

621. A related problem concerns reaching a specific diagnostic conclusion when disorders, (for example, delusional or paranoid disorders) have common features (i.e., making a differential diagnosis). To illustrate, consider the individual who clearly is paranoid; paranoid to the point where the maladaptive beliefs impair the person's daily functioning, thereby justifying *DSM* consideration. To the (untrained) eye, maladaptive paranoid behavior may appear to a product of paranoid personality disorder, however, underneath the ostensible paranoid trait there may be a more serious psychotic condition such that the paranoia is borne of a delusion. Determining whether paranoia is a trait of one's personality (e.g., paranoid personality disorder) or a product of an underlined delusion (e.g., delusional disorder) is a very subtle process. Thus, drawing a distinction between disorders, otherwise making a differential diagnosis, is further complicated by the time constraints surrounding CST evaluations.

raise important questions about whether a diagnostic opinion can contribute meaningfully to the CST finding. Indeed, some mental health law commentators maintain that discerning impairment via diagnostic judgement is relished by clinicians for their own self aggrandizing reasons.[622] In what follows, the process of forming a diagnosis and its influence on CST findings is explored in more detail.

It is now axiomatic that competency to stand trial is concerned with whether the defendant (a) can assist in the defense and (b) understands the charges and legal proceedings.[623] According to Yates, "[c]urrently competency evaluations are generally conducted according to the style of the private practitioner or to the needs/demands of the agency or institution."[624] Given the lack of structure surrounding the CST exam,[625] the process is more likely than not to be highly individualized.[626] Simply put, experts will apply different— and their own— strategies to inform their CST findings.[627] Considering the latitude afforded the mental health practitioner,[628] one style may have the expert eliciting a diagnosis[629] to justify a CST finding despite its validity or reliability.[630] On this point, Grisso argues that "providing a formal diagnosis and description of symp-

622. *See E.g.,* Perlin, Pretexts, *supra* note 606, at 643. Perlin states "less secure mental health professionals are preoccupied with eliciting pathology as a demonstration of their own expertise." *See Id.* at 643. What is often lost is the legal question experts are called to investigate.

623. *See Dusky,* 362 U.S. at 402.

624. *See* Yates *supra* note 569, at 360.

625. *See Id.* at 352–354.

626. *See also* Perlin, Pretexts *supra* note 609, at 643 (noting "professionals with different education and training rely on different sets of data in doing forensic evaluations."); J. Beckman et al., *Decision Making and Examiner Bias in Forensic Expert Recommendations for Not Guilty by Reason of Insanity,* 13 LAW & HUM. BEHAV. 79 (1989).

627. *See* Yates *supra* note 569, at 360.

628. For a general review of potential abuses inherent in competency to stand trial examinations, *see* PERLIN II *supra* note 573, section 14.06, at 226; W. Pizza, *Competency to Stand Trial in Federal Courts: Conceptual and Constitutional Problems,* 45 U. CHI. L. REV. 21, 37–52 (1977).

629. *See E.g.,* M. Perlin, *Overview of Rights in the Criminal Process,* in 3 LEGAL RIGHTS OF MENTALLY DISABLED PERSONS 1879, 1885 (Practicing Law Institute, P. Friedman, ed. 1979) [hereinafter Perlin, Rights] (Discussing issues involving the unreliability of testimony as to diagnosis and competency to stand trial inquiries.)

630. *See E.g.,* Perlin, Rights *supra* note 629, at 1885.

toms is often an important objective, but never a *sufficient* objective, of competency evaluations."[631] In *Carter v. United States*,[632] the court addressed the "chief value" of psychiatric testimony, and opined:

> "The chief value of an expert's testimony in this field, as in all other fields, rests upon the material from which his opinion is fashioned and the reasoning by which he progresses from his material to his conclusion; in the explanation of the disease and its dynamics, that is, how it occurred, developed, and affected the mental and emotional processes of the defendant; *it does not lie in his mere expression of conclusion*..."[633]

In *Carter*, the court emphasizes how the process of reaching a conclusion is more important than the conclusion itself. In other words, by understanding the process of reaching a finding the court is able to attach either more or less credibility to the testimony. Although certainly a noteworthy courtroom plan, this is not always the standing forensic practice as tribunals very often lose sight of substantive values regarding how an expert reaches an opinion.[634] Thus, an empty or poorly developed diagnostic opinion can, at times, be used to support the CST finding.

Although a diagnosis may better explain the expert's reasoning for an opinion,[635] a diagnostic finding (alone) is not dispositive of

---

631. *See* GRISSO II *supra* note 314, at 10.

632. *See* Carter v. United States, 252 F.2d 608 (D.C. Cir. 1957) *citing* Rheingold, *The Basis of Medical Testimony*, 15 VANDERBILT L. REV. 473, 474 (1962).

633. *See Id.* at 617.

634. *See* M. Perlin, *Symposium: The American With Disabilities Act: A Ten-Year Retrospective: "For the Misdemeanor Outlaw": The Impact of the ADA on the Institutionalization of Criminal Defendants wit Mental Disabilities*, 52 Ala. L. Rev.193, 236 (2000) [hereinafter Perlin, ADA]. Perlin states "courts regularly accept patently inadequate expert testimony in incompetency to stand trial cases." *See Id.* at 236.

635. *See* R. Schopp, *Article: Sexual Predators and the Structure of the Mental Health System: Expanding te Normative Focus of Therapeutic Jurisprudence*, 1 PSYCH. PUB. POL. & L. 161 (1995) ("clinicians might be able to state a professional opinion regarding the significance of the psychological disorder for the criteria of legal mental illness...Such testimony may or may not address the ultimate legal issue.") *Id.* at 192.

the legal question of competency to stand trial.[636] Rather than concentrating on assessment protocol that delve into competence related abilities, examiners often center on a process that justifies their expertise (e.g. forming a CST opinion based on a diagnostic conclusion by eliciting pathology).[637] From this perspective, "justifying the process" can potentially supersede the validity of the testimony and, more importantly, neglect the specific criteria attached to the legal question. In addition, a CST exam that centers on a diagnostic conclusion may overlook or neglect the nuances embedded in certain legal standards (e.g., decisional competence and abilities relating to important trial decisions). Thus, for these reasons (i.e., the uncertainty surrounding the CST process and making a diagnosis no matter what), the role of the expert in competency evaluations presents additional fitness-to-stand-trial concerns.

As mentioned previously, the interplay between CST findings, diagnostic conclusions, and expert testimony is complicated further with provisional diagnoses. Even if an "absolute" diagnosis is not achieved (given the limited time for CST evaluation), mental health experts often support CST opinions with a provisional diagnosis or a presumptive "gut-feeling" about the case. According to the *DSM-IV* a provisional diagnosis is used "when there is a strong presumption that the full criteria will ultimately be met for a disorder, but not enough information is available to make a firm diagnosis."[638] We note that the *DSM-IV* explicitly states that provisional findings are presumptive and it is here that a psycholegal problem emerges. In short, the problem with a provisional finding is that once entered in a case by way of expert testimony, the disorder is made real and legitimized, intimating to the court that the defendant may or may not suffer from the illness to which the "expert" unquestionably refers. Rather than providing clarity on the issue of competency to stand trial, such clinical "guesswork" obfuscates the CST issue even further. Ultimately, the question of (in)competency is lost in the muddled world of diagnostic opinion.

---

636. *See* Winick *supra* note 1, at 923, n. 4. *See E.g.*, GRISSO II *supra* note 314, at 16. A diagnosis may have no relation to the issue of competency or conversely a diagnosis may contribute meaningfully to a legal decision about competency.

637. *See* Perlin, Pretexts *supra* note 609, at 643.

638. *See* DSM-IV *supra* note 442, at 3.

5. Sum and Substance: Theoretical Groundwork and Practical Meaning

Although provisional and tentative, two broad themes have been developed in this chapter. The purpose of the first part was to provide an overview for the general features and diagnostic requirements of mental health disorders having psychotic and paranoid characteristics. Clearly, paranoid and delusional mental health conditions are maladaptive yet their impact on cognitive and psychosocial abilities is frequently variable. Recognizing that psychotic and paranoid mental health conditions are encapsulated disorders, we argued that the behavior of the paranoid/delusional person is determined (largely) by the influence of the delusion or the paranoid themes. Barring behavioral difficulties conceived from delusions and paranoid beliefs, cognitive abilities remain preserved and the individual does not demonstrate behavior that is otherwise bizarre. In other words, features and associated features of these disorders are usually difficult to evaluate because they occur on a continuum with normality, are nonspecific, and may be due to a variety of other factors. It follows then that forensic evaluation in the area of psychotic and paranoid disorders requires careful clinical judgement to determine whether specific symptoms are sufficiently persistent to meet the diagnostic criteria.

Given this critical juncture, the second part of the chapter discussed how difficulties with judging paranoid mental health disorders go beyond mere ubiquitous symptoms to include dilemmas with competing clinical and legal objectives in forensic settings, clinical (un)certainty with respect to defining abnormality, CST time constraints/monetary issues, and confusing the CST (legal) issue with diagnostic conclusions. In light of these developments relative to the forensic evaluation of psychotic and paranoid mental health disorders, we argued that clinical practioners will most often use their own CST assessment measures and, as suggested, frequently inform their findings by absolute or provisional diagnoses. Identifying these potential pitfalls underscores the somewhat questionable practice of reaching CST determinations for defendants having psychotic and paranoid mental health conditions. Clearly, our inquiry thus far mostly has been speculative, guided by a careful analytical review of the relevant law and social science literature. However, our position is that this provisional analysis is essential if a detailed case study assessment of Mr. Colin Ferguson, the New York City railway gunman, is to occur. Indeed, as we explain in the subsequent chapter, Ferguson dramatically and provocatively illuminates the troubling interplay between law, psychology, paranoid/delusional mental health conditions, and CST proceedings.

Chapter 5

The Matter of
Colin Ferguson:
A Case Study Inquiry

OVERVIEW

This chapter pays particular attention to the CST dynamics in a pretrial competency hearing. To expose fitness-to-stand-trial tensions described in previous chapters, the high-profile case of Mr. Colin Ferguson, the New York railway gunman, is systematically reviewed and critiqued. Although high-stakes and well-publicized cases represent but a tiny fraction of the thousands of mundane and non-controversial competency matters in general, we maintain that legal disputes garnering the public's attention expose both typical CST examination processes and measures exceeding normal expectation. Accordingly, this investigation considers the value of controversial cases (not their statistical relevance) and asserts that if trial fitness problems arise in high-profile disputes the same limitations are also found (in some capacity) in CST matters lacking this degree of public interest or scrutiny. In other words, high-stakes cases arguably magnify problems occurring in the everyday lived-experiences of defendants undergoing "routine" CST evaluations.[639]

---

639. For those CST cases not subjected to "psycholegal" scrutiny via public interest (or unrest), these defendants become unwitting pawns to such practices as transcarceration. *See generally,* Arrigo, Transcarceration *supra* note 596. *See also* M. Perlin, *"Dignity was the First to Leave":* Godinez v. Moran, *Colin Ferguson, and the Trial of Mentally Disabled Criminal Defendants,* 14 BEHAVIORAL SCIENCES AND THE LAW, 72 1996 [hereinafter Perlin, Dignity]. For example, for cases that do not gather public attention these defendants are often shuffled from involuntary civil commitment, for restoration of

The trial of Colin Ferguson exposed the nation to the worst case scenario involving pretrial outcome difficulties and, in a practical way, demonstrated the unfortunate repercussions in according a delusional defendant a right to waive counsel and proceed *pro se* to trial. Thus, the case of Colin Ferguson illustrates those profound problems relating to a delusional defendant (found competent via the low standard set forth in *Dusky*) who then advances those rights championed by *Faretta* and *Godinez*. Examining these critical issues also identifies the political and ideological reasoning behind questionable CST evaluations[640] and judicial outcomes.[641] Indeed, the case of Colin Ferguson was problematic, not only because it subverted the interests of the parties involved (e.g., accused, victims/witnesses) but because it disrupted the fluidity of the entire adjudicatory process.

---

competence, back to court to ascertain when, if ever, they will be called upon to answer to the charge(s) alleged. As Perlin states, "[i]n such cases, [i.e., non-high-stakes] defendants may very well simply fade away from public consciousness." *See Id.* at 63 *citing* Jackson v. Indiana, 406 U.S. 715 (1972). However, problems evident in more glamorized CST cases will also be present in those cases lacking public concern (e.g., dilemmas trial judges confront in determining credible expert testimony or when trial judges apply questionable CST legal standards).

640. In the clinical evaluation area, social and political forces may influence expert opinions with respect to CST findings, especially when independent contractors are hired by the defense attorney or the A.D.A. representing the state, *see E.g.,* PERLIN II *supra* note 573 § 14.06, at 226. Despite governing ethical guidelines for forensic evaluations, *see generally* American Psychological Association, *Ethical Principles of Psychologists and Code of Conduct*, 47 AMERICAN PSYCHOLOGIST 1597 (1992), objective psychological evaluations are limited by clinicians' own fixed beliefs and further complicated by the desires of the hiring party. In one way, clinicians may feel compelled to advance the desires of the hiring party or, if the clinician's finding are in conflict with the attorney, "couch CST opinions in the most favorable light," discussed *infra*. In yet another way, some suggest mental health experts are "hired guns," so to speak and, for a fee, will flesh out evidence of almost anything asked, *see E.g.,* EVALS. II *supra* note 24, at 3 *citing* Peter Huber, GALILEO'S REVENGE: JUNK SCIENCE IN THE COURTROOM (1991). Given the latitude afforded the clinician in that they use their own assessment measures, *see* Yates *supra* note 569, at 353–354, appeasing the hiring party can often be achieved by way of differential diagnosis, *see supra note* 621 and accompanying text.

641. As previously mentioned, some problems stem from judges shifting their responsibilities for decision making to clinicians; that is, passing responsibility for disposition to clinicians even though CST findings are a legal inquiry not a clinical one. *See* Miller & Germain *supra* note 359, at 377, 378.

In order to review systematically the problems associated with the Ferguson debacle, the legal and psychological circumstances surrounding the case are discussed. Accordingly, we first review the criminal and psychological background of Mr. Colin Ferguson.[642] We then present, in detailed fashion, the psychiatric testimony relied upon by the courtroom experts. Indeed, because this book centers on criminal competency matters, this chapter pays specific attention to those events surrounding Mr. Ferguson's pretrial competency hearing. We then chronicle the closing arguments offered by the defense and prosecution and conclude with the trial Judge's opinion. However, before proceeding with these matters, we discuss our selection of Colin Ferguson for review and critique, the source of the "data" for this analysis and further explain why the data is presented in unabridged form.

A. Why Ferguson: The Issue of Competency, the Data Selection Process and its Unique Presentation

As we have suggested, one case demonstrating the conundrum surrounding CST legal standards, questionable reliance on CST assessments/expert findings, a defendant having paranoid/delusional mental health problems, and suspect judicial decision making is the criminal trial of Mr. Colin Ferguson (a.k.a. Long Island Railroad Gunman). After his arrest and arraignment, in connection with the Long Island Railroad massacre, the hearing court ordered a competency examination.[643] Pursuant to the initial examination, Ferguson was found competent to stand trial, however, once expressing an interest to fire his attorneys and represent himself, the trial court ordered a formal competency hearing to settle, once and for all, the

---

642. The excerpts describing the crime via police testimony and some of the information regarding Mr. Ferguson's background have been organized topically rather than chronologically.

643. After Mr. Ferguson's arraignment, the court ordered a competency evaluation under New York's Criminal Law Procedure 730.30. Pursuant to the order, Ferguson was examined on December 28, 1993. This examination is discussed *infra*.

issue of trial competence as well as Ferguson's requests regarding his defense strategy.

Deciding whether Colin Ferguson was competent encompassed difficult and complex psycholegal matters. Issues surrounding the pretrial hearing included: a defendant having paranoid and delusional mental health problems; a defendant rejecting the CST examination process; a paranoid defendant desiring to waive counsel and conduct his own legal action; and a defendant who passionately rejected the defense of insanity. A would-be nightmare became reality when Mr. Ferguson was deemed competent to stand trial and was subsequently allowed to conduct his own legal action.

The testimony presented throughout this case study is drawn from the recorded transcripts of the original stenographic minutes taken from the pretrial competency hearing (December 6, 1994–December 9, 1994). Materials concerning psychiatric testimony, closing arguments by the defense and prosecution, as well as the opinion of the court are arranged in chronological form. Significant mistakes are followed by [sic] but are included as they appear in the original transcripts. Although some mistakes are spelling errors, the mistakes are included to preserve the message and voice of the speaker, and to demonstrate uncertainty (which goes to the question of credibility). Omission of a word or words or other lengthy deletions are indicated by an insertion of an ellipses.[644] Elsewhere, at times, sentences or paragraphs are combined or separated for clarity. In some instances, words or phrases have been added and set off by brackets. The bracketed language is used to clarify confusing or unclear points or to specify the person to whom the testimony is referring. In some parts, emphasis is added (in bold) to clarify parties or to identify the party objecting to the otherwise two

---

644. With respect to psychiatric testimony, lengthy deletions, at times, are directly a product of discretion. Considering the nature of the evidence embedded in hearing transcripts (the court or attorneys revisiting points, the repetition of questions and answers, and expert qualifications), we chose to present the unabridged colloquies deemed relevant to the issue of competency. In other words, we included testimony dealing with clinical findings, opinions, and conclusions; assessment techniques on the issue of trial competence; and otherwise relevant information informing the CST finding(s). Thus, this case study chooses to delete (via ellipses) segments that repeat and (by discretion) eliminates information that does not add to our understanding of how opinions and findings on CST were achieved (e.g., expert qualifications).

party direct/cross examination (e.g., A.D.A. objecting to a line of questioning by defense counsel during direct or cross-examination) or to identify specific colloquies between the Judge and the defendant.

To assist the reader between question/answer colloquies and to transition and distinguish, for example, the testimony of one expert from another, brief segments are presented describing the person and line of questioning. Although not part of the original stenographic minutes, these segments are provided in order to walk the reader through the somewhat lengthy pretrial testimony. In this way, specific questions are placed in context with the points described in the preceding chapters (types or absence of CST assessment protocol). This notwithstanding, all efforts are taken to preserve the data. This important point is discussed below.

With the exception of the minor editorial adjustments described above, the original testimony from the stenographic minutes is not modified or augmented. Again, this is done in order to preserve the intended meaning of the speaker. Consequently, recounting all the relevant testimony allows for a more exacting psychological and legal analysis (the interpretation of the data) in the subsequent chapter. In making the decision on just how much testimony to recount, we chose to present an unabridged version of the issues dealing with psychiatric testimony. Instead of interrupting the communications (the question/answer exchange between parties) or not allowing the speaker to flesh out points, our case study presents all the relevant testimony and, therefore, leaves little to the reader's imagination. In sum, then, this chapter systematically and thoroughly presents the pretrial hearing dialogue in the Colin Ferguson case, endeavoring to clarify much of the confusion surrounding the dispute on the matter of trial fitness.

Given our preliminary observations on Ferguson, the data for this case study inquiry, and the organization of the pretrial stenographic minutes, we present the case materials in five compact parts. These parts include the following: a synopsis of the crime and the relevant CST psycholegal issues and background information (observed and confirmed in the psychiatric report) concerning Ferguson's behavior before the criminal act; narrative summaries of the expert testimony provided by the three psychiatrists and excerpts from the cross-examination of these witnesses by counsel for the defense and the prosecution; testimony from the closing arguments of

Mr. Kuby for the defense and Mr. Peck for the people; and excerpts from the opinion of the court by presiding judge, Donald E. Belfi. What follows, then, is an extensive discussion concerning the relevant issues in Mr. Ferguson's pretrial competency hearing. Preliminarily, however, information regarding the crime, the critical legal issues (Mr. Ferguson's legal representation) and the matter of competency are discussed.

1. A Synopsis: The Crime, Mr. Ferguson's Legal Representation, the CST Assessment, and the CST Outcome

> "I saw bodies laying on the floor. I saw lots of blood everywhere. People were screaming and yelling. I saw shell casing on the ground, as well as various items: clothing, shoes, like people left the car in a hurry."[645]

On December 7, 1993, Colin Ferguson, a 35 year-old black Jamaican immigrant, killed six train passengers and wounded 19 others on a commuter line in Long Island, New York.[646] When arrested and later checked for identification,[647] a detective found (among other items)[648] rambling notes intimating the act was spurred by a rage against Caucasians, Asians, "Uncle Tom blacks", and many other "racist" people and organizations.[649] The prevailing theme in the notes was racism. Colin Ferguson was originally represented by attorney, Anthony Falanga (eventually fired)[650] and subsequently

---

645. *See* People v. Ferguson 86739 (Cty. Ct., Nassau Co.), Hearing Transcripts [hereinafter Ferguson Hearing Transcripts], Dec. 13, 1994 at 39 (testimony provided by Detective Roderick).
646. After emptying two 15 shot clips and seeking to reload the 9-millimeter hand gun, Ferguson was subdued by three passengers. *See Id.* at 11,12. The incident occurred on the third car of the train as it pulled into Merillon Avenue Railroad station in Garden City L.I., *see Id.* at 19.
647. *See* Ferguson Hearing Transcripts December 13, 1994 at 59.
648. In addition to the notes, Detective Charles Pacini (attached to the Long Island Rail Road Police Department) found a New York State driver's license, a Long Island Rail Road train ticket, and two Long Island Rail Road timetables in Ferguson's right-hand pant's pocket. *See Id.* at 65.
649. *See Id.* at 203, 204 (Ferguson's describing the sheathe of notes.) *See also infra* note 723 (presenting the content of Mr. Ferguson's notes.)
650. *See* People v. Ferguson 86739 (Cty. Ct., Nassau Co.), Pretrial Hearing Transcripts [hereinafter Ferguson Pretrial Hearing Transcripts], December 9,

represented by Mr. Kunstler and Mr. Kuby, two well known New York Attorneys. However, once Ferguson learned Kunstler and Kuby would pursue an insanity defense, based upon the catalyst of "black rage," Ferguson made a specific request to waive counsel entirely.[651] Instead, Ferguson opted to represent himself and prove — despite scores of eyewitnesses and overwhelming evidence — that a mysterious "white Caucasian"[652] stole his gun and committed the shootings.[653]

There was no question that Ferguson was mentally disturbed. The pressing concern, however, was whether a mental impairment or mental defect would prevent Ferguson from understanding the charges and proceedings against him and whether he could assist, if called upon, in the defense. The question, then, was whether Colin Ferguson was competent to stand trial?[654] On December, 6, 1994, a multi-faceted pretrial hearing was conducted to address the CST issue.[655] The hearing hinged on the following psycholegal matters: (1) whether Ferguson was competent to stand trial; (2) if competent, whether Ferguson's application to proceed *pro se* to trial

---

1994, at 437. Ferguson did not cooperate with Falanga and shortly thereafter made a series of allegations against Falanga (none proven to be true) that centered on a racist conspiracy.

651. *See* Ferguson Hearing Transcripts, December 14, 1994 at 202–204.

652. *See* Kuby & Kunstler, *So Crazy He Thinks He is Sane: The Colin Ferguson Trial and the Competency Standard*, 5 CORNELL JOUR. L. PUB. POL.20 (1995)[hereinafter Kuby & Kunstler].

653. *See* Perlin, Dignity *supra* note 639, at 72.

654. After his arraignment on the charges, psychiatrists D'Alessandro and Reichman were appointed by the court to evaluate Ferguson's capacity to proceed to trial. *See* Ferguson Pretrial Hearing Transcripts, December 7, 1994 at 172 (noting pursuant to the court order, a 730 Examination (competency evaluation) was first conducted on December 28th 1993). Following the CST review the experts found Ferguson competent to stand trial. Later, the issue of Ferguson's competency was informally revisited. Relying on Drs. D'Alessandro and Reichman previous CST findings and conversations between the court and the defendant, Judge Belfi ruled (once again) that Ferguson was competent to stand trial. *See Id.* at 454 (discussing the August 19th 1994 competency finding). However, subsequent to this finding, Ferguson made specific requests to waive counsel, strike the insanity defense and proceed *pro se* to trial. *See Id.* at 136. Considering the importance of Ferguson's requests, the defense team made one last effort to prove that Ferguson was incompetent to stand trial. Thus, Mr. Kunstler and Mr. Kuby, for the defense, raised yet again the competency issue which resulted in the formal pretrial competency hearing. *See* Kuby & Kunstler *supra* note 652, at 19, 20.

655. *See* Ferguson Pretrial Hearing Transcripts, December 6, 1994 at 3.

should be granted; and (3) if acting as his own attorney, how to address his position on the defense of insanity, interposed by way of Ferguson's (then-present) defense attorneys, Kunstler and Kuby.

To be considered competent to stand trial in the state of New York (as in most jurisdictions) a defendant must understand the charges against onself, understand the trial proceedings, and assist, if called upon, in one's own defense.[656] These criteria are consistent with those set forth in *Dusky*.[657] Psychiatrists John D'Alessandro and Allen Reichman testified that although Ferguson possessed psychological deficiencies ("possibly suffering from paranoid personality disorder"),[658] Mr. Ferguson was malingering, and they concluded he was rational and did not experience delusions.[659] Based primarily on these reports[660] and on colloquies between the court and Ferguson, Nassau County Judge Donald E. Belfi found Colin Ferguson competent to stand trial. Before reviewing the facts of this case, it is important to consider Mr. Ferguson's personal background. We suggest that this information will help the reader comprehend the rationale developed by the Long Island Railway Gunman and subsequently utilized in his own defense.

2. The Man: Information Sources and Mr. Ferguson's Paranoid and Delusional Behavior

This section attempts to show how Colin Ferguson's mental health problems (e.g., paranoid behavior) not only surfaced subsequent to the shooting but existed for some time prior to the crimi-

---

656. *See E.g.,* A. Goldstein, *LIRR Case a Catch-22 in Reverse*. NEWSDAY, Feb. 3, 1995 at A08–A09.[hereinafter Goldstein I]

657. *See generally* Dusky v. United States, 362 U.S. 402 (1960) *supra* note 6.

658. *See* Ferguson Pretrial Hearing Transcripts, December 9, 1994 at 450–453 (Assistant District Attorney (A.D.A.) Mr. Peck substantiating psychiatrists D'Alessandro and Reichman's testimony that Ferguson's behavior is more consistent with paranoid personality disorder.)

659. Their conclusion was contrary to that formed by the defense-retained psychiatrist, Dr. Richard Dudley, who diagnosed Ferguson as suffering from delusional disorder, persecutory subtype and subsequently found him not mentally competent to stand trial. His evaluation was conducted on May 17th 1994.

660. *See* Perlin, Dignity *supra* note 639, at 72.

nal event. Using data from a psychiatric report and testimony elicited during the pretrial competency hearing, we present and review Ferguson's behavior from 1982 (when he arrived in the United States) to December 7, 1993 (when he open-fired on the Long Island Rail Road). To be clear, this section relies on the psychiatric report provided by Dr. Dudley, the defense counsel's expert witness,[661] as well as testimony elicited from Dr. Dudley during the pretrial competency hearing.[662] As a point of departure, we assert that reviewing excerpts from Dr. Dudley's testimony helps to flesh out several points of interest regarding Mr. Ferguson's pretrial conduct. Before proceeding, however, we briefly explain why this reliance on Dr. Dudley's report and testimony is warranted.

Although evaluated for competency by three psychiatrists (Dr. Dudley for the defense, Drs. D'Alessandro and Reichman appointed by the court and used by the prosecution), Mr. Ferguson, generally, did not cooperate with any of the evaluating mental health professionals. After the initial court-ordered evaluation conducted by Drs. D'Alessandro and Reichman,[663] Ferguson refused follow-up meetings and, thus, prevented efforts in gathering collateral information and evidence on the competency issue.[664] Drs. D'Alessandro and Reichman's, initial meeting with Ferguson lasted approximately one hour and thirty minutes. Regrettably, the interview is limited in scope and it lacks commentary relative to Mr. Ferguson's past experiences and interactions.[665] Similar to those psychiatrists that pre-

---

661. *See* Declaration of Richard G. Dudley, M.D., November 27, 1994[hereinafter DUDLEY] (the psychiatric evaluation was conducted on May 17, 1994).

662. *See* Ferguson Pretrial Hearing Transcripts, *supra* note 648 December 6, 1994 at 5-116 (Providing the pretrial competency testimony offered by Dr. Dudley.) Some of Mr. Ferguson's background is supplemented by court transcripts detailing the custodial interrogation. *See* Ferguson Hearing Transcripts December 14 and 15, 1994 at 18-111. The custodial interrogation was conducted by Detectives Abbondandelo and Daly on December 7, 1993-the night of the shooting.

663. *See supra* note 654 (discussing the initial competency evaluation under New York's Criminal Law Procedure 730.30.)

664. *See* Kuby & Kunstler *supra* note 652, at 21. As discussed in the expert testimony section, the prosecution also relied on Drs. D'Alessandro and Reichman and their testimony, however, this testimony is based exclusively on the initial December 28, 1993 interview and exam.

665. The pitfalls associated with this CST evaluation is discussed in more detail in the subsequent chapter on expert testimony.

ceded him, Dr. Dudley encountered problems as the defendant again refused to participate in a follow-up examination.[666] However, Dr. Dudley, did manage to meet with Mr. Ferguson for three hours and discussed, in detail, important information relative to the accused's behavior and past experiences. Specifically, the background information in the report explains important life experiences and describes the problems Ferguson encountered relating to his occupation, civil law suits, marital and personal relations, the law enforcement community, and the many difficulties he confronted at the colleges and universities Ferguson attended. Thus, the data provided by Dr. Dudley via the psychiatric report and pretrial testimony is used to describe the defendant's behavior; information deemed credible by the court and subsequently admitted into evidence.

This summary does not comment on the relative strengths or weaknesses of Dr. Dudley's report nor does it critique (in this chapter) his courtroom testimony.[667] In addition, this overview is not intended to be exhaustive; rather, its purpose is expository. We locate and describe Mr. Ferguson's paranoid conduct and identify the key interactions he enjoyed, especially with those individuals both within and outside the legal system. Moreover, the information reviewed in this section is clearly relevant for understanding the pragmatics of trial fitness evaluations. Indeed, as we contend, our explication in the following pages makes possible the analysis in subsequent sections addressing expert testimony relative to evaluation methods and a clinician's competency to stand trial findings.

Colin Ferguson was born on January 14, 1958 and raised in Kingston, Jamaica. Mr. Ferguson came to the United States in 1982 by way of California and soon acquired a job at a liquor store.[668] His feelings about racism in the United States began with this first job.[669] It did not take him long to form such opinions. According to

---

666. *See* Kuby & Kunstler *supra* note 652, at 21 n.4 stating, "Mr. Ferguson explained that the only reason he met with the defense psychiatrist in the first place was that he mistakenly believed that the psychiatrist was the eye doctor whom he had requested."

667. A critique and review of the psychiatrists' testimony, however, is provided and discussed in the next chapter.

668. *See* Ferguson Pretrial Hearing Transcripts, December 6, 1994 at 44, 45.

669. *See Id.* at 45.

Dr. Dudley, Ferguson suggested "that people of African descent were treated differently in some real concrete ways and described himself as becoming angry about it [racism] even then."[670] Colin Ferguson soon moved to New York where he married[671] and started a series of jobs working as a bank teller. Not unlike his experiences in California, Ferguson complained of work-related racism,[672] and although he relocated to different banks to escape the prejudice (three to be exact),[673] Ferguson described a repeated pattern in each work setting perpetuating the same sort of bias.[674] Dr. Dudley recounts this cyclic pattern during the pretrial competency hearing.

> DR. DUDLEY: He [Mr. Ferguson] described the first situation as one that had been there during his thirty-day probation period; that he worked hard while white employees were allowed not to work, and he was able to receive an award for services when he was performing well. And then there was a shortage found in his drawer and he described how he began this process of being treated unfairly there; that it was managed differently than it would have [sic] managed for other bank tellers that had much larger difficulties before. His probation was extended.
>
> He was then put at even a more difficult job and, again, talking about how all of this was the result of the racism at the bank. Finally he had to leave that job only to go to another job where he again described the same sort of experience, supervisor being hostile, angry about any person of African descent who was ambitious, who tries to work hard, and tries to do a good job, always waiting for him, looking for him to make errors getting through the probation period. Again there are some other difficulties. He extends his probation period, sends him for all sorts of assessments, humiliates him, embarrasses

---

670. See Id. (Dr. Dudley referring to his interview with Mr. Ferguson.)
671. According to Dr. Dudley's report, Mr. Ferguson married in May 13, 1986.
672. See Id. at 46.
673. See DUDLEY supra note 661, at 4–5.
674. See Id. At the first bank, Ferguson suggested that he would do a large volume of work while his Caucasian counterparts refused to take customers and appeared to "to look busy". At the second bank, Ferguson reported that the head teller seemed unsettled that a black man had ambition. While working at the third bank, Ferguson indicated his work was compromised because he had to work behind a door, a place that the other workers tried to avoid.

him, etcetera to the point where he has to leave again only to
go to a third bank and have a similar sort of situation happen
where he is mistreated, given the worst jobs, and again, has to
leave.[675]

Eventually, Mr. Ferguson left the bank business and started
working for Ademco, an alarm manufacturing company.[676] Again,
Ferguson found difficulties at this job, and eventually filed a griev-
ance with the Equal Employment Opportunity Commission
(EEOC).[677] He later filed a Worker's Compensation claim stemming
from a back and neck injury sustained at work.[678] The Worker's
Compensation case was a long arduous process, further complicated by Mr. Ferguson's paranoid beliefs.[679] The prevailing themes
outlined in Mr. Ferguson complaints involved racism as part of a
grand plan to obstruct his pursuit of long-term objectives. Ferguson's conspiracy theories existed both inside and outside the legal
realm. For example, during the Worker's Compensation case, he described, to the court, a situation involving a conspiracy theory relative to members of the Workers Compensation Board and his attorney. Mr. Ferguson suggested that Board members and others were
preventing him from achieving his objectives. As he explained it:

> [t]he head security guard who wears the white shirt (Puerto
> Rican) and his other guards, many of whom belong to and are
> members of the violent cult group the Hebrew Israelites, have
> illegally barred me from the Board...

> [And with respect to the attorney representing him in these
> proceedings] Mr. Irwin Silverman is my attorney and do I trust
> him? Absolutely not. Since he hates me unto death and does
> not believe that a 'black' who stands up for justice deserves to
> be paid for his injury.[680]

Mr. Ferguson's overall experience during the Worker's Compensation case entails similar instances of distrust and paranoia. Eventu-

---

675. *See* Ferguson Pretrial Hearing Transcripts, December 6, 1994 at
46–47.
676. *See* DUDLEY *supra* note 661, at 5.
677. *See* Ferguson Pretrial Hearing Transcripts, December 6, 1994 at 48.
678. *See* Ferguson Hearing Transcripts, December 15, 1994 at 197.
679. *See* Ferguson Pretrial Hearing Transcripts, December 6, 1994 at 51,
52.
680. *See Id.* at 50–51.

ally, everyone who questioned his paranoid beliefs soon became incorporated into the grand scheme. Dr. Dudley speaks to this very issue during the pretrial competency hearing.

> Dr. DUDLEY: He at every turn in the experience with the Worker's Compensation Board came up with the same sort of sense, whether it was with each of the attorneys that he worked with over time, as well as the various levels really of persons at the board itself, persons from the board, reviewers, the judges, the doctors who were doing the evaluations, again the same sort of response came up. Even when he ultimately got an award from the Worker's Compensation Board still believing that he had not been treated fairly, appealing that award and therefore starting to continue the proceeding all over again.[681]

Mr. Ferguson's problems did not occur only in reaction to his work-related experiences. He also reported problems with various law enforcement agencies and officials.[682] Ferguson reported to Dr. Dudley that representatives from both the Immigration and Naturalization Service (INS) and the Drug Enforcement Administration (DEA) had made contact with his wife, brother, and co-workers with questions regarding the identity of a man in a picture.[683] As Ferguson explained it, the man in the picture was wanted for his connection to drug-related offenses.[684] In the face of his problems with Ademco and various law enforcement agencies, Ferguson's marriage began to suffer and he eventually separated from his wife.[685] According to Ferguson, however, all of his troubles were directly related to a grand conspiracy. Dr. Dudley conveyed to the court the complex workings of this conspiracy as described to him by Mr. Ferguson.

> DR. DUDLEY: But as he talked about all of this [Worker's Compensation case, problems with law enforcement agencies

---

681. *See Id.*
682. *See Id.* at 48, 49.
683. *See Id.*
684. *See Id.* at 48 (Ferguson expressed to Dr. Dudley that it was later learned the man in the picture was of Jamaican descent, and that his wife had told the INS agent that the man in the picture was not Colin Ferguson.) *See Id.* at 48, 49.
685. *See* DUDLEY *supra* note 661, at 5.

and his marriage], again, these incidents got incorporated into a larger belief system and became elaborated as part of this belief system.

More specifically, he began to talk about how this was probably related to the EEOC suit that he had filed against Ademco and that Ademco, in working with these law enforcement entities, had been able to come up with this plan and to have secretive interviews with significant people in his life by coming up with this rouse about trying to identify this particular individual [the man wanted for drug charges].

He [Ferguson] talked about how all of this had been used to destroy his marriage, to humiliate him, to destroy his job. He ended up going down to the DEA trying to find out who was behind this, who started this, and why they were participating in this plot against him, etc. So it became part of the large scheme.[686]

Not unlike his other experiences, Colin Ferguson soon described problems relating to various professors and administrative faculty at the colleges he attended. Mr. Ferguson indicated he attended Nassau Community College for several semesters in 1989.[687] He described how this was a troubling time for him as he was not only working and dealing with the Worker's Compensation case but also attempting to maintain his grades. As a result of the stress, he made arrangements with the school to withdraw from classes without penalty. According to Ferguson one of the teachers (described as a racist) (initially) agreed to not penalize him for withdrawing from his classes but later arranged it so Mr. Ferguson received a failing grade.[688]

Eventually, Ferguson returned to school; however, he soon began to disrupt class sessions, making racist comments to class members and teachers. Incidents occurring in his English class demonstrate typical problems and disruptions. During one class, the student Ferguson called his English teacher a racist in response to her correcting one of his spelling errors. Irene Brenalvirez, the English profes-

---

686. *See* Pretrial Hearing Transcripts, December 6, 1994 at 49, 50.

687. *See* Ferguson Hearing Transcripts, December 15, 1994 at 89.

688. *See* Ferguson Pretrial Hearing Transcripts, December 6, 1994 at 53, 54.

sor, stated that "He seems unable to control his behavior, his responses to minor inconveniences and irritations being entirely out of proportion to their cause."[689] Mr. Ferguson's allegations soon became very broad and sweeping. He filed numerous complaints with various departments, and disrupted numerous offices with the complaints (the Affirmative Action Office). Ferguson eventually left Nassau Community College and enrolled at Adelphi University.

When he enrolled at Adelphi University Ferguson's paranoia persisted. Themes involving racism directed toward the Dean and professors once again materialized. Much like before, Ferguson attributed his problems to racism and a grand plot to keep him from attaining academic objectives. In the pretrial competency hearing Dr. Dudley stated:

> "that [according to Mr. Ferguson] the real problem at Adelphi was that they tried to take his scholarship from him because of his color. They reported that they changed his grades to lower his grade point average; he reported that he was accused of acting as if he knew it all and/or being too ambitious; and he described specific conflicts between him and others (students and teachers)."[690]

During his brief stint at Adelphi, however, Ferguson was able to persuade one professor of South African origin to investigate his numerous complaints. After investigating the matter, the professor was unable to substantiate Ferguson's allegations.[691] As a result, Ferguson rejected the professor's opinion and findings. The Dean and others suggested that Mr. Ferguson seek mental health counseling. He refused and ultimately was expelled from the university.

After several months of flirting with homelessness, Ferguson received some money by way of the Worker's Compensation case. Although he would later appeal the settlement, some of this money was used to travel to California and "re-start his life."[692] While in California, Mr. Ferguson purchased a gun. During his interview with Dr. Dudley, Ferguson explained his need for a gun, noting that

---

689. See Id. at 55 (Dr. Dudley quoting Irene Brenalvirez's observations about Mr. Ferguson classroom behavior.)

690. See DUDLEY supra note 661, at 7.

691. See Ferguson Pretrial Hearing Transcripts, December 6, 1994 at 56.

692. See DUDLEY supra note 661, at 7.

"since people were killed each day in liquor stores and he had been robbed when he worked in the liquor store, he legally purchased a gun."[693] However, Mr. Ferguson was soon called back to New York regarding his Worker's Compensation appeal. He returned to New York (with the gun) on May, 1993 with the intentions of only staying a short while to resolve his case. However, Ferguson noted that the Worker's Compensation appeal suspended any monies from the award; thus, he was "trapped in New York."[694]

Ostensibly, Mr. Ferguson's paranoia and mental health concerns existed prior to the shooting incident. According to Dr. Dudley, the way that Ferguson interacted, interpreted, and processed information was strongly anchored in ideas of paranoid themes involving racism. His allegations were wide ranging, attacking those inside and outside of the legal community. In essence, Dr. Dudley's findings on Ferguson's background indicate that the accused was plagued by perceived incidents of racism, demonstrating repeated patterns of prejudice despite the job or work-setting.

In addition, the Worker's Compensation process reveals a pattern of pervasive distrust and paranoia. Ferguson fired several attorneys and made allegations against all parties involved in the proceedings including: the reviewers on the Worker's Compensation Board, the judges that heard his cases, the lawyers representing him, and the doctors that evaluated his injuries. According to Dr. Dudley, Mr. Ferguson even accused the security guards at the Worker's Compensation Board of being part of a terrorist organization headed by Yahweh Ben-Yahweh.[695] The racist accusations persisted when he attended Nassau Community College and Adelphi University. He accused various individuals at these institutions of conspiring to strip him of an education. Many, including a professor who investigated Mr. Ferguson's allegations,[696] indicated a rapid decline in his

---

693. *See Id.*

694. *See Id.* at 8. During this time, Ferguson also reported problems with his apartment and the people that lived there. Mr. Ferguson indicated that the "bathroom wasn't clean, they were trying to force him out of the apartment, his electricity kept being turned off, etc., all because a white woman had moved into the building." *See Id.*

695. *See* Kuby & Kunstler *supra* note 652, at 20.

696. *See* Ferguson Pretrial Hearing Transcripts, December 6, 1994 at 56 (indicating that not only did this professor investigate each allegation but that Mr. Ferguson was steadfast in his paranoid beliefs despite evidence to the contrary.)

mental health.[697] Approximately two years later, Colin Ferguson's intense feelings about racism reached their boiling point, culminating in the violent and explosive Long Island Railway massacre.

The next section in this chapter describes the court room testimony of the psychiatric experts. The section centers on the issue of competency to stand trial. In addition to fleshing out further Dr. Dudley's testimony, we present the expert testimony provided by the people's witnesses: Drs. D'Alessandro and Reichman. The psychiatric testimony explores the assessment methods used to evaluate Mr. Ferguson's competency and the reasoning for the findings by way of direct and cross-examination.

3. The Expert Testimony

> [I]f he [Mr. Ferguson] wished to be found incompetent you would not have him rejecting the psychiatric examination [but] you would have him running up to psychiatrists, especially a defense psychiatrist...and saying "Mr. Defense Psychiatrist, see how crazy I am? Watch me. Aren't I crazy, Judge? Aren't I crazy, Mr. Psychiatrist?" That is the kind of behavior you would expect if that was Mr. Ferguson's real agenda. You haven't seen that; just the opposite.[698]

As we have already stated, there were two court orders relative to the issue of competency in the case Colin Ferguson. The first was ordered by the court shortly after Ferguson's arrest. Together, Drs. D'Alessandro and Reichman conducted the CST evaluation on December 28, 1993. Based on the findings relative to Drs. D'Alessandro and Reichman's examination and the subsequent colloquies between Ferguson and Judge Belfi, the court ruled that the accused was not an incapacitated person.[699] However, in lieu of Ferguson's desire to fire counsel and proceed *pro se* to trial, the defense filed a motion requesting a formal competency hearing to once and for all settle the issue of competency and address Ferguson's requests on

---

697. *See Id.* at 56.

698. *See* Ferguson Pretrial Hearing Transcripts, December, 9th 1994 at 440–441 (Mr. Kuby's closing arguments regarding the competency issue).

699. *See* Pretrial Competency Hearing Transcripts December 9, 1994, at 455.

defense strategy.[700] This competency motion raised by the defense, and granted by the court, denotes the second CST inquiry in the case of Colin Ferguson. Clearly a more searching inquiry, this CST hearing addressed multiple issues, requiring testimony by mental health experts from both the defense and the people.

On December 6th 1994, the multi-faceted pretrial hearing began addressing the issue of competency and the several requests made by Ferguson.[701] The initial thrust of the hearing involved the competency of the defendant; that is, whether as a result of a mental disease or defect, Ferguson lacked the capacity to understand the nature of the proceedings or to assist in the defense.[702] Second, if Ferguson was found competent, the question was whether or not he would be granted a right to represent himself. And third, if he proceeded to *pro se* the case, the question was whether or not Ferguson would reject the defense of insanity interposed by his then-present counselors, Mr. Kunstler and Mr. Kuby.[703] To resolve these matters, the court relied on evidence elicited at the pretrial competency hearing which centered on clinical forensic expert testimony, and the court's observations of the defendant throughout the proceedings.

Preliminarily, however, before the pretrial hearing began, Ferguson made several comments regarding his sentiments on the competency hearing. Although he had made specific requests to strike the insanity defense and waive counsel, Mr. Ferguson objected to the competency hearing. He thought the hearing "was completely illegal."[704] On December 6, 1994 (the first day of the pretrial competency hearing), the accused offered the following statement to the court:

> "I just wish to indicate to the Court that I view this particular hearing as a moot forum and in fact is a mock trial which exposes me to double jeopardy to my trial in January. [A]lso, I

---

700. *See* Pretrial Competency Hearing Transcripts, December 6, 1994, at 3–4.

701. *See infra* note 651 (once Ferguson made requests to fire his counsel and conduct his own defense the court ordered a formal competency hearing.)

702. *See* N.Y. CRIM. PROC. LAW § 730.10 (McKinney's 1994). Language consistent with the criteria set forth in *Dusky*. The legal issues of Mr. Ferguson competency is discussed *infra*.

703. *See* Ferguson Pretrial Hearing Transcripts, December 6th 1994 at 3–4.

704. *See* Ferguson Pretrial Hearing Transcripts, December 9, 1994 at 495.

wish to indicate that the motion granted in the last hearing [introduction of the insanity defense] should be reflected on the court records as a motion granted to Mr. Kunstler and Mr. Kuby and not to Colin Ferguson."[705]

These statements are powerful, especially with respect to the legal issue of trial fitness. Ferguson's statement to the court not only suggests that he understood but was also mindful of the overall legal procedure.[706] What is more, the defendant renounced the proceedings and the testimony therein, and went on record to say as much, as noted above.[707] These comments highlight Kunstler and Kuby's plight; that is, their struggle to advance the only logical defense (i.e., an insanity plea) on behalf of their client. Moreover, as we will demonstrate, the low threshold competency standard and the questionable CST screening process both illustrate how trial competency and related issues (competency to proceed *pro se* to trial) are problematic psycholegal matters.

The defense introduced testimony by one expert (Dr. Dudley) who evaluated Ferguson per his attorneys' request on May 17, 1994. As previously mentioned, Mr. Ferguson was generally noncompliant during all the CST examinations and refused follow-up meetings with any of the psychiatrists. On this point, Kuby and Kunstler note that "Mr. Ferguson refused to meet with the prosecution's psychiatrist under any circumstances."[708] This notwithstanding, the people called two experts (Drs. D'Alessandro and Reichman) who conducted the first CST evaluation on December 28, 1993, and they relied on their psychiatrists' initial findings to build their own case. We note that the experts who evaluated Colin Ferguson and testified at the pretrial hearing had conflicting opinions concerning the issue of Ferguson's competency to stand trial. Moreover, they based their CST findings on different evaluation methods.

In what follows, we present and explain the expert testimony entered as evidence, the CST findings themselves, the methods for

---

705. *See* Ferguson Pretrial Hearing Transcript, December 6, 1994 at 3.

706. Although the prosecution has the burden of proof (i.e., show fitness by a preponderance of the evidence), it is an easy one to reach. In concert with the competency standard, the low burden is all but achieved when Mr. Ferguson makes these damaging statements to the court.

707. *See* Ferguson Pretrial Hearing Transcript, December 6, 1994 at 3.

708. *See* Kuby & Kunstler *supra* note 511, at 21.

CST evaluation, and the information used to support the psychiatrists' findings. Put another way, this summary does not include all the CST testimony (e.g., we do not present the qualifications of the experts). However, it does present the unabridged statements relevant to diagnostic opinions, information used to inform clinical opinions, CST exam methods, the CST findings, and any other data relevant to the issue of trial competency or related to other points made in previous chapters (e.g., credibility of expert opinions, conflating the issue of competency and insanity). Along these lines, the format we employ provides for narrative summaries of (including important excerpts from) the expert testimony proffered by the three psychiatrists, as well as excerpts from the cross-examination of these witnesses by counsel for the defense and the people.

(a) The Defense Calls Dr. Richard Dudley: Direct Examination by Defense Attorney Mr. Kuby

Colin Ferguson objected to any sort of psychiatric evaluation.[709] According to Kuby and Kunstler, the only reason Mr. Ferguson met with the defense psychiatrist at all was because he presumed Dr. Dudley was the eye doctor whom he had requested to see.[710] After the initial visit, Ferguson refused all forms of follow-up meetings, precluding a complete psychiatric examination.[711] This notwithstanding, Dr. Dudley's initial examination was lengthy (lasting 3 hours), enabling the psychiatrist to supplement findings with collateral data sources involving Ferguson's life before and subsequent to the shooting.[712] Based on all of this infor-

---

709. See Id.

710. See Id. at 21 n.4.

711. See Ferguson Pretrial Hearing Transcript, December 6, 1994 at 9. Dr. Dudley states, "I had anticipated being able to go into some of those in more depth on the second time around, as well as to speak with him about the incident.... he refused the visit." See Id.

712. Collectively, Dr. Dudley reviewed Colin Ferguson's records/file form Nassau Community College covering 1987–1990, the Worker's Compensation case, the records from Adelphi University covering 1989–1991, various notes and letters written by Mr. Ferguson, documents relating to the charges against Colin Ferguson, Report of the 730 examination conducted on December 28, 1993, Dr. Dudley initial exam performed on May 17, 1994, and phone call interviews with various people whom made contact with Mr. Ferguson before the December 7, 1993 incident. See DUDLEY supra note 661, at 1,2.

mation, Dr. Dudley developed a diagnostic assessment and reached a conclusion about Mr. Ferguson's competence to stand trial.[713] Dr. Dudley's findings (especially the reasoning used to support the findings) require direct reference to the pretrial hearing transcripts.[714]

From the outset of the direct examination, Mr. Ferguson proved to a combative defendant. For example, when Mr. Kuby attempted to enter several items into evidence used by Dr. Dudley to render his medical opinion, Ferguson passionately objected, raising legal issues about attorney/client confidentiality. This is what happened during the initial question and answer session between Mr. Kuby and Dr. Dudley.

Q In rendering a psychiatric opinion as to the competency of a defendant one of the things you [Dr. Dudley] review are communications between the defendant and his attorney?

A When available, yes.

MR. KUBY: I would offer that into evidence subject to the same caveat [remain sealed until the Court makes a ruling on competency].

THE DEFENDANT: I object.

THE COURT: People?

MR. PECK: Your Honor, this is communication written to his attorney. He has to waive the privilege.

MR. KUBY: Mr. Peck—

MR. PECK: This is not a communication written to you that you gave us copies of.

MR. KUBY: Judge, the first thing I would note to the Court is these letters in fact attached as exhibits to our motion for an original 730 Examination [competency evaluation] some four or five months ago. So to the

---

713. At the time of the Colin Ferguson pretrial competency hearing, the DSM-III was used by mental health professionals. Since then, it has been followed by the DSM-IV. Notwithstanding the upgraded version, the definitions and diagnostic criteria for delusional disorder, and paranoid personality disorder have not been augmented or changed.

714. See Ferguson Pretrial Hearing Transcripts, December 6, 1994 at 5-65 (Dr. Dudley-direct examination/Kuby.)

extent that there is an objection I think it is several months out of time. They already exist in the court file.

Second, Mr. Peck has no right to assert *jus tertii*, Mr. Ferguson's attorney/client privilege.

Third, one of the things that this hearing is designed to determine is whether or not the defendant is psychologically capable of actually receiving the assistance of counsel and assisting in his own defense, as our psychiatrist will testify. And I know from previous statements the prosecution's psychiatrists have said one of the things you look to is the nature and quality of the relationship between defendant and counsel.

I would also note there is nothing in those letters to us that reveals any specific fact that was not already public knowledge. The letter goes on in some length about Mr. Ferguson's dreams. As to whether or not it is attorney/client privilege, they are in the file, they have been here for four months. Our psychiatrist relied on them and they should be introduced in evidence subject to the same seal as the others.

THE DEFENDANT: Judge, it has not been established that this letter was discussed in the meeting with Dr. Dudley. This is to get a medical opinion from Dr. Dudley concerning his specific meeting at a specific time.

THE COURT: I don't understand that to be the purpose or relevance of it being introduced.

THE DEFENDANT: What Mr. Kuby is doing is entering into the file on the record new evidence. I'm sorry, he is attempting to enter material that was not available to Dr. Dudley at the time that we had a single meeting at the jail.

THE COURT:	…Have you [Dr. Dudley] used the contents of this letter to formulate an opinion as to the defendant's competency at this time?
THE WITNESS:	At least in part.
THE DEFENDANT:	Could he elaborate on that in part?
MR. KUBY:	Judge, if you would like to reserve the decision on this particular exhibit I think we can proceed with the others. This is not essential to the upcoming questions.
THE COURT:	At this time I'm going to reserve decision based upon the possibility of a violation of attorney/client privilege, which Mr. Ferguson indicated that he is not waiving at this time for this purpose.[715]

…

Next, Mr. Kuby explores the sum and substance of Dr. Dudley's findings. Relying on information gathered in his initial meeting,[716] Dr. Dudley presents a diagnosis concerning Mr. Ferguson's mental health condition (delusional disorder, persecutory subtype). The presentation describes delusions and the criteria for delusional disorder as set forth in the *DSM*. In addition, Dr. Dudley discusses Ferguson's behavior in association with non-bizarre delusions, emphasizing associated features (i.e, violent tendencies).

Q Dr. Dudley, based upon the review that you conducted have you determined with a reasonable degree of medical certainty whether Colin Ferguson suffers from a mental disease or defect?

A Yes.

Q What is that opinion?

A It is my opinion that he suffers from a delusional disorder of the persecutory sub-type.

Q What is a delusional disorder?

A Delusional Disorder is a psychiatric condition that is characterized primarily by the presence of what are termed non-bizarre delusions.

Q What is a delusion?

---

715. *See Id.* at 17–20.
716. As noted, Mr. Ferguson refused a follow-up visit, therefore, Dr. Dudley formed his opinion based on the initial 3 hour examination.

A A delusion is a fixed false belief that a person holds onto despite evidence, irrefutable evidence, to the contrary that would refute the belief.

And more often than not it becomes determinative fo the person's behavior in that the person acts on these beliefs and continues to hold onto them despite the fact that acting on these beliefs might be detrimental to them or otherwise interfere with their particular goals and objectives.

Q In your definition you refer to a non-bizarre delusion. Could you please explain to the Court the difference between a non-bizarre and a bizarre delusion.

A A bizarre delusion, such as seen in schizophrenia is a delusion that will be considered totally improbable, totally impossible. So if someone says that they believe that there are green men from Mars living in their TV and attempting to influence their lives, something like that would be considered bizarre.

A non-bizarre delusion in contrast is a delusion that could have grown out of situations that could have happened, but they are exaggerated and made more extreme...that somebody is bothering me, somebody is attempting to harm me in some sort of way.

Q What is the delusion that we are discussing, the non-bizarre delusion?

A The belief that most of the people who he comes in contact with are working against him in an effort to destroy him and that the reason for this is that these non-black persons are working out of racism and many others, also black persons, who he comes in contact with [are] influenced by these beliefs as well and they are also participating in this conspiracy.

Q What is a persecutory sub-type?

A Delusional disorders come in a variety of subtypes. Persecutory is one where the primary delusion, the primary belief, is that one is going to be harmed in some sort of way and/or that persons are working to interfere with the individual's attempts to reach goals and objectives.

Q With persecutory subtype does the afflicted person become violent?

A That can happen. And that persons who suffer from such persecutory delusions often become very angry and violent.

Q ...Did you consult the *Diagnostic and Statistical Manual of Mental Disorders* in rendering your decision, your medical opinion, about Mr. Ferguson's mental state?

A Yes, I did.[717]

...

Q Dr. Dudley, are there criteria for diagnosing delusional disorder persecutory type?

A Yes.

Q Are these criteria listed in the *Diagnostic and Statistical Manual*?

A Yes.

Q What is the first criterion?

A The first criterion is the presence of a non-bizarre delusion. To meet the criterion for persecutory type the prominent theme of that delusion would have to be persecutory in nature.

Q Have you concluded with a reasonable degree of medical certainty that Mr. Ferguson fits that?

A Yes.

Q What about the second criterion?

A The second criterion is that there is an absence of specific diagnostic criteria that would lead the diagnostician to make the diagnosis of schizophrenia instead of delusional disorder.

More specifically what that means is that delusions of course also occur in schizophrenia, although not in isolation. In schizophrenia delusions occur in association with other symptoms: hallucinations, disturbances of speech, disturbances in behavior in what we call negative symptoms of schizophrenia, things like that flattening affect, parsity of speech, movement.

So that one has to look for these when they are delusional in order to rule out schizophrenia. The second criterion for delusional disorder is that you didn't see these other symptoms, and you have no history that the person at some other point had exhibited a sufficient number of these symptoms to meet the diagnostic criteria of schizophrenia.

Q And the third criterion?

A The third criterion really talks about the nature of the dysfunction that a person suffers from a delusional disorder. While they act on the delusion and whatever the action is could be problematic otherwise you don't necessarily see significant impairments in behavior, so the impairments...we see is really a direct result of their acting on the delusional belief.

---

717. *See Id.* at 27–30.

Q Did you find evidence in Mr. Ferguson that he has acted on his delusions?

A Yes.

Q Could you just explain briefly what that type of evidence was?

A His own reports as well as some of the documents that I reviewed indicate his acting on his beliefs.

Q And you indicated that other than that functioning is normal?

A Yes. I mean this is not a disorder that impairs cognitive ability, a person's ability to think. It does not impair intellectual pursuits. And by and large if you are talking about or working outside of the delusional belief itself, you would not see any sort of thinking that is otherwise strange or unusual or bizarre.

Q I ask you to assume for the purposes of this hearing that people have described Mr. Ferguson as extremely intelligent, extremely articulate and—not talking about the judicial proceeding—very lucid. Is that consistent or inconsistent with a delusion disorder?

A It's consistent with the disorder. As I indicated, it is what we call an encapsulated disorder, so to speak and that any behavioral difficulties that may occur are a direct result of responding to the delusion, and outside of that a person can appear quite fine.

Q And could violence be a response to that delusion?

A Yes, it can.

Q In your opinion has violence been a response to Mr. Ferguson's delusion?

A Yes.

Q When did that happen?

A Well, the time most recently in December of 1993.

Q ...Do the events of December 7th provide you with information about Mr. Ferguson's present mental capacity?

A Yes.

Q In what way?

A Well, with this disorder certainly it is important to understand the course of the illness. And as I indicated earlier, one is looking to see a pattern of thinking and responding to those thoughts over time. So that becomes critical in understanding that course of the illness.

In addition to that there are, as I suggested, associated symptoms with this disorder: Anger can occur, violence can occur, lots of litigation. So you are looking for evidence of that over the course of time.

Q With respect to the fourth criterion, what is that?

A The fourth criterion talks about mood disturbances, particularly depression.

Again, this criterion is important to help in a differential diagnosis in that the criterion indicates that while a person with a delusion disorder can be depressed usually it is short-lived in relationship with delusions and occurs during the course of delusional thinking.

Q And did Mr. Ferguson fit that criterion?

A Yes.

Q With respect to the fifth criterion?

A The fifth criterion is an exclusion criterion, rule out criterion. You are supposed to consider whether this delusion difficulty is due to something physiologic, some sort of medical condition, or drugs.

Q Did you find any indication that it was due to a medical condition or drugs?

A No. [718]

Next, Mr. Kuby explores the issue of competency. Specifically, Mr. Kuby poses the question: can Colin Ferguson assist in his own defense? Dr. Dudley discusses competency in light of the signs and conditions associated with delusional disorder.

Q Given his mental illness have you concluded [with a] reasonable degree of medical certainty whether Colin Ferguson is capable of assisting in his own defense?

A Yes.

Q What is that conclusion?

A No.

Q Would you explain why.

A The nature of this disorder is such that the individual, in this case Mr. Ferguson, is unable to develop a relationship with his attorneys that would be based on some volume of trust, and as a result of that he would be unable to really receive from those attorneys the kind of advise and concrete information required to even begin the process of assisting in his defense, because he would not be able to trust that the advice and concrete informa-

---

718. *See Id.* at 33–38.

tion coming from the attorneys is at all accurate and not under some sort of plot to harm him.

In addition to that even if that information and advice could be received then one begins the process of decision making, and trying to make decisions how to best proceed. His ability to do that is impaired by the delusional thinking as well, and he will need to make those sort of decisions and render feedback to the attorneys which would also be impaired.[719]

. . .

On a related subject, Mr. Kuby then asks a series of questions about Mr. Ferguson's experiences with attorneys, in general, intimating Ferguson can not work with attorneys to assist in the defense. Relating Ferguson's current behavior to past behavior, Dr. Dudley also explains why Ferguson is not malingering (i.e., feigning incompetency to avoid standing trial).

Q Based upon your review of the documents and interviews is this the first time Mr. Ferguson has had problems with his attorneys?

A No.

Q Have there been other problems?

A Yes.

Q Could you describe [them] in general?

A Well, in general, for example, with the case that he had with Worker's Compensation Board he went through a series of attorneys with similar sorts of concerns...[A]fter beginning to work with them finding to be racist, finding them to be working against him finding them to be conspiring with others involved in the process in some sort of way, dismissing each one, moving to the next one, dismissing that one and moving to the next one, ultimately needing to defend himself because he is not really able to establish a relationship with any attorney.

Q Dr. Dudley, I ask you to assume for the sake of this hearing that Mr. Ferguson has stated he has a desire to represent himself at this proceeding; that is, his trial for the Long Island Rail Road shooting. Could you state with a reasonable degree of medical certainty whether that decision is based on a rational thought process or whether that decision is based on his delusions?

---

719. *See Id.* at 39–40.

MR. PECK: Objection.

THE COURT: Overruled.

A I would say it is certainly consistent with the existence of a delusional disorder and consistent with the behavior that he has evidenced in the past that in my opinion are related to the delusional disorder. In that sense, yes, I believe it would be associated
with the disorder.[720]

. . .

Q Why is Mr. Ferguson acting out of delusion rather than rational
decision?

A Well, it is really based on, number one, my opinion of the existence of a disorder manifested in a variety of settings over time in
a pretty consistent manner based on the same sort of belief system and evidence that he is doing the same thing here.

Q I ask you to assume for the sake of this hearing that Mr. Ferguson has refused to accept an insanity defense despite overwhelming evidence of his involvement in the Long Island Rail Road
shooting.

Is that decision to a reasonable degree of medical certainty a
product of rational decision making or is that decision a product
of his delusional disorder?

MR. PECK: Objection.

THE COURT: Overruled.

A In this case I believe that it is a product of his disorder.

Q Let me ask you this: Why—can you tell me and tell the court
why it is that Mr. Ferguson just isn't faking this whole thing by
getting here and being as disagreeable as possible, firing attorneys, filing all kinds of papers, and generally resisting the proceedings? Why isn't he just faking this in a desire to be found incompetent so he doesn't have to stand trial to a reasonable
degree of medical certainty, if you know?

A What one looks for really is the nature of the thinking, and its responsiveness to other sources of information, persistence despite
the fact that it's taking one down a road that is ultimately detrimental.

In other words, the treshold [sic] of the decision here is does this
behavior really kind of rise to the level of delusion...differenti-

---

720. *See Id.* at 40–42.

ated from malingering, differentiated from a paranoid personality disorder or other possible diagnoses.

And it is my opinion that his behavior does rise to that level. The severity of it, the severity of the actions that he has taken in response to what he is believing and the persistence of these beliefs despite times others have attempted to intervene, to help him, to try to make sense for him. And his total lack of responsiveness to that. The other thing that is compelling is the fact that over—the persistence of this behavior over time in each setting that he has found himself in that the same sorts of situations have occurred, certainly much before he had any reason to think about this incident. But the behaviors have been very consistent over time with ends that were damaging to him and in ways that interfered with his state.[721]

After chronicling Ferguson's past with respect to racism and social and occupational problems (e.g., work, school, Worker's Compensation case and law enforcement agencies),[722] Dr. Dudley testifies to Mr. Ferguson's behavior at the time of the shooting and explores further the physician's diagnostic opinion (Delusional Disorder, Persecutory Type). On direct, Mr. Kuby discusses personal notes found on Ferguson at the time of the shooting.[723] Dr. Dudley

---

721. See Id. at 42–44.

722. See Id. at 44–56. See also supra notes 659–695 and accompanying text (discussing Ferguson's background) citing, in part, Dr. Dudley's testimony concerning Ferguson's social and occupation problems. See also Declaration of Richard G. Dudley, M.D., November 27, 1994.

723. The personal notes found on Ferguson's person (on the train and after his arrest) list various people and organizations as the cause for the shooting. The notes are titled "Reasons for This" and the "reasons" include: "Adelphi University: Racism; The EEOC's Racism; Workers' Compensation: Racism; NYC Transit Police; NYC Police; The Racism of Gov. Cuomo's staff and Exec. Chamber; The Racism of the Lt. Governor's Staff and Exec. Chamber this includes (REDACTED); Att. General's Office Compensation Appeals." Ferguson also states, "NYC was spared because of my respect for Mayor David Dinkins and Comm. Raymond Kelley who officially [sic] still in office. Nassau County is the Venue. "Also that Chinese RACIST (REDACTED) will never put me to shame again without cause."

Next, Ferguson titles the notes "Additional Reasons for This." Ferguson scribes "the sloppy running of the #2 train it is racism by Caucasians and Uncle Tom Negroes; also the False Allegations Against me by the filthy Caucasian Racist Female on the #1 Line; also: the Racism of (REDACTED) the Legal Aid Society and Court System also Racism of attorney Ms. Abramson [Ferguson's attorney in Workmans' Compensation case] of law firm of Gaffin and Mayo on

explains the content of these communications relative to delusional disorder, persecutory subtype.

Q December 7th 1993 the notes that were found on Mr. Ferguson's person were those consistent or inconsistent with someone suffering from a delusional disorder persecutory subtype?

A They are consistent.

[The notes] have some references to some of these other experiences that we have been talking about and that we talked about, but seemed...just to be evidence of further deterioration.

Q What about the act itself, the act of getting on a train and shooting down everybody on it on December 7th 1993? What does that say with respect to delusional disorder?

A Well, as I indicated, the behavioral disturbances of delusional disorder are usually related to acting on the delusional thinking itself.

And that with regard to the persecutory subtype this acting can often be very angry and violent and so it would be my opinion that that is consistent with the disorder.[724]

...

Next, Mr. Kuby discusses personal correspondence between Colin Ferguson and Judge Belfi—letters directed to the court after Ferguson's arrest. Some of the letters involve an incident in the Nassau County Correctional Facility where Mr. Ferguson was attacked by several white inmates requiring his hospitalization.[725] In addition to the injuries sustained, Mr. Ferguson complained of pervasive eye problems. Although the assault was undisputed, Ferguson quickly

---

Broadway in Manhattan. Those filthy swines that live at (REDACTED) are not my friends once they hear of this they will loot all the evidence in my room such as documents and tapes. I hate them with a passion." Ferguson ends, "also for the corrupt 'Black' attorneys who not only refused to help me but tried to steal my car. Also those so called civil rights leaders such the [sic] Rev. (REDACTED). *See* Defendant's Exhibit B 00001–00008, discovery materials entered into evidence on 12/6/94.

724. *See Id.* at 56–57.

725. Mr. Ferguson was attacked on March 22, 1994 by five inmates within his jail tier. Assistant district attorney Maureen Mulder supervised and prosecuted the inmates connected with the assault. *See* Pretrial Hearing Transcripts, December 7, 1994 at 154, 156. Shortly after meeting A.D.A. Mulder, Mr. Ferguson wrote to Judge Belfi stating "The A.D.A. representing me against five racist inmates of a lynch mob is a racist." *See Id.* at 165.

incorporated and elevated issues regarding his alleged eye injury and related medical appointments to a larger conspiracy devised against him.[726] For example, Mr. Ferguson contrived an elaborate conspiracy theory in light of a cancelled eye appointment that happened by way of a jail emergency. According to Ferguson, the cancellation was no accident. As Ferguson maintained, he was the victim of a complex conspiracy initiated by Kunstler and Kuby, inmates at the Nassau County Correctional Facility, officers in the jail, A.D.A. Peck, and Judge Belfi, undermining his medical interests and, ultimately, preventing the accused from identifying the actual gunman of the Long Island incident.[727] Once again, Dr. Dudley discusses Ferguson's conspiracy theory and the content of the letters relative to delusional disorder, persecutory type.

Q And is it fair to say the [letters to the judge regarding the assault and eye injury] describe Mr. Ferguson's experiences of being taken to the Nassau County Medical Center for an eye examination but before the eye examination began, an emergency forced him to go back to the Nassau County jail?

A Yes.

Q In that letter accusing his attorneys, jail officials and Court, all being a part of a conspiracy to delay independent eye specialist treatment by staging a fake emergency; is that correct?

A That's correct.

Q Is that consistent with a delusional disorder?

A Yes.

Q In what way?

A Again...this emergency indirectly related to him, becomes incorporated into the belief system and elevated really to a much larger conspiracy and scheme against him.

Q Would you describe this kind of delusion as well organized or poorly organized?

A ...Well-organized in a sense that the belief system is consistent over time and presented in ways where at least when we first hear

---

726. *See* Ferguson Pretrial Hearing Transcripts, December 6, 1994 at 58 (Dr. Dudley discussing the association between Ferguson's eye injury and his paranoid belief system.)
727. *See* Kuby & Kunstler *supra* note 652, at 20.

about [the belief system] it is not totally unfathomable. It is when it's elaborated that one sees the extent of the belief system.

Q [Next, Mr. Kuby reads a letter by Ferguson submitted to the court. Ferguson writes:] "The use of television stations and haters to lie against me is part of a conspiracy by the Court, the assistant district attorney and the jail to cover up the fact that a Caucasian committed the crime. My attorney and all of the above-named parties, (attorneys, A.D.A., Court and jail) are therefore attempting to have me go blind to prevent me from identifying the shooter, if I am in fact able."

Is that consistent with delusional disorder?

A Yes.

Q In what fashion?

A The belief really of not being able to treat [the eye injury], not being adequately cared for, the eye injury continues to escalate and it becomes a much larger issue than not just giving treatment. But this is an example of what I mean in that it goes past the issue of is there a plot to not give me treatment, but that then in not giving treatment it then becomes an even larger plot to make me go blind, in this case results in my not being able to identify who really did this.

It just becomes elaborated into a much larger scheme starting with merely this small issue and it gets fed into the rest of the delusional belief system, which now also includes everybody involved in the judicial process, the attorneys, the A.D.A., the Court, so forth.

Q [Mr. Kuby then reads excerpts from another letter written by Ferguson which states] "Based on recent conversations of Mr. Kuby and Mr. Kunstler, together with limited source information I have received, it is clear that not only have Mr. Kunstler and Mr. Kuby conspired with attorneys for the jail, district attorney's office and the Court to cover up the true condition of my eyes, but have carefully railroaded the matter into the racist hands of Judge Belfi, whereby a ruling can be made that nothing is wrong with my eyes."

What does that say with respect to his delusional disorder?

A I would say it lends further support to what I have been saying. And, again, now it becomes further elaborated to also include the judge.[728]

---

728. *See* Ferguson Pretrial Hearing Transcripts, December 6, 1994 at 58–60.

...

Letters supplementing Dr. Dudley's testimony advance the broad sweeping conspiracy theory held by Mr. Ferguson. The sum and substance of Ferguson's conspiracy indicates a complex web of deceit incorporating all parties into a large scheme to destroy him. In one letter directed to the court Ferguson explains the conspiracy and further describes the relation between the assault, Kunstler and Kuby, and the correctional officers at the jail.

Q [Mr. Kuby reads the letter by Ferguson stating:] "I have learned today, Saturday, October 8th 1994, that my present attorneys, Mr. Kunstler and Mr. Kuby, have arranged with officials of the jail to use Lieutenant Santini, shield number 33, and Officer Banschbach, badge 776 to murder me here at the jail.
I am also advised that Mr. Kunstler and Mr. Kuby have arranged with Officer Banschbach [correctional officer]...to allow at least one of my attackers to gain access to my cell area to threaten and abuse me."
What does that say about delusional disorder?

A Well, as I indicated, what happens here, and in this series of letters, is pretty consistent with what happens over time and with the experience that it starts off small and the risk of harm, the threats of harm, the concerns continue to escalate over time, and it is almost predictable based on past experiences that this particular series of letters and concerns about the attorneys the A.D.A., the court system, etc., would eventually get to the point of feeling that it was a life-threatening experience, which is what is certainly indicated in this letter, that his life has been threatened.

In yet another letter, Mr. Ferguson further advances his theory:

Q [Mr. Kuby refers to the letter written by Ferguson on October 11th 1994, which reads:] "I am told that my attorneys Mr. Kunstler and Mr. Kuby are using these officers to break me before trial. This I am told is arranged by Mr. Kunstler and Mr. Kuby in response to my rejecting the so-called 'black rage' insanity defense, them both as my attorneys, and any form of insanity defense.
They have conspired with these officers to murder me after they withdraw from my case. I am also told that my attorneys, Mr.

Kunstler and Mr. Kuby, are sabotaging my case and telling the jail to remove legal documents from my cell."

What does that say about the nature of his delusions as of October 8th or October 11th 1994?

A It says that he is certainly still holding onto the same belief system, and that it has not resolved at all regardless of what has happened.

It also would suggest that just as he begins to state his intent that he will continue to hold onto these beliefs, dispite [sic] outcomes and dispite [sic] how he may be damaged by them, and that the beliefs are essentially at their core consistent over time that everyone is out to harm him.

Q A person in that mental state and possessed of those delusions, is Mr. Ferguson capable of understanding and evaluating rationally what is good for him and what isn't?

MR PECK: Objection.

THE COURT: Overruled.

It does go to the question of competency.

Q To a reasonable degree of medical certainty?

A I believe he is unable to do that because it requires being able to be clear about what situation you are in. And when you have a belief system that tells you that the situation you're in is really part of this large, overwhelming conspiracy against you where everybody is participating in that puts you in a context in which is this belief system, that really interferes with him being able to clearly even understand the context of which he has to make decisions.

And then you add to that the fact that reasonable options that may be available to him also are perceived as part of this same sort of conspiracy and are excluded without even real consideration because of their perceived threat to him.

So you have a context in which decisions are being made that is going to interfere with the decision-making process and you have a thought process that is going to result in the exclusion of options because of the perception of them as part of a plot against you.[729]

---

729. *See Id.* at 61–64.

(b) Cross Examination by Assistant District Attorney Richard Peck

The cross-examination conducted by Assistant District Attorney Peck questioned Dr. Dudley on several issues.[730] Mr. Peck probed Dr. Dudley on materials used to reach the CST finding. Mr. Peck stressed that Dr. Dudley reached a conclusion without speaking to the witnesses on the train, the investigating detective on the case, or Drs. D'Alessandro and Reichman. In other words, Mr. Peck suggested facts relative to the crime were based on information supplied exclusively by defense counsel.

Q Now, when you went in to the examination room the first time you examined Mr. Ferguson, what factual background did you have? What data pertaining to the factual background did you have?

A I believe, I had, as I indicated, some letters that he had written. I believe I was aware of—I know I was aware of the basic facts of the case.

Q From what source?

A Well, Mr. Kunstler and Mr. Kuby gave me the facts. As I indicated I had been contacted by an attorney [Mr. Falanga, Ferguson's first attorney] prior to that that also give [sic] me basic facts.

Q In other words, you got the facts of the case from an attorney?

A Yes.

Q Did you accept those facts to be the truth?

A Yes.

Q You never spoke to a witness on this case, did you?

A No, I didn't.

Q You never spoke to the investigating detective on this case, did you?

A I only read some of the materials, I believe, but I never spoke to an investigator, no.

Q You never spoke to anybody on the train, did you?

A No, I did not.

Q You didn't call Dr. D'Alessandro who did the 730 Examination [competency evaluation], did you, and ask him his impressions?

---

730. *See* Ferguson Pretrial Hearing Transcripts December 6, 1994 at 65–107 (Dr. Dudley-cross examination/Peck).

A I only read the report for the 730.

Q You didn't call Dr. Reichman either; isn't that correct?

A That's correct.[731]

Next, Mr. Peck considered the purpose of Dr. Dudley's examination and explored the idea that Dr. Dudley was assessing both the issue of competency and responsibility.

Q Now, based upon your conversation with Mr. Kunstler and Mr. Kuby there was a purpose; was there not, to your initial examination?

A Yes?

Q That purpose centered around the issue of criminal responsibility; did it not?

A Well, my understanding was that it was a more step-wise purpose than that.

Q Did it center around the issue of criminal responsibility?

A It centered around, number one, whether Mr. Ferguson suffered from any mental disorder or not; and number two, if in fact he did suffer from some sort of mental disorder would that disorder have impacted on his behavior in some sort of way in '93, in December 1993 [referring to the shooting incident], and does it impact on his behavior now.

Q Basically are you saying then that you were concentrating at the time both on a 730 Examination as to his competency, in addition to an examination as to his responsibility at the time?

A Well, at the time of the first evaluation?

Q Yes.

A I was attempting to get some sort of sense as to whether he was suffering from some mental disorder, whereas I suggested to you that my intent was to go back. So my main goal at the time was to determine whether there was a psychiatric disorder or not.

Q That's not exactly the question I'm trying to pose to you. I'm asking you: Were you looking into the area of responsibility or were you looking into the area of competency? That is my question.

A And my answer is that I was first looking into the area as to whether there was a psychiatric disorder and if so did it influence his behavior as it related to responsibility as well as competency.

---

731. *See Id.* at 72–74.

Q Did you, based upon your first examination, diagnosis him as having a psychiatric disorder?

A Based on my May 17th evaluation of him I had suspicions that— pretty strong suspicions—that he had a psychiatric disorder.

Q But it certainly didn't ripen into an opinion with a reasonable degree of medical certainty, did it?

A Alone?

Q Yes.

A Not alone.[732]

Turning to the purpose of the scheduled follow-up meeting (refused by Ferguson), Mr. Peck posed a series of questions involving mental disorders. Mr. Peck underscored the importance of the second examination with respect to reaching a competency determination. On this point, Mr Peck raised concerns that Dr. Dudley based his clinical opinions (diagnosis and CST findings) on the single visit occurring on May 17, 1994.

Q Now, what was the purpose of the your second scheduled examination, which wasn't completed?

A The purpose of the second scheduled evaluation was to continue with the evaluation process. There were some things that we covered that I wanted to talk with him about in more depth, and I was hoping to have an opportunity to do that.

...

Q Well, you wanted more information, didn't you?

A Yes. I indicated there were some questions that I have. I can share those questions with you.

Q Well, you did want a whole lot more information; isn't that correct?

A I'm not sure whether I would characterize it as a whole lot more. I wanted more information.

Q Well, it's important, is it not, in the first instance, to see if someone, as a result of mental disease or defect, either non-responsible or incapacitated, it is important, is it not, for you to know something about the crime, the alleged crime, and something as to whether or not or how the defendant recollects that crime; is it not? Isn't that important for you?

---

732. *See Id.* at 74–76.

A That's important.

Q You didn't have any of that information, did you?

A In what sense?

Q When you wrote the report what information did you have in that regard?

A As I indicated, I had a description of—just a description of the event, and some notes from the investigators, and I had spoken with Mr. Ferguson about it.

Q And he told you that he didn't remember, right?

A That's correct.

Q Did you assume that to be the truth?

A Could or could not have been the truth.

Q I didn't ask you that. I asked you if you assumed it to the truth.

A I made no conclusions about that.[733]

Following this exchange, Mr. Peck questions the purpose of the CST visit as perceived by Mr. Ferguson. Mr. Peck suggests that Dr. Dudley met and examined Mr. Ferguson under false pretenses— Mr. Ferguson believed the defense psychiatrist was the eye specialist for whom he had requested a consult. On this issue, Dr. Dudley explains that Mr. Ferguson had motivations for cooperating with the CST review. The cross examination emphasizes the doctor did not discuss the CST issue with Ferguson or potential outcomes pursuant to a CST evaluation and subsequent findings (e.g., what would happen if found incompetent or not guilty only by reason of insanity). In addition, Mr. Peck stresses the importance of the second exam which Ferguson refused, making a complete exam impossible.

Q Now, what did you tell him, meaning Mr. Ferguson, was the purpose of the examination, if you told him anything?

A I told him that I had been asked by his attorneys to meet with him and to do an evaluation of him...I told him we would be reviewing his history and talking about him over time.

Q And he agreed to talk to you?

A He talked to me the first time, yes.

Q But he told you something else about that, didn't he? He told you that he thought you were there because he wanted you to help

---

733. See Id. at 76–80.

him get some type of better treatment; isn't that correct? You didn't put that in your report, did you?

A I believe what I put in my report was that he was willing to speak with me because he knew I was in fact a physician and that I may be able to help him get some better care.

THE DEFENDANT: Very good.

Q So were you telling then Mr. Ferguson an untruth as to your purpose?

A I think I was suggesting by my report that he had motivations. His motivation . . . for cooperating with me, at least at that time, was in part related to the concern about his physical health.

Q And he basically talked to you with that parameter in mind; isn't that correct?

A No, I didn't say that.

Q Well, let me ask you this: Did you ever discuss with him as to what would happen to him if he were found to be incapacitated or not competent? Did you ever discuss with him that?

A Legally, no.

Q Did you ever discuss with him what would happen to him if he went to trial and were [sic] found not guilty by being absolved of criminal responsibility? Did you ever discuss that with him?

A No, I did not.

Q It was basically then part of the first meeting which you had with him fully expecting to have more meetings once you got background information; isn't that correct?

A I would say it is accurate to say that it was the first meeting with him, I think it's accurate to say that I fully expected that I would be able to see him again.[734]

Next, Mr. Peck poses a series of question involving the materials and information used to inform Dr. Dudley's CST opinion. On this point, Mr. Peck emphasizes the doctor's CST opinion is informed, principally, through Ferguson's background; that is, information before the shooting (e.g., social and occupational difficulties, Workman's Compensation case, and Adelphi University records). Mr. Peck stresses that Dr. Dudley failed to review hearing transcripts concerning a colloquia between the defendant and Judge Belfi oc-

---

734. *See Id.* at 80–82.

curring on November 10, 1994 (Ferguson deemed competent), or records on A.D.A. Riordan's conversation with Ferguson involving the jail house assault. Clearly, Mr. Peck emphasizes the importance of information subsequent to December 7th 1993. The cross examination is designed to refresh the Court's memory that Ferguson understands legal procedure evidenced by statements made to Judge Belfi as well as comments directed to the A.D.A. supervising and prosecuting the jail house assault.

Q You relied on Adelphi college records, right?
A Yes.
Q That happened years before the December 7th [event]; isn't that correct?
A That's correct.
Q You relied on Workman's Compensation records, correct?
A That's correct.
Q That happened months and years prior to the incident; is that correct?
A That's correct.
Q You relied on Adelphi college records which had reference to things happening years before the incident; isn't that correct?
A That's correct.
Q You actually made a phone call to his [Mr. Ferguson's] former boss or co-worker in California and you had a conversation with him; isn't that correct?
A That's correct.
Q But the substance of the conversation that you had with him [Ferguson] pertained to data that happened prior to December 7th; isn't that correct?
A That's correct.[735]

. . .

Q Has [the defense] provided you with the transcript of a proceeding wherein this judge asked Mr. Ferguson certain questions about the indictment and his lawyers, and of things pertaining to his competency, and during that proceeding this judge found him competent? Has Mr. Kunstler or Mr. Kuby ever provided with you that?

---

735. *See Id.* at 83.

A That transcript, no.

Q That would be important to you, right? Wouldn't that be important to you?

A It depends on what is in it really.

Q So it is important only depending upon the contents...Has Mr. Kunstler or Mr. Kuby ever presented to you a memorandum which was given to them by me concerning a conversation that an assistant district attorney had with Colin Ferguson pertaining to his jail house assault?

A I don't believe so.[736]

In addition, Mr. Peck discusses issues regarding Ferguson' memory, statements made to detectives following his arrest, and Ferguson's decisions concerning the gun. On the latter point, Mr. Peck suggests Ferguson considers the difference between right and wrong (i.e., understands the gun is legal in California but illegal in New York and makes the decision to discard the gun) and, thus, demonstrates behavior inconsistent with delusional disorder. The cross examination, once again, stresses inconsistent behavior by Ferguson, designed to support the theory of malingering.

Q Now, Dr, Dudley, it is important, is it not, if someone wants to assist in his defense to be able to relate that which occurred at or about the time the incident occurred? Isn't that correct?

A I believe so.

Q Now the first time you examined Colin Ferguson he told you that he didn't remember anything about December 7th; Isn't that correct?

A Yes.

Q That he said he didn't remember?

A That he said he didn't remember.

Q Did you consider him amnesic at that time?

A I think as I indicated I hadn't drawn a conclusion about that.

Q Well, do you have a conclusion now?

A No, I don't.

Q You had the notes of the detectives; isn't that correct?

A That's correct.

---

736. *See Id.* at 84–85.

Q You were aware, based upon those notes, that Mr. Ferguson said certain things to the detectives; isn't that correct?

A That's correct.

Q Did you ever ask him [Mr. Ferguson] about the notes, both his and the detectives'?

A Not on that visit, no.

Q You expected to do that on the next visit; isn't that correct?

A That's correct.

Q That was very, very important for you to know what his recollection was about the crime; isn't that correct?

A Or whether he would have changed his story or not, yes.

Q …He told you that he bought the gun in California; isn't that correct?

A That's correct.

Q And that it was legal in California, he told you that, correct?

A That he legally purchased it, that's what he said.

Q And then he had to come back to the State of New York for some reason or another and then realized that the gun was illegally possessed in New York and he made plans to dispose of it; isn't that correct?

A That's not what he said to me.

Q What about Coney Island; didn't he tell you he wanted to dump it in the ocean in Coney Island?

A Yes, he did tell me.

Q Why did he tell you he wanted to dump it in the ocean?

A He didn't say he was aware it was illegal.
That's what I'm saying, he didn't say that to me.

Q Didn't he say to you that he finally realized that he would have to stay in New York for a while? He said he took the gun and ammunition that he purchased from the bag that he always stored them in and put them in another bag with the plan of throwing the bag in the ocean at Coney Island? Didn't he say that to you?

A Yes.

Q Basically, then, at least with regard to the gun, he had general concepts of right and wrong; isn't that correct?

A I don't know.

Q You don't know?
Did you ask him why he was disposing the gun in the ocean, why he wanted to do that?

A I didn't ask him that.

Q Why not?

A I hoped to go into that when I saw him the second time.

Q You thought that would be important the second time?

A Why he was disposing the gun?

Q Yes?

A I think that would be an additional piece of important information, of course, yes.

Q In giving—by the way, amnesia is not part of the criteria of delusional disorder, is it?

A Amnesia?

Q Yes.

A No.

Q Because if someone has a true delusion he believes that to be true, right?

A The delusion, yes.

Q ...If someone has a true delusional disorder he doesn't think what he is doing is wrong, does he?

A Well, I would say if someone has a true delusional disorder that they are doing what they feel they have to do.[737]

Other noteworthy exchanges between Mr. Peck and Dr. Dudley concern Ferguson's relationship with his attorneys, and whether Ferguson's distrust was, arguably, based in reality rather than delusions. Mr. Peck argued Ferguson had legitimate reasons to distrust Kunstler and Kuby. During this exchange, defense counsel objected to this line of questioning. In response, Dr. Dudley suggested that Ferguson's distrust was in fact a product of his mental impairment.

Q ...You are under the present impression, are you not, that he [Mr. Ferguson] really doesn't like Mr. Kunstler and Mr. Kuby? Is that not true?

A I don't know that I would use those words.

Q What words would you use?

A I would say that I am under the impression that he really doesn't trust Mr. Kunstler and Mr. Kuby.[738]

...

---

737. *See Id.* at 86–90.
738. *See Id.* at 90–91.

Q Did he ever tell you that he really didn't trust Mr. Kunstler and Mr. Kuby because whatever he told them in a seemingly confidential relationship between attorney and client was disseminated through the media to the world at large which he read? Did you ever discuss that with him?

A Well, we discussed his relationship with Mr. Kunstler and Mr. Kuby. He didn't say that to me however.[739]

...

Q Haven't you read the letters [written by Ferguson to Judge Belfi]? ... [I]sn't he asking this judge to put a restraining order on Mr. Kunstler and Mr. Kuby?

MR. KUBY: Judge, excuse me. I object to two things: one, I object to histrionics; and the second thing I object to is at the time of the meeting he [Mr. Ferguson] hadn't written the letter. The letters hadn't been written yet.

THE COURT: Sustained to the extent not as to the histrionics, but as to the tone that the district attorney is asking the witness.

A I'm reading them now. I hadn't read them obviously at the time.

Q So his distrust could have a basis in reality; is it not true? The basis in reality being the dissemination of a purported confidential relationship between attorney and client?

A A couple of things in response to that: at the time that I met him [Mr. Ferguson], there was already a beginning sense of distrust. He presented at that time [that is, Ferguson's opinions about Kunstler and Kuby were] based on really how much time they were spending with him, what was their commitment to him, etc., and as I indicated, these letters that came later, but the larger issue, of course, is what I attempted to explain earlier which is that this is in fact characteristic of this disorder, and that individuals take things that are in fact experiences that they have and they then become incorporated into it. And it is in fact characteristic of the disorder.[740]

At this critical juncture, Mr. Peck attempts to derail Dr. Dudley on issues relating to paranoid personality disorder, differential diagnosis, and definitions as reported in the *DSM-IIIR* and the *DSM-IV*.

---

739. *See Id.* at 91.
740. *See Id.* at 92–93.

Q Did...Mr. Ferguson ever tell you that he did not want to proceed with the defense surrounding criminal responsibility?

A No.

Q Now, did you say in your testimony that you discounted the diagnosis of paranoid personality disorder?

A I don't believe I said I discounted one. Certainly I considered it in the differential diagnosis.

Q What does that mean?

A That means that as I began to gather information and in the process of thinking through the information that I was gathering I considered a series of disorders.

Q Are you saying that at no time Mr. Ferguson had the symptoms of paranoid personality disorder?

A Say that once more, please.

Q Are you saying that at no time Mr. Ferguson had the symptoms of paranoid personality disorder?

A No, I'm not saying that.

Q So the answer is no?

A The answer is—

Q The answer is no to that question?

A That at no time—could you repeat that?

Q Did he ever have the symptoms of a paranoid personality disorder?

A I don't know.

Q By the way, you quoted from the DSM-IV; did you not?

A Yes I did.

Q Do you recall the definition of a delusion?

A As is in the DSM-IV?

Q Yes.

A I haven't really looked at that.

Q You haven't looked at that?

A In the glossary of terms, no.

Q In other words, you have diagnosed someone as having a delusional disorder and you don't know what the definition of a delusion is?

A I didn't say that.

Q What is it to your understanding?

A To my understanding a delusion is a fixed false belief that a person holds onto and continues to believe despite irrefutable evidence to the contrary.

Q Did they give you a caveat, a warning in the definition of delusion in the DSM-IV?

A Again, as I indicated, I haven't read the glossary of DSM-IV, but certainly in the diagnosis, in the series of diagnoses which are characterized by paranoid thinking of one sort of another, it always refers you back to the other disorders that have similar symptomology for that differential diagnostic purpose. But I haven't read the glossary of terms.

Q DSM-IV is of recent vintage?

A Yes.

Q Are you saying that you never read the glossary concerning the definition of a delusion? Is that what you are saying?

A I'm saying certainly I read definitions of delusions and trained and taught about delusions throughout my psychiatric career. When the DSM-IV came out this year I did not sit down and read the glossary.

Q But you referred to the DSM-IV diagnosis; did you not?

A Yes.

Q And you didn't check back to see what a definition of a delusion was?

A It certainly never occurred to me that they changed the definition of a delusion.[741]

In the next set of questions, Mr. Peck spends some time quizzing Dr. Dudley on the issue of malingering and specifically the association between lying, malingering, and delusional disorder. Dr. Dudley dismisses the idea of malingering suggesting lying is a product of his delusions.

Q Now, you were aware, were you not, that Drs. Reichman and D'Alessandro found him [Mr. Ferguson] to be malingering; isn't that correct?

A Am I aware of that?

Q Yes.

A Yes, I'm aware of that.

Q That was their diagnosis and that was their report with regard to the 730 Examination [competency evaluation]; isn't that correct?

A That's correct.

---

741. *See Id.* at 95–98.

Q And in considering whether or not someone is malingering it is important, is it not, to know whether or not they are telling the truth as to their memory as to what happened on December 7th [day of shooting]; isn't that correct?

A I would say it is correct depending on the circumstances.

Q For malingering?

A May I explain?

Q You believe it depends upon the circumstances? In other words, a person can be lying about the events of the crime and he could still be malingering? He could be lying about the events of the crime and that wouldn't have a bearing on the issue of whether or not he was malingering?

A He could by lying about the events of the crime for other purposes other than malingering, yes.

Q Like what?

A Well, if you're suffering from a paranoid delusional disorder and you think that the people you're talking to are part of that system you may choose to lie to them as part of that.

Q Or that could be a means for just not telling the truth; isn't that correct?

A Pardon?

Q It could be simply a lie because he didn't want to make evidence for himself; isn't that correct?

A He could be lying for a variety of reasons.

Q Therefore, it is important, is it not, for anyone to make proper diagnoses to know whether or not someone related the events accurately immediately after the crime; isn't that correct?

A Well, it's important to try to figure out that in relationship to how they remember the events as you speak to them.[742]

. . .

Q It's important to a psychiatrist to know what a defendant said shortly after the crime pertaining to the incident?

A That's correct.

Q It's very important; is it not?

A Yes.

Q It determines whether or not if he has such a memory, whether or not he can assist in his defense; isn't that correct?

---

742. *See Id.* at 101–103.

A What they do with that information becomes important in making that conclusion [whether one can assist in the defense], yes.

Q It's certainly important to determine whether or not if in fact a defendant said something different later on, whether or not he is malingering at a later time; isn't that true?

A Certainly.[743]

...

Q By the way, when did you come to your opinion in this particular case? On what date?

A I don't remember on what date.

Q Would looking at your report refresh your recollection?

A I don't believe so.

Q Well, can you put it in some sequence as to when you came to your opinion, what month?

A Well, I would say that after I met with Mr. Ferguson the first time and then went back a couple of days later and read my notes and had the interview with him that I felt that he was, I felt, he seemed to be talking about [that] what he was presenting were delusions, and as I read the records, as they became available to me, the chronicity of the disorder — this is a chronic disorder as opposed to schizophrenia, which is more facadic in nature — and the absence of non-delusion specific dysfunctions that were reflected in the record, and the kind of repeated pattern of acting on it, then I became more certain. And so I would say that was by the time I read all of this material it was towards probably the beginning of the fall.[744]

Finally, Mr. Peck queries Dr. Dudley on whether collateral information impacted his final analysis. This line of questioning, once again, raises concerns that Dr. Dudley based his opinion on the single visit occurring on May 17, 1994, without considering other psychiatric opinions or factual information (i.e., conversation between Ferguson and A.D.A. Riordan). In this exchange, the cross examination suggests Dr. Dudley's CST finding was based on limited evaluative data.

Q Did you find it necessary to do other things after the beginning of October in order to finalize your report?

---

743. See Id. at 103–104.
744. See Id. at 105.

A I think it was after that time that I spoke with Mr. Kuby and Dr. Makapela [professor at Adelphi University].

Q Now, at any time — by the way, you acknowledged on your direct examination that you really have incomplete facts in this case; isn't that correct?

A I don't know everything that I would like to know.

Q And if the facts change or are determined to be untrue then your opinion can change; isn't that right?

A Well, certainly if all of the facts I based my opinion on were not true that would affect my opinion, yes, of course.

Q ... If you find that you had additional facts of which were important to you that you didn't have that could impact on your opinion; isn't that true?

A Well, if you're using "impact" in the broadest sense of the word, in the sense it may augment, supplement, change in a variety of different ways.

Q Just one last question, doctor. Referring to People's Exhibit 1 for identification [record concerning jail house assault], is it your testimony that you neither saw that exhibit for identification nor used it in any way in your evaluation of the defendant.

A That's my testimony.

Q And that is, to your knowledge, a report of Assistant District Attorney Riordan acknowledged by Mr. Kuby, acknowledged as being received by Mr. Kuby on September 20th?

A That's what it says here, yes.[745]

(c) The People call Dr. John D'Alessandro Direct Examination by Mr. Peck

Following the arrest of Colin Ferguson in connection with the Long Island Rail Road shooting, Judge Belfi ordered an initial psychiatric examination under NYCPL Section 730.30. As mentioned elsewhere, 730 examinations are used to determine whether or not a defendant is or is not an incapacitated person and as a product of impaired mental status is (in)competent to stand trial. Thus, Section 730.10 of New York's Criminal Procedure Law sets forth the standard for trial (in)competency in New York. The rule states, an

---

745. See Id. 106–107.

"[i]ncapacitated person means a defendant, who as a result of mental disease or defect, is substantially impaired in his or her ability to understand the nature of the proceeding against him/her or to assist in his/her own defense."[746] Following Judge Belfi's court order, the 730 examination was conducted on December 28, 1993. Mr. Ferguson rejected all forms of follow-up exams, therefore the prosecution relied on the 730 evaluation to determine whether Ferguson was competent to stand trial.[747] The two physicians (Drs. D'Alessandro and Reichman) testified that although Ferguson (perhaps) suffered from paranoid personality disorder, the defendant, Ferguson, was malingering and concluded that he was rational and did not experience delusions.[748]

Dr. D'Alessandro (one of the two psychiatrists appointed by the court to evaluate Ferguson on December 28, 1993) was the first to testify on behalf of the people. Key excerpts involving the evaluation methods, preliminary findings, and information reviewed are provided in the following pages.[749]

Q Is there a specific methodology used for 730 Examinations?
A Yes, there is.
Q Would you explain that, please?
A There is a certain set of specific questions that is relevant to ask the individual to ascertain whether they are able to proceed in their court hearing based on whether there is no interference by any mental illness or mental defect.

---

746. See N.Y. CRIM. PROC. LAW § 730.10 (McKinney's 1994).
747. See Ferguson Pretrial Hearing Transcripts, December 7, 1994 at 173. Considering he was unable to meet with Ferguson he based his report on secondary information, and conversations with various witnesses. Dr. D'Alessandro relied on these other sources to supplement his original findings following the 730 examination. See Id. at 174–176. Dr. D'Alessandro reviewed court proceeding observing Ferguson's behavior and statements made to the court, met with various individuals (investigating detectives, jail physicians, correctional officials and officers, detectives on the scene and those who conducted the custodial interrogation), read several letters Ferguson wrote to the Judge Belfi, and reviewed the report written by Dr. Dudley. See Id. This exam is replete with examples of assessment methods lacking structure and subjective bias. These problems will be addressed infra.
748. See R. Toppings, Psychologist: Ferguson's Competency a Fine Line. NEWSDAY, Feb. 5, 1995 at A43.[hereinafter Toppings I].
749. See Ferguson Pretrial Hearing Transcripts, December 7, 1994 at 169–212 (Dr. D'Alessandro-direct examination/Peck)

The specific criteria that is necessary is that the individual is aware of the charges that are made against him; that he recognizes the seriousness or perhaps the lack of seriousness of those charges; knows some of the legal terminology, such as whether these charges are misdemeanors or felonies.

Another important criteria is whether this individual's mental status at that time is based in reality, are they well oriented to time, place and person. Can this individual cooperate with an attorney. Does this individual know their attorney. Do they have a plan...to defend themselves. And can they cooperate with that attorney.

Additionally it is important that the individual is aware of the major roles of the figures within a court and can behave himself appropriately within a court setting. For example, does this individual know the role of the judge, the district attorney or prosecuting attorney; does he know the role of the defense attorney; does he know who the defendant is; does he understand...basic simple concepts, such as what does plea bargaining means [sic]. So, in essence if an individual is able to accurately explain these various procedures and has an understanding of the charges that it is felt that he is capable of proceeding.[750]

Q ...Dr. D'Alessandro, did you conduct, pursuant to court order, a 730 Examination of Colin Ferguson, the defendant in this particular case?

A Yes, I did.

Q Were you assisted by anyone?

A 730 evaluations are performed by either two psychiatrists, two psychologists or a psychiatrist and psychologist. And I performed this evaluation with our medical director Dr. Allen Reichman.

Q Dr. D'Alessandro, when did you conduct this examination?

A We conducted this examination on December 28th 1993.

Q ...Dr. D'Alessandro, based upon that examination did you form an opinion within a reasonable degree of certainty in your field of expertise as to whether or not at that time Colin Ferguson was or was not an incapacitated person?

A I felt at that time that he was not an incapacitated person.

---

750. *See Id.* at 170–172.

Q ...Now, Dr. D'Alessandro, since the December 28th examination...did you try to effectuate through Howard Sovronsky [mental health supervisor in the jail] another 730 Examination of Mr. Ferguson?

A Yes, sir.

Q Was that possible?

A No, sir.

Q Can you explain the reasons why?

A Mr. Sovronsky met with Mr. Ferguson and he refused to participate in another 730 evaluation.

Q That was in the month of August?

A I believe so, sir.

Q Now, Dr. D'Alessandro, do you have a present opinion as to whether or not at this time, right now, Mr. Ferguson is or is not an incapacitated person?

A Absolutely.

Q What is that present opinion?

A My present opinion is that he is not an incapacitated person.

Q Now, Dr. D'Alessandro, since you examined him on the 28th day of December 1993 had you had the occasion to review any mental health records of your department.

A Yes, sir.

Q Have you had the occasion in connection with your opinion here today to review prior proceedings in this case wherein Mr. Ferguson said certain things?

A Yes, I did, sir.

Q Have you had the occasion also to speak to Maureen Riordan about her conversations [she] had with Mr. Ferguson?

A Yes, sir.

Q Have you had the occasion to speak to Dr. Kashimawo, the jail physician, [overseeing Ferguson's medical care] concerning his observations and opinions of Ferguson?

A Yes, I have had that opportunity.

Q Have you had the occasion to read certain letters...that Mr. Ferguson has written to this particular Court?

A Yes.

Q Have you had the occasion to go over in detail with two investigating detectives the content of the conversation that they had with Mr. Ferguson commencing at 7 p.m. on December 7th 1993 [night of the shooting].

A Yes, sir.

Q Is there anything that you recollect at this particular time that you additionally looked at in giving your opinion today?

A I also had a conversation with Lieutenant Anderson from the Nassau County jail. It is Lieutenant Anderson's job to be the liaison between the administration and the jail and Mr. Ferguson, and he has met with Mr. Ferguson on a weekly basis since December 1993.

I also had the opportunity of speaking with Detective Dan Daly...and Detective Abbondandelo, who were the detectives who did the evaluation at 7 o'clock that evening of the incident.

I also spoke with Detective Brian Parpan who was a detective on the scene.

Q In addition, did you review the report of Dr. Richard Dudley?

A Yes, I did, sir.

Q In addition, were you present in court yesterday [December 6th 1994 to observe] Mr. Ferguson exhibit certain forms of behavior with regard to questions and what was going on in court yesterday?

A Yes, I did.

Q Now, Dr. D'Alessandro, you testified that your opinion was that he [Mr. Ferguson] was not an incapacitated person as of December 28th; is that correct?

A That is correct.

Q You testified that it is your opinion within a reasonable degree of medical certainty that he is not an incapacitated person as of today; isn't that correct?

A That is correct.[751]

Next, Dr. D'Alessandro explains the rationale for his findings. Relying on inconsistent statements and behavior evinced by Ferguson in the courtroom, Dr. D'Alessandro suggests Mr. Ferguson is malingering to be found incompetent to stand trial. The following experts recite, in detail, inconsistencies (used to support Dr. D'Alessandro's medical opinion) as reported in the record.

Q Now, in detail, as much detail as you can, Dr. D'Alessandro, can you state the reasons for your opinion?

---

751. *See Id.* at 170–177.

A Yes I can.

Q Would you do so.

A The reasons why I feel this way initiated at the 730 evaluation where Mr. Ferguson behaved in a manner which was inconsistent with an incapacitated person, and led myself and Dr. Reichman to the conclusion —

MR. KUNSTLER: Your Honor, I'm going to object to Dr. Reichman.

THE COURT: Sustained. Strike that.

A — that led myself to the conclusion that Mr. Ferguson at that time was malingering, or in my opinion faking responses, exaggerating his emotional state to the pathological degree, in a way that he was doing it for a specific purpose to mislead the evaluators at that time.

There are several reasons why I came to this conclusion, one of which was his inconsistent behavior patterns throughout the evaluation, and an excessive amount of inconsistent statements and, in fact, lies that were made during the evaluation. And when confronted with these inconsistencies Mr. Ferguson would not respond.

The first inconsistency is that he did not know the specific date of the evaluation. He was then asked the month and did recognize that it was December. However, I then asked him if it was before Christmas or after Christmas. He stated that he did not know.

However, within a five-minute period, as part of his pattern of making numerous complaints about the officials at the jail, he made the statement that the guards at the jail did not give him his Christmas dinner and he was quite upset that he felt that he deserved to have a special Christmas dinner on Christmas. When he was confronted with the fact that he said he did not know whether it was before or after Christmas he put his head down.

Another inconsistency was when he was asked where he was currently being seen, and he indicated that this was at the Nassau County Police Headquarters. He was told [sic] that the policemen had been abusive to him and slapped him. However, when asked who the officials were around him he indicated them correctly as Nassau County Correction Officers, and not policemen.

Another inconsistency was in describing how he received an injury in his Workman's Compensation case. He first described that it was accidental; that he slipped off of a bench. However, within three or four minutes [Ferguson] gave a different story that there was in fact a conspiracy against him and it was purposeful against him.

Mr. Ferguson throughout the evaluation would not answer any specific questions regarding the Long Island Rail Road incident. At one point he did admit to being [on] a train. However, [Ferguson] indicated that no charges were ever made against him regarding this train ride; that... any current charges against him related to Adelphi University and the difficulties he had at that facility.

When we asked Mr. Ferguson specifically about certain legal issues, such as the charges and whether they were misdemeanors or felonies, he stated quote "I know nothing about the law." End quote.

In addition... I read the charges to Mr. Ferguson. He would not respond to them. And as part of the charges was the word "murder." I specifically asked him if he was familiar with the word "murder." He indicated that quote "I don't want to know what it means." He refused to define the word, and once again stated quote "I don't care about that word."

So throughout that evaluation he refused to relate to any aspect of the railroad incident. However, when we wished to address an issue, such as his complaint with Adelphi University or complaints about guards, he was extremely articulate and able to present his position in a concise and intelligent manner, and this presented an inconsistency.[752]

Dr. D'Alessandro continues to present observations stemming from the interview. Next, the doctor explains Ferguson's relationship with attorneys. Addressing issues of trust and the ability to assist counsel, Dr. D'Alessandro describes the defendant's interactions with Mr. Falanga and Mr. Moore—the attorneys who first worked on the case as of December 28, 1993. The following testimony intimates a negative relationship between Ferguson and Falanga but more importantly describes a positive relationship between Ferguson and Mr. Moore. On this point, the expert's opinion suggests that although Ferguson is often suspicious of attorneys, he has

---

752. *See Id.* at 177–180.

trusted counsel in the past. This presentation is designed to suggest Ferguson is able work with attorneys, and, therefore, is able to assist in the defense.

A We also discussed his attorney. At that point it was a Mr. Falanga.

Mr. Ferguson had some difficulties with Mr. Falanga and he wanted Mr. Falanga off the case. He felt that this attorney was just interested in writing a book and getting some notoriety.

However, he had developed a relationship with an attorney by the name of Colin Moore. Mr. Ferguson was quite pleased with Mr. Moore. He frequently, throughout the evaluation, referred to Mr. Moore as his attorney. He stated that Mr. Moore should be answering these questions for him.

He made it very clear that he trusted Mr. Moore, wanted to cooperate with Mr. Moore, and felt quite comfortable and confident with Mr. Moore as his counsel. In fact, at one point he indicated that Mr. Moore was the only individual that he felt any trust for.

As the evaluation went on we also asked him areas such as competency. And we asked him if he was aware what would occur if he was found to be not competent. And he indicated quote "the attorneys won't get paid" end quote.[753]

Continuing the summary, Dr. D'Alessandro describes the assessment method employed during the examination. Although designed to test for malingering or physiological impairment, Dr. D'Alessandro relied on the instrument to supplement his findings on the issue of competency. The structure of the instrument is presented followed by Ferguson's responses and Dr. D'Alessandro clinical findings.

A As the evaluation became continued [sic] I became more and more convinced that Mr. Ferguson was not going to cooperate; was withholding information; was purposefully malingering and trying to present himself in an inappropriate manner.

As a result I decided to present a common psychological tool that is utilized with individuals to help determine whether they are malingering or not.

---

753. *See Id.* at 180–181.

The procedure you utilize is to explain to the individual that perhaps that he is not responding appropriately or could not give adequate representation because he has some memory deficit, and if that is the case we would like to have him participate in a tested procedure to document how much of a memory deficit may be existence [sic].

It is explained to him that it is a rather difficult test, that I would be presenting twenty figures to him, various and different symbols and numbers and letters, and that we would give him as much time as he needed to study this and we would then ask him to reproduce this.

The theory behind this, the acceptable psychological procedure, is that the test is presented in such simplistic form that any individual who could not memorize these twenty figures in thirty seconds would be either organically impaired or profoundly retarded.

Q What are the these twenty figures? I don't think you testified to that. And then proceed.

A The twenty figures are numbers in Arabic form listed one, two, three, four. Under that in capital letters are A, B, C, and D. Under that in Roman numerals are one, two, three and four. And under that in lower case letters is written a, b, c, d. As you can see this requires absolutely no memorization at all. And if you...

Q Let me ask you something; didn't you say sixteen?

A Twenty.

Q Where do you get the twenty? Four by four is sixteen.

A I have another line. The final line... is the only line which requires some memorization. In that is a square, circle, triangle and a rectangle.

So, obviously, anybody who has any recognition of the alphabet and the numerical system does not require any memorization to give a perfect score on this.

The only thing [that] may be there would be some problems with the circle, square, triangle and rectangle, certainly with not [sic] the other numbers. And any individual, as Colin Ferguson did, that he can speak intelligently, that he can present certain ideas, the knowledge we had of his behavior prior to this, he should have had absolutely no difficulty in reproducing this perfectly.

Q ... What was the result?

A The results of this were a totally inappropriate and inadequate production on his part. We gave him a slip of paper. He did not produce it diagonally—excuse me—he did not produce it horizontally across the paper as one would suspect. He wrote in a ragged, diagonal manner and in the first presentation he, after studying this for in excess of five minutes, five to ten minutes, in the first presentation he wrote the Arabic number two, smaller A, smaller B, a circle and a square. Not only is that totally inappropriate, but one does not need to be a trained professional to see that if you can recognize that there are numbers one and two it shouldn't be that hard to know that there is also three and four.

He also presented some of the symbols which were much more difficult to memorize than the numbers and letters which require no memorization at all.

However, we gave him another chance, and I told him, very good, I'm glad to see he [sic] is cooperating. He did as well as he [could] and we presented him back with the test to study one again.

I gave him it and once again he studied this for at least a five-minute period. He then came back and then added on his second trial the smaller C, a triangle, a circle and a rectangle.

Besides the memory this was not done too well perceptually. And I had a dual concern. My primary concern was that perhaps he was suffering from a perceptual motor dysfunction, and there was another concern; that he was shackled by the legs and hands. There was a large long chain between his hands and I feel he had full mobility but I didn't know for one hundred percent sure whether that impeded his response in any way.

But primarily because of the perceptual motor dysfunction question I asked him if he would write for me that my name is Colin Ferguson and he said sure. He took the pen out of my hands, took the paper, and... quite clear, done quite well, done horizontally the way it should be. He wrote "My name is Ferguson," and once again—

Q Ferguson or Colin Ferguson?

A He did not write Colin Ferguson. He wrote "My name is Ferguson." And once again these two things are totally inconsistent; that you could not know A, B, C, D and yet you could use M-Y and right your name and write "Ferguson." And it's inconsistent that someone can be so impaired in one way and then able to write a name, write actually a sentence.

So at that point it totally convinced me Mr. Ferguson was malingering, was not being truthful with us, and led to that diagnosis of malingering.[754]

Dr. D'Alessandro also conducted other simple tests. Mr. Ferguson was asked to memorize and recite letters, and numbers. The results were mixed.

A He was asked some other simple tests, which he performed verbally. He was able to memorize and repeat back one, two, three. I asked him "I'm going to give you three letters." I gave him F.B.I. and U.S.A. and he was able to repeat those.

I also gave him some random numbers which he was not able to repeat. The first sequence I gave him was one, four, seven, two, three. And he responded four, two, three. I then gave him two, five, eight, three, four and he responded five, eight, three, four.[755]

Dr. D'Alessandro also administered some analogy abstracts and asked Mr. Ferguson to explain them.

A The final inconsistency in his presentation to us on December 28th was I gave him analogy abstracts. Analogies are commonly used in psychological evaluations and testing. And I asked him to explain the meaning of these to me. On two of them he could not respond appropriately, however, on two he did.

Q Now, for this record, doctor, could you get into that in a little more detail. What analogy?

A I asked him "What does this mean, Colin, "strike while the iron is hot?" And he did not respond.

I also asked him to explain "one swallow does not make a summer," and he could not explain that in abstract sense.

However, I then asked him what does "a stitch in time saves nine" mean? And he stated that it means "Do it now. It's better now than later." I also asked him to explain what the statement "two heads are better than one" means and he stated that it means..."You do better if you work together."

That's evidence right there of higher cognitive functioning. That would be inconsistent with his other productions and representations to us.

---

754. *See Id.* at 181–186.
755. *See Id.* at 186.

So it was basically for these reasons that we felt that he was—
that I felt that he was purposefully not cooperating, purposefully
trying to mislead, which is also an indicator of an individual who
has a plan, who has a nerve, who has a reason, who has an
agenda where he purposefully goes out of his way to mislead examiners so that this also led me to believe that he was certainly
competent, that he was not incapacitated, and could certainly
continue with the court process.[756]

In conclusion, Dr D'Alessandro suggested the problems Mr. Ferguson demonstrated were more consistent with an adjustment disorder.[757] To support his findings (malingering and that the defendant was competent to stand trial), Dr. D' Alessandro described to
the court how he conducted interviews with various persons, read
letters, and reviewed court proceedings to reach his ultimate conclusion. Dr. D'Alessandro gathered (from this information) more inconsistent statements suggesting Ferguson was mindful of his situation and knowledgeable about legal procedure.[758] On this latter
point, Dr. D'Alessandro discusses some of Ferguson's statements,
describing his knowledge about the law and, once again, his ability
to cooperate with counsel—Mr. Moore.

A I also reviewed some court transcripts that I found extremely infor-
mative. The first being which occurred in the court on August 19th
1994. I believe this was directly after Mr. Ferguson had refused the
second 730 evaluation on August 15th, and during that time he in
comparison to what he told me during the evaluation that he knew
nothing about the law, he certainly in this court document appeared quite articulate and quite knowledgeable about the law.

---

756. *See Id.* at 186–187.
757. *See Id.* at 189. Dr. Mannetti [the treating psychiatrist at the Nassau
County Jail] originally diagnosed Mr. Ferguson as having an adjustment disorder [a transitory state triggered by some form of change in life circumstance;
the stressor often complicates an individual's ability to function]. After discussing Mr. Ferguson's behavior with other mental health experts of the Nassau County Jail (e.g., Mr. Sovronsky, and Dr. Kashimawo), Dr. D'Alessandro
found no evidence Mr. Ferguson's behavior resulted from delusions. *See Id.* at
189–191.
758. *See Id.* at 193–197. Dr. D'Alessandro relied on information conveyed
by the detectives involved in the criminal complaint, Nassau County Jail officials, and court transcripts detailing Mr. Ferguson's ability to file legal motions.

He certainly was aware of Judge Belfi asking him some specific questions that were appropriate to a competency evaluation and Mr. Ferguson answered accurately. He appeared to know the charges against him. He knew the role of the district attorney. He stated that he [could] cooperate with attorneys. However, did not wish to cooperate with his present attorneys.

This was quite consistent with the December 28th statement on his part that he felt trust and confidence in attorney Mr. Colin Moore and wanted that individual to represent him. And there was no doubt in my mind that he would be able to cooperate fully with Mr. Moore.[759]

. . .

Referring to Ferguson's letters written to Judge Belfi and additional statements made in court, Dr. D'Alessandro explains that Ferguson's current problems in cooperating with defense counsel are a product of his poor relations with Kunstler and Kuby and specifically the 'black rage' defense.[760]

Q In addition, I also reviewed over forty letters of printed form by Mr. Ferguson to Judge Belfi, in which they were very suspicious and paranoid in nature dealing with apparently a major issue now, the fact that he is not cooperating with his present attorneys, and if he is not able to cooperate with his present attorneys that he is therefore incompetent to proceed.

His letters are ripe with complaints concerning their own political agenda and the fact that they have taken certain confidential information and revealed it to the media therefore presenting Mr. Ferguson as a mentally unstable individual, and apparently he has some desire not to be presented in that manner and not to be represented by a black rage defense, which he thought was inappropriate.

Along these same lines I reviewed the letter that [was] written by Mr. Ferguson to the judge on August 19th, 1994...And what

---

759. *See Id.* at 97–98.
760. *See Id.* at 199–201.

I felt was of extreme significance and importance were the first two paragraphs of this.

Q What do you mean by that? Can you explain that doctor?

A There was concern that he could not cooperate with his current attorneys and that in some way he was an incapacitated person because he would not accept their defense plan, and that he therefore could not cooperate and therefore would be found incompetent.

...This is Mr. Ferguson writing on August 19th 1994.

"Please know of a surety that the so called 'black rage' defense is the creation of the sick minds of my attorneys and my decision to reject it is final and irreversible." New paragraph.

"I will, however, request that the options for all other possible defenses be left open for new attorneys, if I am so forced to seek. This paragraph serves, therefore, as a motion to extend the deadline set for September 19th 1994, at which time options for an insanity defense are closed."

Q Does that have significance to you in whether or not he on a cognition basis is weighing the options of which he wants to choose in this case?

A Absolutely.

Q Explain that.

A He is rejecting the black rage defense but he is leaving open other options, one of which is perhaps an insanity defense, and one of which is, as he was saying yesterday, is a different type of defense that may be developed with a new attorney that he was unaware of what they could be.[761]

...

Q What about your personal observations of him yesterday?

A My personal observations of him in the courtroom yesterday certainly led me to believe this is an individual who understood the proceedings, had what appeared to be appropriate objections that were considered by the Court and will be considered more formally at a later date.

I also heard him informally shouting across the courtroom to his attorneys and questioning whether he had the right to plead

---

761. *See Id.* at 199–201.

guilty and what would happen if he pled guilty and is this an option for him.

So obviously he is weighing the different options that he has and yet has also made it very clear that he is not really interested in this black rage defense.[762]

Lastly, the direct examination critiques Dr. Dudley's CST findings and opinion, centering on Dr. Dudley's already proffered diagnosis: delusional disorder, persecutory subtype. The cross examination is designed to highlight assessment shortcomings regarding Dr. Dudley's CST evaluation of the defendant. Points of interest involve differential diagnosis, CST time constraints, and CST structural limitations; that is, Dr. Dudley's disregard for issues relative to 730 assessments (e.g., what is the role of the judge, defense counsel, A.D.A.). Dr. D`Alessandro concludes that Mr. Ferguson does not suffer from delusions; rather, his behavior is more consistent with paranoid personality disorder. Dr. D'Alessandro's closing observations are presented in the following pages.

Q Now, doctor, you sat here yesterday [competency hearing December 6th, 1994] through the testimony of Dr. Dudley; did you not?
A Yes, I did.
Q And you heard him give his opinion that Mr. Ferguson has a delusional disorder; is that not correct?
A That's correct.
Q Do you have an opinion that he does not have a delusional disorder?
A Yes, I do.
Q What is that opinion with regard to delusional disorder whether or not he has it or doesn't have it?
A I believe there is strong evidence to suggest that he is not suffering from a delusional disorder
Q Can you explain the reasons for that?
A Several reasons: number one, there are other disorders that are extremely similar to a delusional disorder. And the differential diagnosis is quite difficult and time consuming. And there is no way, in my opinion, that Dr. Dudley could make that differential diagnosis ruling out the strong possibility that Mr. Ferguson is

---

762. *See Id*. at 202–203.

suffering from a paranoid personality disorder, which I personally feel is more appropriate.

Q ...Is a delusional disorder a psychotic disorder?

A A delusional disorder is a psychotic disorder.

A paranoid personality disorder is a personality disorder.

Q And the person is in touch with reality with regard to one of them.

A Yes.

Q Which one?

A There is a loss of reality with the delusional disorder.

Q Is there a loss of touch with reality with regard to the personality disorder?

A Not usually.

A Proceed.

Q Dr. Dudley only had three hours of interview with Mr. Ferguson. And I am not suggesting that a trained psychiatrist such as Dr. Dudley could not arrive at a decision in a three-hour period if he knew he only had [a] three-hour period.

If an individual knows that you have a limited time to do an evaluation you would so structure your evaluation to get the most crucial and prominent data that you would need to make the differential diagnosis within that period of time. And I believe that if Dr. Dudley had proceeded in that manner he would most likely have considered seriously other diagnoses.

However, unfortunately, he went in on the assumption that he would have several meetings with Mr. Ferguson. As a result it was not made clear to me the purpose of this initial evaluation, but it generally appeared to me to be an information gathering and a history taking session which is appropriate and acceptable as an initial evaluation.

I did not get the impression that this was a 730 evaluation. It certainly did not follow the format of a 730 evaluation. In fact, none of the questions that are appropriate to that type of evaluation were asked. It may have occurred on a second or third interview.

Therefore, I think it is premature for Dr. Dudley to have arrived at a definitive diagnosis of a delusional disorder.

I had certain other difficulties with a delusional disorder. As the DSM-IV indicates, this disorder usually occurs in later adulthood. Not that it could not occur earlier, but in a normal form it occurs in a much older age than Mr. Ferguson. While personality disorder is more consistent with early adulthood.

In addition—and this is of primary concern to me—also...the evidence that he has lied to us, he has been a malingerer. There is absolutely no doubt that he has manipulated the system, attempted to lie, attempted to present facts that are not true. A usual factor in this delusional system is that the individual truly believes those delusions to be true. Now, Mr. Ferguson says they are true, but to be quite honest with you I have a lot of difficulty in believing that Mr. Ferguson truly believes that these statements or even some of the things that he has written to Judge Belfi are accurate.

Just because he wrote them or just because he has stated them does not mean that he believes them.

They can once again be part of this malingering pattern, could once again be part of this pattern of attempting to mislead us. So I'm not convinced of that. And that would certainly require further investigation.

Another issue which leads me to seriously question the conclusive diagnosis of delusional disorder is based on some of Mr. Ferguson's history. Where consistent with a paranoid personality disorder, such an individual is difficult to get along with, [the individual has] a chip on their shoulder, is overly suspicious, is looking to bring up any attitude, is looking to make...a big issue out of little things. In general [is] making a real pain in the neck out of themselves.

In all of the examples that are brought up, if someone is delusional and truly delusional they can walk into a room or walk into a setting and very quickly develop that delusional system without any interaction from the other individuals. Yes, there can be some triggers but they do not necessarily need actions [from] others to develop their system.

It seems to me from the review of Dr. Dudley's report and some of the information that I received that the situations that he has run into at work, at Nassau Community College, at Adelphi, in his relationship with his wife, in the immigration service was that initially the contacts were fine and there were no problems. However, due to Mr. Ferguson's inappropriate behavior consistent with a paranoid personality disorder...authority figures began to react towards him in a negative manner due to his inappropriate behavior, an it was then that he began to react and state that there was a conspiracy that they are out to get him; that all of these things are going on and yet [Dr. Dudley] never takes into consideration the real strong possibility that with further investigation [it] could most likely be proven that his [Mr. Ferguson] actual behavior was so inappropriate as to precipitate the responses of these other individuals, and that's kind of—that is inconsistent with a delusional disorder, and very consistent with a paranoid personality disorder.

Therefore, I really have [difficulty] in fully accepting Dr. Dudley's diagnosis for these reasons, and am strongly leaning towards a diagnosis of a paranoid personality disorder.[763]

(d) Cross Examination by Mr. Kunstler

The cross-examination by William Kunstler challenged Dr. D'Alessandro's testimony on many fronts.[764] These queries are presented in the following pages. Amid the cross-examination, Mr. Kunstler addressed more substantive questions involving paranoid beliefs and racism. On this point, Mr. Kunstler explored Ferguson's repeated pattern of firing his attorneys in both the Worker's Compensation case and the current criminal matter.

Q Dr. D'Alessandro, as a professional man, is it your testimony that facing that evidence against him that his decision to proceed on a not guilty bases, whether it was a Caucasian that he said did it or not, that that is indicative of a competent person who understands fully the nature of the charges against him and the seriousness of it, the evidence, and so on—
MR. PECK: Objection.
THE COURT: Overruled.
MR. KUNSTLER: I haven't finished.
Q — you think that is evidence of competency?
A I don't know if that is his true feeling.
I know that his true feeling and belief is he has an agenda to relieve you and Mr. Kuby as his attorneys.
This has been the theme throughout the entire process. It has been the theme through every letter. I think he is utilizing every possible maneuver that he can think of and he is an intelligent and manipulative man to do that.

---

763. See Id. at 203–208.
764. See Ferguson Pretrial Hearing Transcripts, December 7, 1994 at 212–258 (Dr. D'Alessandro-cross-examination/Mr. Kunstler).

So I can sit here and say that I feel this is his true belief.

Q And I might add, do you know that every single attorney that has ever represented him in the United States he has discharged?

MR. PECK: Objection.

Q I'll go—do you know about Christine Lee [attorney Workman's Compensation case]?

A No.

Q Do you know—

THE COURT: Objection overruled.

Q — about Mr. Silverman and Brounstein before the Worker's Compensation Board?

A I believe I heard the name Silverman in this court yesterday.

Q Did you know that he [Mr. Ferguson] got rid of those attorneys?

A No, I'm not aware of that.

Q Did you know about Mr. Falanga? You know he got rid of Mr. Falanga?

A Yes.

Q What about Smith and Dunne? Do you know that he hadn't even consented to see them?

A No.

Q And with reference to Colin Moore, whom you said that he was the only attorney that you think he trusted—

A No, I didn't say that.

Q What did you say?

A I said that Mr. Ferguson told me this was the only attorney he trusted.

Q Didn't he also tell you that he thinks people got to him and turned him against him [Mr. Ferguson]?

A He said that too.

Q What?

A He said that also.[765]

In addition, Mr. Kunstler examined the basis for Dr. D'Alessandro's findings. In particular, he questioned the value afforded Ferguson's inconsistent statements and how these incongruous statements impacted Dr. D'Alessandro's clinical opinions. As is evident from the excerpts below, Mr. Kunstler revisited these statements relative to

---

765. *See Id*, at 218–220.

Ferguson's perceived conspiracy theory, drawing attention to the consistent theme of racism.

Q ... You talked about a lot of inconsistencies in what he told you during that interview in December; isn't that correct?

A That's correct.

Q And a lot of what you have told the Court is based on those inconsistencies; isn't that correct, the analysis of those inconsistencies?

A I presented those as inconsistencies.

Q But there was one thing that he was entirely consistent on, wasn't he, and that was the fact there was a conspiracy against him everywhere; isn't that correct?

A He mentioned the conspiracy, but I did not get the impression that he had an overall concept of a universal conspiracy.

Q Refer to your report..."Mr. Ferguson consistently went back to his conspiracy theories, but yet was unwilling to supply any specific details." Didn't you write that?

A Yes.

Q That was the only consistency that he had, consistently went back to his conspiracy theories?

A There were other consistencies. He didn't like his attorneys and the guards were beating him. This was one of many things. But, yes, there was this element of conspiracy that he had.

Q Isn't that feeling that there is a universal conspiracy against you one of the aspects of the persecutory type of a delusional disorder?

A That is one of the criterion, yes.[766]

Next, Mr. Kunstler questioned Dr. D'Alessandro's objectivity, and explored the limited time Dr. D'Alessandro spent with Ferguson for the competency exam. In addition, Mr. Kunstler explored a contradiction relating to malingering and Ferguson's legal strategy. This contradiction suggested that Ferguson was feigning incompetency and insanity while he rejected an insanity defense so that the defendant could conduct his own legal action. In the following passages, Dr. D'Alessandro stresses uncertain motives (i.e., evolving desires

---

766. *See Id.* at 222–224.

concerning the trial's outcome) to explain Ferguson's inconsistent statements and behavior.

Q Dr. D'Alessandro, you indicated, I think on direct, that you have conducted a great many 730.30 evaluations [competency evaluations]; is that correct?

A Yes, sir.

Q How many would you say?

A In excess of a hundred.

Q How many of those have you found incompetent?

A We haven't kept those statistics.

Q You haven't found any incompetent?

A No.

Q How many have you found incompetent?

A Close to fifty percent.

Q Fifty percent?

A I don't know if that figure is exact.

Q With reference to Colin Ferguson your examination took how long? Three hours?

A Hour and-a-half.

Q Hour and-a-half, wasn't it?

A That's correct.

Q Now, you indicated I think somewhere along the way, and if I misquote you please tell me, you indicated that you thought a further examination would be required to reach a definitive opinion in this case, further examination of Colin Ferguson?

A Not to reach the decision of malingering.

Q Malingering.

Let's get to malingering. In your original opinion you said he was malingering. Malingering from what?

A Severe mental illness and not knowing—

Q He was trying to fake insanity you mean?

A Yes. Yes, sir.

Q Is he trying to fake insanity today when he wants to reject an insanity defense, proceed *pro se* on a reasonable doubt defense?

MR. PECK: Objection. We are on the issue of competency.

THE COURT: Overruled.

Q Is he faking insanity today as well?

A I think sometimes he is.

Q So you think he is faking insanity to reject any insanity defense and wanting to proceed *pro se* on a reasonable doubt standard?

A It is my opinion that forsaking an insanity defense may in fact be a rational decision and an appropriate decision.

Q You think an appropriate decision is to go to trial with what you know about the evidence in this cause on a reasonable doubt standard?

A It's very possible that it is a rational and a real decision, and I'll explain why.

Q Go ahead.

A There are two options. Either he is going to be found guilty, if he proceeds without an insanity defense, at which point he would then spend the rest of his life in jail; or there is the possibility if he decides to take an insanity defense and is found innocent by reason of mental illness he would spend the rest of his life in a mental institution.

And it is very possible that an individual can make that as a rational decision that I would prefer to spend my time in jail than in a mental hospital.

Q Then why doesn't he plead guilty?

A He may very well plead guilty. He was certainly suggesting that yesterday.

Q All right.

When you sat in the courtroom you thought he suggested that he was going to plead guilty—that he was considering pleading guilty?

A He was asking questions about whether he had the right to do so, and I couldn't get the whole swing of the conversation but certainly I got that impression.

Q So I take it back in December of 1993 [referring to the CST evaluation] he was faking it in order to show that he wasn't sane and would spend the rest of his life in a mental institution and today he is faking it to show he isn't insane so he could go to jail for the rest of his life? Is that what you're telling us?

A I think you have to look at the context of things. When we saw him it was very soon after the incident. He hadn't spoken to other inmates, he hadn't consulted, he hadn't been able to think it through. And it's very possible that at that point he wished to come across as incompetent and therefore was malingering and now he is presenting a different scenario.

Q He wants to be held to be competent and also malingering?

A I never said he was malingering today.

Q What is he doing today? Is he malingering?

A I think in many instances he is not malingering. I think in some instances he is. I would have to look at each situation as an isolated case.

Q You're saying essentially that a decision to proceed with a reasonable doubt case would be essentially a rational decision?

A I'm saying it's very possible for an individual to make a rational decision that if I'm going to have to spend the rest of my life incarcerated I would rather do it— for whatever reason that individual may have—I would rather do it in a jail than in a mental institution.

There is also the occurrence that an individual—and I certainly don't know if it's real—has the self-pride that I don't want to be identified as a crazy person, I would rather be just a criminal and go to jail.

Q How do you explain him saying he is innocent and that a Caucasian did it? How does that fit into your thought process?

A That is a statement he made. I don't know if that is going to be his final presentation.

Q Everything is a statement that he made, isn't it, that we have been discussing today?

A Sure.

Q If we throw into your scenario the fact that he says he is innocent and that a Caucasian was the killer on the railroad a year ago today, does that in any way change your opinion?

A I don't know if he truly believes that.[767]

• • •

Mr. Kunstler suggests the consistent racist theme affects Ferguson's behavior and, thus, indicates a delusional disorder, persecutory subtype. Dr. D'Alessandro questions whether Ferguson believes his racist theories, a criterion necessary for a diagnosis of delusional disorder.

Q [In reference to the letters, Mr Kunstler asks,] did you notice all of the references to racism?

---

767. *See Id.* at 225–230.

A Yes.

Q Lets go through some of those.

He said that the court officers in this courtroom were racist, didn't he?

A Yes.

Q And then carry it one step further, he stated that the television stations were racist that covered these proceedings? ... Do you remember that phrase?

A No.

Q To go on, ... "Judge Belfi, I wish to end by saying that racism will not prevail and your attempts to protect the racist lynch mob that injured my eyes will only serve to remind the world you are just another little man, the little racist with the lynch mob mentality and justice whose life more miserable than mine."

Do you remember that?

A No.

Q With reference—I read you some. I'm going to read you more with reference to did you take those into consideration on judging this man's competency?

A I didn't use the letters to judge his competency.

Q Did they play any role in your decision?

A I already made the decision that he was competent to stand trial on December 28th. That was presented to the court?

Q Sorry. You also made the decision that he is not suffering from any delusional disorder; isn't that correct?

A No, I did not.

Q Have you made that now?

A No, I have not.

Q I think we are still up in the air whether—

A No. I said I would not diagnose him as having a delusional disorder, and that many of the symptoms he exhibits are not consistent with a delusional disorder. So I think that by making the diagnosis of a delusional disorder at this time is inappropriate and not accurate.

...

Q Now, you're familiar, of course, with the DSM-IV?

A Yes.

Q And I just want to ask you if you subscribe to this aspect of it, and I'm reading now from subtypes under delusional disorder. I'm reading from persecutory type, "this subtype applies when the central theme of the delusion involves the person's belief that she or he is being conspired against, cheated, spied on, followed, poisoned or drugged, maliciously maligned, harassed, or obstructed in the pursuit of long-term goals."

Do you agree with that?

Q Agree with what? That that is a statement in the DSM?

A And describing the persecutory subtype?

Q Right. Under delusional disorders.

A Yes, sir.

Q There is certainly evidence in those letters, in fact, you found essentially the only consistent statements he made were people were conspiring against him.

A I think that the difference is you read a word there that says believes and that is what I'm not sure of whether he believes in these delusions.

Q You say Mr. Ferguson consistently went back to his conspiracy theme.

A Right. That doesn't mean he believes them. That means he goes back to them. It could also be part of a ploy. I have no idea at this point.

Q Doctor, you were going on what he told you, weren't you?

A That's all I have to go on.

Q When you say in answer to my questions, I don't know whether he believes that or doesn't, and in answer to Mr. Peck's question you didn't put that word in whether he believes it or not, did you?

MR. PECK: Objection to the form.

MR. KUNSTLER: I'll withdraw it, Judge.

THE COURT: Sustained.

Q You will admit to me that you reported back to the Court that he consistently went back to his conspiracy theories.

A Yes.

Q And that is true also, is it not, in the various letters that he wrote to Judge Belfi?

A That was the theme of the letters.

Q Consistent theme?

A That was the theme of his letters.

Q That the lawyers are out to murder him?

A He did make that statement.

Q And he also indicated that the jail authorities are out to assist in his murder and assist in letting people into his cell to harass, injure or kill him?

A That statement was in the letters.[768]

In the subsequent exchange, the cross-examination explores further the content of the letters penned by Ferguson. Mr. Kunstler and Dr. D'Alessandro quibble over linguistics (i.e., whether Ferguson uses the term "racist" as an adjective or a noun) but eventually discuss the content of these letters relative to delusional disorder and Ferguson's anger.

Q ...In writing to Judge Belfi, and I believe this was on September 23rd 1994, he [Mr. Ferguson] said, "[I]t is evident that your hate for me has seriously affected your judgement and decision making and it is therefore in the best interest of justice to excuse yourself from my case."
Do you remember reading that?

A I see it now.

Q Does it ring a bell?

A Yes. In general.

Q ...A letter on the 23rd of September, same day as the preceding letter, by the way, he [Mr. Ferguson] says, "[J]udge Belfi, I strongly object to racism and the unfair manner in which you conducted the hearing on September 20th 1994, in which I sought to gain court approval for the use of an independent retinal specialist."
Do you remember reading that?

A Yes, I do.

Q ...[Mr. Kunstler also refers to another excerpt, where Ferguson writes], [I]t seems also that the Court, and my attorneys are attempting to prevent me from defending myself *pro se*."
Do you see that?

A Yes.

Q Now...this is a letter of October 11, 1994. You see where he states: "Earlier today saw an interesting development in my case which I began to watch very carefully. I have — something — continued to secure all boundaries with prayer to the almighty God as a defense against a racist and corrupt criminal justice system."
Do you see that?

---

768. *See Id.* at 231–235.

A Yes

Q And by the way do you remember seeing that at all?

A I had—I couldn't read that, that copy.

Q ...[Mr. Kunstler referring to yet another excerpt, Ferguson writes] "[I]n a conversation today by phone Mr. Kuby reminded me that Judge Belfi found me to be a manipulator. My response to Mr. Kuby, and the Court, is I will not concern myself with sick utterances from a racist judge, who by virtue of that, should be disqualified from my case."

Do you see that there?

A Yes, I do.

Q With reference to a diagnosis of delusional disorder would you take those into consideration?

A No. It sounds to me he is using racism as an adjective and any time anybody disagrees with him or doesn't even in an appropriate way question him he calls them a racist. He is using these terms as adjectives.

Q You don't think he means it?

A No, I think he means it. I don't think he means it as a racist. I think he means it as a slur, as an adjective. He uses it in every other word, every statement...

Q Everyone is a racist and everyone—

A I think he is using it as an adjective rather than as a noun. That is the way it is presented.

Q Is that a serious answer?

A It's an absolutely serious answer.

   If you look at the letters it is used as an adjective, not as a noun. Show me one time it's used as a noun.

Q Is there a difference in your mind if he says Judge Belfi is a racist judge or Judge Belfi is a racist?

A Slight.

   ...

Q Don't you think it reflects somewhat on his mental condition?

A Yes. But he is angry.

Q That he is angry?

A He is angry and he wants his way and when he is not going to get his way like a spoiled little boy he is going to stamp his feet and say everybody is a racist.

Q Or pick up a gun and kill six people and wound nineteen.

   MR PECK: Objection

THE COURT: Sustained.[769]

Next, Mr. Kunstler questions Dr. D'Alessandro's CST finding and
Ferguson's desire to proceed *pro se* to trial. In addition, the attorney
once again focuses on the psychiatrist's objectivity. On this latter
point, Mr. Kunstler poses questions about Dr. D'Alessandro's CST
experiences for the court. In conclusion, Mr. Kunstler centers on the
limited scope of the physician's investigation. Mr. Kunstler underscores Dr. D'Alessandro's failure to review historical information
concerning Ferguson's work experiences and the problems occurring at the colleges and with the Worker's Compensation case.

Q ...Did you think wanting to go *pro se* is part of a competency
evaluation, plays a role?
A He never told me he wanted to go *pro se*.
Q You read the letters?
A That doesn't mean he wants to do it.
Q Doctor, whether he told you "I want to go *pro se*" that is differ-
ent from telling Judge Belfi that he wants to go *pro se*?
A Yes. He wants to get rid of his attorneys and he has an agenda
and he will say and do anything to get rid of his attorneys.
That is his current agenda. It is made very clear in all of the let-
ters and in all of his recent activities.
Q So if he told you that and didn't write it you had just indicated it
would mean a difference to you, right?
A I would investigate it further. I would just not take it as a statement.
Q Well, you have the letters...I just read you one of them where he
says he wants to go *pro se*. That wouldn't trigger [for] you a further investigation?
A Absolutely. But I didn't have that opportunity. I would like to
have that opportunity.
Q All right.
A I think that I would like to have another competency evaluation.
We have wanted to have one since August, I would like to have
one now.

---

769. *See* at 236–240.

Q Without it you really can't reach a definitive opinion, can you?

A Without it I can rely on my initial opinion, which is valid that he was competent, and with the additional information that I have obtained since then, based on my initial competency evaluation, he is still competent.

Q Don't you feel, doctor, as a professional man, a little uneasy in not having a further examination of Colin Ferguson before you reached a final decision?

MR. PECK: Objection.

THE COURT: Overruled.

A I would like another evaluation but in lieu of not having the opportunity to do that I feel quite competent with my opinion.

Q By the way, are you an employee of the county?

A I am an—no.

Q Do you get paid by the county when you do these evaluations?

A Yes. I'm an independent contractor.

Q And you have done these, at least a hundred of them?

A Yes.

Q Could you just tell us what you get for that?

A I get an hourly rate.

Q What is the hourly rate?

A Forty-six dollars.

Q Forty-six dollars.

And you submit that to the county and they pay that?

A Yes, sir.

Q You're an independent contractor. Do you do this also for defense counsel?

A I have done that, privately consulted with defense counsel.

Q For defense counsel. About how many times?

A On just 730s [competency evaluations] or—

Q I'll stick to 730s?

A Privately maybe only four or five times.

Q All the rest have been as you have done here for the court?

A Independent evaluators for the court, yes.[770]

...

Q Did you go through the files of Adelphi?

---

770. *See Id.* at 241–244.

A No, sir.

Q What about Nassau Community College?

A No, sir.

Q Did you contact any of his former employers, for example, in California—

A I did not.

Q — or in New York?

A I did not.

Q Did you contact the Workman's Compensation Board or look at any of their files?

A No.

Q I take it then that you did not know that there were recommendations along the line from some of these people in some of these organizations or institutions who felt that he required or should consult a psychiatrist?

MR. PECK: Objection.

THE COURT: Sustained.

Q Don't you think, doctor, that some of this information with reference to the things you did not look into might have been helpful to you?

A Just based grossly on the information that I had in Dr. Dudley's report, and my opinion that there is evidence to suggest he is not suffering from this, and that there has to be other considerations.

Q There is also evidence to suggest that he might be suffering from that?

A It's possible, yes.[771]

(e) The People Call Dr. Allen Reichman: Direct Examination by Mr. Peck

Echoing Dr. D'Alessandro's testimony, Dr. Reichman draws similar inferences concerning Mr. Ferguson's mental health and the issue of trial competence.[772] The people (through direct examination of

---

771. *See Id.* at 256–257.

772. As mentioned, Dr. Reichman conducted the initial 730 evaluation with Dr. D'Alessandro.

Dr. Reichman) once again critique Dr. Dudley's CST exam, discuss the issue of malingering, and revisit Ferguson's indiscriminate use of the term racist. Although Dr. Reichman does not rule out a mental health condition (given the limited time for evaluation),[773] he challenges the more debilitating delusional disorder introduced by Dr. Dudley and suggests Ferguson's behavior is more consistent with paranoid personality disorder. Based on the preliminary 730 evaluation, Dr. Reichman concludes Ferguson is competent to stand trial. The direct examination by Mr. Peck fleshes out the reasoning and methods for Dr. Reichman's CST finding.[774]

Q Dr. Reichman, in connection with this particular case did you have an occasion to facilitate an order by a judge of this district court to examine and do a report on the competency of Colin Ferguson?

A Yes.

Q And, Dr. Reichman, based upon your examination of Colin Ferguson — which was on what date?

A December 28th 1993.

Q Based upon that examination of Colin Ferguson did you form an opinion within a reasonable degree of certainty in your field of expertise as to whether or not Mr. Ferguson, as a result of mental disease or defect, lacked capacity to understand the proceedings against him or to assist in his own defense?
Did you form such an opinion?

A Yes, I did.

Q What was that opinion, please?

A My opinion was that he did not lack capacity to understand the charges against him or to participate in his defense.

Q Now, I want you to limit yourself to the basis for your opinion as of December 28th, and I'm going to ask you some questions after that.

---

773. As noted, Ferguson refused the second 730 evaluation ordered by the court on August 15, 1994. *See* Ferguson Pretrial Hearing Transcripts, December 7, 1994, at 197. Like Dr. D'Alessandro's before him, Dr. Reichman's describes CST findings based on the initial 730 evaluation conducted on December 28, 1993.

774. *See* Ferguson Pretrial Hearing Transcripts, December 7, 1994 at 258–278 (Dr. Reichman-direct examination/Peck).

With regard to your opinion as of December 28th [1993] could you give the Court the basis for your opinion as to his competency...?

A Basically my opinion was based on the fact that Mr. Ferguson appeared to be uncooperative with the examination for the purpose of presenting himself as someone who was not competent to stand trial.

I believe that to be the case because the statements that he made during the course of the competency evaluation were evasive, he made frequent reference to a conspiracy, and I saw his reference to conspiracy as a closer of responses.

He would give a non-response by simply labeling something as a conspiracy. I found that his statement that he was not charged with anything to be in conflict with statements he had made just days prior to that, and I found that part of his responses were lacking in credibility.

I was forced, therefore, to assume that Mr. Ferguson was malingering, and because he was malingering he appeared to have the competency to understand the charges and to cooperate with his attorney if he chose to do so.

Q Dr. D'Alessandro was with you during this examination?

A Yes.

Q And you sat through the testimony of Dr. D'Alessandro—

A Yes.

Q You gave him certain tests with regard to his mental capacity?

A Yes. We [Dr. Reichman and Dr. D'Alessandro] gave him a paper and pencil test, which was really a test to rule out the possibility of some organic brain dysfunction which might account for his total lack of responding to the questions he was being asked.

The responses that he gave, as Dr. D'Alessandro testified, were inconsistent and clearly showed initially the presence of what would have been a severe organic impairment, but it was clear to us that Mr. Ferguson did not have such an impairment.

He was oriented as to time and person. He was intelligent. He was articulate. He was able to make responses.

I had spoken to him about two weeks prior to the 730 examination and I got a whole different set of responses[775]

---

775. See Id. at 261–264.

...

Q [Dr. Reichman refers to a conversation with Mr. Ferguson approximately a week or two prior to the competency evaluation]...At that time, Mr. Ferguson complained about the treatment he was receiving in the jail and he said that the guards, the night corrections officers, were abusive to him.

He also said he felt he was being tried in the media, or something to that effect; that the media was portraying him as a bad person and he, I believe, made specific reference to a person in the media, Peter Jennings, I think it was. And he made an oblique reference to the December 7th incident.

He didn't specify what it was, but it was clear to me on the basis of speaking with him at that time, that he knew why he was in jail and that he knew it had to do with a shooting that had occurred on the Long Island Rail Road and because of that he was being dealt with unfairly in the press. All of this was completely at variance with what he told me in the 730 Examination. And it was also at variance with a statement he made to Dr. Mannetti [jail mental health clinician] eight days prior to the 730 Examination.

At that time he told Dr. Mannetti that he wanted to be found competent and he wanted the legal process to move along. He also mentioned that he thought it was likely that he was going to wind up spending the rest of his life in prison. And that was a statement he made eight days prior to the 730 examination.

When I see [sic] him on December 28th he tells me he is not charged with any criminal offense and that the only reason he is in jail is because of some dispute he had with people at Adelphi.

If I had not gone any further in the examination I would have considered that to be evidence of malingering.[776]

...

Q Now, Dr. Reichman, do you have an opinion as you sit here today as to the present capacity of Mr. Ferguson to stand trial?

A I have an opinion, which is based on my examination of December 28th 1993, and not refuted by other information that I have received since then.

---

776. *See Id.* at 264–265.

Q ...Doctor, in giving your testimony here today have you relied on one, the examination of December 28th and the two other examinations, brief examinations done by doctors before that time, Mannetti and yourself?

A Yes.

Q [A series of questions also established that Dr. Reichman relied on several sources to form his opinion. Specifically, Dr. Reichman reviewed court transcripts, interviewed investigating officers, Nassau County Jail officials and mental health experts, reviewed letters written by Mr. Ferguson, observed court room testimony provided by Dr. Dudley and reviewed his report, and observed Mr. Ferguson's demeanor and conduct in court.]

...Now, based upon all of these factors, all of these indicia, Dr. Reichman, has your opinion that you formulated as of December 28th, has it in any way altered?

A No, it has not.

Q Could you explain in as great as detail as possible the reasons for that?

A To begin with Dr. Dudley's examination was done so far as I could tell for the purpose of evaluating in an overall way Mr. Ferguson's mental state in all likelihood for the possibility of consideration of a not responsible psychiatric defense.

It does not appear to have been done primarily as a examination of his competency to stand trial.

Dr. Dudley, as Dr. D'Alessandro had previously testified, fully intended to come back and see Mr. Ferguson again to complete his examination.

It may be or may not be, I don't know, that he might have gotten around to asking him the requisite questions for determination of a person's competency to stand trial. It is clear to me that he didn't specifically put those questions to Mr. Ferguson nor did he get responses which would lead him to be able to make a determination of whether he is competent to stand trial.

The second thing is that Dr. Dudley's diagnosis as a delusional disorder, persecutory type has not been confirmed either by his continued examination, [Ferguson refused the follow-up] or by an examination of any of the material that I have seen or that I believe Dr. Dudley used in the process of forming his opinion.

I believe that the diagnosis of delusional disorder is possible but it is certainly not the only diagnosis worthy of consideration.

In fact, it seems as likely or perhaps more likely that Mr. Ferguson suffers from what is called a paranoid personality disorder, which has already been indicated in testimony as not being a mental illness and not characterized by delusional ideation.[777]

On direct examination, Dr. Reichman spends some time describing the general and defining characteristics of paranoid personality disorder emphasizing that, although maladaptive, these characteristics are not based on delusions.

Q Do you know, can you recite the criteria, diagnostic criteria, for paranoid personality disorder, doctor?...

A ...Basically a paranoid personality disorder is one of a whole class of personality disorders. So to begin with you have to understand what a personality disorder is...A personality disorder is a condition in which an individual's traits—now, just to back up a little bit, traits are defined as enduring patterns of relating things and forming attitudes which are set down early in the life of a person and become pretty much so identified by late adolescence and early adult life.

A personality disorder exists when those traits have become inflexible and maladaptive.

In other words, the playing out of those traits in a person's daily living causes them difficulty in their adaptation to life situations, to interpersonal relationships, and to any one of a number of other ordinary life pursuits.

So that is what is meant by the term "maladaptive." When these traits are so rigid and inflexible and maladaptive they are referred to as constituting a personality disorder.

Paranoid personality disorder is one of many other personality disorders.

In a case of a person with a paranoid personality disorder they perceive responses on the part of other people as threatening, as demeaning, as negatively directed toward them.

They can perceive others as being part of a conspiracy against them...

Q How would you differentiate a delusional disorder from a paranoid personality disorder?

---

777. *See Id.* at 266–269.

A A delusional disorder has delusions, that is why they call it a delusional disorder. A delusion is a false fixed belief which is not changeable by logic or persuasion.

An individual with a paranoid personality disorder distorts what happens to him. He doesn't make it up out of whole cloth. He takes something that actually occurs and makes it into — because that is his nature, that is his personality, those are his traits — he makes it into something that is negatively directed towards him. That is what a paranoid personality disorder does.

A delusional disorder is characterized by a person taking something that may not have happened and out of whole cloth making it into something which is negatively directed toward him with no basis in reality.

The distinction is sometimes very fine and rather difficult to make. When I examined Mr. Ferguson on December 28th 1993, I did not formulate a diagnosis of delusional disorder or paranoid personality disorder.

Q Was that your function at that time?

A It was not particularly my function.

If I had gotten enough information to make these diagnoses I would have been willing to do that.

Since Mr. Ferguson did not cooperate fully with the examination, he did not respond sufficiently to reveal enough of himself in terms of personality to make any such diagnosis. I was not able to do that.

So at that point in time the only thing I could say with clarity is that he was malingering and that he had demonstrated on previous occasions the ability to understand the charges against him and by inference the ability to cooperate with an attorney, if he chose to do so.

Q I believe you mentioned that based upon the data which you learned after December 28th; in other words, the material I just made mention of, you talking to detectives, you reading the letters, and things like that, that you testified that his behavior, his conduct, is more consistent with paranoid personality disorder. Is that not what you said?

A I think it wasn't so much his conduct with the detectives. He didn't appear to be very paranoid at all at the time that he spoke to the detectives initially, but his letters are clearly very paranoid.

Q What I'm trying to get at, doctor, with regard to Colin Ferguson and what you know about him now, either through talking to the detectives, looking at data, looking at court transcripts, can you give reasons why Mr. Ferguson fits in with that diagnostic criteria?

A Well, he fits in to the diagnostic criteria of paranoid personality disorder because he is paranoid.

He interprets things in a paranoid way. That is what people with a paranoid personality disorder do. There is often a kernel of truth to the things that he says, for example, he is being at times mistreated in the jail. That is not a delusion. There is some of that actually going on.

He will enlarge upon it and perhaps exaggerate it.

He was allegedly assaulted in the jail and suffered some kind of injury. He saw that as a conspiracy.

It certainly was not a benign act that was done to him. So his seeing it as a conspiracy is something which arises from an incident that actually occurred and he just puts the paranoid interpretation on it and that's what paranoid personality disorder people do.

His letters to the judge are also very tinged with paranoid material. He makes reference to all sorts of racism that is occurring around him. Unfortunately, there is racism that occurs in the world. He is much more apt to see racism than an individual who doesn't have a paranoid personality disorder, just as he is more inclined and more able to and predisposed to see other negative things going on around him than an individual who lacks this disorder.

It is not clear to me on the basis of his letters that he is making all this stuff up.

...he is taking things that are happening and distorting them, and seeing them in a paranoid way.

It is clear that he is a very paranoid individual. But I don't think there is anything in these letters, in any of these letters, which clearly establishes the presence of a delusional disorder.[778]

Next, Mr. Peck establishes a connection between Drs. Reichman and D'Alessandro's CST findings. Lastly, the direct examination dis-

---

778. *See Id.* at 269–275.

cusses Mr. Ferguson's ability to assist in his defense, intimating Ferguson meets the first prong of the competency standard. On this point, Dr. Reichman testifies that Ferguson not only considered the black rage insanity defense, but anticipated the inadequacy of it as a legal strategy.

Q Now, you have heard Dr. D'Alessandro testify?
A Yes.
Q You have heard questions and answers being given by him concerning material with regard to background material and his answers with regard to background material?
A Yes, I did.
Q If I asked you the same questions would your answers be similar to Dr. D'Alessandro?
A I think in large part they would. I can't give you a blanket yes to that.
Q Did you agree with the conclusions of Dr. D'Alessandro —
A Yes
Q — with regard to his competency?
A Yes, I did
...
Q Have you seen in Mr. Ferguson's conduct his ability to consider various options in the case?
A I have seen one reference in a letter that he was considering certain options. I have heard him consider another option in court yesterday which was that of pleading guilty.
I think that he has stated at certain times and contradicted himself at other times that he would consider a psychiatric defense, and then at other times he has said that he would under no circumstances consider that defense. But I think it is no different from the inconsistency that he has shown in other areas.
Q What about any conversations that you were made privy of [sic] with regard to the testimony of Maureen Riordan Mulder [A.D.A. representing Ferguson regarding the jail house assault]?
A Yes. In that instance he was talking about the black rage defense and he said he didn't think that was going to work. Basically that was the gist of what he was saying, and that if he used that defense he would certainly — I don't know if he used the word "certainly" — be found guilty.
Q Do you consider that an option?

A I consider that an option that he considered and rejected.[779]

(f) Cross Examination by Mr. Kuby

Suggesting Dr. Reichman's findings understated the severity of Ferguson' mental health condition, the cross examination was designed to show that Ferguson's paranoid behavior impaired his ability to assist in the defense. On this point, Mr. Kuby revisited the people's theory of malingering and, once again, suggested the theory was in conflict with Ferguson's requests regarding his defense strategy. In other words, the people's experts argued that the defendant was malingering (in a deliberate attempt to be found incompetent), even though Ferguson made explicit requests to reject an insanity defense, fire his counsel, and proceed *pro se* to trial.[780] In what follows, some of the more noteworthy exchanges between Mr. Kuby and Dr. Reichman during the cross-examination are presented.[781]

* * *

Q In your report you indicated that you thought he was malingering in a deliberate attempt to be found incompetent, right?
A Right.
Q And the inference there—and stop me if I'm mistaken—the import of your report, the inference is that he would then rather go to a psychiatric institution than go to jail; is that correct?
A No, not at all.
Q Well, if the result is going to be if he is deliberately malingering, deliberately attempting to be found incompetent, then he is going to be sent to a mental institution; is that correct?
A That's correct.

---

779. *See Id.* at 275–278.
780. *See Id.* at 280. Dr. Reichman states "[I]t is often difficult to know what Mr. Ferguson truly believes. It didn't make a great deal of sense back in December [the initial 730 evaluation] that he wanted to appear not competent when he had said eight days previously that he was anxious for the case to move forward and he wanted to be competent. *See Id.* at 283–284.
781. *See* Ferguson Pretrial Hearing Transcripts, December 7 and December 8, 1994 at 278–305 (December 7th 1994) and 371–392 (December 8th 1994) (Dr. Reichman-cross examination/Kuby).

Q Now, what you are saying is he is rejecting an insanity defense because he—because he wishes to go to jail for the rest of his life over a mental institution?

A First of all, I didn't say that. Dr. D'Alessandro said that.

Q You disagree with Dr. D'Alessandro?

A I think it is a possibility. I don't know whether he wants that or doesn't want it. It is a possibility. Dr. D'Alessandro did not say that that is what he wants either.

That is one reason that he might be rejecting an insanity defense. It doesn't necessarily have to be the reason, but it is a possible reason.

Q ... One possible reason he is rejecting an insanity defense is because he is possessed of paranoid delusions and he believes everybody is conspiring against him, that's another possibility?

A That's another possibility.

Q Fine.

You did speak to the detectives in this case; is that correct?

A Yes.

Q And they told you basically what happened; is that correct?

A Yes.

Q With respect to the shooting on the train?

A Yes.

Q From the indication that you received from them there is no doubt that Colin Ferguson is the person who shot the bullets and killed the people; is that correct?

A That's correct.

Q You're aware that Mr. Ferguson now states he is rejecting an insanity defense; is that correct?

A That is something he said at various points in time.

Q ... Do you believe with a reasonable degree of medical certainty that when Mr. Ferguson is saying that he rejects an insanity defense that he is in fact rejecting that defense?

MR. PECK: Objection.

MR. KUBY: Judge, I have to be able to ask him.

THE COURT: That question I will allow.

A All I can say for sure is that is what he is saying.

It is often difficult to know what Mr. Ferguson truly believes. It didn't make a great deal of sense back in December that he wanted to appear not competent when he had said eight days previously that he was anxious for the case to move forward and he wanted to be competent.

So, from one day to the next it is difficult to say what Mr. Ferguson's belief is and what his agenda is...Because he keeps contradicting himself so I don't know what he really wants at this point.

Q But you certainly, as you sit here, know that he has expressed a desire to reject an insanity defense?

A Yes.

Q And based on what you know of the case the insanity defense is the only defense open to him; is that correct?

MR. PECK: Objection.

Q Based on what you knew.

THE COURT: Sustained.[782]

Next, Mr. Kuby discusses the relationship between delusional disorder, persecutory subtype and abilities associated with trial competence. In addition, Mr. Kuby questions the association between paranoid personality disorder and trust. On this point, the litigator questions whether the defendant must have some degree of trust to assist in the defense. Detailing Ferguson's pattern of hiring and firing attorneys, Mr. Kuby intimates that the accused (as a product of his mental health condition) did not trust attorneys and, thus, could not assist in his defense.

Q Have you ruled out with a reasonable degree of medical certainty that Mr. Ferguson is suffering from delusional disorder persecutory type?

A I have not ruled it out completely. I think that it exists as a possibility.

Q And, in fact, you have said it is your feeling that it is as likely or perhaps more likely that he is suffering from a paranoid personality disorder?

A Yes.[783]

...

Q It is also fair to say, isn't it, that somebody suffering from a delusional disorder persecutory type has delusions of persecution; is that right?

A Yes.

---

782. *See Id.* at 280–284.
783. *See Id.* at 285.

Q And under those circumstances when a person believes that everybody, including his own attorneys, are conspiring against him is a person under those circumstances competent to stand trial?

A If a person believes—I think there is a built-in contradiction to your question. And I will explain. It is not characteristic of a person with a delusional disorder to believe that everybody is against him, the whole world is against him. That is more evidence of a paranoid personality disorder that kind of global, vague notion...In a sense, I really can't answer that question because of that contradiction.

Q Can I amend the question?

A Please.

Q In that case let us assume that somebody is suffering from a delusional disorder and they believe that the judge and their attorneys and the prosecutor are conspiring against them.

A If they believe that.

Q Right.

A And it is a delusion.

Q Yes.

A Then I think the likelihood would be that they would not be competent.

Q ...They have to genuinely believe that this conspiracy is taking place; is that right?

A Yes. Absolutely.

Q And, secondly, it has to be a delusion?

A Yes.

Q And a delusion is a firm, fixed belief, firm fixed false belief, it is unshakable dispite [sic] obvious incontrovertible evidence to the contrary; is that right?

A That's correct.

Q ...Would you agree that in order for a defendant to assist in his own defense he has to have some degree of trust in the advice he is getting from his lawyer?

A I think for a defendant to be competent he can't totally mistrust his attorney. He may not be too happy with some of the decisions that are made and still be competent, but if he doesn't trust anything that his attorney is doing then he needs to get a new attorney.

Q And let us assume further he gets a new attorney and he doesn't trust that one either?

A Then I guess he has got to go and get somebody else yet again.[784]

...

Q I ask you to assume that somebody such as Mr. Ferguson has seven or eight different attorneys, and with each and every one of those attorneys it became impossible, or he was unable to form any relationship of trust until the point that he ended up accusing those attorneys of engaging in illegal and conspiratorial conduct. Given that sort of background would you believe that a defendant is still competent to stand trial?

MR. PECK: Objection.

THE COURT: Overruled.

A The way you have put the question I would say such a person would not be competent.

However, I would like to add something—

Q Please.

A ...First of all, I think there is a very basic difference between a multiple murder trial and a Worker's Compensation matter. And I really have a hard time lumping all of these experiences with lawyers together.

I think Mr. Ferguson has expressed the desire to not have you and Mr. Kunstler represent him in response to the proposal to use a black rage defense.

That doesn't necessarily mean to me that he will automatically reject any other lawyer that is chosen. I can't say on the basis of the fact that he has expressed this intention that he is therefore not competent and will never be able to agree or trust any other attorney. I'm not in a position to say that.

Q Are you aware that prior to our representation of him he had a Mr. Falanga representing him?

A Yes.

Q Are you aware that he expressed dissatisfaction with Mr. Falanga as well and discharged Mr. Falanga?

A Yes.

Q Are you also aware that he expressed paranoid type accusations against Mr. Falanga, he was only into writing a book, he doesn't really care about me...Are you aware that he expressed those allegations against Mr. Falanga?

---

784. *See Id.* at 286–290.

A Yes.

Q Are you also aware that he consulted with attorneys named Smith and Dunne in this case?

A Yes.

Q Are you aware that when they made an appointment to go back out to see him at the Nassau County jail he refused to see them?

A I did hear something to that effect.[785]

...

Q Six separate lawyers with four different firms; is that right?

A Right.

Q He has been unable or unwilling or he certainly has not cooperated with any of them; is that right?

A I don't know. I'm not in a position to say.

Q You do know that he now stands poised ready to proceed *pro se*?

A That's what he said, yes.

Q How many different lawyers would it take for him to reject before you were convinced to a reasonable degree of certainty that this isn't some sort of an act and genuinely can't bring himself to establish trust with an attorney? Give me a number?

MR. PECK: Objection.

THE COURT: Sustained.

Q Did you review the Worker's Compensation records in this case?

A No.

Q You didn't.

Are you familiar with the fact that he went through three separate attorneys and/or legal representatives in that proceeding?

A I believe I heard something to that effect, yes.

Q Discharging all of them and ultimately proceeding *pro se*; is that correct?

A That is what I heard happened, yes.

Q Does the Worker's compensation issue combined with what you have seen in this case, doesn't that suggest to you that in fact Mr. Ferguson is incapable of establishing a relationship of trust with an attorney?

---

785. See *Id.* at 291–293. In a series of questions Mr. Kuby presents the various attorneys Colin Ferguson contacted regarding the current criminal matter including: Mr. Falanga; Mr. Kunstler; Mr. Kuby; Mr. Dunne; Mr. Smith; and Mr. Moore. See *Id.* at 294.

MR. PECK:	Objection.
THE COURT:	Overruled.

A I don't know if I'm prepared to say that he is incapable. I think it is possible that if he hears what he wants to from an attorney then he may be able to proceed with him. Whether that will actually happen or not of course I can't tell.

Q What does he want to hear?

MR. PECK:	Objection.
THE COURT:	Objection sustained.
MR. KUBY:	Judge.

Q You are not prepared at this time to say he is incapable of relating to an attorney; is that correct?

A That's correct.

Q The evidence thus far indicates that that may very well be a possibility; is that correct?

A Yes.

MR. PECK:	Objection.
THE COURT:	As a possibility, overruled.

A Yes. The evidence suggests as a possibility, yes.[786]

...

Q When you conducted your original examination you came to the conclusion that Mr. Ferguson was malingering for the purpose of being found incompetent to stand trial; is that correct?

A Not exactly.

He was malingering for the purpose of appearing to be not competent to stand trial.

I don't know whether he had thought it through to the extent that he was considering what would happen if he were found not competent or whether he really wished to be found not competent. I think what he was doing was just not cooperating with the process. It didn't seem to me that he had any direct notion of what was going to happen an why he was doing it.

Q You're not prepared to say that it was his conscious purpose at that time to be found incompetent so he would go off to a mental institution and avoid trial?

A No, I'm not saying that. I'm not saying that.[787]

---

786. *See Id.* at 294–297.
787. *See Id.* at 299.

...

Q Are you familiar with the reason that Colin Ferguson has stated he will not plead insanity?

A I'm not sure I'm familiar with his true reason, no.

Q Well, I will ask you to assume that the reason he has stated that he will not plead insanity is because he didn't commit the crime, some white person committed the crime.... Are you familiar— some Caucasian did it. Are you familiar with the fact that he has made that statement?

A Yes.

Q I ask you to assume for purposes of the next question that Colin Ferguson genuinely believes that to be true, and given that assumption would you say with a reasonable degree of scientific certainty that rejecting an insanity defense for that reason is a rational decision?

MR. PECK: Objection

THE COURT: Overruled

A If you're asking me to make this rather large assumption, which I have a lot of trouble making but for the purposes of your question I will force myself to make the assumption, and assuming that were the case, that is not a rational decision.[788]

Next, Mr. Kuby revisits Dr. Reichman's assessment process and further questions how Ferguson's perceived conspiracy theory informed the CST findings. Mr. Kuby also discusses the seeming impermanence of the defendant's preoccupation with his delusional beliefs; questions designed to suggest that Ferguson's paranoid ideology was not prominent during the brief exam.

Q ...Doctor, in formulating your decision did you consider Mr. Ferguson's statement that a conspiracy of racist whites and blacks are out to harm him?

A Yes.

Q And did part of your assessment turn on whether or not Mr. Ferguson genuinely believes that statement?

A I don't think so. I think that in certain contexts he may believe that there is a conspiracy operating such as that.

---

788. *See Id.* at 300–302.

But he uses the term so frequently and so vaguely that I would have trouble making a statement, a blanket statement, that he does believe that or doesn't believe it.

It depends what is going on at the time which prompts him to say that. And I think in any event if he does believe it, it is a distortion of something that is actually happening. And it is his way of interpreting something that is going on. He labels it a conspiracy and he uses that term rather loosely.

THE DEFENDANT: Objection, Judge. There was not enough time in the meeting between the defendant and the doctor for him to establish a credible medical opinion.

THE COURT: Mr. Ferguson.

THE DEFENDANT: When the defendant was chained and handcuffed.

THE COURT: You're not in a position to make any statements. When and if you are to represent yourself in this proceeding you will have an opportunity to make objections and ask questions.

As of now Mr. Kuby is still your attorney and he will do the questioning and make the objections.

Q ...Let me ask you this, then: Would you agree with the following statement: Especially in the persecutory subtype the disorder may be chronic, although a waxing and waning of the preoccupation with the delusional beliefs often occurs. Would you accept that as a correct statement?

A That is probably something that is written in the DSM-IV. I think it is true.

But I think what that statement really means is that a person, even a person with a delusional disorder, experiences different things from day-to-day and there may be things which arouse this delusional idea and there may be things which don't. So it appears to the observer that the condition waxes and wanes because there are times when he is voicing the delusion and there are other times when he is not.

Q I'm sorry. I don't understand that answer. I thought that one of the hallmarks of a delusion was that it was not in response to something that actually occurred; that it was something confabulated out of whole cloth. Wasn't that your testimony yesterday?

A Yes. It is a belief in something and the belief tends to be permanent.

If you remind a person with a delusional disorder of something and make reference to it he is going to continue to believe that idea that he has got. That doesn't necessarily mean that he thinks about it all the time.

Q So some days a person will encounter incidents that will set him off and the delusional behavior will be more pronounced, and other days things won't set it off and it will be less pronounced?

A Right.

Q And so it is fair to say that the fact that he did not appear to be delusional to you in — excuse me, how long were you in his presence?

A Hour and-a-half.

Q The fact that he was not delusional for an hour and-a-half on December 28th is not dispositive of whether or not he has delusional disorder persecutory type; is that correct?

A That — as I said then, the presence or absence of delusions was not something that was clearly determined at the time of the examination because of his lack of cooperation... The lack of complete cooperation at the time that the 730 Examination was done made it impossible to make that determination.

There was nothing in the examination that clearly suggested the presence of a delusion.

Q ...Is it your testimony that at that at time when you examined him he may have been in a delusional state but you did not have enough — well, is it your testimony that at that time he may have been in a delusional state?

A No. I saw no evidence that he was in a delusional state.

Q Did you have enough information to make a determination one way or the other?

A I had enough information to differentiate between true delusions and these kind of vague references that he was making.

It is possible that if he had been more open he would have revealed some findings that were more consistent with a delusional state. I can't say.

Q Is it fair to say, going back to my original question in this area, is it fair to say that the presence or absence of delusions on that day and time that you saw him that is not dispositive of whether or not he is suffering from a delusional disorder persecutory subtype?

A If he displayed evidence of delusional thinking at that time I would have to suspect that he had either a delusional disorder or a schizophrenic disorder paranoid type.

He did not display any indication that led me to believe that either one of those diagnoses was present.

Q ... The fact that he did not have delusions at that particular time does that enable you to rule out the presence of delusional disorder persecutory subtype?

A I think insofar as that examination was concerned it was ruled out. One always has the opportunity to learn things at subsequent examinations or by later history that a certain condition may exist.

At that point in time I think that I was sufficiently able to rule out the existence of such a disorder at that time.[789]

The cross examination also underscores time constraints with respect to the initial 730 evaluation (Dr. Reichman's hour and one-half CST review), and the limited scope of Dr. Reichman's examination (disregarding Ferguson's background information suggesting that the defendant was paranoid prior to the shooting). In addition, Mr. Kuby discusses Dr. Dudley's findings and explores the divergent opinions between Drs. Dudley and Reichman.

Q Given the importance you just stated of taking a thorough history, under those circumstances did you examine—did you talk to any people who had known Colin Ferguson prior to the shooting?

A No.

Q Did you examine any records of the university he had attended prior to the shooting?

A No.

Q Any of his previous writings prior, except for those found at the time of the shooting?

A No.

Q Did you in fact examine the writings that were found on him at the time of the shooting?

---

789. *See* Pretrial Hearing Transcripts December 8, 1994 at 375–381.

A At the time of the shooting I had not seen those writings. I had not seen the writing at the time of the shooting when I did the 730 Examination, no.

Q Did you subsequently examine those writings?

A Yes.

Q You testified that you discounted Dr. Dudley's findings of delusional disorder persecutory subtype; is that correct?

A I didn't say I discounted them.

I said that I did not feel on the basis of his examination he was able to make a diagnosis definitively and, therefore, I did not make the assumption that that disorder existed on the basis of his report or his testimony.[790]

Q ...[A]nd there were several reasons that you stated, on direct examination, as to why you felt that; is that correct?

A Yes.

Q And one of them was because Dr. Dudley's examination was done for the purpose of ascertaining, I believe you said, and overall state of mind or something like that?

A Yes.

Q In fact, Dr. Dudley stated, did he not, that his purpose was to determine in the first instance whether Colin Ferguson had a mental disease or defect?

A Yes.

Q Not an overall state of mind, but a specific mental disease or defect; is that correct?

A Well, I believe, If I recall correctly, in his testimony that is one of the terms he used, his overall mental state.

Q Another reason that you indicated that you weren't in a position at this time to agree with Dr. Dudley's diagnosis was because he did not do a full examination; is that correct?

A ...I said I did not agree with his conclusion that Colin Ferguson was not competent to proceed because he did not do a 730 Examination.

Q But in fact he spent more time with Colin Ferguson than you did; is that correct?

A That's correct.[791]

...

---

790. *See Id.* at 381–383.
791. *See Id.* at 381–384.

Q ...According to your testimony a delusion is a false belief that has no basis in reality?

A ...That is contrary to the facts which exist in external reality and is not persuadable or changeable by reason or logic and contradictory to the evidence present.

Q And there are two generalized types of delusions: bizarre and non-bizarre; is that correct?

A There are many different types of delusions, but that is one categorization that is used. Bizarre, that differentiates between schizophrenia and delusional disorder.

Q And non-bizarre delusions are delusions of things happening that actually do happen in real life?

A That could happen.

Q Yes, that could.

A That sometimes do happen that are believable to the extent that people have experienced such things.

Q Is it fair to say that in a delusional person genuine events that they experience or that they perceive are interpreted in the context of a delusional structure? Is that a fair statement?

A That I think that would be a fair statement, yes.[792]

...

Q So if somebody such as Colin Ferguson, for example, were taken to the hospital for purposes of an eye examination and for whatever reason the examination was curtailed and he was brought back to the jail, if he then believed or then, assuming that he then believed that the emergency was staged by his lawyers, the judge and the district attorney's office to make it look like he was getting proper medical care, when he wasn't in order to cause him to go blind so he couldn't identify the Long Island Rail Road shooter, would you classify that as a delusion?

MR. PECK: Objection.

THE COURT: Overruled.

A What you just described could conceivably fall in the category of delusional thinking, but it might be a misinterpretation of reality. For example, if he went to the hospital for treatment and if he interpreted that as part of a conspiracy that wouldn't necessarily be a delusion.

---

792. *See Id.* at 385–386.

That would be a distortion of the sort that can be found in individuals with a paranoid personality disorder which, as I said, seems highly likely in Mr. Ferguson's case.

Q I'm asking you to not just consider the fact that he regarded the trip to the hospital as part of the conspiracy.

I'm asking you to consider the following: he is taken to the hospital for purposes of an eye examination that he requested, before the examination gets under way it is important because he is taken out of the jail. I'm asking you to assume that he then interprets that to mean, a number of people, including the judge, prosecutor, defense lawyers, are involved in a specific conspiracy to stage this phony emergency so it looks like he is getting proper medical care for his eyes when in fact he is not getting proper medical care for his eyes, the purpose of that being that he goes blind so he can't identify the Long Island Rail Road shooter. That sounds much more delusional than it sounds paranoid; is that right?

A It's still a distortion. That whole scenario that you described is not necessarily a delusion because it all is based on something that is going on, and it is all a misinterpretation of facts that actually took place.

It could be or could not be a delusion.

...The fact that he may misinterpret what happens as being malevolently directed toward him is not necessarily a delusion.

Q Right.

I understand it might be, it might not be. How do we tell?

A Sometimes it is a rough call.[793]

A series of questions addressed the issue of differential diagnosis, and the ubiquitous characteristics associated with delusional disorder. Finally, Mr. Kuby questions whether individuals can be intelligent and articulate and still suffer from delusional disorder, persecutory subtype?

Q It's important, right? It's important whether he [Mr. Ferguson] is simply paranoid or delusional? It's important?

A It's important, but if you isolate one single incident it doesn't make the diagnosis.

---

793. *See Id.* at 387–390.

You have got to have a consistent pattern of delusional thinking in order to really be comfortable about making that diagnosis.

If you see one thing which is a pretty close call, and may or may not be a delusion, and you don't see a pattern of consistent occurrences of things that are clearly delusional then you are on thin ice in making that kind of diagnosis.

Q If you do see such a pattern demonstrated, not just when a defendant is arrested and needs a defense, if you see such a pattern before that person ever got into trouble with the law, ever ended up in the courtroom, you would be much more comfortable in making the diagnosis of delusional disorder; is that correct?

A ...It is correct to the extent that if your hypothetical includes consistent occurrences that are clearly identifiable as delusional thinking then I would agree with it, yeah.

Q And, also lastly, being highly intelligent is not in any way inconsistent with delusional disorder; is it?

A No, it is not.

Q And, in fact, being extremely articulate is not inconsistent with delusional disorder?

A No.

Q Is it still fair to stay...one can still formulate a plan, engage in very deceptive and even intricate behavior, behavior that shows more forethought and planning, and still be suffering from delusional disorder persecutory subtype; is that correct?

A As a hypothetical question that is correct.[794]

4. Closing Arguments

Following the conclusion of the expert testimony, lawyers for both sides of the case presented closing arguments to the court [Judge Belfi]. The next section presents excerpts from the closing arguments for the defense (Mr. Kuby) and the people (Mr. Peck).

(a) Closing Argument by Mr. Kuby for the Defense

Mr. Kuby's closing arguments center on obvious mental illness and underscore Ferguson's pattern of paranoid and delusional be-

---

794. *See Id.* at 390–392.

havior before and subsequent to the shooting (e.g., hiring and discharging attorneys). In light of legal difficulties fueled by paranoid delusions, Mr. Kuby concludes Ferguson is not able to cooperate with counsel. In addition, Mr. Kuby questions the value of the medical opinions provided by the people's experts. On this point, Mr. Kuby challenges Dr. D'Alessandro's objectivity, as a witness, and emphasizes that Dr. Reichman's clinical opinion and CST findings are informed by a brief CST exam which failed to consider information pertaining to Ferguson's background. The closing statements are designed to suggest the people's experts neglected the historical pattern involving Ferguson's delusions of racism and the resulting problems (i.e., difficulties relating to education, employment, and the Workman's Compensation case and appeal). Excerpts from Mr. Kuby's closing arguments follow.[795]

> Colin Ferguson is insane. And of that there can't be any serious doubt. A sane person doesn't take a loaded pistol and massacre a train load of people he never met. Period. Colin Ferguson is also very intelligent, but that doesn't make him any less insane. He is also extremely articulate. That doesn't make him less insane.

> The only question we are here to resolve today is this one: how crazy is he? We have had three days of hearings in this case and [have] debated over [whether] Mr. Ferguson [is] delusional or just very paranoid. We tossed around terms of idea fixation or actual delusions, and we quibbled over definitions such as paranoid personality disorder or delusional disorder.[796]

> * * *

> Now, in this country and in our legal system we like to lay claim to the notion that we have a certain degree of enlightment. We say we don't try people who are incompetent, who are incapacitated. To do that would be hearkening back to English and French Common Law where they used to try mules who kicked their owners and would string them up in full view of our other mules presumably as an object lesson so the other mules would learn.

---

795. See Ferguson Pretrial Hearing Transcripts, December 9, 1994 at 426–445 (closing arguments/Mr. Kuby for the defense).
796. See Id. at 426–427.

We require people to understand the nature of the pleadings against them and to be able to participate in their own defense before we put them on trial. The prosecution has the burden of proof by a preponderance of evidence that Mr. Ferguson is competent.

Now, there is no doubt that Mr. Ferguson knows he is in a courtroom, knows he is facing charges, knows what those charges are. We are not contesting that. We have never contested that. That is only one element of competency.

The other element of competency is he able to assist in his own defense? And the courts have defined that term..., as whether the defendant has sufficient present ability to consult with his attorney with a reasonable degree of rational understanding.

Mr. Ferguson does not. He suffers from delusional disorder persecutory type. He has firm and fixed and unshakeable delusions of persecution. He is incapable of forming any relationship on the basis of trust.

He is incapable of trusting another attorney, any attorney, enough to rationally evaluate the advice that attorney provides.

And everyone who tries to help Colin Ferguson always ends up in exactly the same position: sooner or later they become part of the racist conspiracy, they are being accused of doing crazy and absolutely untrue things. Everyone, always without exception, white, brown, black and otherwise, we all become a part of the conspiracy to deprive him of an education, to blind him, to murder him, and to make the Number 2 train run improperly, the craziest kinds of things. You have seen this over and over again.

Everything that Mr. Ferguson is told, no matter how well-meaning it is, ends up being filtered through the dark and murky and distorting lens of his own paranoia. And we know this to be true based on absolutely everything we know about Colin Ferguson.

We know it from Dr. Richard Dudley, who is a psychiatrist of remarkable achievement and professional standing, who has conducted the longest, most in-depth examination of Colin Ferguson that anybody has ever conducted. He spent more time with him. And he is also the only psychiatrist to take the time to review the records from Adelphi University, from the Worker's Compensation Board, from Nassau Community College, to talk to people who knew Colin Ferguson before Colin Ferguson needed some sort of legal defense.

And Dr. Dudley tells the Court that Colin Ferguson is suffering from delusional disorder persecutory subtype. He very carefully took us through all of the criteria for that diagnosis as set forth in the Diagnostic and Statistical Manual.

As you listen to the definition, Judge, just listen: non-bizarre delusions apart from the impact of those delusions, the behavior is not obviously odd or bizarre. There is a central belief that the person is being conspired against, cheated, obstructed, the smallest things may become exaggerated, and the focus of the delusional system, it is often on some injustice that must be remedied by legal action and the affected person to be engaged in the repeated attempts to appeals in court or often resentful and angry and may resort to violence.

My God, Judge, you listen to that and you say, "Gee, do we know somebody who fits that description." Yes, we do. It's Colin Ferguson. It's a description tailor-made for Colin Ferguson. It is exactly the kind of person we have seen.

I would submit that the testimony of Dr. Reichman is also instructive on this point. His testimony ultimately was very equivocal. When I asked him about delusional disorder persecutory type he said well he thought paranoid personality disorder was just as likely, perhaps more likely.

He also acknowledged that Colin Ferguson was very paranoid...I asked him about Mr. Ferguson's interpretation of [the incident involving his eye injury and the trip to the hospital] and how Mr. Ferguson interpreted that as you [Judge Belfi] and the D.A. and myself and Mr. Kunstler all constructing this fake emergency to have Mr. Ferguson brought to the hospital then brought back to the jail without eye care so that he would go blind, so that he couldn't identify the actual Caucasian shooter on the Long Island Rail Road train.

What did Dr. Reichman say about that? He said it sounds very much like a delusion. He couldn't diagnosis it without more information. He needed to see a pattern. And with commendable honesty he admitted he had not reviewed any of the documentation of Mr. Ferguson's aberrant and bizarre and delusional behavior that took place prior to December 7th [1993].

Even Dr. D'Alessandro, who I submit was the most biased witness we saw in this case, even he was sufficiently uncomfortable with his own diagnosis; that he said it would be very useful to do another competency evaluation upon everything we now know about Colin Ferguson, everything we learned about him since the original competency evaluation on December 28th 1993.[797]

* * *

You have Colin Ferguson, a crazy man, rejecting the defense of insanity for an utterly irrational reason. He maintains he didn't do it dispite [sic] overwhelming and absolutely irrefutable evidence to the contrary.

...Even Dr. Reichman admits that if Colin Ferguson is rejecting an insanity defense for that reason it is not a rational decision.

So I ask you judge, is the insanity defense only available to someone sane enough to claim it? If you're looking for a pattern to Colin Ferguson's delusional behavior, if that is what one needs to make this diagnosis, well we certainly have a pattern.

First look at the lawyers. For the Worker's Compensation Board Mr. Ferguson hires Lee Braunstein to represent him on a claim. Mr. Braunstein does so. He thinks he settled the case. Mr. Ferguson immediately rejects the settlement that he agreed to and fires Mr. Braunstein claiming he engaged in legal acts absolutely inapplicable to his claims. Of the judges involved in the Compensation Board, they were all racists. He hires a new representative, Christine Lee....she has a tenure of two months. We don't know what the problem is. There is a new lawyer on the scene, Irwin Silverman. What does he say about him? Well in a letter to the Worker's Compensation Board, in which Mr. Ferguson is complaining that even the security guards at the Board are members of a violent cult group the Hebrew Israelites, he says Mr. Silverman "hates [me] to death and does not believe that a black who stands up for justice deserves to be paid for his injury." He fires him and ultimately represents himself.

...What about this case? Well we see Anthony Falanga, the first attorney. This was an attorney who didn't speak to the

---

797. *See Id.* at 427–433.

press, who didn't coin the term "black rage," who made no public statements or utterances about his client. No cooperation from Mr. Ferguson. And, again, Mr. Ferguson makes up a wild series of allegations about Mr. Falanga, none of which are true.

Mr. Falanga gets discharged, and Mr. Ferguson calls us up and asks us if we would take the case. We agree to do so. And after a very short honeymoon we too become the people who are conspiring against him, dispite [sic] our efforts to retain an eye care specialist and ultimately are successful at getting a specialist. We are accused of making him go blind and accused of conspiring with you [Judge Belfi] and ultimately accused of being part of a murder plot with the D.A. and Nassau County Sheriffs' Department and the Court....

Judge, this is not a man who is capable of rationally accepting and evaluating information and advice that he is given....

Now, I know what Mr. Peck is going to get up and argue that Colin Ferguson is malingering. We have heard that word a lot in this case, that this is all some sort of clever ploy by Mr. Ferguson to achieve some sort of unstated objective, that is basically what Dr. D'Alessandro said. But the problem with making that agreement is you have to figure out what the point is.

Dr. D'Alessandro said that Colin Ferguson was malingering in order to be found incompetent so there would be no trial.

But Mr. Peck has argued, and I expect he is going to argue again, that Colin Ferguson does want to go to trial, he [Mr. Peck] insists he [Mr. Ferguson] is not incompetent, he wants to go to trial, he wants to face the charges, he would rather go to jail than a mental institution.

It absolutely makes no sense, this allegation of malingering.

What does make sense, and Dr. Dudley and Dr. Reichman and Dr. D'Alessandro acknowledge it might be true, is that on December 28th when he was in chains and shackles and a group of court-appointed psychiatrists came to examine him, that he was not going to cooperate with them because he perceived, and in this case somewhat rightly, that they were not out to help him; that they were part of this conspiracy against him, he deliberately understated his abilities to perform these simple cognition examinations.

If Mr. Ferguson wished to be found incompetent you would have expected that he would not be assisting so hard...he is competent. If he wished to be found incompetent you would not have him rejecting the psychiatric examination [but] you would have him running up to psychiatrists, especially a defense psychiatrist, and running up to him and saying "Mr. Defense Psychiatrist, see how crazy I am? Watch me. Aren't I crazy, Judge? Aren't I crazy, Mr. Psychiatrist?" That is the kind of behavior you would expect if that was Mr. Ferguson's real agenda. You haven't seen that; just the opposite.

Now, Mr. Peck is going to argue, I believe, what he has indicated in the course of his questioning and that is Mr. Ferguson isn't suffering from delusions; that he is suffering from some sort of lesser form of mental illness. Dr. Dudley says he is delusional. Dr. Reichman says he is not sure. He really isn't. He would like more information. At least one episode may have been a delusion. He would like to see a pattern....

The essential feature of a delusion, according to the DSM, is that it is unshakable, no matter how much evidence one amasses to the contrary, no matter how much information one is given that [the] delusion is not true, [the person does not] abandon that delusion. That is the nature of delusional disorder. And I would ask Mr. Peck to show one example in Mr. Ferguson's life where ... Mr. Ferguson was confronted with evidence that he was wrong [and] he then changed his position. Never happened, Judge. Not at the Worker's Compensation Board, not at Adelphi University, not at Nassau Community College, not with his previous lawyers, not here, not today, never. That is because Mr. Ferguson suffers from delusions.

Now it is certainly true that Colin Ferguson is capable, more than capable, of planning, recognizing legal processes and utilizing them ... People with delusional disorder persecutory subtype love to litigate. That is one of the features. [a] constant seeking of redress through the legal system. The DSM says so. Mr. Ferguson's life has been one long attempt to obtain redress for legal and imagined grievances. That hardly disproves the diagnosis. That, in fact, helps to confirm it....

I know that there is tremendous pressure from the community, from the district attorney's office, to have a trial in this case. We just lived through the anniversary of the shooting and we hear people calling for a trial. I know it is hard to resist that call, but you should.

Judge, don't think for one moment that by putting Mr. Ferguson on trial and having him go forward with his crazy defense, and having him get convicted, and having him go off to jail, don't think for one moment that is going to deter some other madman, some other insane person, from committing some act that may take place. The nature of insanity is that it is not amenable to reason, it is not susceptible to lesson, it is not susceptible to deterrence.

Colin Ferguson has never been treated psychiatrically. So we don't know whether [he] can be restored or stabilized through medical care, through psychiatric treatment whereby he would actually be capable of sitting at a table, conferring with counsel and making rational decisions. But you know it is worth a try, Judge, because otherwise, he is going to go to trial.

This insane defense he has he didn't do it, he will get convicted and go to jail and it is almost certain, Judge, that two or three or four or five or ten years from now someone will murder him in jail... and this whole proceeding will be a footnote. We will have one more interview with the families of the victims and that will be the end of it. That won't be justice. That won't be a form of law. That won't be a procedure that any of us should feel good about or comfortable with.[798]

* * *

The trial that we are going to have here, if Colin Ferguson is found competent to stand trial, is going to be an obscene and a tragic spectacle. I know that the prosecutor is anxious to strike Mr. Ferguson's insanity defense and the prosecutor wants to go forward no matter what because at the end of the day it is a lot easier to prove that Colin Ferguson did the shooting than it is to show that he is sane. But the trial of a crazy man, representing himself, with an irrational defense is not going to be a trial for which the prosecution can take or should take any joy. It is going to demean everyone it touches. It's going to debase us all. It's going to be [a] horrific spectacle and it doesn't have to happen.

I'm asking you to stop it and declare this man mentally incompetent and send him to a mental institution where he belongs.

Thank you, Judge.[799]

---

798. *See Id.* at 442–444.
799. *See Id.* at 434–445.

(b) Closing Argument by Mr. Peck for the People

Mr. Peck's closing argument emphasizes the poor relationship between the accused and Mr. Kunstler and Kuby. Mr. Peck stresses that Ferguson is oriented to time, date, and place (e.g., the defendant knows the anniversary of the shooting), and argues further that Dr. Dudley's findings of delusional disorder are false. Mr. Peck draws attention to Ferguson's legal decisions as evidenced in conversations with A.D.A. Riordan Mulder where the defendant explains his rationale for rejecting the "black rage" insanity defense (i.e., because he could not win). The closing arguments suggest that Ferguson's legal decisions, although not appropriate nor strategic, are calculated and, thus, not a product of delusions. In addition, Mr. Peck intimates that Ferguson perhaps suffers from paranoid personality disorder not delusional disorder— the psychotic disorder interposed by Dr. Dudley. Mr. Peck concludes by indicating that a decision to reject a mental health defense is a considered judgement (i.e., Ferguson's desire not to be labeled mentally impaired) and, more importantly, is the defendant's right. Excerpts from Mr. Peck's closing arguments follow.[800]

> Judge, Mr. Kuby throws around the terms "insanity" and "competency" as if they were equal. Now, that is not the test. You know it is not the test and I know it is not the test. The test is whether or not he can assist in his own defense.
>
> Now that doesn't necessarily mean his lawyer's defense, and that is the heart of the problem. If you look at the history of this case it is the lawyer's defense that Ferguson has the problem with.
>
> Now look at his letters...and look at the whole history of the case. But what do we know? We know one thing: that he certainly is oriented as to date, time and place. We know that. That is a consideration you [Judge Belfi] have to make...I believe it was Tuesday [December 6th 1994] when he said to you look tomorrow is going to be one year and I don't want to come to court—very, very oriented as to date, time and place...He has written formal motions to you with regard to

---

800. *See* Ferguson Pretrial Hearing Transcripts, December 9, 1994 at 426–454 (closing arguments by Mr. Peck for the people).

what constitutes the denial of a speedy trial motion. He has written formal motions to you with regard to testimony in the grand jury. He knows what is going on.....

Now, the history and analysis of this case is very, very important and your [Judge Belfi] personal observations of the defendant are very, very important. Basically what Dr. Dudley is saying is that the defendant was delusional back in December, was delusional before, is delusional throughout and is delusional right now. That is what Dudley is saying. He is saying it is everything. Is that a fact?...Does the testimony in this case bear that out? Hardly.

Look at the testimony from Maureen Riordan Mulder [A.D.A. assigned to investigate and prosecute the inmates who attacked Colin Ferguson in the jail]. What does she say? She says she has been on...the case involving the jail-house assault for a long time. Apparently Mr. Ferguson has an interest in that case. And she was able to converse with him very, very well because he has a motive to be interested in that particular case.[801]

* * *

He says to her [A.D.A. Maureen Riordan Mulder] "you don't use any black rage defense in Nassau County because you are going to be found guilty." What does that indicate? It means that he is telling Riordan that I have analyzed my possible defense here, "I have analyzed the suggestion from my lawyers, but I have rejected it because I can't win." That is not necessarily the mark of a delusional man. That is a mark of a man who is listening to and weighing his options.

Now, in this court of law for the first time I believe Mr. Kuby has called him [Mr. Ferguson] insane. In this court of law right now. You can see from the tone of the letters and the history of this particular case that what Mr. Ferguson is most annoyed with, and he asked you [Judge Belfi] on numerous occasions to shut them up by means of a restraining order, what he is most annoyed with is Mr. Kunstler and Mr. Kuby making public statements which are disseminated in the media telling the world that he is crazy; that he is insane. That is the general theme. And if you talk about whether or not someone...is a little paranoid about that, that has a definite basis in reality.

---

801. *See Id.* at 445–447.

Now, if it has a definite basis in reality then it is not delusional at all. As a matter of fact, Mr. Kunstler and Mr. Kuby have fueled the fires as to what is going on before you right now because they keep it up. I'm not saying...in fairness to them, that this is not good strategy on their part as lawyers. But what I am saying is that when they take completely divergent views from the view of their client it is going to make the divergence between them greater, and that is what is happening. And this defendant has been asking you for months to bring this matter to a head and to relieve them [Kunstler and Kuby]. That is not delusional at all. Perhaps it is certainly reflective of a paranoid personality disorder, perhaps. But it is his choice.

Now, what did the psychiatrists and psychologists say? They basically said, based upon all of the information that they had, Mr. Ferguson has told them different stories at different times and they felt he was malingering. And they gave you the reasons for that at the time. And that means December 28th [1993] that he was malingering. And then they studied all of the materials, the material...that happened by way of transcripts that was set before you [Judge Belfi], and based upon all of the evidence now it is their opinion that he is competent. He certainly knows, he certainly understands the nature of the proceedings. But they also say something else. They try to tell you, and they try to tell us, what is the basis for Mr. Ferguson's mental problem, if any. And what they say is it is more consistent with paranoid personality disorder because by his very nature Mr. Ferguson is confrontational. And when he confronts people in that manner they react differently to him as they would to someone else.

And then he perceives that in some way as a reaction against him. Judge, that is not a delusion. That is paranoid personality disorder, if it exists.

...So far as Adelphi is concerned what did the Dean say? He said that they have a system of due process rights established in the school whenever there is a problem. He complied with that. He participated in it. Was he delusional then? The man is making choices. He is entitled to do that.

With regard to the psychiatrist [Dr. Dudley]...he said he originally spoke to him for three hours and got an awful lot of background information and he scheduled another examination of him and really wanted another examination of him. Dudley is playing solitaire with a deck of thirty-nine cards.

That is what he is doing. He really doesn't have the facts upon which to base an examination.

What are the diagnostic criteria for paranoid personality disorder? Let me read it into the record: A pervasive distrust and suspiciousness of others, such that their motives are interpreted as malevolent, beginning by early adulthood and present in a variety of contexts as indicated by the following: one, suspects without sufficient basis that others are exploiting, harming or deceiving him; two, is preoccupied with unjustified doubts, with the loyalty or trustworthiness of friends or associates; three, is reluctant to confide in others because of unwarranted fear that the information will be used maliciously against him or her; four, reads hidden meaning or threatening meanings into remarks or events; five, persistently bears grudges, unforgiving of insults, injuries or slights; six, perceives attack on his or her character or representations that are not apparent to others and is quick to react angrily or counter attack; seven, has recurrent suspicions without justification regarding fidelity of spouse or sexual partner. Except for number seven, this fits Colin Ferguson to a tee.

...According to D'Alessandro he is manipulating this system. You saw that. We had a hearing lasting two days with regard to his eyes. They are perfect. You saw that yesterday when he was examined by a doctor. His health was perfect throughout. Every consideration has been given to him concerning all of these allegations that he is making.

He understands you. He understands me. But basically, Judge, what is at the heart of it, and you can see by his behavior, there is a certain amount of ego and pride attached to this man. And he doesn't want to be labeled someone who is insane, who has a mental disorder. That is his choice.

Thank you.[802]

---

802. *See Id.* at 448–454

5. Opinion of the Court: The Issue of Competency, Addressing Ferguson's Requests to Proceed Pro Se, and Strike the Insanity Defense

As previously noted, the primary issue before the Court was whether Colin Ferguson was a mentally incapacitated person and, as a result, was not competent to stand trial. In other words, the question before Judge Belfi was whether the people (Mr. Peck) met their burden (established by a preponderance of the evidence) that Mr. Ferguson was *not*, as a result of mental disease or defect, substantially impaired in his ability to (1) assist in his own defense and (2) understand the nature of the proceedings against him.[803] In a perfunctory decision, Judge Belfi found Colin Ferguson competent to stand trial.

In addition to the initial matter involving competency, the pretrial hearing (from December 6–9, 1994) also addressed Ferguson's request to proceed *pro se* to trial and his position on the defense of insanity as raised by Kunstler and Kuby. We present the relevant excerpts regarding Judge Belfi's CST ruling and the subsequent colloquy between Judge Belfi and Mr. Ferguson on the matter of the collateral requests.[804]

(a) Judge Belfi's Ruling on the Competency Issue

Based on all of the evidence elicited at this hearing, the arguments of counsel, the observations of the defendant made by the Court throughout all of the earlier proceedings the numerous colloquies…the Court and defendant on August 19th 1994, wherein the Court [Judge Belfi] found the defendant to be competent; and on November 10th 1994 reassurance to the defendant that the November election of Governor-Elect Pataki and his position on the death penalty would not apply to the defendant, the Court finds pursuant to Section 730.10

---

803. *See* N.Y. CRIM. PROC. LAW § 730.10 and 730.30. Note Section 730.10 and 730.30 of New York's Criminal Procedure Law (defining an incapacitated person and incompetency) adheres to the criteria set forth in *Dusky*.

804. *See* Ferguson Pretrial Hearing Transcripts December 9, 1994 at 454–495 (Judge Belfi's opinion on CST and collateral issues/Ferguson's request to proceed *pro se* and Ferguson's application to strike the insanity defense).

and 730.30 of the C.P.L. (criteria that must be met to be considered incompetent/incapacitated person), that the defendant is not an incapacitated person; in that he does not as a result of mental disease or defect lack capacity to understand the proceedings against him and to assist in his own defense.

The Court having found the defendant to be competent the criminal action against him must proceed.[805]

(b) Collateral Issues: Judge Belfi's Ruling on Ferguson's Request to Proceed Pro Se and Application of the Insanity Defense.

THE COURT:	The second thrust of this hearing, Mr. Ferguson, is a request by you to proceed *pro se*.
THE DEFENDANT:	Yes.
THE COURT:	You still reiterate that request and is that still your desire?
THE DEFENDANT:	Absolutely.
THE COURT:	There are a number of questions I want to ask you in reference to it so that at some subsequent time it will be available to an appellate court, if that point is reached.[806]

In addition to general background questions (e.g., age; education; work history; legal history and specifically his involvement in the Worker's Compensation case),[807] the Court raised more substantive inquires about Mr. Ferguson's ability to represent himself and the potential pitfalls of proceeding *pro se* to trial. In what follows, we present excerpts from the exchanges between Judge Belfi and Mr. Colin Ferguson.

THE COURT:	To the best of your recollection you have never had a situation where you represented yourself in any type of hearing; is that correct?

---

805. *See Id.* at 454–455.
806. *See Id.* at 455.
807. *See Id.* at 455–457.

THE DEFENDANT: Not in the hearing itself, but I have done my own appeals to the Worker's Compensation Board. I have challenged the Equal Opportunity, EEOC as far as that, but that is outside of any type of hearing situation. At the board I did my own appeal.

THE COURT: Have you ever been involved in any other type of legal proceeding?

THE DEFENDANT: Do you have a specific definition of what you expect a legal proceeding to be?

THE COURT: Anything involving a court, judge, hearing room?

THE DEFENDANT: Except for the Worker's Compensation Board, traffic violations.

THE COURT: Have you represented yourself in traffic violations in a court?

THE DEFENDANT: Yes.

THE COURT: You understand that as intelligent as you may be, you lack normal training and education as an attorney?

THE DEFENDANT: I understand that.

THE COURT: And do you understand the lack of that knowledge is because you have never obtained it by legal education?

THE DEFENDANT: That's correct.

THE COURT: You also understand that the lack of this knowledge might cause you to be prejudiced during the trial, should you choose to represent yourself?

THE DEFENDANT: Yes.
I understand that, but would expect to be given all of the rights available to a regular attorney and the privileges that belong with that.

THE COURT: That goes without saying. That would happen. But you understand that you're not necessarily, in my opinion based upon your background, aware of all of the rights you might be entitled to, whereas an attorney would be aware of those rights?

THE DEFENDANT:	That is also correct, but I would approach you on that matter and I would expect to receive your assurance as to what I would be entitled to.
THE COURT:	You would rely upon the Court should you proceed *pro se?*
THE DEFENDANT:	I would rely upon your integrity and also the integrity of the Court. I see it as a whole synergy, therefore I would expect that you would be truthful to me. If not, I believe it would be an issue for the appellate court. I would also require a record of whatever we discuss, except that I ask perhaps a meeting in chambers and you would make a decision as to whether or not I would be able to.
THE COURT:	Are you presently under the influence of any alcohol or any drugs or have you taken any drug?
THE DEFENDANT:	No. It's no—no. I'm not delaying the answer to that, but it seems to me in jail it's impossible, but I'm not into that kind of thing. Never will be.
THE COURT:	Have you ever been treated for any mental illness or disorder?
THE DEFENDANT:	No, I have not.[808]

---

808. *See Id.* at 459–461. A question and answer session between Judge Belfi and Mr. Ferguson also touched on many aspects concerning jury selection and a potential change of venue. *See Id.* at 463–466. Specifically Judge Belfi pointed out that "in the state process the pool will only consist of panelists from where the crime was committed, or if there was a change of venue the residents of that county where the venue has been changed." Ferguson responded "...And I would have expected based on twenty-twenty hindsight that it would only be Brooklyn residents, because I believe I would be more comfortable with Brooklyn residents as part of the total jury pool to be selected...Justice is served on an equal basis. I believe there should be no discrimination as far as the defendant is concerned." *Id.* at 466.

Following this exchange, Judge Belfi questions, "Do you accept the fact that should there not be a change of venue you would be tried by Nassau County residents?" *See Id.* at 466. Mr. Ferguson states "I would have to abide by your ruling. Of course whatever is available to me I'll exercise and we'll take it from there [intimating a possible appellate issue]." *See Id.*

...

THE COURT:	Do you realize that other defendants have represented themselves and have been unsuccessful?
THE DEFENDANT:	I have not looked at specific facts or statistics on that, but I feel as if I can handle this matter.
THE COURT:	Do you also understand that should you be found guilty the fact that you appeared *pro se* or alone may not be a ground from which you can appeal?
THE DEFENDANT:	That is not something that I looked at in coming to my decision to go *pro se*. I believe I can depend on my integrity and my confidentiality as perceived within myself and I believe I can be a—for want of a better word—a formidable opponent to Mr. Peck.
THE COURT:	Why do you wish to proceed *pro se*; to be a formidable adversary for Mr. Peck?
THE DEFENDANT:	Absolutely not.
	I stated my feelings as far as my inner expectations. But your question, to answer your question, it has nothing to do with that. I believe I can prove my innocence. I believe I can be acquitted. And I believe I could do a better job than anyone else. I believe integrity is more important, more than raw expertise. Raw expertise without integrity is detrimental to the defendant.[809]

...

In the face of confusion, Judge Belfi poses a number of questions involving the impact of Ferguson's emotions during the course of the trial. Lucid one moment, unintelligible the next, Colin Ferguson's response to the question of general risks in proceeding *pro se* to trial provides a curious exchange.

---

809. *See Id.* 466–468.

THE COURT:	Do you understand the risks of proceeding *pro se*?
THE DEFENDANT:	I would depend on you to inform me of those risks.
THE COURT:	Because you are personally involved you may—you may not be able to maintain the objectivity required of an attorney in the conduct of a trial. Do you understand an attorney acting in your behalf would be obliged to maintain such objectivity?
THE DEFENDANT:	On instant analysis of what you said, and immediate response, I would say yes indeed there are such risks. But I would question your integrity, and the integrity of the Court, if you want to ask of the assessment, that is the attorney to intervene without first debating the issue of my involvement, there would therefore have to be supporting basis for that, because of course I believe you would be tempted—with no disrespect to you, Judge, this is not disrespectful—I ask you not to see that way, for the Court intervene at a time when there is no need and to take-over the proceedings to my detriment. I would ask that you resist that temptation.
THE COURT:	Do you understand what I indicated about personal involvement and your personality might affect your ability to be objective?
THE DEFENDANT:	That is always a possibility, but I will diligently seek to avoid that.
THE COURT:	Do you also understand that you will be emotionally involved and you may be unable to control your behavior and/or exercise the discipline necessary to ensure that you get a fair trial?
THE DEFENDANT:	I believe the prevailing circumstances would far outweigh that. I believe just my inability,

for example, to not adequately represent myself based on lack of expertise I believe the other matters which have been brought before the Court would far outweigh that.

For instance, the matter of can Ferguson get a fair trial in Nassau County? What about the way in which the Court has handled the proceedings thus far? I believe an appellate court would have no problem putting aside my inadequacies and look at the bigger instances of injustice toward me.

THE COURT: Do you think you could control your emotions during the trial?

THE DEFENDANT: Absolutely. I don't think you have found any instance that I have not been able to control it here. I have been friendly towards everyone. I have complained, yes. That is my right. And notwithstanding it's very very difficult for me in the situation at the jail, and I am also subjected to inhuman treatment, etcetera, I believe we can work that out.

I do not believe I could ask any officer to go back retroactively in time to correct an injustice against me. I'm willing to have them start at a new setting and turn over a new leaf and begin from there. I'm prepared to deal with them on that basis.[810]

Judge Belfi emphasizes the trial is more restrictive than the competency hearing. In this instance, Ferguson shifts the conversation to include issues of security and, specifically, whether he can remove the shackles during the trial proceedings. The judge questions whether security issues were the basis on which the defendant chose to conduct his own legal action.

---

810. *See Id.* at 468–471.

THE COURT:	Do you know that the Court would be more restrictive insofar as any discussions you might want to have or questions you want to ask in the presence of a jury than it has been in the give and take of the hearings that have gone on up until today?
THE DEFENDANT:	Let me just test my understanding of what you just said.
	You would be, for instance, referring to an approach to the bench for discussion or to discuss a motion for example? Are you referring to that?
THE COURT:	Yes.
THE DEFENDANT:	If there is a legal basis to deny me of that I would have to take a look.
	However, my main concern would be the removal of shackles. For instance, I believe that body movement is a language within itself which constitutes speech which is covered under the First Amendment, freedom of speech.
	Therefore, if Mr. Peck has the ability to enhance his verbal presentation to the jury with his body movement, which I say is very articulate, that I be afforded the exercise of freedom of speech.
THE COURT:	Do you understand absent any security reason that if you were to be represented by an attorney at the trial in all likelihood you would not have shackles on you?
THE DEFENDANT:	Pardon me?
THE COURT:	Do you understand that if you were represented by an attorney and there were no security reasons why you should be shackled that you would not be shackled during the course of a trial with an attorney representing you?
THE DEFENDANT:	I think you're at this time giving me almost a combination of something that is seemingly hypothetical and futuristic

which, under the circumstances, no one has said to me in any way or form there are security reasons why I should or should not be. I cannot answer the question effectively not unless you said to me specifically that you have seen them or know of reasons why that should be so, then I can respond to that.

THE COURT: Do you understand the thrust of my question has to do with whether or not you're shackled or unshackled that has nothing to do about whether you should be represented by a lawyer or not?

THE DEFENDANT: You're saying—you're asking me do I understand that for instance if Mr. Kuby were to represent me I would not necessarily be shackled not unless you had reasons—

THE COURT: Exactly.

THE DEFENDANT: — to have security around me?

THE COURT: Exactly.

THE DEFENDANT: No one approached me with that kind of discussion. I'm saying it's impossible for me to answer your question unless you first come to me and say this is going to be the case based on my findings or feelings. Then I could answer the question effectively. I do ask if I go *pro se* I could be afforded the same freedoms as Mr. Peck.

THE COURT: As I said, you would be afforded the same freedoms within the boundaries and confines of your behavior and security precautions. But by virtue of the fact that you are going *pro se* is not going to give you any more liberty than had you been represented by an attorney throughout the trial. In other words, I'm suggesting to you just for the reason to forego security is not the reason to give up a right to have an attorney representing you.

THE DEFENDANT: No one said that is the reason. Which in my letters to you—which I hope to see copies of all of them, to the extent I need to know how many got to you—I think that is the reason or even suggest there might be a suspicion otherwise.[811]

...

The next gambit of questions addresses Ferguson's ability to maintain his train of thought per objection by the District Attorney.[812] Judge Belfi also discusses the defendant's right to raise objections during the proceedings and the appropriate and expected behavior during these motions and rulings (e.g., not arguing with the Court's decision following an objection).

THE COURT: Would you assure me that you will not engage in conduct which would prevent a fair exhibition of the issues in this trial?

THE DEFENDANT: Just a bit of humor here, object to form. You phrased it that way.

But conduct, I would need you to perhaps state an instance, an example, of something you would look at as not appropriate conduct during the process.

THE COURT: Arguments that might not be appropriate objections, and then attempting to argue the Court's ruling after you made an objection.

THE DEFENDANT: I believe that sustaining the assistant district attorney's objections when there is no basis for it will eventually help me at the appellate level.

---

811. *See Id.* at 471–474.
812. *See Id.* at 475–477. Judge Belfi states "Basically what I was suggesting is if you are to either be questioned by somebody assisting you [legal advisor] or if you were to testify in a narrative form there may be an objection and it may be an appropriate objection, and you may become distracted and lose your train of thought, which probably would not happen should an attorney be involved with the objection..." *See Id.* at 477. Ferguson answers "I believe that could be remedied by a request for a read back." *See Id.*

Equally, if I ask a question that by law is legally acceptable and you wish to exercise malice toward me by overruling it and allowing it, allowing an objectionable question to go through for Mr. Peck, it will be to the detriment of the Court, because it will not be an issue for—it will be an appellate issue, I would say.

THE COURT: You understand that should you disagree with any decision I make or for any reason whatsoever that the Court is not going to allow any disruptive behavior during the course of the trial?

THE DEFENDANT: I understand completely.

This is why my responses were such that it will be on record. And I think that you would know that and I would know that and Mr. Peck would know that so I would allow you to make as many errors as possible.[813]

...

Next, Judge Belfi considers the question of stand by counsel and Mr. Ferguson's position on the matter if in fact the defendant's application to proceed *pro se* to trial is granted.

THE COURT: Do you wish to have an attorney with you during the trial and be permitted to consult with that attorney at any time during the trial?

THE DEFENDANT: Just for my information, do you separate an advisor from say a stand-by attorney?

THE COURT: An advisor or stand-by attorney I think are the same words.

THE DEFENDANT: Same thing?

---

813. *See Id.* at 477–479. Judge Belfi also clarifies that Ferguson understands the potential punitive outcomes relative to a guilty finding. Judge Belfi states "Do you also understand that, I'm sure you do, if you are convicted you are exposing yourself to possible substantial jail time?" Ferguson replies "Indeed, yes. I understand that completely." *See Id.* at 479.

THE COURT: Yes.

THE DEFENDANT: Okay.

THE COURT: As acting *pro se* you would be representing yourself. I'm asking you whether or not you would want somebody to be available should you have a question of law, should you have a question that you would like to ask that advisor in private? And that advisor of course would be an attorney.

THE DEFENDANT: I will respond in this way: regardless of what is said, I do not consider myself a malicious person.....What I have to say is I would easily accept if Mr. Kunstler and Mr. Kuby [as my advisors]....They already know what is in the file.

Of course, I understand their relationship is contrary to mine without question.

However, their abilities, their record indicates that there is no one better to seek legal advice and information from.

I believe that these two gentlemen have the ability and wherewithal to separate the issues that were ugly before the court in terms of my attempting to relieve them, and having been successful, I believe they can rise above that and provide for me, because they so love their profession, that they will do a good job.

As a matter of fact, I believe I will be getting a gift of a book. I do not mind it. I would prefer to have these gentlemen on their time. If they can't show up at a particular date, that's fine. I do not expect them to bend to the extent of my whims or fancies.

THE COURT: If the Court were to grant your application and allow you to proceed *pro se* any attorney that the Court would appoint to advise you would have to be present at all

	times and be available to you at all times whether you choose to talk to them or not.
THE DEFENDANT:	Would Mr. Kuby answer that question for you? Would you allow him? He would know best.
THE COURT:	I think Mr. Kuby has indicated that if appropriate he and Mr. Kunstler would act as your advisors, if the Court grants your application [to proceed *pro se*], and would be available knowing full well that it is their obligation to be present during every time you appear in court and whenever there is any proceeding involved in the case.[814]

...

THE COURT:	There is no doubt in your mind that you wish to proceed *pro se*?
THE DEFENDANT:	There is no doubt in my mind.[815]

...

THE COURT:	...Based upon the totality of the circumstances, I believe your request is unequivocal to proceed *pro se*. I think you have made a knowing and intelligent waiver of the right to have counsel present. You have indicated to the Court that you are going to proceed in a fair and orderly exposition of the issues involved in this case. You made a timely assertion of your right to proceed *pro se*, and I must say to you I grant your request with great reluctance because I think it is going to be a very unfortunate situation, a very difficult trial. This is a very difficult case. I think it is a case that cries out for representation by able counsel, as you already have, and my

---

814. *See Id.* at 481–484.
815. *See Id.* at 487.

own personal advice to you is that I think
you are doing a foolish thing. But you do
have the right to proceed *pro se* and I feel
that you made an intelligent and unequivocal waiver of that right.
Is that still your desire to go *pro se?*

THE DEFENDANT: It is still my desire to go *pro se.*[816]

The final issue addressed by the Court concerned the insanity defense interposed by Kunstler and Kuby. The exchange, however,
was filled with a curious set of responses by Ferguson. Of particular
interest was the accused's obsession with the process of "withdrawing" the insanity defense as an option. Ferguson failed to understand or, more accurately, refused to accept that Kunstler and Kuby
had previously introduced the defense as a possible option which is
a customary practice when insanity is contemplated. Asserting that
the competency hearing was illegal, Ferguson failed to comprehend
that the issue of an insanity defense had to be revisited. This exchange is testament to the fact that Ferguson's seemingly knowledgeable and intelligent application of the law often dovetailed into
a perceived conspiracy theory (e.g., the attorneys applied the insanity defense so they could deny him of his rights).

THE COURT: The final issue I think we have to resolve
right now is that a defense of mental disease or defect, commonly known as an insanity defense, has been interposed by Mr.
Kunstler and Mr. Kuby while they were
representing you.
Is it your desire to continue to have that
defense available to you or is it your desire
to withdraw that defense, that notice of
that defense and the ability to use that defense?

THE DEFENDANT: My position has not changed. I said to the
Court at no time did I authorize the use of
an insanity defense or authorize the presentation of such papers and motions to

---

816. *See Id.* at 492.

the Court, and will continue to view it that way. So in my mind it is not a case of now withdrawing my intent to use an insanity defense. My position is that I have never, ever authorized the use of one, and therefore those papers should not have been entered into the court proceedings whatsoever.

THE COURT: Just mechanically, for purposes of clarity of the record, even though you state you did not authorize it, as now acting as your own attorney do you withdraw that request?

THE DEFENDANT: Again, we are now getting into legalities here as to wording.

THE COURT: I think it is a simple yes or no question.

THE DEFENDANT: The use of the word "withdraw" suggests previous action and a reversal of that action. I'm saying that there is not going to be a reversal of the action. It's a constant position that has never changed. In other words, from my perspective no such document has been entered, no such intent has been entered, the hearing was completely illegal, the competency hearing.

I would like the Court to strike it.

THE COURT: Your application is granted [withdrawing the insanity defense].[817]

6. Summary of Ferguson's Pretrial Competency Hearing

Colin Ferguson (a.k.a. the Long Island Railroad gunman) was accused of murdering six train passengers and attempting to murder nineteen others on a commuter line in Long Island, New York. Afer his arraignment on the charges, psychiatrists were appointed by the

---

817. *See Id.* at 494–495.

court to evaluate whether Ferguson was an incapacitated person and, as a result, was incompetent to stand trial. Pursuant to the court order (December 28, 1993), the doctors conducted a brief exam and concluded Ferguson was mentally fit to stand trial. As the case moved closer to trial, however, Ferguson requested to waive counsel, proceed *pro se* to trial, and strike the insanity defense. Given the import of these requests, the defense team raised yet again the issue of competency which resulted in a formal hearing to resolve the matter.

In the pretrial competency hearing, the defense called Dr. Dudley who testified that Ferguson suffered and continued to suffer from delusional disorder, persecutory sub-type. To support the findings, the defense expert relied on psychiatric evidence indicating a long pattern of paranoid beliefs and delusions. Although Ferguson refused a follow up examination,[818] Dr. Dudley asserted that Ferguson maintained his paranoid delusional beliefs in the face of irrefutable evidence. The clinical expert concluded that because Ferguson was suffering from delusional disorder, persecutory subtype he was not competent to stand trial and specifically not able to assist in the defense.

Since Ferguson refused any subsequent CST exams, the prosecution called Drs. D'Alessandro and Reichman who conducted the initial competency exam for the Court. In the pretrial competency hearing, the clinical forensic experts for the people testified that Ferguson was rational and did not experience delusions. They concluded that Ferguson was malingering. Their main evidence of malingering included inconsistent thought and contradictory statements. For example, on some occasions Ferguson could memorize simple symbols and numbers; on other occasions he could not. The defendant also chose to explain the meaning of some analogies and then not others. To further support their contention of malingering, Drs. D'Alessandro and Reichman suggested that Ferguson had an expressed purpose and plan to mislead the doctors during

---

818. As mentioned, Dr. Dudley evaluated Ferguson on May 17, 1993 per request by the defense to gather general information on Ferguson's mental status. The initial thrust of the exam was to determine whether Ferguson suffered from a mental disorder. Since Ferguson refused follow-up examination, Dr. Dudley relied on the three hour meeting to determine whether Ferguson was an incapacitated person and as a result was incompetent to stand trial.

the CST review. In sum, the prosecution's experts testified that Ferguson understood the trial proceedings, the charges against him, the penalties, the role of court officials, and could assist in the defense. During cross-examination, the experts conceded that Ferguson perhaps suffered from paranoid personality disorder; however, they ultimately concluded that the accused was neither incapacitated nor incompetent.

Following the three-day competency hearing, Nassau County Court Judge Donald E. Belfi determined that the defendant was competent to stand trial. Belfi's conclusion was based on a single psychological report, testimony provided by the three evaluating experts, the previous competency findings, and his own questioning of Ferguson. After the defendant was found fit for trial, Ferguson struck the insanity defense interposed by Kuby and Kunstler, exercised his constitutional right to waive counsel, and decided to proceed *pro se* to trial.

Chapter 6

A Psychological and Legal Analysis: The Controversial Case of Colin Ferguson

OVERVIEW

The pretrial competency proceedings in the Colin Ferguson matter underscore the troubling connection between a defendant having paranoid and delusional mental health concerns, clinical evaluation methods/expert testimony, and questionable judicial decisions. In what follows, we provide a detailed analysis of where and how the psychological assessment of and legal standards for competency produced problematic outcomes in the administration of justice. Indeed, this chapter explains why Mr. Colin Ferguson was able to *pro se* his case, and how this determination was an outgrowth of the bizarre decision that found him competent to stand trial.

In order to facilitate an inquiry into these matters, chapter 6 is divided in to two main segments: a psychological investigation and a legal analysis. In these respective parts, general models, theories, and perspectives are described relative to ongoing competence-related concerns and then applied to the case of the Long Island Railroad gunman. In other words, the psychological and legal commentary that follows explores several noteworthy, compelling, and thorny theoretical positions on the matter of trial fitness and then demonstrates their practical meaning and significance by revisiting the relevant psycholegal issues in the Colin Ferguson pretrial competency proceedings. The section on psychological issues examines such matters as models of forensic evaluation, lack of uniformity in CST assessment practices, provisional diagnostic findings, ultimate legal issues and absolute clinical forensic opinions, and the presumed objectivity of the expert. The section on legal issues discusses such matters as New York case law precedent and legal limits, political influences in judicial decision making, the role of expert services in the courtroom, credibility rather than uniformity in CST examinations, the Ferguson trial and appeal, and the intersection of psychology, law, and competency to stand trial.

A. Psychological Analysis: An Overview of the Relevant Issues in the Case of Colin Ferguson

Thus far, a review of the expert testimony (via direct and cross examination) indicates that the court, in the face of competing psychiatric opinions, found Colin Ferguson competent to stand trial. In this section we explore the role of mental health experts in CST evaluations in general, especially as this relates to the expert clinical forensic courtroom testimony in the case of the Long Island Railroad gunman. As we contend, problems stemming from the trial fitness assessment methods go well beyond mere structural limitations (i.e., not using CST evaluation protocol) and include appending courtroom conclusions to the language of the ultimate legal question of competence, couching expert opinions in their most favorable light, and basing CST findings on provisional diagnostic judgements. These limitations are of particular interest when reviewing the case of Colin Ferguson.

As previously documented in the Ferguson pretrial hearing transcripts, various cross-examination gambits disclosed many instances in which CST assessment issues and the objectivity of the experts were questioned.[819] However, to avoid repetition of case materials, this section examines the more glaring problems embedded within the psychiatric testimony. These matters include the following: credibility of expert services; deficient or absent CST mea-

---

819. The systematic presentation of the direct and cross-examination is replete with examples exposing CST evaluation problems and instances that call into question the expert's objectivity (e.g., Dr. D'Alessandro's frequent work for the court).

sures; testimony addressing the ultimate issue of competency; framing expert opinions in their most positive fashion, and bolstering CST findings with provisional diagnostic conclusions.

1. Models for Forensic Evaluation and Direct and Cross-Examination Testimony: The Lack of Uniformity, the Issue of Competence, and Colin Ferguson

To comprehend the practical problems affiliated with the expert services rendered in the Colin Ferguson competency hearing, it is essential to examine models guiding mental health professionals in areas of forensic assessment. In their instructional text, Melton et al. discuss models in writing forensic reports,[820] and ways to convey these findings by way of direct testimony and cross-examination.[821]

In writing a forensic report, Melton et al. identify a six step process, including: (1) circumstances for the referral; (2) date and nature of clinical contacts; (3) collateral data sources; (4) relevant personal background information; (5) clinical findings; (6) psychological-legal formulations.[822] Separating factual information and descriptive materials (understood by clinical observation) from theoretical and inferential formulations, this format offers a sound way for the examiner to link the clinical data to the legal question in the referral.

When providing expert testimony by way of direct examination, a popular design is modeled after an inverted pyramid.[823] In this scheme, the preferred method organizes and presents the findings pursuant to the exam.

> the expert begins by describing evaluation techniques and the data those techniques have produced; then proceeds to inferences; and ends with the "peak," the summary conclusion. If

---

820. *See* EVALS. II *supra* note 24, at 524; Robert Bluglass, *The Psychiatric Court Report*, 19 MED. SCI. & L. 121 (1979). *See also* GERALD H. VANDENBERG, COURT TESTIMONY IN MENTAL HEALTH: A GUIDE FOR MENTAL HEALTH PROFESSIONALS AND ATTORNEYS (1993).
821. *See* EVALS. II *supra* note 24, at 524.
822. *See Id.*
823. *See Id.* at 531.

tests or laboratory procedures were used, the clinician should be prepared to discuss their validity and to describe the method of test development.[824]

In order to stave off more unpredictable cross-examinations, Melton et al. advise careful preparation of the materials.

> In general, the most important way of coping with this type of attack [cross-examination] is careful preparation... [C]onducting a careful evaluation, becoming familiar with the reliability and/or validity of tests used, going over one's deposition testimony, and consulting with the referral attorney should be part and parcel of the witness's pretrial work.[825]

Although direct and clear, the models in writing forensic reports and for conveying those findings via courtroom testimony suggest that there is general utility in evaluating whatever psycholegal matter emerges. However, we note that it is here that a considerable forensic dilemma becomes evident. Indeed, when writing reports the methodology indicates that particular areas should be addressed (e.g., circumstances for the referral, clinical findings); however, these instructional accounts fail to indicate that *certain* psycholegal matters require the use of *specific* assessment protocol. In a similar way, recommendations for courtroom testimony emphasize the issue of credible evidence. However, from this perspective, models for report writing and courtroom testimony stress general guidelines, ignoring the more important and weighty question of the evaluation method itself. As a result, the emphasis placed on general utility means that forensic examiners are able to conduct (freely) individualized assessments that have little or no structure. Consequently, the court is often confronted with conflicting findings via testimony gleaned from subjective test procedures. What is lost in the process is the issue of method in evaluation and, moreover, how exacting legal inquiries require specific evaluation procedures.

The need for targeted attention in psycholegal matters is perhaps best exemplified with the legal issue of competency to stand trial and the evaluations conducted to assess one's trial fitness. While general guidelines are often embraced by mental health practition-

---

824. See Id.
825. See Id. at 532.

ers (e.g., models in writing forensic reports and testimony), regrettably they are often shaped to meet only individual needs. Thus, practically speaking, the lack of uniformity allows "rogue" evaluations and testimony to dominate the forensic domain of competency to stand trial. Indeed, as Perlin asserts, "[i]n practice the standard of fitness to stand trial becomes discretionary with the psychiatric experts and lacks objective standard or explicit form."[826]

We note that in chapter 3 the evolution on the use of CST assessment instruments and the increased explanatory and predictive capabilities of the more contemporary protocol (i.e., MacCAT-CA) were presented in considerable detail, relative to *Dusky's* two-prong standard. As we explained, the more recent and recommended instruments endeavor to assess the *understanding* and *assisting* component embedded in *Dusky,* while examining the more practical issue of decisional competence. However, what has yet to be explicitly discussed is how these new instruments developed with decisional competence in mind comport with the everyday realities of those whose trial fitness is called into question. Notwithstanding those studies endorsing the notion that contemporary protocol are better equipped to assess competence-related abilities, the current practice trend recognizes that mental health professionals implement highly individualized checklists based on subjective scores and judgements. In other words, the clinical forensic literature has yet to address systematically the practical implications (and limitations) of the very instruments they recommend; instruments that are sound in theory but are, nonetheless, ostensibly deficient in application. As a result, different mental health experts frequently present to the court competing conclusions (in reports) and provide absolute opinions (in testimony) based on their unique methods for assessing competence to stand trial.

In sum, the absence of uniform measures complicates CST determinations when forensic examiners fail to implement standardized assessment protocol (affirmed by empirical research) that adequately evaluate important competence-related abilities (decisional competence). Individualized assessments inadequately evaluate

---

826. *See* IDENTIFICATION *supra* note 60, at 469 n. 92 *citing* Vann & Morganroth, *The Psychiatrist as Judge: A Second Look at the Competency to Stand Trial,* 43 U. DET. L.J. 2–3 (1965).

whether the defendant is making important strategic trial decisions (waiving the right to counsel) based on a mental illness. As one might expect, these limitations are further compounded when the accused evinces symptoms relating to certain mental health disorders (e.g., when the paranoid/delusional defendant waives counsel based on conspiracy theories). Moreover, leading accounts in the clinical forensic literature do not highlight potential CST assessment problems such as these and, consequently, the seminal research continues to perpetuate a process that ostensibly enables CST examiners to utilize those methods most familiar or comfortable to them. In short, we submit that what is needed is uniformity. In order to substantiate our concerns regarding individualized assessment methods informing and impacting CST evaluations, we review the fitness-to-stand-trial evaluations in the case of Colin Ferguson. As we demonstrate, the problematic and divergent styles for rendering such exams were prominently displayed in this case for this defendant.

2. Generalizing to Ferguson: Lack of Uniformity in CST Assessment Protocol, Provisional Diagnostic Findings, and Expert Services

The expert clinical forensic testimony in the case of the Long Island Railroad gunman exposes both assessment difficulties and further identifies validity and credibility problems relative to these services. More importantly, a review of the expert findings indicates that examiners conducted (highly) individualized assessments. These subjective CST procedures produced questionable results ultimately based on individual discretion. As we explain, the findings regrettably suggest that other issues were at play. Indeed, as we subsequently argue, the individualized CST assessments in the Ferguson case were implemented, to some extent, to meet the desired ends of the parties for whom the experts were employed. This section reviews these troubling matters.

The determination of incompetency reached by Dr. Dudley in his forensic report was based on his having conducted an extensive clinical interview. Although he addressed relevant background information derived from collateral data sources (e.g., Adelphi records, work history), Dr. Dudley neglected to discuss with Ferguson key aspects on the matter of competency (e.g., what would happen to the defendant if he was not found fit to stand trial). Conflating issues of responsibility and competence, Dr. Dudley searched for a relationship between Mr. Ferguson's criminal behaviors and a mental illness, and generalized the scope of the exam to involve multiple psycholegal issues.[827] As Dr. Dudley explained,

> CF's [Colin Ferguson] history, his behavior at/around the time of the murders, and his behavior since the murders have been such that the question has been raised as to whether he suffers from some form of mental illness that may have contributed to these behaviors. Therefore, CF's attorneys have referred him to this psychiatrist for an evaluation.[828]

Throughout the report, Dr. Dudley addressed matters pertaining to Ferguson's paranoid beliefs (e.g., personal notes and conversations with people who interacted with the accused). Dr. Dudley's clinical findings indicated that the defendant suffered from delusional disorder, persecutory type and, thus, his behavior both past and present was a result of this disorder. In conclusion, Dr. Dudley's psycholegal formulations linked his diagnostic finding to multiple issues. He suggested the utility of an insanity defense and intimated that the defendant was not competent to stand trial because he could not assist in the case. As Dr. Dudley therefore stated:

> ...It is the opinion of this psychiatrist that CF (Colin Ferguson) was suffering from a Delusional Disorder, Persecutory Type on 7 December 1993, and that as a result of this disorder he lacked substantial capacity to understand that what he was doing was wrong. It is also the opinion of this psychiatrist that CF continues to suffer from a Delusional Disorder, Persecutory Type and that as a result, he is unable to assist in his own defense.[829]

We note that Dr. Dudley's individualized assessment was limited in structure and was far-reaching in terms of what it attempted to

---

827. This practice is not uncommon in mental health examinations concerning the issue of competence. According to one study, of 106 reports audited regarding competency evaluations, none addressed the issue of competency, the explicit reason for the referrals. See A.L. McGarry, *Competency to Trial and Due Process via the State Hospital*, 122 AM. J. PSYCHIATRY 623 (1965).

828. See DUDLEY *supra* note 661, at 1.

829. See *Id.* at 14.

test. Although the initial thrust of Dr. Dudley's exam was to determine whether Mr. Ferguson was suffering from a mental disorder (and to his credit he did make such a case), the psychiatrist failed to evaluate the legal aspects associated with competency. Indeed, there is no evidence to suggest that *any* CST assessment instrument was employed and the direct and cross-examination testimony seem to indicate that this expert was not considering the use of any CST assessment protocol, even if the defendant had acceded to and complied with a follow-up meeting. Given the poorly structured evaluation of Ferguson, we maintain that Dr. Dudley's incompetency finding was informed largely by his own (subjective) opinions.

Similar to Dr. Dudley, the experts for the people also erred in various ways regarding their investigation on the issue of Ferguson's competence to stand trial. The pitfalls in Drs. D'Alessandro and Reichman's CST findings and opinions were best illustrated during cross-examination testimony. The cross-examination revealed that both Drs. D'Alessandro and Reichman failed to research important background information; data supporting claims that the accused, in the past and at the time of the pretrial hearing, had suffered from intense paranoid delusions of racism. Instead, Drs. D'Alessandro and Reichman spent the better bulk of their (brief) 90 minute interview focusing on the issue of malingering. The psychiatrists employed a simplistic tool used to eliminate possible neurological impairment, resulting in a finding that Ferguson was feigning mental illness. Clearly, the absence of rapport-building influenced the troubled interaction between Ferguson and Drs. D'Alessandro and Reichman on December 28, 1993. Indeed, the people's experts failed to establish any sort of working relationship with the defendant and, instead, subjected him to a pencil and paper test and a memory exam. Arguably, these instruments insulted Ferguson's intelligence, leading him to reject categorically the CST process altogether.

Similar to the defense expert, Drs. D'Alessandro and Reichman failed to use any traditional or contemporary CST instrument. Although they addressed the requisite questions pertaining to competency (i.e., understanding the charges and ability to assist with the defense), their CST findings were informed (largely) by their frustration with a noncompliant defendant. Administering their minimally useful tests, the individualized assessments they produced failed to adequately account for specific competence-related abilities. Indeed, during the pretrial hearing, both experts for the people testified that

Ferguson was neither incapacitated nor incompetent and, further, presented a weak argument on the relationship between the defendant's paranoid tendencies (substantiated in Ferguson history prior to the incident) and his requests to fire defense counsel. Moreover, Drs. D'Alessandro and Reichman rendered ultimate opinion conclusions based largely on competing statements made by Ferguson during the initial 730 assessment (e.g., conflicting statements made to the interviewing doctors and A.D.A. Riordan Mulder). Given that these experts rendered ultimate legal opinions on the issue of competency, we now address this disturbing psycholegal matter.

3. Ultimate Issues, Expert Services, and Ferguson

Another CST concern involves the practice of clinical forensic experts framing their findings in the language (and logic) of ultimate legal issues. On this score, the insights of Melton et al. are useful as they explain the problems stemming from opinions couched in this language.[830] Preliminarily, these commentators address the "ultimate issue" question by referencing the APA's recommendation on the matter which states that, "since it is not within the professional competence of psychologists to offer conclusions on matters of law, psychologists should resist pressure to offer such conclusions."[831] In addition, Melton et al. state that when faced with ultimate legal judgements (e.g, declarations of incompetency or insanity), psychologists do not have the expertise nor the responsibility to respond to such matters. Instead, they suggest that clinicians should indicate the limits of their expertise, focusing solely on their clinical data and professional opinions regarding the mental health of the client.

Another recommendation cited by Melton et al. suggests that practitioners state that their opinions are not based on scientific fact but, instead, are to be considered advisory only. This is especially important when responding to questions regarding "reasonable medical certainty" or "reasonable scientific certainty."[832] Below is

---

830. *See* EVALS II. *supra* note 24, at 543.
831. *See Report of the Task Force on the Role of Psychology in the Criminal Justice System, Recommendation 5*, in WHO IS THE CLIENT? (John Monahan ed. 1980).
832. *See* EVALS II. *supra* note 24, at 543–545.

an example of how a clinician should respond to an attorney posing an "ultimate-issue" question.

Attorney:	Doctor, are you saying that Mr. Doe should be committed to the state hospital for treatment?
Doctor:	Whether he *should* be committed is a decision a judge must make. It is beyond my skills as a psychiatrist to say that Mr. Doe is mentally ill and dangerous *enough* that his freedom should be restricted and treatment provided involuntarily. However, if it is the court's decision that he does need involuntary treatment, then I consider the most appropriate treatment setting to be a locked hospital ward.

In this example (and recommendation), the utility of recognizing the psychiatrist's limitations and emphasizing the judge's role in decision making regarding the ultimate legal issue is underscored.

When returning briefly to the Ferguson pretrial transcripts we note that the psychiatric experts were confronted with questions regarding the ultimate legal issue of competency. To avoid repetition of case materials only exacting excerpts are re-presented relative to the ultimate legal questions and responses on the matter of trial fitness. We recognize that although all of the experts offered opinions on this issue, the more noteworthy responses were provided by the experts for the people. Following a short colloquia affirming Dr. D'Alessandro's expertise as a psychiatrist, on direct examination Mr. Peck posed the following ultimate issue question to this psychiatrist. Seeking to elicit the full impact of D'Alessandro's testimony, Mr. Peck asked:

Q Dr. D'Alessandro, based upon that examination (initial 730 exam) did you form an opinion within a reasonable degree of medical certainty in your field of expertise as to whether or not at that time Colin Ferguson was or was not an incapacitated person?

A I felt at that time that he was not an incapacitated person.... [833]

---

833. *See* Colin Ferguson Pretrial Hearing Transcripts, December 7, 1994 at 173.

Once again, after establishing Dr. Reichman's expertise as a witness (e.g., degrees obtained, aspects of experience and training), Mr. Peck posed a similar question; however, this time he asked the doctor about particular aspects of competence as a legal issue (i.e., whether Ferguson understood the charges and whether he could assist in the defense). We note that this query fuels a misguided assumption; namely, that Dr. Reichman's conclusion was a scientific fact rather than an "advisory" suggestion.

Q Based upon your examination of Colin Ferguson—did you form an opinion within a reasonable degree of certainty in your field of expertise as to whether or not Mr. Ferguson, as a result of mental disease or defect, lacked capacity to understand the proceedings against him or to assist in his own defense?
   Did you form such an opinion?
A Yes, I did.
Q What was that opinion, please?
A My opinion was that he did not lack capacity to understand the charges against him or to participate in his defense... [834]

Direct testimony provided by Dr. Dudley indicates that he responded to ultimate legal issues as well. Dr. Dudley's response to queries centered on mental illness and particular aspects of the competency construct. Although the litigator's questions were not specifically tailored to a direct response on the legal issue of competency, the queries did attempt to elicit scientific certainty. Following a short question and answer exchange affirming Dr. Dudley's qualifications, the psychiatrist described his diagnostic findings.

Q Dr. Dudley based upon the review that you conducted have you determined with a reasonable degree of medical certainty whether Colin Ferguson suffers from a mental disease or defect?
A Yes.
Q What is that opinion?
A It is my opinion that he suffers from a delusional disorder of the persecutory sub-type... [835]

---

834. *See* Colin Ferguson Pretrial Hearing Transcripts, December 7, 1994 at 261.
835. *See* Colin Ferguson Pretrial Hearing Transcripts, December 6, 1994 at 27.

Later, Mr. Kuby posed ultimate issue questions consistent with criteria embedded in the incompetency doctrine.

Q Given his mental illness have you concluded to as [sic] reasonable degree of medical certainty whether Colin Ferguson is capable of assisting in his own defense?
A Yes.
Q What is that conclusion?
A No.[836]

Considering that the CST exams administered in the case of the Long Island Railroad gunman were fraught with structural limitations informed by troubling, if not flawed, evaluative practices, it is quite remarkable that any of the psychiatrists elected to offer ultimate legal opinions on the issue of competence in either their reports or their testimony. Unlike the recommendations identified in the forensic literature (avoid ultimate issue responses), all the experts provided quick and direct opinions expressed in language consistent with the ultimate legal issue of trial fitness. In sum, then, the doctors involved in the Ferguson pretrial competency proceedings rendered ultimate opinions based largely on provisional diagnostic conclusions couched in a way that was most consistent with their diagnostic findings. In the next section we address those thorny problems raised when mental health professionals are called on to work for the courts. In short, we discuss the dilemma of mental health experts whose forensic evaluations and clinical findings amount to an advocacy stance for the hiring party, and how diagnostic conclusions are employed to either maximize or minimize one's mental health condition.

4. Couching the Expert Opinion in the Most Favorable Light and Attorney Strategy

The implications of CST psychiatric evaluations and testimony run much deeper than just examining assessment utility and clinical opinions on ultimate legal issues. They are also influenced by social and political forces.[837] Despite governing ethical guidelines for

---

836. *See Id.* at 39.
837. *See E.g.*, PERLIN II *supra* note 573 § 14.06, at 226.

forensic assessment,[838] objective psychological evaluations are complicated by the outcome desires of the litigators.[839] Brodsky and Poythress speak to this very issue:

> "Mental health professionals who testify regularly find themselves subjected to pressures to join the attorney in the adversarial process. Afer all, the attorney who has engaged the experts is the person with whom the personal relationship has been established...It is not unusual, therefore, for some experts to find themselves committed to defending "their" attorney's position in a fierce and vigorous manner."[840]

Thus, from the above perspective, clinicians may feel compelled to advance an interposed legal strategy. Indeed, given the latitude afforded practitioners who apply their own CST assessment measures,[841] appeasing the hiring party can often be achieved by emphasizing differential diagnoses and diagnostic criteria. On this latter point, although mental health professionals may be unable to provide an absolute diagnosis (in light of CST time constraints), examiners can highlight the symptomatology (or the absence of it) in either the forensic report or in direct testimony. Thus, mental health professionals can preserve the integrity of the defense or prosecution's case (when findings are not consistent with the attorney) by couching CST findings "in their most favorable light." Indeed, discretionary assessments permit highly individualized opinions, allowing experts to phrase reports or to offer testimony consistent with coveted legal outcomes. In what follows, we present evidence suggesting that the experts involved in Colin Ferguson's assessment produced suspect CST findings designed, in part, to advance the legal aims of the attorneys who employed them.

---

838. *See generally* American Psychological Association, *Ethical Principles of Psychologists and Code of Conduct*, 47 AMERICAN PSYCHOLOGIST 1597 (1992).

839. To put the point more crudely, some suggest mental health experts are "hired guns," so to speak, and, for a fee, will flesh out evidence of almost anything asked. *See E.g.,* Peter Huber, GALILEO'S REVENGE: JUNK SCIENCE IN THE COURTROOM (1991).

840. *See* S. Brodsky & N. Poythress, *Expertise on the Witness Stand: A Practitioner's Guide*, in PSYCHOLOGY, PSYCHIATRY AND THE LAW: A CLINICAL AND FORENSIC HANDBOOK 389, 391 (C.P. Ewing ed. 1985).

841. *See* Yates *supra* note 569, at 353–354.

5. Generalizing to Ferguson: Advancing Legal Theories, Paranoid and Delusional Disorders, and Pejorative Affect

In the Ferguson case, the experts were called on to assess the issue of competency for an individual demonstrating paranoid and delusional mental health characteristics. In chapter 4, we systematically discussed paranoid and delusional mental health disorders. We explained that making a clinical distinction between delusional disorder, persecutory subtype and paranoid personality disorder was often a fine line, complicated by dimensions of personality, degrees of impairment, and similar symptomatology. We submit that the intricate and subtle distinctions explored in this chapter were present in the case of Colin Ferguson.

Despite ubiquitous traits, the defendant's social and occupational relations clearly indicated that he had and continued to suffer from a mental health condition consistent with either a paranoid or delusional mental health disorder (i.e., delusional disorder, paranoid personality disorder, or paranoid schizophrenia). However, diagnostic findings alone did not address the CST issue or dispose of this legal inquiry by itself. According to New York statute, a person is incompetent to stand trial only when he or she "as a result of mental disease or defect, lacks capacity to understand the proceedings against him [or herself] or to assist in his [or her] own defense."[842] Instead of recognizing a clear mental impairment, the experts in Ferguson's CST review concentrated on the first part of the test, failing to assess competence-related abilities and, in particular, Ferguson's ability to assist in the defense.

Focusing specifically on the testimony offered by the experts for the people, their clinical judgements and CST findings were informed largely by a finding of malingering, minimizing Ferguson's paranoid behavior. In the face of historical information suggesting a more debilitating condition, Drs. D'Alessandro and Reichman failed to investigate Ferguson's background data and failed to test for and later rejected (in court) the diagnosis of delusional disorder,

---

842. *See* N.Y. CRIM. PROC. LAW § 730.10 (McKinney's 1994).

persecutory subtype. Instead of recognizing what was an obvious mental impairment or instead of conceding that time constraints precluded a provisional diagnostic finding, the doctors elected not to move forward with tests and questions about competence-related abilities. Ironically, however, in rejecting the diagnosis of delusional disorder the experts later testified that Dr. Dudley did not weigh the issue of differential diagnosis and, specifically, did not consider the mental health condition of paranoid personality disorder.

From this perspective and instance, a preliminary diagnostic finding (albeit absolute or provisional) can be used to refute a diagnosis already introduced to the court. For example, the prosecution's experts did not observe the same behavior as the defense expert and, therefore, suggested that a different disorder was operating (i.e, paranoid personality disorder), thereby casting doubt on the defense expert's conclusion (i.e., delusional disorder, persecutory subtype). In sum, then, we see how the lack of uniform CST measures is further compounded when experts rely on questionable diagnostic findings (or the absence of them) to inform their clinical judgements and courtroom testimony. In other words, the respective mental health experts in the Ferguson case emphasized distinct types of mental illness that the defendant was suffering from and based their different competency findings on these clinical judgements. Thus, it appears that rather than offering greater clarity on competence-related abilities, the practice of introducing various disorders (if only for the purpose of arguing the absence of another) clouded, indeed obfuscated, the CST issue even further, leading to a battle of the experts.

Focusing specifically on the expert for the defense, Dr. Dudley based his analysis on delusions and paranoid obsessions but failed to discuss the trial fitness issue with Ferguson. Indeed, Dr. Dudley concentrated on establishing the presence of a mental impairment (over a three hour period) and then decided to comment on the criminal incident; an inquiry not expressly requested in the original referral. In direct testimony, Dr. Dudley advanced the theory that Mr. Ferguson suffered from a delusional disorder, persecutory subtype and testified to the ultimate legal issue involving competence-related abilities. Stated differently, Dr. Dudley commented on competency issues not addressed during the clinical forensic evaluation. Although he identified a mental impairment he failed to implement the appropriate CST protocol. As such, Dr. Dudley only drew attention to his principal diagnostic finding of delusional disorder, persecutory subtype. Thus, in the face of questionable CST assessment practices, this defense expert asserted an ultimate (legal) opinion, thereby conveying to the court misguided confidence in his findings.

A related problem in CST evaluation practices and psychiatrists/psychologists testifying in the courtroom is the pejorative affect attributed to certain disorders, and how attorneys advance diagnostic findings through direct and cross examination testimony. In other words, certain disorders sound worst than others and litigators use this knowledge when building their case. Thus, the decision to introduce one disorder over another may be based on the pejorative connotation of the diagnosis.

For example, the direct and cross-examination indicate that the attorneys strategically presented (the defense) and critiqued (the prosecution) the diagnosis of delusional disorder, persecutory subtype. Given that this condition is classified as a psychotic disorder, the degree or intensity of this condition suggests that it is more profound (and debilitating) than a paranoid personality disorder. In other words, the generic meaning attached to delusional disorder is often equated with "madness," given that it is an Axis I psychotic disturbance. However, paranoid personality disorder suggests maladaptive personality traits. Thus, as one might expect and as evidenced during Ferguson's pretrial hearing, Mr. Peck (for the prosecution) emphasized malingering and the Axis II paranoid personality disorder, especially since he sought a judicial finding of competence. Moreover, as one might anticipate, Mr. Kuby (for the defense) stressed the more debilitating Axis I delusional disorder, given that he sought an incompetency ruling.

Based on the above observations, we recognize that legal decision making involving a defendant of questionable mental health might hinge significantly on the nature and elements of a particular diagnosis. Further, in light of the CST time constraints witnessed in the Ferguson case, either a delusional disorder or a paranoid personality disorder could have been supported, especially when considering the impact of degrees of impairment and the common traits these disorders possess. Moreover, these diagnostic findings could have been further justified through the process of differential diagnosis. Arguably, then, a skilled attorney and a trained expert can convincingly persuade the fact finder of either disorder, especially when the right questions are asked and the right answers are tendered. On this matter, we maintain that a legal strategy to advance one disorder over the other may be determined principally (although not necessarily exclusively) by the pejorative connotation the diagnosis engenders and, moreover, may be entertained strategically to advance the desired ends of the attorney. The question, then, is why does all this matter? In other words, des it make a difference if Colin Ferguson suffered from a delusional disorder, persecutory type, paranoid personality disorder, or even paranoid schizophrenia? Indeed, shades of illness are still illness. We assert that Ferguson's choice making processes, especially in terms of his critical legal decisions (i.e., discharge counsel and proceed *pro se* to trial), suggest that his paranoid beliefs precluded him from assisting in his own defense.

In sum, then, the experts quibbled over differential diagnoses and diagnostic criteria. While the three psychiatrists were able to meet with the defendant, the CST examinations were fraught with serious evaluative and diagnostic problems. As previously mentioned, these findings were informed by single examinations with the examiners reaching clinical judgements in a matter of hours.[843] More importantly, however, the experts conducted highly individualized assessments that lacked structure and failed to explore important competence-related abilities (i.e., decisional competence). Indeed, the experts neglected to investigate the relationship between paranoid and delusional tendencies and Ferguson's requests to waive counsel and proceed *pro se* to trial. The psychiatric examinations and courtroom testimony suggest that the mental health professionals arrived at questionable findings and, ultimately (by way of individualized assessments and differential diagnoses), framed their ultimate legal issue opinions in ways that merely advanced the aims of the respective litigators. Thus, in the final analysis, rather than offering greater conceptual and practical clarity on the decisional element of competency, the experts for both the defense and the people

---

843. Another component complicating the examination process is the non-compliant defendant who rejects the CST process. Although an interesting topic in its own right, a treatment on statutes and case law regarding CST compliance or the right not to comply is beyond the scope of this investigation. However, *see generally* Kuby & Kunstler *supra* note 652, at 21. Kuby and Kunstler briefly describe the state and federal codes in mandating CST reviews for the otherwise non-compliant defendant. This dilemma is discussed with the Ferguson case in mind.

produced suspicious CST findings, calling into question the validity and credibility of their clinical judgements altogether.

B. Legal Analysis: An Overview of the Relevant Issues in the Case of Colin Ferguson

This portion of chapter 6 examines the CST legal dynamics that occurred in the pretrial competency hearing of Mr. Colin Ferguson. Relying on legal precedent in the state of New York, the first section not only describes the case law holdings Judge Belfi used to justify his CST ruling (decisions consistent with *Dusky, Faretta,* and *Godinez*), but explains why the defendant was able to *pro se* his own criminal dispute and how this determination was an outgrowth of the questionable decision that found him competent to stand trial. We contend that reviewing the pre- and post-*Godinez* precedent setting case law in New York reveals that while Judge Belfi's CST determination was supported by legal precedent, the New York case law was fraught with the same limitations that plagued the *Godinez* decision (e.g., setting a low standard to waive counsel and proceed *pro se* to trial.)

We also examine, although somewhat speculatively, how Judge Belfi's competency determination in the Ferguson matter and the subsequent rulings that flowed from this finding (i.e., the defendant's right to proceed *pro se* to trial, striking the insanity defense) were influenced by social and political forces. As we contend, the Court's failure to locate conclusive evidence of competence despite competing and problematic diagnostic conclusions, clinical judgements, and expert testimony raises troubling questions about judicial politics and how other dynamics ultimately influenced the trial's outcome.

The legal analysis portion of chapter 6 also addresses the issue of offering expert testimony in a court of law where case law holdings provide guidelines to determine the credibility of this testimony. Along these lines, we discuss how CST proceedings are complicated when expert testimony is generalized to focus principally on the issue of witness credibility, especially when the value of the expert's evaluation methods in relation to specific legal inquiries are minimized or ignored. Although this observation could easily enough apply to an array of psycholegal assessment practices, we specifically consider the interplay between the judicial decision making process and competency to stand trial evaluations. Based on this analysis, we assert that judges who focus on credible evidence often lose sight of the importance of the CST assessment protocol employed in a particular case. Indeed, as we argue, emphasizing witness credibility at the expense of assessment utility, once again helps underscore the ongoing problems in competency to stand trial criminal proceedings. Moreover, recognizing what the court values (i.e., credibility) and what the court ostensibly does not value (i.e., uniform assessments) suggests that mental health examiners will continue to freely engage in their own individualized CST assessment practices. Thus, as we intimate, when these circumstances are coupled with the vague and ambiguous language embedded within the legal construct of competency (see chapter 2), it is not surprising that judges differently (and problematically) interpret forensic evaluations.

In order to better appreciate Judge Belfi's questionable decision making on the issue of Colin Ferguson's fitness for trial, we present some of the more noteworthy events in the criminal case and the appellate outcome. Accordingly, some of the key statements made by the defendant are recounted. Moreover, we summarize the legal difficulties stemming from Ferguson's trial, demonstrating the judicial dilemmas that emerge when a judge interacts with a delusional litigant who then employs those rights afforded to him by *Faretta* and *Godinez* (i.e., relinquishes counsel and proceeds *pro se* to trial). Indeed, our discussion on these matters reveals what can happen when a paranoid/delusional defendant is found competent to stand trial and allowed to conduct his own defense.

We conclude chapter 6 by revisiting and examining the interplay between the relevant psychological and legal factors in the case of the Long Island Railroad gunman. In particular, we explain how these critical psycholegal issues produced a flawed competency finding and, more importantly, a travesty in the administration of courtroom justice. This analysis is relevant as it creates the necessary backdrop against which to recommend criminal justice policy reforms on the matter of competency to stand trial. These policy recommendations are delineated in chapter 7.

1. The Court's Pretrial Hearing Decision and New York Legal Precedent

On December 9th 1994, in the face of overwhelming evidence to the contrary, Judge Belfi not only found Colin Ferguson competent to stand trial but also granted his application to proceed *pro se* to trial. His failure to find conclusive evidence that Ferguson was competent, in light of the considerable testimony indicating otherwise, raises concerns about Judge Belfi's overall ruling. At first glance, the decision appears to preserve the defendant's rights (i.e., his right to waive counsel given *Faretta* and his right to proceed *pro se* to trial given *Godinez*). Indeed, Judge Belfi's ruling finds support in New York state decisions; decisions supporting the finding that if one is informed of the risks and consequences of representing oneself, a knowing and intelligent defendant is not only competent to stand trial but is also competent to act as his or her own attorney.[844] Con-

---

844. For New York state decisions before *Godinez see, E.g.*, People v. Reason, 37 N.Y.S. 2d 353–354 (App. Div. 1975) (Following a determination of competence, combined with "a full and searching" inquiry that the defendant made a knowing and intelligent waiver and also "new the risks and advantages" of conducting his own defense, is sufficient to support the waiver). *See Id* at 355, 356. Thus affirming conviction, where the appellate court held the defendant "could not argue that he was not competent to act as attorney pro se." *See Id.* at 351. *See also E.g.*, People v. McIntyre, 36 N.Y.S. 2d 10 (1974) (convictions reversed where defendant was improperly denied his right to self-representation; "defendant's motion was unequivocal and timely made; *his waiver of his right to counsel was knowing, intelligent, and voluntary*; and he had not forfeited the right to proceed pro se by engaging in disruptive conduct that would prevent a fair and orderly trial") (emphasis added) *See Id.* at 10.

For New York State decisions after *Godinez see, E.g.*, People v. Schoolfield, 196 N.Y.S. 2d 111 (App. Div. 1994) (If a defendant is competent to stand trial he is competent to conduct his own defense so long as the waiver is knowing and intelligent and he understands the risks and advantages of proceeding pro se) *See Id.* at 116–117; *See also* People v. Vivenzio, 62 N.Y.S. 2d 776 (App. Div. 1984) ("A criminal defendant is entitled to be master of his own fate and 'respect for individual autonomy requires that he be allowed to go to jail under his own banner if he so desires and if he makes the choice with eyes open'," *quoting, in part, from* United States ex rel. Maldonado v. Denno, 348 F2d 12, 15 (2nd Cir. 1965); People v, Meurer, 621 N.Y.S. 2d 422, 423–424 (App. Div. 1994) (affirming conviction, after defendant found competent to stand trial, trial court found that decision to waive counsel was made in a knowing, intelligent, and voluntarily manner and defendant was informed about the risks and consequences of proceeding pro se.)

sequently, Judge Belfi's decision seems reasoned enough to withstand the potential threat of appellate inquiry, especially on the matter of competency to stand trial as informed by psychiatric testimony. Indeed, under New York state case law precedent, a defendant is competent to stand trial if the people show, based on the somewhat low burden of a preponderance of the evidence, that the accused was not an incapacitated person,[845] and establish the defendant's fitness through the expert testimony of two psychiatrists.[846] Moreover, in *People v. Breeden,* the court of appeals held that, "where the court is presented with conflicting evidence of competence [per psychiatric testimony] great deference is accorded its findings."[847] In other words, significant discretion is afforded judges who must weigh conflicting expert psychiatric testimony when reviewing the matter of trial fitness.

Another prevailing issue in the Ferguson case, relevant to Judge Belfi's CST ruling and subsequent findings, was the fundamental difference of opinion between the accused and his attorneys on the matter of a mental status defense strategy. While Ferguson was vehemently opposed to such a legal approach, Mr. Kuby and Mr. Kunstler were strongly in favor of this defense tactic. However, the Judge did not consider this conflict relevant to the issue of the defendant's trial competence, and Belfi's position ostensibly finds support in the prevailing case law. Indeed, consistent with other "state-friendly" decisions, in *People v. Allen* the appellate court held that even though "the defendant . . . disagreed with his attorney's theory of the case [this] d[id] not establish that he lacked the capacity to stand trial."[848]

---

845. Although the people bear the burden to prove a defendant's competency to stand trial, the threshold is low (preponderance of the evidence). *See* People v. Supino, 202 N.Y.S. 2d 454 (App. Div. 1994) (the people have the burden of establishing the defendant's fitness "by a preponderance of credible evidence that the defendant is not an incapacitated person.") *See Id.* 454; *See* People v. Orama, 150 N.Y.S. 2d 505, 541 (App. Div. 1989); People v. Allen, 135 N.Y.S. 2d 823 (App. Div. 1987).

846. All the people or state have to do is establish that a defendant is competent to stand trial through the expert testimony of two psychiatric examiners. *See E.g.,* People v. Pulecio, 237 N.Y.S. 2d 633 (App. Div. 1997); People v. Vandemark, 225 N.Y.S. 2d 716, 717 (App. Div. 1996) (when competency is in question, "defendant must be examined by two qualified psychiatric examiners") *See Id.* at 716.

847. *See* People v. Breeden, 115 N.Y.S. 2d 715 (App. Div. 1985).

848. *See* People v. Allen, 135 N.Y.S. 2d 823 (App. Div. 1987).

Thus, Judge Belfi's CST decision in the case of Colin Ferguson finds support from the precedent case law of New York on the matter of reconciling conflicting expert psychiatric testimony and on the matter of addressing competing perspectives regarding defense strategy. Admittedly, our comments here are somewhat limited; however, the holdings to which we direct our attention focus on some of the more pressing and troubling concerns in the Ferguson dispute. In the following section, we speculatively consider what additional forces may have influenced Judg Belfi's decision making in the case.

2. Political Influences in Judicial Decision Making and Limitations with New York Precedent

Judge Belfi's ruling in Colin Ferguson's pretrial competency hearing appears consistent with prevailing New York case law, thereby obviating potential appellate review challenges. However, as we contend, this does not make Judge Belfi's decision any less suspicious or, for that matter, any more precise. Indeed, various political and social factors ostensibly prompted his court rulings and these matters must also be examined.

From a political perspective, it is reasonable to assume that Judge Belfi found the defendant competent to stand trial because of the heinous nature of the crime he was accused of committing. Several innocent people were brutally and senselessly killed. From a social perspective, the ruling was perhaps a response to the pressure from the public at large (certainly in the state of New York) enraged by the defendant's behavior and clamoring for a trial already significantly delayed. Arguably, preserving and acknowledging the defendant's constitutional rights functioned most especially to satisfy the public's relentless outcry for redress in the matter. On this score, when Judge Belfi found Ferguson competent to stand trial and granted the defendant's motion to represent himself, he likely neutralized critics repulsed by the idea that a "mad" gunman would be criminally tried and convicted. If we are indeed correct on this front, we suggest that what was lost in this troubling decision was the spirit of the incompetency doctrine. As the court in *Frith's Case* held:

> [t]hat no man shall be called upon to make his defence at a time when his mind is in that situation as not to appear capa-

ble of so doing; for, however guilty he may be, the inquiring into his guilt must be postponed to that season, when by collecting together his intellects, and having them entire, he shall be able so to model his defence as to ward off the punishment of the law[849] ...

The decision making of Judge Belfi elsewhere suggests that other social and political dynamics were afoot. Indeed, immediately after the Judge found Ferguson competent to stand trial and granted his ancillary requests (i.e., to proceed *pro se* to trial and to strike the insanity defense), the defendant expressed an interest in invoking a notice of alibi. Mr. Kuby expressed Ferguson's request to the judge as follows:

> MR. KUBY: Judge, in continuing with what I do think has become almost a serial exercise, Mr. Ferguson has been informed by me prior to this that if he wishes to issue a notice of alibi, he was not on the train, he was somewhere else, he had a limited time period within which to do that...
>
> THE COURT: I will give you until next Wednesday, that will be December 14th. Should it be your desire to interpose an alibi defense[850] ...

Although at trial Ferguson argued his original theory (i.e., that a mysterious "white Caucasian" gunman committed the massacre) his request to issue a notice of alibi raised further doubts about the defendant's then mental health and called into question Judge Belfi's finding that Colin Ferguson was competent to stand trial. What we question here is why Judge Belfi allowed the proceedings to continue and why he refrained from pursuing the matter of competency again, especially given the complete implausibility of the defendant's notice of alibi?

In part, the answer redirects us to the governing case law underpinning Judge Belfi's CST finding. To be clear, these appellate court rulings are not without problems and include the administration of legal standards that lack content as well as the enforcement of precedent not applicable to defendants with mental health conditions. Indeed, New York Criminal Procedure and the legal decisions

---

849. *See Frith's Case supra* note 50, at 318.
850. *See* Ferguson Pretrial Hearing Transcripts, December 9, 1994 at 495–496.

pertaining to trial fitness in the state mirror the federal holdings found in *Dusky*, *Faretta*, and *Godinez*. Thus, the law pertaining to competency to stand trial in the state of New York is flawed in much the same was as is the law on this matter as articulated by the United States Supreme Court. As we explain below, these limitations are evident in two pivotal ways.

First, according to section 730.10 of New York's Criminal Procedure Law, a person is found not competent to stand trial only when he or she, "as a result of mental disease or defect, lacks capacity to understand the proceedings against him [or herself] or to assist in his [or her] own defense."[851] This code merely recites the criteria set forth in *Dusky*, absent any additional or useful elaboration. Consequently, the problems previously identified in *Dusky* (i.e., a legal standard lacking meaningful content as reviewed in chapter 2) also apply to the Criminal Code employed in New York. For example, a defendant can have paranoid and delusional symptoms, can be intelligent, and can be articulate; however, despite these attributes the defendant may not be able to assist in the defense by virtue of his or her own paranoia. In short, the application of the *Dusky* standard generalized to other states like New York confounds rather than clarifies the administration of courtroom justice. Indeed, the limitations associated with *Dusky* regrettably were realized in the case of Long Island Railroad gunman.

Second, in *People v. Reason*,[852] the appellate court opined that a defendant found competent to stand trial is necessarily competent to waive his or her right to counsel and proceed *pro se* to trial. However, this legal opinion is replete with problems not unlike those identified in *Godinez*. In *Reason*, the court reached its conclusion based on a decision that was not applicable to a defendant having a (debilitating) mental health condition. Briefly, the defendant appealed the case claiming that the court erred when denying him his constitutional right to counsel as he lacked the capacity to conduct his own defense.[853] The appeals court affirmed the conviction, arguing that once the defendant was found competent to stand trial he "knowingly waived his right to counsel."[854] As such, the accused

---

851. *See* N.Y. CRIM. PROC. LAW § 730.10 (McKinney's 1994).
852. *See* People v. Reason, 37 N.Y2d 351 (App. Div. 1975).
853. *See Id.* at 351.
854. *See Id.* at 356.

had no room to complain about the case outcome, given that he conducted his own defense.

However, not unlike the problems identified in *Godinez*, the appeals court in *Reason* relied on a non-mental health case (*People v. McIntyre*)[855] to support its decision. Simply stated, the appellate court in *Reason* determined that a defendant with a mental health condition could conduct his own defense (if a knowing and intelligent waiver was made), basing its position on case opinion that had absolutely no relationship to psychiatrically disordered defendants whose competency to stand trial was at issue. As the court in *Reason* explained:

> [I]n *McIntyre* we indicated that a defendant in a criminal case may invoke the right to defend *pro se* provided: (1) the request is unequivocal and timely asserted, (2) there has been a knowing and intelligent waiver of the right to counsel, and (3) the defendant has not engaged in conduct which would prevent the fair and orderly exposition of the issues. *In that case there was no question of the defendant's competence to stand trial since that issue had not been raised.* We believe the same standards should apply when, as here, [the court made the determination that the defendant, Reason, was competent to stand trial]. At that stage the only so-called competency question remaining is whether the decision to waive counsel— implicit in the assertion of the right to defend *pro se*—has been made competently, intelligently and voluntarily.[856] (emphasis added)

The muddled logic employed in *People v. Reason*, is very similar to the rationale found in *Godinez v. Moran*, (1993).[857] As described in chapter 2, the *Godinez* court lumped all defendants together with respect to their constitutional right to waive counsel. Indeed, rather than drawing a distinction between defendants suffering from and not suffering from mental impairments, the *Godinez* court uni-

---

855. *See* People v. McIntyre, 36 N.Y2d 10 (1974).

856. *See* People v. Reason 37 N.Y2d 351, 354–355 (App. Div. 1975) (emphasis added) *quoting, in part, from* People v. McIntyre *supra* note 668, at 17. For a review of the Supreme Court case establishing the competent, intelligent, and voluntary criteria to waive counsel, *see* Johnson v. Zerbst, 304 U.S. 458 (1938).

857. As described elsewhere, in *Godinez* (a case involving a mentally impaired defendant) the Supreme Court relied on *Faretta* (a case not involving a mentally impaired defendant) to articulate the standard.

formly applied the *Faretta* criteria concluding that as long as an accused voluntarily and intelligently relinquished counsel, the defendant could proceed *pro se* to trial. We submit that regardless of whether this failure to differentiate categories of defendants occurs at the state level (i.e., *People v. Reason*) or at the United States Supreme Court level (*Godinez v. Moran*), the results are the same: defendants with questionable mental health standing will proceed *pro se* to trial.

Thus, the force of legal precedent, suspect and, indeed, flawed as its was, led Judge Belfi to render his CST determination and ancillary court rulings in the Colin Ferguson dispute. Therefore, from our perspective, the judicial decision making in this case demonstrates how legal precedent not only failed the defendant but undermined the very purpose for which the justice system was conceived. Indeed, as long as state and federal law continue to address inadequately, incompletely, and inappropriately the intersection between competence to stand trial, mental impairment, and a defendant's right to waive counsel and *pro se* the case, casualties like Ferguson will not only reoccur but they will become a matter of routine.

3. The Role of Expert Services in the Courts and Legal Decisions: Emphasizing Credibility Not Uniformity in CST Assessments

In addition to the previously articulated limitations attributable to the CST assessment process,[858] a pivotal question surrounding the role of mental health professionals in the courts is the credibility of their expert testimony.[859] Historically, legal holdings have set forth criteria advising courts when to strike questionable expert tes-

---

858. As previously discussed, the contentious process includes the binding yet discrepant legal standards and the clinical methods used to assess trial competency (e.g., interviews discerning abilities to assist and understand as compared to structured measures to tap decisional competence, otherwise— decisions pertaining to the trial such as plea bargaining, testifying, or waiving counsel).

859. *See* PERLIN II *supra* note 573 section 14.07 at 228; IDENTIFICATION *supra* note 60, at 469–471.

timony.[860] For example, in *People v. Brock*, the court clearly enumerated several guidelines on this very issue:

> (1) the correctness or adequacy of the factual assumptions on which the expert testimony is based; (2) possible bias in the experts' appraisal of the defendant's condition; (3) inconsistencies in the experts' testimony, or material variations between experts; and (4) the relevance and strength of the contrary lay testimony."[861]

Designed to aid judges and to inform them about the limits of expert testimony, the observations expressed in *People v. Brock* are both enduring and compatible with more recent decisions.[862] We note, however, that none of these cases review and interpret this matter, mindful of specific psycholegal issues such as a clinical forensic expert's assessment of one's trial fitness. Admittedly our concern here understandably falls outside the scope of *Brock*; however, the absence of case law on the subject indirectly contributes to the type, degree, and intensity of complications that plague competency evaluations and controversial CST outcomes.

Given the holding in cases like *Brock*, judges appear more interested in the general issue of credibility (e.g., expertise, trustworthiness) than they do with the methodology employed to assess a particular psycholegal problem. We maintain that what is lost in this process is the expectation that uniform instruments should be implemented to measure specific psycholegal matters (e.g., MacCAT-CA for competency). In the context of CST evaluations, legal holdings that emphasize credibility and minimize the importance of uniformity in CST evaluations enable forensic examiners to freely conduct individualized assessments, thereby preventing judges from

---

860. *See* PERLIN II *supra* note 573, section 14.07 at 228.

861. *See* Brock v. United States, 387 F.2d 254, 257, 258 (5th Cir. 1967).

862. *See* Bundy v. Dugger, 675 F. Supp. 622, 634 (M.D. Fla. 1987), *aff'd*, 850 F.2d 1402 (11th Cir. 1988), *cert. denied*, 488 U.S. 1034 (1989) (case affirming *Brock* factors). *See also* People v. Doan, 141 Mich. App. 209, 366 N.W.2d 593, 595 (1985). the court ruled that it is error for an expert to: "(1) express an opinion on the legislature's intent in adopting certain statutory language; (2) quantify (using IQ measurements) mental retardation where the legislature had chosen to define it descriptively; and (3) base his expert opinion on such colloquial and imprecise expressions as going bananas or being out in left field." *See Id*, at 595–598. *See also* Addkinson v. State, 608 So. 2d 304, 308 (Miss. 1992).

ascertaining whether an adequate (and appropriate) competency assessment was conducted in the first instance. Clearly, then, practices such as these significantly contribute to the ongoing problems surrounding competency to stand trial legal findings: judges do not know the value of using particular assessment protocol as applied to specific psycholegal questions, and the absence of uniform evaluation standards serves only to confound rather than to clarify the fact finder's CST determinations. As we demonstrate in the next section, Judge Belfi's inability to recognize where and how the psychiatric experts failed to implement the appropriate assessment instruments is clearly evident in the Colin Ferguson pretrial competency proceedings.

4. Generalizing to Ferguson: Minimizing the Importance of CST Assessment Protocol

As we previously stated, the mental health experts in the Colin Ferguson case utilized deficient CST assessment measures, predicating their findings on provisional diagnostic conclusions. Dr. Dudley arrived at an incompetency determination by conducting an extensive clinical interview. Although addressing relevant background information derived from collateral data sources (e.g., Ferguson's work history and scholastic records), the psychiatrist either ignored or overlooked key aspects regarding the issue of competency (e.g., what would happen if the defendant was found incompetent). In short, Dr. Dudley failed to implement any instrument recognized as a standard CST assessment tool.

Similar to Dr. Dudley, the experts for the people also erred in their assessment practices. The limits of Drs. D'Alessandro and Reichman's CST findings and opinions were best illustrated in the brevity of their forensic evaluation and their unwavering and near obsessional commitment (especially Dr. D'Alessandro) to the presence of malingering in the case. Both psychiatrists failed to research important background information; information clearly supporting the claim that Ferguson had and continued to suffer from paranoid delusions about racism. Instead, Drs. D'Alessandro and Reichman spent the better part of their (brief) 90 minute interview addressing whether the defendant had made contradictory statements indicative of malingering. On this point, Drs. Reichman and D'Alessandro employed a simplistic tool used to eliminate possible neurological impairment, supporting their belief that Ferguson was feigning mental impairment. Regrettably, absolutely no CST instrument was implemented by the witnesses testifying on behalf of the prosecution.

Based on the expert testimony of the two court-appointed psychiatrists and based on Judge Belfi's exchange with the defendant, Colin Ferguson was declared competent to stand trial and competent to represent himself. Although Judge Belfi's decision was consistent with prevailing New York state case law, the ruling demonstrated not only the practical limits of legal precedent but the dispositive weight afforded expert psychiatric testimony regarding CST determinations. Indeed, in the case of the Long Island Railroad gunman, the credibility assigned to what the psychiatrists said was more significant for purposes of the Judge's competency finding than was the assessment process by which these psychiatrists evaluated competence-related abilities. Our observations here are not intended as an indictment of Judge Belfi. To be clear, we recognize that the case law in this area centers on witness credibility (e.g., *Brock*) rather than clinical evaluation methods. Thus, it is quite likely that Judge Belfi was oblivious to the importance of employing particular CST assessment protocol when addressing specific psycholegal inquiries. But this realization only serves to underscore our point: lower court judges will continue to search for misguided evidence (i.e., psychiatric witness credibility) to reach conclusions (i.e., competent vs. incompetent) derived from inadequate sources (i.e., existing legal precedent), until such time as the law-psychology community makes clear that specific psycholegal issues require the application of exacting assessment instruments. We assert that the trial, appeal, and outcome in the Colin Ferguson case amply illustrate our perspective.

5. The Aftermath: The Trial, the Appeal, and the Outcome

In the following section we select out excerpts from the criminal trial of the Long Island Railway gunman to showcase the defendant's paranoid mental health condition. The trial is replete with examples of Ferguson's paranoid behavior, illustrating the limitations that attach when a constitutional right to self-representation is afforded a mentally impaired defendant. In short, the Colin Ferguson case demonstrates what can happen when a paranoid and delusional defendant is found competent to stand trial and then allowed to proceed *pro se* to trial, consistent with prevailing case law. Ultimately, the proceedings beg one critical question: how could the defendant have been found competent to stand trial, much less granted the opportunity to conduct his own defense?

Although Judge Belfi declared that Ferguson was not incompetent (i.e., not incapacitated), the accused's paranoid delusions became appreciable and problematic from the outset of the trial. In his opening statement, Mr. Ferguson made the following announcement: "There are 93 counts in the indictment only because it matches the year 1993. Had it been 1925 it would have been 25 counts. This is a case of stereotype victimization of a black man. A subsequent conspiracy to destroy him. Nothing more."[863] Often rambling incoherently, Ferguson made various incriminating statements during his 14-minute opening argument. Strategically, for example, he gave up much ground when admitting that he owned the 9-millimeter handgun used in the shootings. On this point, Ferguson stated that he feared his (Brooklyn) neighbors would steal the gun from his home; therefore, he transported the weapon to friends in Westbury, Long Island for "safe harbor."[864] Ferguson's explanation here was quite revealing. It was an early and vivid example of what was yet to come; that is, paranoia about other people and paranoia about a government conspiracy.

Ferguson's ability to assume the role of attorney was initially somewhat convincing; however, as the trial progressed so, too, did his paranoid thought patterns. For example, in his opening statement, the defendant set forth his would-be defense theory. He argued that while on the commuter line, he fell asleep and the gunman removed the weapon from his (Ferguson's) bag and opened fire. "Awakened by gunfire," the defendant/attorney explained, "I sought to run for cover like any other person on that train."[865] In

---

863. NATIONAL PUBLIC RADIO, WEEKEND EDITION, FEB, 1995.

864. *See* D. Wise, *Accused Train Gunman Claims He Is Scapegoat*, N.Y. L. JOUR., Jan. 27, 1995 at 1.

865. *See Id.*

this context, then, Ferguson's theory suggested he was also a victim much like other passengers, but was victimized in a different way. Intimating that he was the casualty of a wide-ranging conspiracy, Ferguson argued that a white gunman (part of the governmental plot against him) was responsible for the shooting. "Scapegoated by the government" the accused proclaimed that he had been targeted by the Immigration and Naturalization Service and other law enforcement agencies for "a number of years."[866] Thus, according to Ferguson, he was wrongfully accused, was clearly framed, and, therefore, was thoroughly innocent of the criminal charges against him.

Appearing lucid one moment and incoherent the next, the defendant typically referred to himself in the third person, as "Mr. Ferguson, the defendant." He often objected to responses provided by the prosecution's witnesses (many victims of the attack), informing Judge Belfi, for example, that "[the] witness is becoming argumentative."[867] Ferguson insisted he was not the triggerman on the Long Island Railroad, despite numerous testimonial accounts to the contrary. One after the other, the witnesses/victims testified about the shooting, the injuries they sustained, and the absolute certainty they possessed that the defendant, Colin Ferguson the attorney, was the person responsible for the horrible shootings.[868] For example, Mr. Casazza, the last witness to be called by the prosecution and cross examined by the defendant, clearly demonstrates the troubling nature of these exchanges. Consider the following devastating response elicited by the defendant during his cross examination. Ferguson asks: "Was it your testimony that you did not see a weapon at the time you were shot? Mr. Casazza responds: "I saw it peripherally...I was looking at your face. Obviously you were holding the weapon, but I was looking at you right in the eye, and I couldn't believe that you were standing over me with this weapon...."[869]

Uniformly considered a trial of form over substance, Ferguson mounted long, rambling narratives accusing police officers and po-

---

866. *See Id.*

867. *See* G. Baum, *The Trial of Accused Sniper Colin Ferguson Has Taken on the Absurdist Ambience of a Eugene Ionesco Play,* L.A. TIMES, Feb. 10, 1995, at E1.

868. *See Id.*

869. *See* J. T. McQuiston, *Advisor Says L.R.R.R. Suspect Prefers Conviction to Insanity Finding,* N.Y. TIMES, Feb. 10, 1995, at B5.

litical figures of conspiring against him.[870] For example, during a presidential visit to Manhattan, President Clinton congratulated three men who subdued Ferguson in the commuter line. The three men and another shooting victim were also greeted by former Governor Mario Cuomo.[871] In light of this information, the defendant/attorney attempted to subpoena Clinton and Cuomo, contending that these politicians should be called as witnesses "because they had certain conversations with witnesses in my case."[872] Indeed, Ferguson bizarrely attempted to draw upon these developments as further evidence of and support for his theory that a governmental conspiracy was in place to destroy him.

As Colin Ferguson's mental state deteriorated in the court room, his conspiracy theory expanded in substance but not in logic. The defendant's all-encompassing conspiratorial plot eventually led him to invoke the power of supernatural forces, including his intent to subpoena a parapsychologist and an exorcist who would testify that the government had implanted a microchip in his head, and, as a result, rendered him "lasered out by a remote-control device."[873] Even with these obvious indicators of severe mental impairment, the proceedings continued. After a month-long trial, Ferguson eventually appealed to the sympathy of the jury in his closing argument. He sought redemption and, most assuredly, an acquittal.

> Vindicate Mr. Ferguson. Do not destroy his life more than it has already been destroyed...I now can put my life in the hands of fact-finders, jurors who will look at me and see me as a human being and do to me what is needed to put me back in society...to be productive.[874]

---

870. *See* F. Biddle, *In Ferguson, TV Gets New Spectacle*, BOSTON GLOBE, Feb, 16, 1995, at 1.

871. *See Id.*

872. *See* Legal Communications, Ltd., *Railroad Shooter Wants Clinton, Cuomo Subpoenaed*, NATIONAL NEWS, Jan.19, 1995, at 4.

873. *See* Perlin, Dignity *supra* note 639, at 73. *See* McQuiston, *Commuter Killing Trial Goes to Jury: Ferguson Gives Incoherent Summation*, HOUSTON CHRONICLE, Feb. 17, 1995, at A2; M. Goldstein, *LIRR case a "Catch-22" in Reverse*, NEWSDAY, Feb. 3, 1995, at A08–A09; R. Toppings, *Psychologist: Ferguson's competency a fine line*, NEWSDAY, Feb. 5, at A43. J. T.

874. *See* S. McCarthy, *Ferguson: Madness or Just Manipulation?*, NEWS-DAY, Feb. 22, 1995, at 6.

The jury convicted Ferguson on six counts of murder, nineteen counts of attempted murder, criminal possession of a weapon in the second degree, and reckless endangerment. He was sentenced to over 300 years in prison.[875]

As anticipated, Ferguson presented several arguments to the Appellate Division in the state of New York. Consistent with the unfolding of his criminal case, he argued that his conviction should be reversed, principally on the grounds that he should not have been found competent to stand trial and, thus, not allowed to proceed *pro se* to trial. On February 30, 1998 the New York Supreme Court of Appeals affirmed his conviction. In a perfunctory ruling the Court directly addressed each of Ferguson's contentions and systematically explained away the Long Island Railroad gunman's appeal. As the Appellate Court summarily stated:

> "The [trial] court properly determined, after a hearing, that the defendant was competent to stand trial...Contrary to the defendant's contentions, neither the fact that the defense-retained psychiatrist disagreed with the conclusion of the two court-appointed experts, nor the fact that the defendant opted to reject a "black rage" insanity defense dictated a ruling that he was unfit for trial...In addition, the defendant's decision not to pursue an insanity defense does not, in and of itself, indicate incompetence. [Finally, as the appeals court opined] the court properly permitted the defendant to appear *pro se*, since a defendant who is competent to stand trial is necessarily competent to waive his right to counsel and proceed *pro se*."[876]

The Colin Ferguson trial and outcome vividly illustrate the systemic legal problems that can (and do) occur in pretrial competency hearings. Indeed, this case reflects the type and degree of troubling courtroom fall out that follows in the wake of flawed CST determinations. As we have shown, the forensic expert's role in the matter of trial fitness, Judge Belfi's questionable decision making, the limitations of legal precedent, and the effects of self representation by defendants experiencing obvious and debilitating paranoid and delusional symptoms, significantly compromise prospects for the

---

875. *See* M. Fan, *315 2/3 Years For Ferguson; Protesting to the End, LIRR Killer Sentenced*, NEWSDAY (Nassau & Suffolk ed.), Mar. 23, 1995, at A4.
876. *See* People v. Ferguson, 248 N.Y.S. 2d 725 (App. Div. 1998).

administration of justice. Indeed, as a veritable showcase for incompetency, the adjudication of Colin Ferguson as fit-to-stand-trial compromised the rights of the accused, further traumatized the victims and their families and, in the final analysis, made a mockery of the entire criminal adjudicatory process.

6. Sum and Substance: Revisiting the Legal and Psychological Assessment Dynamics in the Ferguson Case

The purpose of this chapter was to provide a detailed psychological and legal assessment of the Colin Ferguson pretrial competency proceedings. As we have shown, the pretrial CST hearing of the Long Island Railroad gunman exemplifies and underscores the troubling intersection between naive competency standards, questionable reliance on competency screening instruments and/or expert testimony, defendant's experiencing acute and chronic paranoid and delusional mental health problems, and the judicial decision making process. This chapter demonstrated where and how the prevailing case law (e.g., various New York state appellate decisions) and the psychological fitness evaluation process produced a flawed competency to stand trial outcome. In addition, the chapter explained why Ferguson was able to *pro se* his case, and how this finding was an outgrowth of Judge Belfi's controversial decision that found the defendant competent to stand trial and competent to represent himself. We note that precisely because the Ferguson case was a media-generated, highly visible spectacle, the limits of law and psychology were that much more apparent. Well-publicized and controversial cases have a profound ability to put not only a particular defendant on trial but also the process by which one's guilt is measured and assigned.[877]

The Ferguson case is an example of a defendant who, following a competency hearing, proceeded *pro se* to trial and, eventually, because of initial, undetected paranoid and delusional symptomatology became mentally unstable without the benefit of a subsequent CST hearing. Ferguson's initial ability to assume the role of attor-

---

877. *See* Arrigo &Bardwell *supra* note 18, at 29.

ney was persuasive; however, ultimately it was not convincing. On the one hand, the prosecutors concluded that this courtroom behavior was a ruse in order for the defendant to prove that he was insane.[878] On the other hand, Ferguson's former defense counsel, Mr. Kuby, argued that the trial was an exercise *in* mental illness rather than a trial *about* mental illness.[879] Despite the competing opinions on Ferguson's psychiatric state, the case demonstrates that neither psychological impairment nor legal functioning abilities are good predictors for meaningfully assessing competence-related abilities. For the remainder of this chapter, therefore, we briefly summarize some of the more salient points raised in our psychological and legal analysis.

Ferguson's pretrial competency hearing demonstrates the inadequacy of existing CST evaluations (i.e., individualized assessment methods) designed to assess competence-related abilities. The case also illustrates the problems posed by *Dusky* and its progeny, especially as reflected in the precedent setting case law of New York state. These are holdings that affirm the position that a defendant found competent to stand trial is "necessarily competent to waive his right to counsel and proceed *pro se.*"[880] In addition, the bizarre courtroom behavior exhibited by the defendant during the unfolding of the criminal suit challenges the veracity of the common law rule referenced by Justice Kennedy who concurred with the decision in *Godinez*. In short, Kennedy opined that "trial courts have the obligation of conducting a hearing whenever there is sufficient doubt concerning a defendant's competence."[881] If the delusional antics Ferguson displayed during the trial did not constitute "sufficient doubt," one can only speculate about the conditions under which the invocation of this common law rule would be applicable.

---

878. *See* L. Caplan, *Beyond Reasonable*, 28 LAW AND ORDER, 18–30 (1995).

879. *See Today's News*, N.Y. L.J., Apr. 6, 1998.

880. *See* People v. Reason, 37 N.Y.S. 2d 353–354 (App. Div. 1975) (Following a determination of competence, combined with "a full and searching" inquiry that the defendant made a knowing and intelligent waiver and also "new the risks and advantages" of conducting his own defense, is sufficient to support the waiver. *See Id* at 355, 356. Thus affirming conviction, where the appellate court held the defendant "could not argue that he was not competent to act as attorney pro se." *See Id*. at 351.

881. *See* Godinez v. Moran, 509 U.S. 389, 408 (1993) *citing, in part,* Drope v. Missouri, 420 U.S. 162, 180–181.

Whether highly individualized CST evaluations are used or whether vague and impractical legal precedent influence competency determinations, we submit that the process of ascertaining trial fitness remains egregiously flawed for purposes of administering justice. In light of this perspective and given the preceding analysis upon which it is based, recommendations for criminal justice policy reform are most assuredly warranted. Accordingly, in chapter 7 we comment on where and how law and psychology can (and must) rethink their behavior regarding CST determinations. Along these lines, specific and practical policy remedies are delineated relative to the role of forensic mental health professionals, judges and attorneys, and defendants whose psychiatric state is called into question during the course of a criminal trial. Along the way, we explore the utility of these recommendations by assessing what their impact might have been had they been employed in the case of Colin Ferguson.

Chapter 7

Criminal Justice Policy and the CST Process: Strategy for Reform

OVERVIEW

Recommending changes to existing crime and justice policies on the basis of selective, high-profile cases is by no means simple. Indeed, it is difficult to generalize where and how reform is warranted when such revisions are based on limited cases. This notwithstanding, controversial cases magnify where the legal (and psychological) system is flawed.[882] Media-driven cases draw out attention to the process by which justice is rightly or wrongly administered, prompting, sometimes even demanding, modifications when courtroom results are questionable, bizarre, or tragic. As Caplan pointed out in reaction to Colin Ferguson's appeal, "The Ferguson [matter] is likely to do for the competency question...what the John Hinckley trial did for the question of the insanity defense: jump start reform."[883] Thus, the forensic mental health policy recommendations we describe stem from the knowledge that the case outcome for the Long Island Railroad gunman symbolized deep-seated problems with CST legal standards and their corresponding clinical assessment methods. In what follows, several reform measures related to both of these matters are presented.

---

882. *See* A.M. Dershowitz, REASONABLE DOUBTS: THE CRIMINAL JUSTICE SYSTEM AND THE O.J. SIMPSON CASE. NEW YORK: TOUCHSTONE (1997).
883. *See* Caplan, *supra* note 878, at 18.

To appropriately situate our inquiry, this chapter is divided into a number sections. We begin by discussing how lawyers can avoid some of the problems associated with fitness evaluations, mindful of the clinical forensic specialist's assessment role in the overall decision making process. Nest, we emphasize how evaluators can (and should) assume an information-oriented rather than an expert opinion-oriented perspective in matters pertaining to one's competence to stand trial. In addition, we identify and explain several practical legal policy reforms, relevant to a CST finding wherein the defendant assumes a more active role in the trial process (e.g., waives counsel and pursues self-representation). In discussing these legal strategies for change (e.g., the court's prerogative to appoint standby counsel, the defendant's right to select counsel of choice following revocation of the right to proceed *pro se* to trial, hybrid representation), we revisit the case of Colin Ferguson. Our purpose here is to specify the practical utility of implementing the recommended, proactive psychological and legal policy remedies.

A. Lawyers and Pragmatic Solutions Regarding Competency Laws, Evaluators, and Competency to Stand Trial

As described in chapter 3, defining and measuring competence to stand trial or adjudicative competence is a complicated task that often produces questionable findings. Indeed, as outlined in that chapter, the array of psycholegal difficulties has led to significant concerns with the assessment instruments themselves and with the outcomes they produce when fitness evaluations are conducted. Not only do the limits of the clinical tools complicate CST proceedings but the (flawed) competency laws routinely undermine other system needs wherein fitness evaluations function as a short-cut to expedite treatment[884] or to

---

884. See J. Gellar & E. Lesser, *The Process of Criminal Commitment for Pretrial Psychiatric Examination: An Evaluation*, 135 AMERICAN JOURNAL OF PSYCHIATRY 53–60 (1978); see ROESCH & GOLDING, *supra* note 16, at 56. Competency laws are used as a convenient means to bypass civil commitment procedures, especially when law enforcement officials and legal

achieve punitive ends.[885] In addition, defense attorneys inappropriately raise competency motions to avoid capital punishment, as a potential mitigating factor with respect to sentencing or as a tactical maneuver to avoid a lengthy prison term.[886] Moreover, the CST process is complicated and confounded by the attitude of (some) judges who routinely grant competency motions when the issue is raised, fearing that to overrule such motions might constitute grounds for appeal and reversible error.[887] These observations on the misappropriation of CST evaluations again magnify why the issue of criminal competency presents courts with complex pretrial dilemmas.

In addition to circumventing other system needs or furthering questionable agendas, the CST process creates practical problems for the defendant. These problems are linked to existing civil commitment laws and the psychological test information contained in the fitness evaluations. The dilemmas associated with assessment procedures and the findings generated in CST reports are discussed below, accompanied by several recommendations. Ultimately, the intent is to suggest how lawyers can avoid some of the pitfalls associated with the CST process.

---

parties feel there is a need for immediate treatment. *see also* Winick & DeMeo, *Competency to Stand Trial in Florida*, 35 U. Miami L. REV.31, 39 (1980); *see also* Golding et al., *supra* note 14, at 322. CST evaluations are also approved to ensure immediate treatment in response to more strict civil commitment statutes. *Id.* at 322.

885. See R. Slovenko, *The Developing Law on Competency to Stand Trial*, 5 JOURNAL OF PSYCHIATRY AND LAW 5, 165 (1977). Prosecutors and judges may use evaluation commitment for preventive or long-term detention, or to deny bail. *Id.*; EVALS. II *supra* note 24, at 128.

886. *See generally* P. Chernoff & W. Schaffer, *Defending the Mentally Ill: Ethical Quicksand*, 10 AMERICAN CLINICAL LAW REVIEW 505–31 (1972). *see also* Roesch & Golding *supra* note 15, at 49.

887. See ROESCH & GOLDING *supra* note 16, at 191–193 (table 6.28). Roesch and Golding's survey on judicial attitudes found the majority of polled judges believed defense counsel either misunderstood the legal criteria of competency (53%) or raised competency motions with intent to delay trial (67%). This notwithstanding, the judges granted the motions. *Id.* at 192. *See also* Winick I, *supra* note 1, at 925. Winick also explains how the existing CST process is extremely expensive with respect to evaluation and treatment costs. *See Id.* at 928–938.

1. Assessment Procedures

Although competency issues are most often raised by the defense counsel, any party, including the court, can order a fitness evaluation, *sua sponte*.[888] However, if the court does introduce the issue, an uninformed attorney can make egregious mistakes, especially if deficient about the law and how it functions in regard to competency evaluations. Using Federal statutes as an example, if the court puts forth the issue of trial fitness the defendant must undergo a competency evaluation. According to the statute, "the court may commit the person to be examined for a reasonable period [i.e., thirty days not to exceed forty-five days] to the custody of the Attorney General for placement in a suitable facility."[889] Although seemingly clear, these provisions create opportunities that can potentially infringe on an accused's liberty interests, especially for defendants not in custody. Although the provisions recommend that the examination take place in a facility close to the court,[890] the defendant can be placed in a federal prison to be evaluated by government doctors. If the attorney is not acquainted with the nuances of these provisions, she or he may fail to challenge appropriately or effectively the court's reasoning for custodial commitment. If, however, the defendant *is* in custody, the uninformed attorney may fail to convince the director of the facility why an extension beyond the thirty day examination period is warranted, lacking the requisite legal knowledge for a showing of good cause for the same.[891] Given

---

888. *See* EVALS. II *supra* note 24, at 126; S. Eizenstadt, *Mental Competency to Stand Trial*, 4 HARV. C.R.-C.L.L. REV. 379 (1969). *See also* Pate v. Robinson, 383 U.S. 375 (1966) (Supreme Court held trial court must raise the competency issue if the court's own evidence or information provided by the defense or prosecution raises a "*bona fide* doubt" as to the defendant's competence to stand trial.); Drope v. Missouri, 420 U.S. 162 (1975) ("The import of our decision in Pate v. Robinson is that evidence of a defendant's irrational behavior, his demeanor at trial, and any prior medical opinion on competence to stand trial are all relevant in determining whether further inquiry is required, but that even one of these factors standing alone may, in some circumstances, be sufficient.") *See Id.* at 180.

889. *See* 18 U.S.C. sect. 4247 (b).

890. *See* 18 U.S.C. § 4247 (b) ("Unless impracticable, the psychiatric or psychological examination shall be conducted in the suitable facility closest to the court.")

891. *See Id.*

these considerations, the defense counsel should first raise the issue of competency, especially for defendants not in custody. In addition to having input with regard to selecting an examiner,[892] defense counsel can press for an examination in either an in-patient or out-patient setting.

2. Assessment Findings

We also argue that the competency evaluation itself presents potentially devastating problems. Briefly, once the defendant is examined, a report is filed to the court with copies provided to the defense attorney and, more importantly, to the prosecuting attorney. Since these evaluations often investigate the pending indictment,[893] statements made by the accused are located in the report. In other words, incriminating statements made by the defendant may be provided to the prosecutor unintentionally and subsequently used against the defendant during the trial. Similar to the points previously described, clinical forensic accounts in the literature suggest that examiners often relate information (by virtue of a CST exam) that could work against the defendant in at least three ways[894]:

> (1) when the evaluator testifies at trial and repeats confessions or admissions of fact implicating the defendant in the crime with which he is charged, (2) when the prosecution uses the statements to impeach the defendant's credibility in case he testifies at trial, and (3) when the prosecutor, prior to trial, used the information (available through discovery) to add to his knowledge of the defendant.[895]

---

892. For defendants in custody, and if the court "finds it appropriate, [the evaluation may be conducted] by more than one such examiner. *See Id.* For this reason, the attorney may file a motion for request of an outside examiner, especially if s/he has concerns over the government doctors' ability or objectivity.

893. Indeed, as previously discussed the most recent and recommended assessment instrument, the MacCAT-CA, includes six appreciation items concerning the defendant's beliefs and perceptions with respect to their own legal situation.

894. *See* B. Weiner, *Mental Disability and the Criminal Law*, in S.J. BRAKEL., J. PARRY & B. WEINER, THE MENTALLY DISABLED AND THE LAW 702 (American Bar Foundation, 3d. ed. 1985). *See also* PERLIN II *supra* note 570 § 14.04, at 220.

895. *See* D. Bennett, *A Guided Tour Through Selected ABA Standards Relating to Incompetence to Stand Trial*, 53 GEO. WASH. L. 375, 399 (1985)

Clearly, then, detailed knowledge of courtroom procedure and strategy can have important, if not deleterious, implications for criminal defense lawyers and their clients. In what follows, three important recommendations are discussed regarding what defense attorneys should do under these circumstances. In brief, these include: (1) know the evaluator; (2) become familiar with CST protocol; and (3) understand the interaction between CST laws and CST assessment instruments. Although provisional and speculative, we contend that if implemented appropriately the proposed recommendations could help minimize the risks associated with damaging information elicited during a CST review.

First, attorneys should carefully select who they choose to evaluate their client, using experts specializing in the area of competency to stand trial. Litigators should investigate the background of the licensed psychologist or psychiatrist, ensuring that they choose a specialist both qualified and objective in terms of the person's evaluation practice.[896] Second, attorneys should become familiar with CST protocol. Once conversant, litigators can then ask questions such as: "How will you evaluate my client"; "What assessment protocol or format do you use?"; and "To what extent will your examination query the current charges involving my client?". Acquiring this necessary acumen will enable the attorney to screen-in appropriate experts. Finally, reviewing the subtleties of the competency laws practiced and the CST assessment instruments employed relative to one's jurisdiction helps lawyers skillfully advise their clients about the general fitness evaluation process before the exam occurs. Al-

---

(citing F. Berry, *Self-Incrimination and the Compulsory Mental Examination: A Proposal*, 15 Ariz. L. Rev. 919, 929 (1973).

896. *See* D. Mossman, *Is Expert Psychiatric Testimony Fundamentally Immoral?*, 17 INT'L J. L. & PSYCHIATRY 347 (1994) in PERLIN *supra* note 15, at 14. (Although Mossman's article centers on ethical status of testimony with respect to moral conflict, he states "[B]eing a 'hired gun' whose opinions are formed by and available for large fees, or being influenced by one's potentially correctable biases about crime, criminals, types of clients, or judicial outcomes, or claiming expertise for one's opinions when none is justified, are practices that are very troublesome and obviously wrong.") The idea that some forensic psychiatrists are not subjective or "play only on one side of the fence" is an important issue but, nonetheless, beyond the scope of this book. However, for a review concerning this topic, *see generally* American Psychiatric Association's Council on Psychiatry and Law, *Peer Review of Psychiatric Expert* Testimony, 20 BULL. AM. ACAD. PSYCHIATRY LAW 343, 344–45 (1992).

though certainly contingent upon many issues (e.g., degree of mental impairment, defendant's willingness to work with counsel), consultation in this regard may prevent the admission of potentially devastating and incriminating statements.[897]

B. Psychological Assessment and CST Rulings

A competency to stand trial determination is a profound conclusion that can dramatically impede or halt the flow of the criminal adjudication process.[898] When such pretrial decisions are reached, concerns for both the defendant and the victim surface.[899] When CST burdens are met, the court takes measures to ensure that the defendant will not be subjected to an unfair trial. This is accomplished by remanding the accused to a mental health facility.[900] In theory, this procedure is defined as a measure to avoid an unjust or biased trial in the interest of the accused. Ostensibly, however, other agendas are endorsed through the operation of commitment procedures for those found incompetent to stand trial. Specifically, incompetent to stand trial detainees undergo protracted psychiatric treatment for various lengths of time to determine if and when they will become fit to go forward with their criminal case.[901]

---

897. Admittedly, the latter suggestion is not realistic in many situations given the nature of the inquiry; however, informing the client about such information is prudent in some instances. For example, if another party (i.e., the prosecution or the court) raises doubt about a defendant's incompetence, consultation is a safe measure to inform the accused that incriminating questions may arise during the evaluation. This notwithstanding, we suggest that the specific context and the lawyer's discretion should determine whether providing such information would or would not preserve the integrity of the defense.

898. *See E.g.,* Nicholson & Kugler *supra* note 153, at 355. *See also* Winick I *supra* note 1, at 925.

899. *See generally* R. Bonnie, *The Ferguson Spectacle Demeaned System,* 17(23) THE NATIONAL LAW JOURNAL. A23 (1995).

900. *See* D. Davis, *Treatment Planning for the Patient Who is Incompetent to Stand Trial,* HOSPITAL & COMMUNITY PSYCHIATRY. 268 (1985).

901. *See Id.* at 268. *See also* Jackson v. Indiana, 406 U.S. 715 (1972). Although *Jackson* (1972) attempted to address problems associated with indefinite confinement, the court did not set limits on the duration of commitment, thus many defendants are still subjected to indefinite confinement. *See* Nicholson & Kugler *supra* note 153, at 355; Davis *supra* note 900, at 268.

1. Shades of Paranoia: Paranoid or Delusional, Does It Really Matter When Assessing Competence-Related Abilities?

The previously articulated recommendations address some of the concerns that surface with respect to assessment procedures, assessment findings, and the defense attorney's role in both matters. However, other critical psycholegal issues emerge involving the clinical evaluation of trial fitness and a courtroom determination of the issue. Indeed, the judicial weight assigned to diagnostic findings, especially when defendants demonstrate paranoid and delusional symptoms, is also of concern. On this point, we maintain that the distinction between paranoid and delusional tendencies are (mostly) irrelevant in the context of CST clinical evaluations and courtroom judgements. To be clear, we assert that the pivotal issue when assessing one's mental state for purposes of a trial and when reaching a judicial determination on this issue should not hinge on a specific or even provisional diagnosis. Rather, the clinical and diagnostic findings should only consider the impending problems related to the defendant's decisional competence and his or her ability to assist with the defense.

This matter is compounded further with the paranoid litigant. At the risk of belaboring the point made throughout this text, paranoid and delusional mental health conditions involve ubiquitous traits that often go undetected, especially in light of the problems plaguing the CST process (e.g., low standards, CST time constraints, inadequate clinical evaluation measures). Consequently, the judicial weight afforded the examiner's clinical assessment of one's competency to stand trial must be reconsidered.

Whether a defendant has paranoid beliefs, is delusional, suffers from either bizarre or non-bizarre delusions is really of limited importance. Thus, specific diagnoses (e.g., paranoid personality disorder, paranoid schizophrenia, or delusional disorder, persecutory type) made under time constrained conditions are equally unimportant. Indeed, it should be axiomatic by now that defendants suffering from shades of paranoia are often able to understand what is going on around them (Prong 2 of *Dusky*) but, nevertheless, are unable or are not willing to assist in the defense process (Prong 1 of *Dusky*). As stated in chapter 4 when discussing mental health disorders, paranoid and delusional symptomatology occur along a continuum and, thus, present mental health examiners with a troubling decision about what is or is not normal. However, defendants with such disorders are frequently found competent to stand trial and, because of their paranoia, they experience deep-seated conflicts or other rifts with their attorneys, often desiring to conduct their own defense. Thus, the question is whether shades of paranoia really matter in competency determinations? Clearly, behavior demonstrating paranoid beliefs disrupts the flow of the legal process and prevents the defendant from receiving a fair trial. Indeed, these issues were imminent concerns in the Colin Ferguson case. Given these troubling factors, we submit that psycholegal policy reform on this matter is most assuredly needed.

Circumstances such as those just described raise questions about the efficacy and legitimacy of the CST hearing altogether. The Ferguson case lends support to these observations. The clinical evaluation issue in the Ferguson case was whether he was, *throughout the duration of the trial*, mentally competent to stand trial. His courtroom conduct and self-representation suggested that he was not. This notwithstanding, Ferguson was found guilty, producing controversy among the lay public and within legal circles. Curiously, a finding of incompetency may have provided Ferguson adequate time and respite sufficient for him to then move forward with the legal dispute, potentially producing a courtroom outcome absent considerable doubt and suspicion. At the very least, an incompetency finding would not have (initially) resulted in trying and convicting a defendant, physically present in the courtroom but mentally absent, especially in terms of advocating skillfully on his behalf.

2. Informational Value and Competency Assessments

In light of the limitations contained within various psychological assessment instruments (as noted in chapter 3) and the corresponding problems stemming from long-term civil commitment and/or detainment, we suggest that the CST process, and the evaluation of psychological fitness, needs to be significantly reformed. Preliminarily, however, we contend that difficulties with the proper administration of justice are (largely) the product of inaccurate or questionable determinations that one is mentally fit to stand trial. In other words, although there are fundamental liberty interests at stake if one is wrongfully found incompetent to stand trial (i.e., protracted and unnecessary civil confinement), these concerns address constitutional questions beyond the scope of the present text. Rather, the concern here is chiefly with the psychological outlets and legal protections availed to defendants wrongfully found fit to stand to trial. Thus, we recommend that the clinical assessment of fitness not be given the kind of authoritative and controlling weight judges typically afford it. The intent behind standardizing CST instruments (or the misguided attempt to standardize CST instruments) suggests that data should be presented to the court in the most simplistic manner possible. This is why judges value expert testimony in relation to competency matters,[902] and seldom disagree with expert opinion.[903] Agreement rates between judges and CST forensic experts are not only confirmed in the literature,[904] but are operative in actual competency cases. Indeed, the most frequent conclusion reached about the class of defendants identified as incompetent is that their fate (largely) depends on opinions rendered by clinical forensic experts.[905]

In contrast to the elevated status the forensic evaluator's testimony receives (i.e., value judges attach to ultimate legal opinions), a strategy that acknowledges only the informational value clinical forensic assessments offer in CST proceedings should be endorsed.[906] As previously discussed, Melton et al. maintain that

---

902. *See* G. Melton, L. Weithorn, & C. Slobogin, COMMUNITY MENTAL HEALTH CENTERS AND THE COURTS: AN EVALUATION OF COMMUNITY BASED FORENSIC SERVICES. (1985).

903. *See* J. Reich, & L. Tookey, *Disagreements Between Court and Psychiatrist on Competency to Stand Trial*, 47 JOURNAL OF CLINICAL PSYCHIATRY. 29–30 (1986).

904. *See Id.* at 29.

905. *See* EVALS. II *supra* note 24, at 129 (noting "whomever examining mental health professionals characterize as incompetent is likely ultimately to be found incompetent.").

906. *See* Arrigo & Bardwell *supra* note 18, at 32. Although many jurisdictions utilize an "informational" approach rather than relying on the determinative quality of clinicians' opinions (unpublished information, personal communication from Thomas Grisso), we argue that our previous recommendation is not a standardized procedure nor is it readily apparent from our own experiences. Thus, we contend that "ultimate opinions" reinforce the practice that

"clinicians should attempt to avoid offering legal conclusions about competency, or, if the court orders otherwise, should couch their conclusions in cautious terms."[907] In this regard, evaluators should not feel derelict when mis-diagnosing mental impairment or minimizing troubling traits associated with certain mental disorders, and jurists should not feel responsible when incorrectly finding one fit to stand trial.

The significance of this psychological assessment recommendation takes on greater practical meaning when considering the legal reforms needed to make it work. Indeed, the utility of clinical forensic evaluations as data to consult rather than depend on can only be implemented effectively if certain courtroom practices are in place. In the next section we introduce several legal policy remedies along these lines. Moreover, we consider their practical utility by revisiting what their impact would have been, if implemented, in the Ferguson matter.

C. Legal Policy Remedies

In an earlier section of this book, the important and controlling case law on the matter of competency to stand trial was examined. As the review and analysis disclosed, the CST hearing can produce judicially sanctioned, though flawed, outcomes wherein defendants effectively "shoot themselves in the foot."[908] In other words, by exercising one's constitutional right to self-representation, as articulated in *Faretta*, defendants potentially forfeit their ability to have their case argued persuasively under the law and succumb, regrettably, to the perils of using "[t]he system of criminal justice [as an] instrument of self-destruction."[909] These outcomes can be particularly thorny when the defendant is mentally impaired.

---

many trial judges shift responsibility for the final disposition of the case to clinicians when making competency judgements. This suggests that the issue of trial competence is, practically speaking, a clinical rather than a legal question. This is where the problem lies.

907. *See Id.*
908. *See* Decker, *supra* note 178, at 483.
909. *See Faretta*, 422 U.S. at 840. (Burger, C.J., dissenting).

While it is true that not all cases raising competency concerns are publicized (e.g., Ferguson), less visible cases involving competency matters also disrupt the legal proceedings to some meaningful degree.[910] Put another way, even when defendants are able to craft a well-founded courtroom strategy, verbal outbursts, bizarre behavior, incoherent thoughts, unusual logic, and/or physical assaults can be damaging, if not devastating, to the trial's outcome. The likelihood of an adverse verdict is appreciable when the accused conducting the defense is of questionable mental health status.[911] The Ferguson trial and verdict substantiate this claim. However, these legal problems are also appreciable and problematic in other less publicized CST cases. The related case of *United States v. Jennings*[912] amply illustrates the myriad of problems associated with certain psychiatrically disordered defendants exercising their *Faretta* rights. Indeed, the *Jennings* case vividly demonstrates the problems that arise when a combative defendant with questionable mental health (reluctantly) invokes his constitutional right associated with *Faretta*. As the *Jennings* case discloses, these legal problems are compounded when judicial determinations on the constitutional right to proceed *pro se* to trial are informed by one's dubious mental health or disruptive behavior as evinced by the defendant.

Prior to jury selection, the defendant, Edward Jennings, entered a motion to substitute counsel but the waiver was denied.[913] Upon learning the news, Jennings struck his attorney "in the side of the head with a closed fist, causing counsel to reel to the courtroom floor."[914] Six U.S. marshals were needed to restrain Jennings successfully. The trial judge subsequently determined that the accused had waived his Sixth Amendment right to counsel.[915] The following

---

910. *See* Decker *supra* note 178, at 487.

911. *See Id.* at 487, 488.

912. *See* United States v. Jennings, 855 F. Supp. 1427 (M.D. Penn. 1994).

913. *See Id.* at 1432. Jennings wanted to substitute counsel due to a fundamental disagreement over defense strategy. Specifically, Jennings had intentions of asserting an insanity defense and counsel did not feel such a defense would have any merit. "Jennings' basis for an insanity defense was the stress he claimed to feel from the alleged threats from the corrections officers." *See Id.* at 1442.

914. *See Id.* Jennings later expressed to marshals that his original intent was to "bite counsel's ear off," but opted otherwise given the chaos that would inevitably follow. *See Id.* at 1440.

915. *See Id.*

day, Jennings threatened "to cut the throat of his counsel and 'drink his blood,' to 'slaughter' corrections officers, and to murder the Assistant United States Attorney."[916] Given the nature of his conduct, the defendant was placed in a secure holding cell so that he could participate in jury selection, *in absentia*.[917] While confined in the cell, Jennings continued to engage in unruly and disruptive behavior. He threw water on the speaker units, rejected any communications from the court or from court personnel, and "threatened to throw a cup of urine at the marshal."[918]

Several days later, the accused was transported to the courthouse, where he proceeded to conduct his own defense. The jury found Jennings guilty on all counts of the indictment. Although he appealed claiming inadequate representation, the U.S. District Court affirmed the trial court's decision that the defendant had indeed waived his right to counsel.[919] The case of Edward Jennings is just one of many that raises significant questions about the efficacy of self-representation for mentally impaired, though presumably competent, defendants.

As previously discussed, a similar problem presented itself in the Ferguson matter. Although his courtroom antics did not rise to the volatile level displayed by Jennings, the trial judge (Judge Belfi) did *not* insist upon a subsequent hearing to assess the defendant's CST standing, despite obvious indicators to the contrary (e.g., incoherent logic, unusual thoughts during the trial). Indeed, although Ferguson's essential strategy involved racial prejudice, his courtroom demeanor as a (psychologically impaired) litigator sent a clear message that he *was* to blame for the six murders and nineteen attempted murders occurring in the New York train.

---

916. *See Id.*

917. *See Id.* at 1445 (Because Jennings was conducting his own defense, the court wired the cell for sound and provided paper and writing utensils so that he could participate in the proceedings.).

918. *See Id.* at 1445.

919. *See Id.* at 1433. Jennings' defense efforts consisted of his own testimony that he did not contest the government's case against him. In fact, Jennings acknowledged the wrongful nature of his actions and stated "that he would do things much worse in the future." *See Id.* It is interesting to note that the issue of trial competence was never raised. Indeed, this is surprising considering his erratic and violent behavior during pretrial proceedings and, further, given the illogical reasoning employed in his own defense efforts.

The relevance of the outcomes in the respective cases of Edward Jennings and Colin Ferguson are linked to one's constitutional right to waive counsel and proceed *pro se* to trial, following a CST judicial determination. Although the decision in *Faretta* constitutionally guaranteed the right to self-representation, it failed to provide the needed guidance for lower courts to discern the scope of this right and its attending procedures.[920] Similarly, the *Godinez* decision acknowledged the significance of decisional competence, ruling that a defendant's trial fitness and competence to plead guilty were subsumed within the same unitary formulation set forth in *Dusky*, and that a defendant's ability to make decisions was also embedded within that standard.[921] Even though the *Godinez* ruling clarified some aspects concerning decisional competency, the Court's unfortunate silence regarding which abilities were required for it, "invites further conceptual interpretation and continuing controversy."[922]

In what follows, several legal policy recommendations applicable to the area of forensic mental health are outlined, addressing the shortcomings associated with *Dusky*, *Faretta*, and *Godinez*. We draw heavily on related federal and United States Supreme Court decisions that assess the rights of criminal defendants whose mental health standing is not challenged. As we assert, if the logic of these corollary cases was routinely implemented, this would curtail some of the more thorny problems associated with defendants who *pro se* their criminal cases, especially those who choose the path of self-representation despite having their competency previously questioned. Moreover, as we demonstrate, these reforms are consistent with our policy position on how psycho-diagnostic findings are to be employed in CST proceedings. We acknowledge at the outset that each of these recommendations is tentatively and speculatively discussed, requiring more systematic analysis prior to implementation. However, in order to contextualize our policy ideas, we examine their utility in relation to the CST process in the Colin Ferguson case.

---

920. *See* Decker *supra* note 178, at 488.
921. *See* Hoge et al., I *supra* note 360, at 146.
922. *See* N. Poythress, R. Bonnie, S. Hoge, J. Monahan, & L. Oberlander, *Client Abilities to Assist Counsel and Make Decisions in Criminal Cases: Findings From Three Studies*, 18 LAW AND HUM. BEHAV. 437, 438 (1994).

1. The Court's Prerogative to Appoint Standby Counsel

Requiring standby counsel in a *pro se* defense can reduce problems associated with defendants whose mental health has been previously called into question.[923] Indeed, one implication of *Faretta* is that the court can exercise its discretion and appoint standby counsel to assist the *pro se* defendant.[924] In the subsequent case of *McKaskle v. Wiggins*,[925] the Supreme Court articulated the role of standby counsel for defendants who engage in self-representation. Specifically, the Court addressed the conditions wherein standby counsel could offer assistance over the *pro se* defendant's objection while still respecting the defendant's *Faretta* rights.[926] The Court held that the accused's *pro se* rights were not violated, despite standby counsel's unsolicited involvement.[927] In support of their position, the Court opined: "[p]articipation by counsel to steer a defendant through the basic procedures of trial is permissible even in the unlikely event that it somewhat undermines the *pro se* defendant's appearance of control over his own defense."[928] The *McKaskle* holding is important with respect to CST determinations, particularly when defendants whose mental health status is doubtful waive counsel and present their own defense. Moreover, this ruling demonstrates its courtroom utility relative to defendants who proceed *pro se* to trial for questionable reasons.

In a discussion concerning motivational factors for defendants who request to conduct their own defense, Decker[929] describes a

---

923. *See* Corinis *supra* note 183, at 287 (suggesting the utility of mandating standby counsel for defendants whose mental health is questionable).

924. *See Faretta*, 422 U.S. at n. 46 (stating that even over the objection of the accused, a State can "appoint a standby counsel to aid the accused if and when the accused requests help, and to be available to represent the accused in the event that termination of the defendant's self-representation is necessary.") (citing United States v. Dougherty, 154 U.S.App.D.C. 76, 87–89, 473 F.2d 1113, 1124–1126 (1972).

925. *See* McKaskle v. Wiggins, 465 U.S. 168 (1984).

926. *See Id.* at 170.

927. *See Id.* at 946 (noting defendant was able to make his own appearances as he saw fit, and further found standby counsel's participation within reasonable limits). *See Id.* at 188.

928. *See Id.* at 184.

929. *See* Decker *supra* note 178, at 485–487.

number of emerging themes inspiring the *pro se* defendant. In brief, some of these reasons include: a general act of defiance; having nothing to lose given the heinousness of one's prior acts; furthering one's own secret agenda including the advancement of a radical political belief; and suffering from mental illness.[930]

Consistent with the underlying policy purpose of our investigation, mandating standby counsel is especially important for defendants making such *pro se* requests as a product of their mental illness. Indeed, while delusions and related psychopathological traits may significantly distort or circumscribe an accused's reasoning ability, they may not, however, impact judicial determinations of competency. Thus, while some defendants can be found fit to stand trial, they may conduct their defense based on irrational beliefs or delusional themes. For example, a psychiatrically disordered defendant's fear of being labeled "mentally ill" may function as the primary basis for proceeding *pro se* to trial.[931] Relatedly, in some instances, defendants harbor paranoid delusions believing that everyone is "out to get them." Thus, they relinquish their right to counsel and conduct their own defense. The Ferguson trial provides such an example and demonstrates the significance of *McKaskle's* implications.

Although Judge Belfi assigned Ferguson numerous advisors, the benefits of standby counsel were not evident in the trial. This is not to imply that the controversial outcome was the result of *McKaskle* implications; that is, whether standby counsel was or was not appointed. Rather, the troubling outcome was a product of what the lawyers failed to do in their advisory role and what Judge Belfi failed to do when opting not to recognize Ferguson's (obviously) impaired mental status. As such, we contend that standby counsel interests (via *McKaskle*) were not realized because of the defense attorneys and, more importantly, because of the judge. Consequently, in what follows, the interplay between the Colin Ferguson trial and

---

930. *Id.* (Decker citing many case examples illustrating the various motivating factors surrounding defendants who proceed *pro se* to trial).

931. As discussed *infra* in the supplemental case study analysis, Theodore Kaczynski was in constant conflict with his attorneys and ultimately pled guilty to the "unabomber" crimes because he did not want to be portrayed as mentally ill. *See* Arrigo & Bardwell *supra* note 18, at 28.

standby counsel is briefly discussed. In particular, we identify the reasons why standby counsel was not effective in the case of the Long Island Railroad gunman and conclude that mandatory standby counsel should have been operating in this legal matter.

Kunstler and Kuby participated initially as standby counsel, however, convinced that their client was suffering from delusional disorder, persecutory sub-type the attorneys soon resigned their position. Understandably, Kunstler and Kuby could not bear the prospect of watching their client assume responsibility for the case in an awkward, inexperienced, and unqualified way. Later, Ferguson would require the services from a variety of attorneys to assist him on procedural issues.[932] Although at one time the defendant had five in-court advisors (standby counselors), they failed to indicate to Judge Belfi that Ferguson's courtroom antics clearly demonstrated that he was incompetent for purposes of self representation. Indeed, two of the attorneys remained throughout the duration of the trial, yet surprisingly the issue of the defendant's trial fitness was not raised.

In addition, as discussed in chapter 6, Ferguson argued that he was the victim of a mass governmental conspiracy. As such, he eventually tried to subpoena high ranking politicians, including former President Clinton and then governor of New York, Mario Cuomo. The defendant's delusional themes of conspiracy became appreciable and problematic from the outset of the trial; however, this apparently was not enough for Judge Belfi to raise the issue of competency himself.

Given the nature of Ferguson's bizarre behavior, the application of standby counsel was not the problem in this case. Instead, the difficulty with the case of the Long Island Railroad gunman stemmed from what the in-court advisors failed to do. Their inactivity made the presence of standby counsel simply ineffective. Stated differently, the attorneys providing in-court advising should have been more vigilant in monitoring Ferguson's *current* capacity to stand trial. Moreover, they should have interceded, on several obvious occasions, insisting that the judge order a subsequent CST

---

932. *See Court TV: Tape New York v. Ferguson, Murder on the 5:33: The Trial of Colin Ferguson,* Log timecode 26:20.

exam. Thus, what we draw attention to is the fact that while Ferguson had at his disposal several attorneys to assist him on basic legal procedure, competency concerns throughout the trial were ignored. As we have documented, the defendant's far-reaching conspiracy theories and other courtroom escapades, supplied countless opportunities to revisit and reexamine the issue of trial fitness. Regrettably, however, this did not happen.

Relatedly, Judge Belfi, in the face of clear paranoid and delusional evidence, ignored and/or overlooked Ferguson's bizarre behavior and mental state. In short, Judge Belfi failed to reconsider the issue of competence. Consequently, the fantastic trial continued to the detriment of the defendant, the victims and their families, and the entire adjudicatory process.

Based on the foregoing commentary, we maintain that standby counsel *should* be applied in cases like that of the Long Island Railroad gunman. Accordingly, the logic contained in *McKaskle* provides a much needed and fertile legal basis for preserving the defendant's autonomy (as required by *Faretta*), while addressing concerns related to the *pro se* defendant who operates out of a framework of delusional thoughts and beliefs. Moreover, with respect to judicial concerns, *McKaskle* helps ensure the integrity of the trial process and the decorum of the court.[933] Indeed, if courts can impose standby counsel "to relieve [the] judge of a need to explain and enforce basic rules...or to assist counsel [the defendant/attorney] with routine obstacles...,"[934] then clearly its rationale is applicable in other, more troubling contexts. Under the conditions set forth in *MsKasckle*, it is not unreasonable to mandate such in-court advisors for all *pro se* defendants whose competence has already been called into question. Simply put, the application of *McKaskle's* logic to cases of CST defendants whose mental health status nonetheless remains questionable at best during trial, would enable standby counsel to reassert the question of competency, giving rise to a subsequent hearing on the matter.

---

933. Among other advantages, standby counsel "ensure[s] the defendant's compliance with basic rules of courtroom protocol and procedure." *See Id*. at 183.

934. *See Corinis supra* note 183, at 287.

2. Defendant's Right to Select Counsel of Choice Following Revocation of the Right to Proceed *Pro Se*

During a criminal proceeding, defendants who engage in self-representation can have this right revoked as it is not absolute.[935] Revocation is particularly problematic when standby counsel has been appointed and the defendant seeks to retain counsel of choice.[936] The Court addressed this matter in *United States v. Romano*.[937] In *Romano*, the district court made clear that the defendant had the right to retain counsel of choice before the trial commenced; however, if the defendant, Romano, waived her right to counsel and subsequently lost her *pro se* status, in effect she then would have "waived the right to retain counsel of her choice."[938] This is precisely what happened in the case and the court, over the objection of the defendant, appointed a standby attorney to assume the defense.

As a point of departure, the district court found the defendant, Romano, in contempt and argued that she raised subjects that would confuse and prejudice the jury.[939] In her opening statement, Romano exclaimed:

---

935. See *Faretta*, 422 U.S. at 834 n. 46 ("the trial judge may terminate self-representation by a defendant who deliberately engages in serious and obstructionist misconduct").

936. See Decker *supra* note 178, at 533.

937. See United States v. Romano, 849 F.2d 812 (3d Cir. 1988). Briefly, Romano and three others (the self proclaimed "Epiphany Plowshares") a political group in protest of miliary action were arrested and indicted for entering a military installation and damaging government property. Among other things, they damaged military aircraft and specifically broke control panels, equipment controls, and severed hydraulic lines, poured blood in the cock pits, left pamphlets and bottles, scribing various political epitaphs. The damage exceeded $160,000. See *Id.* at 813.

938. See *Id.* at 816. Specifically, once revoking the defendant's *pro se* status (finding the defendant to be in contempt), the district court appointed standby counsel to take over the representation for the accused. Here the district court relied on *Faretta*. See *Faretta supra* note 176, at 834 n. 46.

939. In *Romano*, the Court of appeals agreed with the district finding of contempt (by way of a limine order) arguing "the court would be remiss if it failed to screen what the jury is exposed to because of te potential for jury confusion and prejudice.... A trial judge has a duty to limit the jury's exposure to

[Y]ou will hear testimony about the blood, which was spilled on the aircraft, representative of the millions who will die needlessly, in illegal, immoral atomic war. Of the thousands that were slaughtered now in the war that we perpetrate in other lands... We intend to put forth in testimony that we also made banners to take with us to proclaim the basis for our action to witness to the truth, the rightness and the legality of our action; releasing captive Jews from Nazi death camps or dismantling those gas chambers... What this case is really about is the slaughter of innocent people.[940]

On appeal, the United States Court of Appeals for the Third Circuit held that while the district court

did not err in implementing and enforcing the in limine order [a vehicle used to prevent confusing and prejudicial statements as evidenced in Romano's opening statement], we do find that the district court's failure to allow Romano the opportunity to retain counsel of choice [following the loss of *pro se* status].... [violated] Romano's rights under the Sixth Amendment.[941]

Revocation of the defendant's *pro se* status and the issue of counsel of choice, following forfeiture of the *pro se* right, is significant in cases where there is some question about the accused's competency. As previously noted, standby counsel, in and of itself, may not be sufficient to advance the administration of justice. The Ferguson trial substantiates this claim. Indeed, for mentally ill defendant's with certain symptomatology (e.g., flight of ideas, paranoid delusions) standby counsel alone can frustrate a defendant's desires, particularly in instances where the accused does not want to pursue certain trial strategies and their attending implications (e.g., avoiding the defense of insanity). Accordingly, for some mentally ill defendants subsequently found competent to stand trial, questions about psychiatric impairment can cause such serious problems for the *pro se* litigant that the court finds itself compelled to revoke the defendant's right to self representation, thereby instructing standby

---

only that which is probative and relevant and must attempt to screen from the jury any proffer that it deems irrelevant." *See* Romano at 815.

940. *See Id.* at 814. n.4.

941. *See Id.* at 820 citing *United States v. Laura*, 607 F. 2d 52, 56 (3d Cir.1979) (recognizing "the most important decision a defendant makes in shaping his defense is his selection of an attorney.")

counsel to assume (significant) responsibility for the legal defense. However, under these circumstances, the defendant may become so frustrated with counsel's intent to pursue, for example, an insanity defense, that the accused may display unruly behavior and subsequently may be found in contempt of court. Thus, standby counsel "may literally stand by to take over in case the defendant loses the right to self-representation."[942] Given the preceding comments, we submit that the facts in the Colin Ferguson trial are consistent with and lend support to the appellate decision in *Romano* and its generalizability elsewhere. Indeed, *Romano* is relevant on the issue of abrogating Ferguson's *pro se* status and for granting the accused the right to select counsel of choice, following the *pro se* revocation.

To reiterate, following *Romano*, the defendant still retains the right to choose counsel of choice. Thus, in cases involving *pro se* defendants with prior CST concerns, the accused would retain some control over the defense strategy. In light of the previously recommended legal policy reform; namely, mandating standby counsel for all *pro se* defendants whose competency is called into question, the application of *Romano* in cases such as these helps curtail courtroom problems stemming from a defendant's particular mental illness.

To illustrate this point, consider the case of the Long Island Railroad gunman. If Judge Belfi had been inclined to revoke Ferguson's *pro se* status, given his chronic and acute paranoid behavior, under *Romano* the defendant would still retain the option to choose an attorney rather than accept, without his consent, one appointed by the Court. As previously mentioned, Ferguson had several courtroom advisors and, in particular, two attorneys served in this capacity throughout the duration of the trial. Thus, the defendant did have access to alternative counsel, independent of those litigators with whom he had prior conflicts (e.g., Kunstler and Kuby). In this context, then, the accused would have retained some control over the defense, without having to rely on counsel he previously fired. Under these circumstances, the case would have proceeded, arguably without the type, degree, or intensity of courtroom antics formerly displayed by Ferguson the attorney. In sum, we contend

---

942. *See* Decker *supra* note 173, at 525.

that allowing a defendant, not subjected to a CST reexamination, suffering from a paranoid or delusional disorder to select his or her standby counsel of choice potentially diffuses trial difficulties that might otherwise relate to mentally impaired themes (e.g., governmental conspiracy theories, fear of being portrayed as psychiatrically ill).

Notwithstanding the potential benefits just described by way of *Romano*, we maintain that Judge Belfi's failure to revoke Colin Ferguson's *pro se* status was the most devastating factor impacting the case's controversial outcome. Despite obvious signs that Ferguson suffered from and was guided by paranoid delusions, his criminal trial continued without the benefit of a subsequent CST review. Having alienated himself from the jury (e.g., he referred to himself in the third person and cross-examined the victims of the crime in which he was charged), the mounting evidence of Ferguson's debilitating psychological condition did not prompt Judge Belfi to revoke the defendant's right to self representation. Indeed, Ferguson's opening statements bizarrely connecting the counts in the indictment to the year of the trial (i.e., 93 counts for 1993) were at least comparable to the information proffered by Romano in her initial argument. In *Romano*, the result was the revocation of the accused's *pro se* status. Moreover, in *Romano* the issue of mental impairment was not in question but the defendant still lost her right to self representation by virtue of incoherently articulated political ideology. From our perspective, it stands to reason that if defendant Romano's political logic resulted in the revocation of her right to proceed *pro se* to trial; a defendant whose psychiatric fitness was not questioned in the first instance, then Ferguson's paranoid and delusional logic displayed throughout the trial, following his CST determination, should have produced the same outcome. Under these conditions, the revocation of Colin Ferguson's *pro se* right would more than likely have resulted in a subsequent CST review, arguably resulting in a more accurate incompetency finding.

3. Hybrid Representation

In some jurisdictions, trial courts may exercise their discretion and allow the accused to assume some of the defense attorney functions.[943] This is known as "hybrid" or "mixed". representation.[944] Although it is not constitutionally guaranteed, hybrid representation is constitutionally permissible.[945] Admittedly, there are problems stemming from the use of mixed representation (e.g., it is not particularly efficient, attorneys have to deal with the vicissitudes of under- and non-legally trained defendants); however, the doctrine is suggestive for cases wherein questions persist about the defendant's competence to stand trial.[946]

Although Ferguson passionately wanted to present his case to the jurors personally, his obvious mental impairment contributed to his own courtroom demise. Given the flawed predictive capability of diagnostic instruments assessing fitness to stand trial and the potential problems stemming from standby counsel (i.e., how much assistance can an in-court attorney really offer a *pro se* defendant who is delusional?), a more meaningful solution may be hybrid representation. Had Ferguson been allowed to invoke this legal option, he and his "co-counsel"might have been able to develop a more cogent (race-based) defense, and the verdict may have been more consistent with what Ferguson anticipated. Invoking this right not only respects the defendant's autonomy but evinces utility as it can reduce the adverse impact defendants undoubtedly confront when using "the courtroom as a platform for personal expression."[947] If nothing else, involving attorneys by way of hybrid counsel in cases where "Ferguson factors" figure prominently (i.e., paranoid and

---

943. *See* United States v. Kimmel, 672 F. 2d 720, 721 (9th Cir. 1982); United States v. Ramos, 21 F.3d 426 (4th Cir. 1994) ("As many courts have noted, a trial judge's decision to permit 'hybrid' representation or a co-counsel structure is well within the district court's discretion, and a court is free to permit or deny such representation in accordance with the individual circumstances of the case." (Citing United States v. Sacco, 571 F. 2d 791, 793 (4th Cir. 1978); United States v. Treff, 924 F. 2d 975, 979 n. 6 (10th cir. 1991); United States v. Halbert, 640 F. 2d 1000, 1009 (9th Cir. 1981)). *See* Decker *supra* note 178, at 539 n. 327.

944. *See* Decker *supra* note 178, at 537, 538.

945. *See Id.* at 539. *See also* J. Pearson, *Comment, Mandatory Advisory Counsel for Pro Se Defendants: Maintaining Fairness in the Criminal Trial,* 72 CAL. L. REV. 697, 713 (1984).

946. *See* V. Berger, *The Supreme Court and Defense Counsel: Old Roads, New Paths—A dead End?,* 86 COLUM. L. REV. 9, 41 (1986).

947. *See* Grisso II *supra* note 29, at 362 citing Miller & Germain *supra* note 359, at 371, 372.

delusional mental health concerns and/or CST defendants wanting to proceed *pro se* to trial), provides an alternative vehicle by which litigators can raise correctly and appropriately the question of trial fitness.

4. States Are Free To Adopt Higher Competency Standards

Notwithstanding the recommended legal policy remedies, the best course of action regarding defendants found competent to stand trial who then *pro se* their case is to require separate fitness standards for the respective inquiries (i.e., competence to stand trial, competence to waive the right to counsel). In other words, establishing separate guidelines based on the legal risks involved for a given competency matter works in the interest of the defendant, the witnesses, the (potential) victims, and the overall administration of justice.

As we previously argued and demonstrated in chapter 2, the sole reliance on a unitary standard (i.e., the *Dusky* formulation for competency inquiries) is both illogical and inefficient. Moreover, the ambiguous *Dusky* measure concentrates on current knowledge as it relates to assisting counsel and understanding the trial proceedings. Although the *Godinez* decision acknowledges decisional competence, it categorizes these abilities under *Dusky* so that the umbrella phrase, "competence to stand trial," encompasses all psycholegal abilities related to fitness and the law. However, as Justice Blackmun aptly noted in *Godinez*:

> "[t]he reliability or even relevance of such a finding [i.e., competent based on the ability to assist counsel] vanishes when its basic premise— that counsel will be present—ceases to exist. The question is no longer whether the defendant can proceed with an attorney, but whether he can proceed alone and uncounseled."[948]

Blackmun's dissent admonished the Court's "monolithic approach to competency" and argued "[c]ompetency for one purpose does

---

948. *See Id.* at 413 (Blackmun, J., dissenting).

not necessarily translate to competency for another purpose."[949] Accordingly, we contend that states should adopt higher standards for fitness inquiries, consistent with the specialized needs of their respective jurisdictions, for CST defendants who then elect to represent themselves in a criminal trial.

The next chapter supplements our law, psychology and policy analysis of the Long Island Railroad gunman, by briefly examining another controversial, and more recent, criminal competency case. This is the matter of Theodore Kaczynski (a.k.a. the unabomber). As we reveal, Kaczynski not only reaffirms the kind of problems that surface relative to routine CST assessment procedures (e.g., adhering to controlling legal standards and following current trends in forensic evaluation practices) but also represents a trial fitness review that exceeded expectation with respect to the protocol used to assess competency.[950] As we contend, if psycholegal dilemmas occur in high profile cases (i.e., Ferguson and Kaczynski) where much is at stake for the proper administration of justice, then the same difficulties will also be present in less publicized disputes.

In addition, as we demonstrate, the supplemental case considers how the alternative assessment solutions and legal remedies provisionally examined in this chapter could have curtailed those problems stemming from a delusional and paranoid defendant (i.e., the unabomber) wanting to proceed *pro se* to trial. Along the way, we consider points of similarity in the pretrial competency hearing and trial of Colin Ferguson and the guilty plea and verdict of Theodore Kaczynski

---

949. *See Id.* at 413 (Blackmun, J., dissenting).
950. In the face of media scrutiny, a judge presiding in a high profile case (wishing to avoid possible reversal on appeal) is likely to be very cautious knowing, full well, each step in a competency review is under the proverbial microscope of the lay public and the legal community.

Chapter 8

Beyond Ferguson: New Directions and Competency to Stand Trial

OVERVIEW

The problems engulfing the Ferguson dispute are also apparent in a host of other criminal matters where the presenting issues include trial competence and legal representation. Thus, the purpose of this chapter is to show how problems identified in Ferguson can be generalized to other (high profile) CST courtroom disputes. Clearly, several cases mentioned throughout this book accomplish this task. Indeed, some of these cases underscore problems with the legal standards themselves while others draw attention to the competency evaluation process and the role of psychiatry in the courts.[951]

However, for purposes of this chapter, we examine the veracity of our law, psychology, and policy analysis by considering yet another controversial legal action embodying CST evaluation concerns similar to those found in the case of the Long Island Railroad gunman. This is the matter of Theodore Kaczynski (a.k.a. the unabomber). As we contend, in one respect the supplemental case indicates that the competency limitations discussed throughout this volume (actualized in the Ferguson matter) most definitely apply to high-stakes disputes. In addition, though, we argue that the generalizability of our analysis from Ferguson to Kaczynski further substantiates our

---

951. Indeed, on this matter we have made these points drawing support from United States Supreme Court cases and other federal and state appellate case law.

claim that the everyday realities of CST defendants are fraught with the same assessment problems that ultimately affect competency determinations and trial outcomes. Then, too, as we explain, the "unabomber" case provides an important backdrop against which to evaluate the legitimacy and applicability of our proposed criminal justice policy remedies for purposes of addressing and reforming the issue of criminal competency in general. Accordingly, we now turn to the case of Theodore Kaczynski.

A. Theodore Kaczynski

The supplemental case of Theodore Kaczynski demonstrates (for reasons similar to yet different from Colin Ferguson) the limitations with competency standards, CST assessment instruments, a paranoid and (potentially) delusional defendant wishing to control the defense, and psychiatry's role in the courts. Indeed, in the face of criticism engendered by the Ferguson outcome,[952] the unabomer legal dispute indicates that in many ways pitfalls and problems with the psycholegal construct of competency to stand trial still occur today. However, more disturbing, and similar to the Ferguson matter, the Kaczynski case shows the troubling connection between prosecutorial and judicial decision making[953] when a defendant with questionable mental health seeks to waive counsel and proceed *pro se* to trial. Assessing the behavior of the court on these matters is especially significant given the prospects for "grave appellate error"[954] that did, as we contend, eventually materialize.[955] Accord-

---

952. *See generally* Perlin, Dignity *supra* note 639; *See also* Decker *supra* note 178, at 523.

953. For example, on this point Finnegan observed that Judge Burrell who presided in the case "was said to be haunted by the thought of poor Lance Ito [the judge in the O.J. Simpson double homicide murder trial], undone in the national spotlight by bunglers and demagogues [and therefore] denied his [Kaczynski's] request for new counsel." *See* W. Finnegan, *Defending the Unabomber*, New Yorker, Mar. 16, 1998, at 52, 60.

954. *See Id.* at 60.

955. For example, during the pretrial stage of the case, Kaczynski requested to waive his right to counsel and instead proceed *pro se* to trial. For reasons relating (clearly) to judicial politics, Judge Burrell denied the request as "untimely." *See* J. Newman, *Doctors, Lawyers, and the Unabomber*, 60 MONTANA L. REV. 67, 79 (1999).

ingly, in what follows, we provide a brief synopsis of the relevant facts in the Kaczynski case and outcome. We also assess the points of convergence and divergence in the respective matters of Ferguson and Kaczynski. Although this subsequent commentary is mostly provisional and clearly speculative, we argue that the unabomber case describes (similar to Ferguson) how the CST process failed the defendant and the system of courtroom justice.

1. Synopsis of Kaczynski: Background and Crimes

In 1971, Theodore Kaczynski, a Harvard graduate and doctor of philosophy in mathematics, resigned his teaching position at the University of California, Berkeley, opting instead to settle in rural Lincoln, Montana.[956] In a secluded one room cabin, Kaczynski developed and harbored deep-seated obsessions that a technocratic elite controlled the economic and political structures within the United States. Believing that those in power would not listen to reason, Kaczynski elected to retaliate by unleashing a series of bomb attacks from 1978-1995.[957] His efforts were mostly directed toward various universities, targeting computer scientists, behavioral psychologists, geneticists, and public relations executives; however, he also attempted to sabotage the flight of a major airline carrier.[958] Given the intended targets, the would-be revolutionary was assigned the pseudonym of "uabomber" (*un*iversities and *a*irplanes), and he was elevated to the Federal Bureau of Investigation's (F.B.I.) ten most wanted list where he remained for the better part of twenty years.[959]

A self-proclaimed member of an anarchist group called the "Freedom Club,"in 1993 Kaczynski wrote to the New York *Times*

---

956. *See Id.* at 70. For a review of Kaczynski's life *see* R. D. McFadden, *Prisoner of Rage—A Special Report: From a Child of Promise to the Unabomber Suspect*, N.Y. TIMES, May 26, 1996, at 1.

957. *See* W. Glaberson, *The Unabomber Travesty*, N.Y. TIMES, Jan. 10, 1998, at A08–A09 [hereinafter Glaberson, Travesty].

958. *See* Finnegan *supra* note 953, at 62. Designed to explode at a certain altitude, the bomb placed on the plane failed to detonate; however, it did set mailbags on fire resulting in an emergency landing. *See Id.*

959. *See* N. Gibbs, *Tracking Down the Unabomber*, TIME, April 15, 1996, at 37–46.

rejecting technology and modern society and encouraged a revolution in the name of "Wild Nature."[960] In the face of empty leads, Kaczynski became the focus of the largest and most expensive manhunt in American history.[961] In 1995, the unabomber threatened to send a bomb to an unspecified destination with the "intent to kill" if either the *Washington Post* or *New York Times* did not publish Kaczynski's "ideological" *magnum opus*, now universally recognized as the "Manifesto."[962] At the risk of provoking the unabomber to greater violence, the Attorney General and the Director of the F.B.I. agreed to publish the manuscript titled, "Industrial Society and Its Future;" a 35,000 word essay railing against the industrial revolution and technology's influence on society.[963]

Despite the F.B.I.'s futile attempts to apprehend the unabomber (spanning over 18 years), the case finally broke when Kaczynski's brother, David, compared the "Manifesto" with letters and journals written by his older brother (Theodore) in years past.[964] In 1996, Theodore Kaczynski was arrested and charged with 16 bomb attacks that killed 3 people and injured 23 others. In the wake of the defendant's apprehension, the government made clear they would seek the death penalty, following conviction.[965]

2. Relevant Psycholegal Issues and the Trial's Outcome

From the outset, the unabomber case was fraught with complex psychological and legal issues. Questions surfaced regarding Kaczynski's mental health and his relationship with defense coun-

---

960. *See* Finnegan *supra* note 953, at 52.
961. *See Id.*
962. *See* THE UNABOMBER, INDUSTRIAL SOCIETY AND ITS FUTURE, THE UNABOMBER'S MANIFESTO [hereinafter cited MANIFESTO], available at <http:www.unabombertrial.com/manifesto/index.html>.
963. *See* Gibbs *supra* note 959, at 41, 44.
964. *See Id.* at 44. Following a search of Kaczynski's cabin, the F.B.I. seized bomb materials, the original copy of the manifesto and journals documenting Kaczynski's bomb "experiments." *See* Finnegan *supra* note 953, at 52, 62.
965. *See* M. Coyle, *Unabomber's pen pal: Ted Wants a New Trial.* NEWSDAY, Feb. 15, 1999, at A1–A2.

sel.[966] These matters soon became one and the same as a profound conflict developed between Kaczynski and his attorneys over a mental defect defense. Kaczynski wanted to avoid being portrayed as a "sickie"[967] while his defense team intimated that a mental status defense would either be the case in chief or implemented during the penalty phase.[968]

However, as the pre-trial case evidence mounted (e.g., information suggesting Kaczynski crafted and planned the bombs, detailed journals documenting Kaczynski's bomb "experiments"), the defense team anticipated the futility of trying to prove that their client was legally insane. In effect, the defense team recognized that the guilt phase was moot[969] and, instead, directed their attention to the penalty phase, alleging that Kaczynski's mental status was impaired.[970] From this perspective, if and when Kaczynski was found guilty, proof of "impaired capacity" would serve as a mitigating factor during the penalty stage.[971] While the attorneys advanced their "impaired capacity" defense plan, the tension between Kaczynski and his counselors grew and eventually erupted when the accused rejected in open court any form of an impaired mental status defense.[972] These very volatile and contentious psycholegal matters consumed much of the pretrial phase of the case.

Interposing requests for new counsel and imploring the judge to rule on who ultimately controlled the mental status defense, the unabomber endeavored to identify options to resolve the obvious and deep conflict involving the defense team and Kaczynski on the issue of the mental health evidence. Judge Garland Burrell who presided

---

966. *See* R. A. Zitrin, *Who Really Spoke for Ted Kaczynski?*, THE CONN. L. TRIBUNE, NEWS, Feb. 9, 1998.

967. *See* C. Hubert & D. Walsh, *Kaczynski Gives Lawyers Little Help Saving His Life*, SACRAMENTO BEE, Nov. 23, 1997 (quoting from Kaczynski's journals). *See also* Finnegan *supra* 950 at 54–55. In his journals, Kaczynski described a fear that his bombing campaign would be received as the work and product of a "sickie."

968. *See* United States v. Kaczynski Pretrial Hearing Transcripts, January 22, 1998.

969. *See* Finnegan *supra* note 953, at 52.

970. *See* Newman *supra* note 955, at 68.

971. *See Id.*

972. *See* Finnegan *supra* note 953, at 54.

over the Kaczynski matter denied the defendant's request for new counsel, suggesting that it was "untimely" and further ruled that his lawyers were entrusted with determining whether or not a mental status defense was warranted in the case.[973]

As a result of the Judge's ruling and to escape the impending presentation of a mental status defense, Kaczynski (evidently that very evening) attempted suicide.[974] In the wake of his failed attempt, the defendant invoked his *Faretta* right the following day, requesting to waive his right to counsel and conduct his own defense.[975] Presumably, the only way Kaczynski could prevent the mental status defense from unfolding was to proceed *pro se* to trial.[976] In response to Kaczynski's request, the defense argued that the defendant's inability to endure a mental health defense was *prima facie* (clear) evidence that he was not competent to stand trial.[977] In addition, the defense argued that a psychiatric evaluation was required to determine whether Kaczynski was fit to stand trial and, thus, competent to waive his right to counsel. Collectively, these circumstances produced a court-ordered competency evaluation.

Pursuant to the court order, Kaczynski's competency examination was conducted by Dr. Sally Johnson. She tendered a "provisional" diagnosis of schizophrenia, paranoid type.[978] However, in the clinical opinion on the legal issue of competence, Dr. Johnson concluded that Kaczynski was competent to stand trial and, further, competent to represent himself.[979]

In addressing the ultimate legal issues concerning trial fitness and Kaczynski's request to proceed *pro se* to trial, Judge Burrell rendered a CST finding; however, he denied Kaczynski's request to rep-

---

973. See *Id.* at 60.
974. See C. Hubert & D. Walsh, *Kaczynski Reportedly Tries to Take Own Life*, SACRAMENTO BEE, Jan. 9, 1998.
975. See Newman *supra* note 955, at 75–76.
976. See *Id.* at 76.
977. See *Id.* at 78.
978. See Forensic Evaluation of Dr. Sally Johnson, M.D., Jan. 16, 1998.
979. See Finnegan *supra* note 953, at 60, 61. In her competency evaluation, Dr. Sally Johnson suggested Kaczynski's suicide attempt was a rational preference for death over life. Accordingly, she concluded the suicide attempt was not evidence to support an incompetency finding. See Newman *supra* note 955, at 93 n. 4., *citing* United States v. Kaczynski, 1998 WL 226796, at 9 (E.D. Cal. May 4, 1996).

resent himself on the grounds that it was, once again, "untimely."[980] In addition, Judge Burrell suggested that the request was a deliberate attempt to manipulate the court and delay the proceedings.[981] Following this judicial determination, Kaczynski pled guilty in federal court to the criminal counts associated with the bombings, including the three fatalities. The unabomber was sentenced to life in prison without the possibility of parole.[982]

On appeal, Kaczynski argued that the plea was coerced, that he should have been granted his *Faretta* right, and, further, that he had the right to bar his counsel from presenting a mental status defense.[983] In a fifty-eight page handwritten brief, Kaczynski explicitly asked the Ninth U.S. Court of Appeals to withdraw his guilty plea, reopen the case, and order a new trial.[984] Kaczynski's legal brief argues why he accepted the initial plea arrangement and further describes why he attempted suicide while awaiting trial. On this latter point, Kaczynski indicates in the brief that defense counsel informed him of their intended legal strategy and their plan to portray him "as a grotesque lunatic...[and to] broadcast [the characterization] nationwide.... [T]his...prospect...anyone might have found unendurable [and] [s]uicide to avoid public humiliation [wa]s by no means unknown."[985]

The Appellate Court decided to revisit the Kaczynski matter, ruling that the defendant raised a valid constitutional concern when his right to self-representation was denied. However, despite their initial review, the United States Court of Appeals for the Ninth Circuit held: "The district court's denial of defendant's habeas petition was affirmed where his guilty plea was not rendered involuntary on account of the wrongful denial of his self-representation request or because of anticipation of evidence about his mental condition."[986] Although Kaczynski has yet to appeal based on the absence of trial

---

980. *See* United States v. Kaczynski, Pretrial Hearing Transcripts, Jan. 22, 1998 available at <http://www.unabombertrial.com/transcripts/012298kz.html> at 12.

981. *See Id.*

982. *See* Arrigo & Bardwell *supra* note 18, at 28.

983. *See* Coyle *supra* note 965, at A01–A02.

984. *See* United States v. Kaczynski, 239 F.3d 1108 (9th Cir. 2001).

985. *See* CNN.com, *Kaczynski Says Guilty Plea Coerced, Asks For New Trial*, Available: http://www.cnn.com/2000/US/01/18unabomber.plea.ap/.

986. *See* United States v. Kaczynski, 239 F.3d 1108 (9th Cir. 2001).

fitness (i.e., incompetence), his strong feelings against the label of mental illness suggests that he is not likely to raise the CST issue in the future.

Given the preceding summary of the case, we note that the Kaczynski matter is an example of a defendant who, following a competency hearing and CST finding, asserts his right to waive counsel electing instead to proceed *pro se* to trial. These actions are consistent with the logic of *Dusky*, *Faretta*, and *Godinez* and the decision in Ferguson. However, the district court (i.e., Judge Burrell) and the Ninth Circuit Court of Appeals rejected these requests. We question why the unabomber's requests were denied.

Preliminarily, we assert that embedded within Kaczynski's plea agreement were a number of complex (and contentious) political issues, reflecting the Court's concern for the outcome in this high profile, media manufactured, and ideologically-charged case. In short, we submit that there was considerable fear among law makers that the unabomber, as a paranoid schizophrenic, would conduct his own legal action, potentially resulting in a finding of insanity or a hearing to assess his trial fitness. These results would only prolong the case; something the government (and certainly the conscience of America) did not want. Ultimately, Kaczynski agreed to a plea arrangement with the government, obviating the criminal trial proceedings altogether. Perhaps more troubling and contrary to the Ferguson result, the Kaczynski case indicates how a competency finding influences prosecutorial maneuvering and judicial decision making, significantly (and problematically) impacting the trial's outcome.

B. Revisiting Kaczynski's Paranoia: Opposing Views and Profound Evidence

This section discusses the issue of Kaczynski's mental health. We briefly present arguments from those who believed he was not mentally ill and from those who argued that he was. In the latter instance, we offer *profound evidence* suggesting that Kaczynski suffered from a mental health disorder that included paranoid and delusional symptomatology. As we explain, this analysis enables us to better appreciate the psycholegal problems plaguing the unabomber case and further demonstrates the similarities between Ferguson and Kaczynski.

1. Opposing Views: Pathologizing Radical Ideology or Recognizing Debilitating Mental Illness

Some commentators contend Kaczynski is not mentally ill and raise questions about the role of psychiatry in the courts and the pathologizing of radical "ideology" by lawyers and the media.[987] Kaczynski's lengthy creed (i.e. the Manifesto) railing against technological and industrial society has even been likened to a dissenting treatise not unlike the teachings of political philosophers in the past. For example, in reaction to the Manifesto, James Q. Wilson the right-wing social scientist stated: "The argument is subtle and carefully developed, lacking anything even faintly resembling the wild claims of irrational speculation that a lunatic might produce.... If it is the work of a madman, then the writings of many political philosophers—Jean Jacques Rousseau, Tom Paine, Karl Marx—are scarcely more sane."[988]

In a similar vein, Michael Mello, another dissenting voice, has argued that Kaczynski's lawyers, the media, and the judicial system effectively muffled the unabomber's voice, instead (erroneously) portraying him as a madman.[989] While some recognize a "clash of wills and world views" between Kaczynski and his defense team,[990] others acknowledge the legal conundrum concerning the unabomber's limited defense options.[991] Kaczynski's lawyers could have advanced theories of incompetency and insanity (against the defendant's wishes) or put the unabomber's anti-technology views on trial

---

987. See E.g., Finnegan supra note 953, at 54. As previously already stated, Kaczynski rejected the idea of being portrayed as mentally ill and found this type of defense reprehensible in many ways. Fearing his bombing attacks would be received as the work of a madman, Kaczynski wrote in his journal "many tame, conformist types seem to have a powerful need to depict the enemy of society as sordid, repulsive, or 'sick.'"

988. See Finnegan supra note 953, at 61, citing James Q. Wilson.

989. See M. MELLO, THE UNITED STATES OF AMERICA VERSUS THEODORE JOHN KACZYNSKI (1999).

990. See Finnegan supra note 953, at 54.

991. See Newman supra note 955, at 69.

(against the lawyers wishes), exposing him to a likely conviction and a probable death sentence. Theories such as those just described were never tendered in a trial (i.e., the defendant pled guilty); however, the consensus among many is that Theodore Kaczynski was denied his day in court.[992]

Although we agree that the legal outcome in the Kaczynski case was flawed, we do not subscribe to the more political and philosophical explanations that thus far have been offered. In other words, we endorse the same conclusion (i.e., the defendant was denied his right to represent himself) but come to this perspective in a different and somewhat less complicated way. Indeed, consistent with the theme developed throughout this book, the problem plaguing the Kaczynski case stems from the inadequacy of the CST process in general. To be more specific, the disturbing outcome is a product of the low standard by which competency is measured and the deficient ways mental health experts evaluate trial fitness. However, before addressing these matters, we describe the reasons why Kaczynski suffered (and continues to suffer) from a paranoid and delusional mental health condition.

(a) Revisiting Kaczynski's Paranoia

What follows is a brief description of the relevant evidence solidifying the argument that Kaczynski suffered from a paranoid and delusional mental health disorder. We argue that his mental impairment was not only present subsequent to his arrest but explain where and how it existed for some time prior to his arrest. On this score, we provisionally discuss Kaczynski's background, his journal entries, letters written by the unabomber attempting to obtain mental health assistance, and psychiatric opinions occurring after his arrest (i.e., observations independent of Dr. Johnson's CST review which we examine later).

(b) Profound Evidence

As previously mentioned, Kaczynski left his teaching position at Berkeley, California in 1971, relocating to rural Montana. He built and lived in a cabin (comparable in size to the current cell he now

---

992. See Finnegan *supra* note 953, at 52; MELLO *supra* note 989, at 21; Newman *supra* note 955, at 100.

occupies) for more than twenty-four years. During this period, Kaczynski cultured anti-technology views, penned arguments against industrial progress, and crafted instruments of destruction. In an effort to practice what the unabomber preached, Kaczynski targeted various universities and airlines with his packages of destruction. In documenting his applied work, Kaczynski scribbled "lab notes" of "bomb experiments" and their consequences.[993] Calculated and methodical, the entries profile the mind (and personality) of the unabomber. Without a doubt, the journal entries provide concrete evidence supporting Kaczynski's mental instability.

For example, in response to the first fatal bombing, Kaczynski wrote: "Excellent, Humane way to eliminate somebody. He probably never felt a thing. $25,000 reward offered. Rather flattering."[994] Commenting on yet another bombing, Kaczynski attempted to reconcile a growing personal conflict that his attacks were not indiscriminate, not in vain, but served a purpose. Kaczynski spoke to this very issue when describing the 1985 attack on John Hauser, an air-force pilot and graduate student of electrical engineering. As Kaczynski wrote:

> I was relieved to read what kind of guy sprang the trap. I had worried about [the] possibility that some young kid, undergrad, not even [a] computer science major, might get it. But this guy is clearly [a] typical member of the technician class. Might even be one of those guys that has flown those fucking jets over my home. This gives great relief to my choking, frustrated anger and sense of impotence against the system...Relief of frustrated anger outweighs uncomfortable conscience. I would do it all over again.[995]

The victim, Hauser, suffered permanent injury to his arm and hand, ending his career as a pilot and dashing his dreams of becoming an astronaut. After reading a newspaper clipping about the victim Kaczynski wrote:

> Hauser's arm was severed or nearly severed. Tips of three fingers torn off. Use of arm and hand will be permanently im-

---

993. See Finnegan *supra* note 953, at 62.

994. See Government's Sentencing Memorandum, *United States v. Kaczynski*, No. CR-S96-259 GEB, 1998 WL 21667 (E.D. Cal. Doc. April 30, 1998).

995. See Finnegan *supra* note 953, at 62, citing Kaczynski's journal entry.

paired...He was afraid his "dream" was ruined. Dream was to be an astronaut. Imagine a grown man whose dream is to be an astronaut. I am no longer bothered by this guy partly because I just "got over it" with time, partly because his aspiration was so ignoble.[996]

Kaczynski's journals are replete with similar examples detailing his thoughts as he doled out death and destruction. During his seventeen year bombing campaign, Kaczynski ultimately killed three persons and injured twenty-three others. The unabomber's systematic journal accounts offer us a provocative and chilling portrait of the disturbing thought processes of a mentally impaired person. Clearly, Kaczynski's heinous and deplorable actions were not the machinations of a political philosopher; rather, they were more aptly the product of a person suffering from a deteriorating mental health condition. Indeed, his journal entries were an attempt to reconcile his crazed behavior with his desperate need to believe that there was a viable reason for his madness.

Presumably, this crazed behavior would suffice to convince a reasonable person that Kaczynski suffered from acute delusions about technology. However, other ancillary data gathered before and subsequent to his arrest indicates that the unabomber experienced chronic paranoia and delusions. Indeed, unbeknownst to many, questions concerning Kaczynski's mental health surfaced before his arrest. Between 1988 and 1993, he wrote several letters sent to psychiatric centers in Montana in which he explained that he suffered from depression and insomnia.[997] The letters illustrate Kaczynski's acute level of cognitive functioning, however, embedded within them are themes of paranoia.

For example, in a letter post-marked July 12, 1991, he wrote in part:

....To begin with, I must tell you frankly that I am highly skeptical about the theories by which talk therapists (illegible) to explain their patients' problems, and I'm not going to pay large sums of money to listen to speculative explanations based on

---

996. *See Id.*
997. *See* Excerpts form Letters Written by Theodore Kaczynski available at <http://www.unabombertrial.com/documents/letters111497.html>.

psychoanalytic theories or to be told that I have 3,288 different personalities. In fact, the main cause of my problems seems reasonably clear (though questions about contributing factors can be raised), and I am interested in a concrete and practical approach to getting over the problem.[998]

On another occasion, in a letter postmarked October 6, 1993, Kaczynski wrote how he continued to experience some discomfort from his symptoms. As he explained:

"I am suffering from insomnia, which is causing me serious hardship and which I suspect is due to some form of (redacted). I am seeking referral to a psychiatrist or other doctor who could diagnose and treat this problem...I don't want to pick a psychiatrist at random out of the yellow pages, because I might pay a hundred dollars or more for a visit to him only to find that he is, for example, a freudian who tries to tell me that I have insomnia because I am unconsciously punishing myself for oedipal feelings or some such nonsense. So it would be extremely helpful to me if you could give me the name of a psychiatrist....who might diagnose and treat my insomnia.[999]

Kaczynski's decision to seek assistance from mental health professionals is curious because after his arrest he stated that psychiatrists were "the enemy."[1000] Moreover, although his worries about the psychoanalytical paradigm appear to be within reason, the unabomber would later put these writings in context. In other words, the content is more consistent with his delusional claims against mental health professionals (i.e., psychiatrists are "the enemy") than it appears, and his writings in the Manifesto (e.g., "The Psychology of Modern Leftism") bear this out.[1001]

Following his arrest, Kaczynski (per his own requests) met with several psychiatrists searching for answers to somatic complaints. Indicating that he experienced a general sleep disturbance, a sensitivity toward sound, and intense anxiety in anticipation of going to trial, the accused met with a psychiatrist to resolve these prob-

---

998. *See* Excerpts form Letters Written by Theodore Kaczynski available at <http://www.unabombertrial.com/documents/letters111497.html>.

999. *See Id.*

1000. *See infra* note 1003 and accompanying text.

1001. *See generally* MANIFESTO *supra* note 962 (citing a heading).

lems.[1002] One doctor addressed his symptomatology, and diagnosed Kaczynski as suffering from schizophrenia, paranoid type. During this initial meeting, the defendant demonstrated paranoid tendencies and put his previous skepticism about mental health professionals in perspective. As Dr. Foster, the treating physician, explained:

> His paranoia about psychiatrists made it very difficult to broach his psychiatric symptoms with him in a direct way. In fact, early on in our sessions, he looked me in the face and said, 'You are the enemy.' As I have previously indicated, after significant efforts to build a relationship with Mr. Kaczynski, when I finally addressed his symptoms with any degree of specificity, he refused to see me further.[1003]

Although Kaczynski disliked those working in the mental health profession, he agreed to meet with other doctors but only for the purpose of supporting his contention that he was not mentally impaired. When subsequent psychiatric opinions were contrary to his own, Kaczynski discharged them. Many of these clinical meetings are fraught with examples suggesting that the unabomber suffered from paranoid schizophrenia and even neurological deficits. Dr. Karen Bronk spoke to these very issues.

> My own testing was authorized by Mr. Kaczynski only because he believed that it would prove that he did not suffer from any neurological deficit impairing his social functioning. He was surprised and dismayed when this examiner provided him with the test results which showed that neurological impairments affected his ability to recognize and interpret the meaning of nonverbal social communication... [After Dr. Bronk provided clinical conclusions inconsistent to those of Kaczynski] he informed me in writing the very next day that he would no longer need my professional services.[1004]

Following the exchange with Dr Bronk, Kaczynski refused to submit to any additional mental health evaluations and even declined to cooperate with the government's experts pursuant to a

---

1002. *See E.g.,* Newman *supra* note 955, at 70.
1003. *See* Declaration of David V. Foster, M.D. available at <http://www.unabombertrial.com/documents/dvfoster111797.html>.
1004. *See* Declaration of Karen Bronk, Ph.D., available at <http://www.unabombertrial.com/documents/froming111797.html> as cited in Newman *supra* note 947, at 71.

court order requiring a mental health examination.[1005] Taken as a whole, Kaczynski's bizarre journal entries, his letters to mental health professionals, and his meetings with psychiatrists after his arrest provide *profound evidence* that the accused was an individual plagued by paranoid and delusional mental health symptoms. Indeed, the experts, including Dr. Johnson, who conducted the court-ordered CST evaluation, all concluded that Kaczynski suffered from paranoid schizophrenia.

C. The Ferguson and Kaczynski Cases: Revisiting the Legal and Psychological Dynamics in the CST Process

This section compares the relevant CST psycholegal issues in Kaczynski's pretrial hearing and non-trial to those previously identified in the Ferguson case study. As we contend, these disputes support our contention that the case law, clinical assessment, and judicial decision making dynamics pertaining to criminal competency matters are seriously and egregiously flawed. Moreover, as we document, these disputes reveal the troubling interplay between trial fitness assessment practices and legal findings and defendants with paranoid and delusional mental health problems. As we explain, this comparative analysis demonstrates how distinct cases can succumb to the same CST limitations, although for different and comparable reasons.

In comparing the cases, two broad themes are evident. First, the Kaczynski dispute shows us how CST problems identified within the Ferguson matter are indeed generalizable to other (high profile) criminal competency cases. Indeed, similar to Ferguson, the unabomber's pretrial hearing involved various competence issues (i.e., competence to stand trial, competence to waive the right to counsel), a court-ordered CST assessment, and major strategic decisions pursuant to the trial fitness finding that ultimately determined the dispute's outcome (i.e., Kaczynski's request to waive counsel and proceed *pro se* to trial subsequently rejected by the Judge resulting

---

1005. *See* C. Hubert & D. Walsh, *Kaczynski Balks at Court-Ordered Psychiatric Exam*, SACRAMENTO BEE, Oct. 25, 1997.

in the plea arrangement). Second, and perhaps most interesting, is how the Kaczynski case contributes to our understanding of current trends in the CST process. Similar to Ferguson, the more recent unabomber case suggests that the trial fitness limitations systematically explored throughout this book (and actualized in the Ferguson case study) are, in many ways, still operative today.

Elsewhere, we have argued that the CST process is fraught with problems; including, limitations with the standards used to determine competence-related abilities (i.e., *Dusky*) its progeny (i.e, *Godinez*), and limitations with paranoid and delusional defendants whose paranoia impedes their own defense efforts. Relatedly, these psycholegal dilemmas have resulted in both the courts relying on clinical forensic experts to conduct (flawed) CST evaluations, and lawyers manipulating these opinions to advance their own strategic courtroom agendas. As we explained, these factors raise troubling questions about psychiatry's role in the courts. Similar to the Ferguson dispute, the Kaczynski case demonstrates, in another practical sense, this troubling interface. Thus, in what follows, we briefly analyze these critical psycholegal issues as they relate to both the Ferguson and Kaczynski matters.

1. The Comparative Analysis: CST Problems Achieved in Similar and Different Ways

The Ferguson case is an example of a defendant who, following a competency hearing, proceeds *pro se* to trial and, eventually, because of initial undetected paranoid symptomatology becomes mentally unstable without the benefit of a subsequent CST hearing. In addition, Ferguson demonstrates the inadequacy of existing psychological instruments that assess one's mental functioning abilities for purposes of a trial. The clinical evaluation issue in the Ferguson case was whether he was, *throughout the duration of the trial*, mentally competent to stand trial. His courtroom behavior and self-representation suggested that he was not. This notwithstanding, Judge Belfi allowed the trial to continue despite criticism from the lay public and the legal community.

With respect to pretrial competency dynamics, the case of Theodore Kaczynski closely resembles the limitations that surfaced in the trial fitness hearing of Colin Ferguson. For both individuals, paranoid and delusional mental health concerns, constitutional rights, and clinical diagnostic practices, all impacted the CST examination and the ultimate competency determination. However, unlike Ferguson, the Kaczynski dispute additionally addressed two thorny matters: who controlled the mental status defense; and whether the accused possessed a right to self-representation as set forth in *Faretta*. Both of these contentious issues make the relationship between Kaczynski and the CST process quite troubling, though for reasons other than those previously identified in the Ferguson dispute.

The Kaczynski case is an example of a defendant who, following a competency determination, asserts his right to self-representation but agrees to a plea arrangement with the government, obviating the criminal trial proceeding altogether. It is clear that the government's willingness to broker a plea arrangement with Kaczynski successfully avoided the likely confusion that would have surfaced had no deal been struck and Kaczynski opted for the path of self-representation. Indeed, Judge Garland Burrell's request for an initial psychological assessment found the defendant competent to stand trial. But, in the face of a competency evaluation and finding, Burrell denied Kaczynski's request to proceed *pro se* to trial.

One can only speculate whether the prosecutors and judge in the unabomber case, similar to attorneys in the Ferguson trial, feared that the proceeding would eventually raise questions about the mental state of the defendant, producing unwanted delays with the trial and, perhaps, a judicial finding that sufficient doubts existed as to the competency of Kaczynski, resulting in a hearing to determine the matter. A decision from a subsequent competency hearing could have produced a legal finding that Kaczynski was *not* competent to stand trial, subjecting him to sustained civil confinement until such time as he was declared competent by hospital psychiatrists. To be clear, given the contentious and volatile nature of the Kaczynski matter, this outcome was far from acceptable to federal prosecutors concerned with obtaining a clear and unequivocal conviction. In a far less sinister way, one could reasonably surmise that Judge Burrell, aware of the courtroom antics displayed in the Ferguson case, simply did not want Kaczynski's trial to spiral into a circus, thereby making a mockery of the justice system.

The Ferguson and Kaczynski cases illustrate the ongoing problems posed by the CST legal construct and the practical ineffectualness of CST instruments used to clinically and psycho-diagnostically assess competency in media-manufactured cases. When coupled with the vague and ambiguous language of the legal standard itself, it is not surprising that lower court judges unevenly apply the standard and differently interpret forensic evaluations. Moreover, we note that while both defendants were convicted, they have filed (or did file) appeals,[1006] clearly suggesting that the clinical assessment of competency did not help give closure to their respective cases. Thus, from our perspective, had a finding of incompetency been issued, it may very well have provided the defendants with adequate time and respite sufficient for them to then move forward with their legal disputes, potentially producing courtroom outcomes absent the considerable doubt, suspicion, and speculation that exists today.

The Ferguson and Kaczynski cases also make clear why a conclusive clinical diagnosis is not important for purposes of assessing competence-related abilities. As both legal disputes illustrate, paranoid traits and delusional themes continue to impact, indeed taint, a defendant's capacity to assist in the defense by virtue of the individual's psychiatric illness. In other words, a defendant during a CST review may, at that time, understand the charges and may appear, at that time, capable of assisting in the defense; however, eventually, these individuals are likely to form paranoid (and conspiratorial) opinions about the advocacy of their attorneys. As we indicated, this troubling circumstance was certainly evident in the Ferguson and Kaczynski matters. Thus, questions persist about whether (and when) such defendants will become incompetent to stand trial in the future. Interestingly, given our analysis of the Long Island Railroad gunman and the unabomber, judges tend not to tolerate these disturbing developments. Indeed, neither Judge Belfi (for Ferguson) or Judge Burrell (for Kaczynski) reconsidered the issue of trial competence, given the courtroom and pretrial escapades that ensued in these respective cases. From our perspective it was regrettable that the common law doctrine as outlined in *Drope* was not applied in either of these legal disputes. As the Court asserted there, "trial courts have the obligation of conducting a hearing whenever there is sufficient doubt concerning a defendant's competence."[1007] Thus, one can only speculate about what the outcomes in these cases may have been had different (and more exacting) case law standards and clinical assessment practices been employed.

1006. As previously discussed, Ferguson seemingly exhausted all competency issues and his conviction was affirmed.

1007. *See* Drope v. Missouri, 420 S. Ct. 162, 180–181 (1975).

In what follows, we apply the previously outlined criminal justice policy remedies as articulated in chapter 7 to the case of Theodore Kaczynski. In particular, these recommendations, introduced by way of and examined in the Ferguson case, consider where and how law and psychology must rethink the doctrine of criminal competence to stand trial. To resituate this discussion, we briefly revisit the recommendations as outlined in Ferguson but, more fundamentally, focus on how the policy reforms could have circumvented the controversy that surrounded the Kaczynski matter.

2. Generalizing the Proposed CST Assessment and Legal Reforms

Not only do the limits of the clinical tools complicate CST proceedings but other more insidious problems exist relating to the underlying motives for requiring these evaluations. Elsewhere, we argued that expert services are routinely used per requests by the prosecution and defense wherein fitness to stand trial findings function as a short-cut to achieve strategic trial objectives and outcomes. For example, litigators use such clinical expertise to craft and support the legal theory underpinning a given case. In this context, then, expert opinion and testimony either corroborates or invalidates a contention regarding the defendant's mental health status.

As we previously documented, "the battle of the experts" consumed much of the pretrial competency hearing in the Ferguson matter. In fact, the judicial CST determination was largely informed by the (methodologically misguided) opinions of the forensic examiners. What we are troubled by is the extent to which courts nonetheless rely on such "evidence," especially given the problems we have identified with ongoing clinical assessment practices.

In response to these (and similar) CST shortcomings, we have called for drastic reforms (e.g., overturn problematic legal standards, regard expert testimony as informational only), and have assessed the merits of our remedies (e.g., hybrid representation, appoint standby counsel) in relation to the case of Colin Ferguson. In this section, however, we apply our policy recommendations to the case of Theodore Kaczynski. As we explain, our strategies for change not only suggest a viable alternative for the unabomber, but signal a sustainable basis by which to implement reform more generally on the matter of criminal competence to stand trial.

(a) Kaczynski and Psychological Assessment Reform

In chapter 3 we examined various CST assessment protocol and identified several problems in evaluating competence to stand trial. Generally speaking, some of these problems entailed important limits when screening for certain competence-related abilities (e.g., the defendant's ability to make trial decisions), and significant difficulties when examiners routinely implement their own individualized measures. A constant theme investigated throughout our inquiry on these matters has been that uniform CST assessment instruments are absent in practice. Consequently, concerns with evaluation practices, diagnostic findings, and judicial determinations are manifold. Indeed, circumstances such as those just described raise serious questions about the efficacy and legitimacy of the CST process altogether.

Consistent with the discussion on assessment reforms in the Ferguson matter, we recognize the informational rather than the dispositive value clinical forensic assessments offer in criminal competency proceedings. Thus, this same position obtains in the case of Theodore Kaczynski. In the following section, we describe the impact of our perspective on the latter case's outcome.

(b) Kaczynski's CST Review

Revisiting Kaczynski's CST examination further illustrates how our proposed trial fitness assessment reform (i.e., acknowledge the informational rather than dispositive value of such clinical forensic evaluations) is a worthwhile policy recommendation on the matter of criminal competence. Indeed, this inquiry demonstrates that the CST assessment problems identified in the Ferguson matter are still occurring today in many important ways. In order to accomplish our evaluative task, we investigate the nature of the CST assessment finding as performed by the court appointed psychiatrist, Dr. Sally Johnson.

The competency evaluation conducted in the Kaczynski case was performed by Dr. Sally Johnson, the assistant warden for mental health services at the Federal prison in Butner, North Carolina.[1008] Dr. Johnson had previously testified for the government in a num-

---

1008. *See* Finnegan *supra* note 953, at 61.

ber of high-profile and controversial cases including those involving Jim Baker and John Hinckley.[1009] Although Dr. Johnson had been characterized as a fair expert witness by many in the court system, one defense attorney involved in the Hinckley trial observed that the government solicited her services for particular reasons: the governement "picks her when they want a certain result, and she gives it to them."[1010]

In January, 1998, Kaczynski agreed to a competency evaluation to assess whether he understood the legal proceedings leveled against him. Based on the request of Judge Burrell, Dr. Johnson examined Kaczynski to determine if he was competent to stand trial and, thus, competent to waive his right to counsel. After a somewhat lengthy review, Dr. Johnson diagnosed Kaczynski as suffering from schizophrenia, paranoid type; a diagnosis consistent with Dr. Froming's conclusion for the defense.[1011] In addition, Dr. Johnson concluded that Kaczynski was competent to stand trial. In the hearing on January 20, 1998, the defense and the government stipulated that Kaczynski was competent to stand trial, based on Dr. Johnson's report.[1012]

The competency finding outlined in Dr. Johnson's report takes on greater meaning when evaluated against the legal standards for which trial fitness abilities are based (i.e., *Dusky* and *Godinez*), as well as the character of Kaczynski's paranoid and delusional behavior. In short, excerpts reveal the troubling connection between problematic legal standards and defendants having paranoid and delusional symptomatology. In her report, Dr. Johnson indicated that,

> ... despite the presence of significant mental illness historically and residual evidence of such problems at the present, Mr Kaczynski is able to understand the nature and consequences of the proceedings against him, and is able to assist his attorneys in his defense.[1013]

However, elsewhere in the report, Dr. Johnson stipulated that

---

1009. *See Id.* at 61.

1010. *See Id.* (Finnegan citing Hinckley's defense attorney Vince Fuller.)

1011. *See* Newman *supra* note 955, at 71 (Newman notes other doctors concurred with this diagnosis including Dr. Foster and Dr. Amador who met with Kaczynski prior to the court-ordered CST evaluation.)

1012. *See Id.* at 79.

1013. *See* Forensic Evaluation of Dr. Sally Johnson, M.D., Jan. 16, 1998 available at <http://www.unabombertrial.com/documents/psych_report3.html>.

[i]t is likely that Mr. Kaczynski will present some challenges during the trial process, regardless of whether he is represented by counsel or proceeds *pro se*...He will continue to demonstrate his ambivalence and suspiciousness, and is likely to over value some information that may arise...He does not have much insight into the fact that acquiring new representation will not necessarily resolve the types of conflicts he currently has with this defense team, who remain his main support system at this time."[1014]

These two statements are inconsistent. Indeed, how can a defendant suspicious and ambivalent toward his defense attorneys, assist them, if called upon, in his own legal action? Indeed, the competing statements produced in Dr. Johnson's report beg one critical question: what purpose did the CST evaluation serve, if any? Perhaps these seemingly contradictory statements provide the "data" sufficient to justify any decision a judge makes on the issue of trial competence. More generally, however, the conclusions outlined in Dr. Johnson's report suggest two important things. First, her CST findings demonstrate how clinicians adhere to the competency legal standard, even at the risk of offering competing, confusing, and/or contradictory statements. Second, her clinical opinion suggests that defendants suffering from a paranoid and delusional mental health condition can be competent to stand trial; however, during the unfolding of the case, the individual is likely to become incompetent in the future. Specifically, her findings intimate that the accused will become incompetent in the sense that the individual will, during the course of the trial, be unable to assist with the defense by virtue of general suspiciousness towards others, including one's lawyers. Under these circumstances, we are again led to ask whether her clinical assessment and diagnostic findings were really of any courtroom significance.

3. Problems with the Assessment and Generalizing the Informational Approach

Similar to the problems identified in the Colin Ferguson case, the criminal competency action of Theodore Kaczynski embodies both

---

1014. *See Id.*

clinical assessment difficulties and legal standard limits. In particular, the unabomber matter signifies the type of psycholegal problems that surface when a defendant evinces acute and chronic paranoid and delusional mental health symptoms, wherein the controlling case law (i.e., *Dusky*, and *Godinez*) is utilized to render clinical assessment judgements and CST judicial determinations.

From our perspective, the pivotal forensic evaluation issue in the Kaczynski case was whether the competency screening process produced an accurate result. Despite Dr. Johnson's competency finding and expert opinion on the ultimate legal issue, Judge Burrell denied Kaczynski's request to waive counsel, claiming that the request was "untimely." Why? We contend that at best the Judge's ruling suggests that the Court was not prepared to watch the accused circumvent criminal responsibility by benefitting from a *pro se* defense that subsequently would be compromised by his own debilitating mental impairment. Thus, by logical extension, this means that Kaczynski's competency determination indeed may have been flawed (at least in the Judge's eyes), and that Burrell's decision to not grant the defendant his self representation request was designed to prevent the CST determination from backfiring on the prosecution and the Court. On this matter we draw attention to the limits of legal precedent and the law's inability to adequately assist forensic examiners who psycho-diagnostically assess trial fitness.

In addition, however, the Kaczynski evaluation shows how a defendant can be intelligent and articulate and can use those very skills and/or attributes to conceal an enervating paranoid and delusional mental health condition. Regrettably, as we have argued, accounts in the clinical forensic literature are lacking with respect to CST instrument utility as applied to specific legal inquiries. Indeed, similar to Ferguson, the examiner in the Kaczynski case neglected to use any type of established CST protocol. Although Dr. Johnson appeared to conduct an exhaustive interview (22 hours) and administered a battery of tests, she failed to implement anything remotely approximating an instrument that would assess competence-related abilities.[1015]

1015. *See* Forensic Evaluation of Dr. Sally Johnson, M.D., Jan. 16, 1998 available at <http://www.unabombertrial.com/documents/psych_report3.html>. Dr. Johnson's assessment is a fine example of a psychiatrist administering a highly individualized CST assessment. To be clear, she spent considerable time

In sum, then, the CST evaluation conducted by Dr. Sally Johnson provides us with yet another vivid example of how contemporary CST protocol are sound in theory but are deficient in application. To be sure, if accomplished and experienced experts such as Dr. Johnson neglect to employ any assessment protocol in media-manufactured and politically-charged case like those of the unabomber, one can only speculate about the conditions that would give rise to the invocation and utilization of CST instruments as validated through empirical study. Stated differently, if such assessment tools as the MacCAT-CA are not implemented in high-profile cases where much is at stake for the administration of justice especially in terms of the outcome, then these competency instruments are not likely to be used in other CST cases where the public's (or the government's) investment in the dispute is considerably less apparent.

Given the limitations associated with various psychological assessment instruments and the corresponding problems stemming from possible long-term civil commitment and/or detainment, we maintain that, similar to our position in Ferguson, the CST process and the evaluation of psychological fitness need to be significantly reformed. Preliminarily, as we have argued, difficulties with the proper administration of justice are (largely) the product of inaccurate or questionable determinations that one is mentally fit to stand trial.[1016] In other words, the concern here is with the psychological

---

with Kaczynski. Indeed, the report states, "during this evaluation Mr. Kaczynski was interviewed by the examiner on eight occasions...with a total interview time of approximately 22 hours...In addition to the clinical interviews, formal review was conducted of previous medical evaluations, as well as previous neuropsychological and psychological testing results. Additional psychological testing administered during this evaluation included the Minnesota Multiphasic Personality Inventory-2 (01/12/98), the Millon Clinical Multiaxial Inventory-II (01/12/98), the Beck Depression Inventory (01/15/98), and the Draw a Person Picking an Apple from a Tree projective drawing (01/15/98)." See Id. at 3. However, these psychological inventories by and large assess personality (e.g., borderline, hostile, aggressive, paranoia) and depression. Interestingly, of all these tests, not one assesses competency. Perhaps the interview touched on issues relating to competency (e.g., "what does the judge do?"), however, no formal test of competency was administered.

1016. Although there are fundamental liberty interests at stake if one is wrongfully found incompetent to stand trial (i.e., protracted and unnecessary civil confinement), these concerns address constitutional questions beyond the scope of the present examination.

outlets and legal protections availed to defendants wrongfully found fit to stand to trial. Thus, we recommend that the clinical assessment of fitness not be given the kind of authoritative and controlling weight judges typically afford it. In contrast to the elevated status the forensic evaluator's testimony receives (i.e., an ultimate opinion often used to resolve the case), a strategy acknowledging only the informational value clinical forensic assessments offer in CST proceedings should be endorsed. In this regard, evaluators should not feel derelict when mis-diagnosing mental impairment or minimizing troubling traits associated with certain mental disorders. For example, in the context of the Kaczynski assessment, an information approach might have emphasized the impending problems associated with the defendant's paranoia, intimating that he in fact did not meet the first prong set forth in *Dusky* (i.e., the ability to assist in the defense).

The utility of this psychological assessment recommendation takes on greater practical meaning when considering the legal reforms needed to make it work. Indeed, the significance of clinical evaluations as data to consult rather than depend on can only be effectively implemented if certain courtroom practices are enacted. Consistent with our discussion in Ferguson, the next section revisits the three interposed legal policy remedies to demonstrate their generalizability to Kaczynski and beyond.

4. Proposed Legal Reforms and Kaczynski

The case of Kaczynski shows the troubling connection between competency to stand trial outcomes and prosecutorial and judicial decision making when dealing with a brilliant, yet mentally impaired, defendant.[1017] To be sure, Judge Burrell required the services of an expert psychiatrist to establish the unabomber's trial fitness. Ironically, however, the Court, in the face of Dr. Johnson's competency finding and the respective litigators' stipulation that Kaczynski had a right to represent himself, denied the defendant his request on this matter. On its face, Judge Burrell interpreted Kaczynski's request as untimely and reasoned that the petition was a calculated

---

1017. *See* Arrigo & Bardwell *supra* note 18, at 27–30.

decision to delay the trial.[1018] At the risk of being portrayed as a madman and following the Judge's ruling on the *pro se* issue, Kaczynski agreed to an unconditional plea arrangement, resulting in life in prison without the possibility of parole, and no appellate action on the constitutionality of the search of his cabin.

It is clear that Kaczynski felt considerably constrained to work within the legal parameters identified for him by his defense team. As Tony Serra, an attorney who consulted with Kaczynski, observed:

> "[Kaczynski] believed that the public defenders [like the prosecutors] were conspiring... to silence him and prevent him from espousing the ideology that 'explained' the homicides. He believed that it was ultimately the right and the left hands, so to speak, of government seeking the same objective in chilling his opportunity to be heard."[1019]

However, even if Kaczynski had been allowed to conduct his own legal action, other problems would have surfaced. In other words, when a defendant is found competent to stand trial, self representation can compromise the rights of an accused. In short, the absence of a legal background and restricted access to resources can seriously undermine the appropriate handling of a complex criminal case. For example, although a defendant can refuse the assistance of court-appointed counsel, "no constitutional rights exists mandating that the prisoner... be provided access to a law library" or any other legal materials.[1020] Conversely, if a defendant accepts (or is forced to accept) the assistance of government-financed counsel, the person "may not reject the method provided and insist on an avenue of his [or her] choosing."[1021] This issue of compromised legal rights was particularly apparent in the Kaczynski case.

For now, one can only speculate about how successful Kaczynski might have been (and what legal materials he would have had at his disposal to effect these results) had he been granted a right to *pro se*

1018. *See* Newman *supra* note 955, at 79.
1019. *See* Finnegan *supra* note 953, at 61 (Finnegan citing Tony Serra).
1020. *See* United States ex rel. George v. Lane, 718 F.2d 226, 227 (7th Cir. 1983).
1021. *See* United States v. Wilson, 690 F.2d 1267, 1270–1273 (9th Cir. 1982).

his case to trial. What is clear, however, is that the unabomber was not allowed to exercise his right to self-representation and he was not allowed to develop a defense strategy beyond the parameters set forth for him by his attorneys. As a result, he vigorously pursued a federal habeas corpus petition to set aside the controversial plea. His position is that had he been permitted to work outside the limits of court-appointed representation, he would have been acquitted.[1022]

Each of these legal problems, magnified by the publicity surrounding the Kaczynski dispute, raises significant questions about the efficacy of self-representation and, in particular, those rights afforded a defendant by way of *Faretta* and *Godinez*. As discussed in the context of Ferguson, three legal policy remedies are applicable to this area of forensic mental health. Similar to our analysis of the Long Island Railroad gunman, we submit that these reforms are applicable to the Kaczynski case and are consistent with the policy position on how psycho-diagnostic findings are to be used in CST proceedings. What follows, then, is a brief discussion exploring how the Kaczynski case would have produced different results had standby counsel, the right to select counsel of choice following revocation of the right to proceed *pro se* to trial, and hybrid representation been available to and implemented on behalf of the defendant. As we conclude, these recommendations suggest how the complicated legal and psychological dynamics embedded within the Kaczynski matter could have been minimized if not altogether avoided.

(a) Kaczynski and Standby Counsel

Similar to Ferguson, the Kaczynski dispute represents another justification for standby counsel and for limiting the court's reliance on forensic diagnostic evidence. To be clear, standby counsel helps address the ongoing problems stemming from CST evaluations and expert opinions. More fundamentally, it neutralizes the weight assigned to questionable ultimate opinions and conclusions rendered by clinical forensic experts. Standby counsel can appropriately and strategically challenge ultimate legal opinions tendered by psychia-

---

1022. *See* M. Coyle, *Unabomber's Pen Pal: Ted Wants a New Trial*, NEWSDAY, Feb. 15, 1999 at A1–A2.

trists/psychologists on the CST matter, thereby preventing judges from making competency determinations based on the face validity of forensic evaluations.[1023]

The United States Supreme Court articulated the role and function of standby counsel for defendants who engage in self-representation in the case of *McKaskle v. Wiggins*.[1024] As we previously explained when reviewing this case, the Court addressed the conditions wherein in-court advisors could offer assistance over the *pro se* defendant's objection. The *McKaskle* Court concluded that "the *pro se* defendant is entitled to preserve actual control over the case he [or she] chooses to present to the jury.... [and standby counsel cannot] make or substantially interfere with any significant tactical decisions."[1025] Clearly, this decision is important when competency to stand trial determinations are at issue, particularly for defendants who elect to proceed *pro se* to trial and subsequently experience obvious mental health problems (e.g., Colin Ferguson and Theodore Kaczynski).

In the unabomber dispute, substantial weight was given to the psychological fitness evaluation when deciding on the matter of the defendant's competency. However, despite Dr. Johnson's trial fitness clinical finding, Judge Burrell denied Kaczynski's petition to proceed *pro se* to trial. Given the problems stemming from his guilty plea and verdict, standby counsel arguably would have produced an entirely different outcome. Indeed, "counsel may serve as a resource, consulting with the client outside of the courtroom or seated at the client's side, available for assistance."[1026]

We contend that had Judge Burrell granted the defendant his right to self-representation and permitted standby counsel to intervene consistent with the decision in *McKaskle*, the government would have been less suspicious of (and unnerved by) a mentally impaired, though competent, Theodore Kaczynski who wanted to

---

1023. One implication of *Faretta* is that the Court can exercise its discretion to appoint standby counsel. As the *Faretta* Court observed: "[A] State may appoint a "standby counsel" to aid the accused if and when the accused requests help, and to be available to represent the accused in the event that termination of the defendant's self-representation is necessary." *See Faretta*, 422 U.S. at 834 n. 46.

1024. *See* McKaskle v. Wiggins, 465 U.S. 168 (1984).

1025. *See Id.* at 178.

1026. *See* Decker *supra* note 178, at 525.

proceed *pro se* to trial.[1027] Again, under these circumstances, the administration of justice likely would have produced considerably different trial results. As Decker (1996) notes in relation to standby legal assistance:

> "[t]he *pro se* defendant must be allowed to control the organization and content of his own defense, to make motions, to argue points of law, to participate in *voir dire*, to question witnesses, and to address the court and the jury at appropriate points in the trial."[1028]

This is precisely what Kaczynski wanted. Had the presence of standby counsel been in effect for the unabomber, his personal defense strategy needs and the demands for justice would have been more meaningfully realized."[1029] Indeed, had the court considered the advantages of standby counsel, we submit that Kaczynski's recent efforts to appeal on the basis of a coerced plea and the denial of his right to waive counsel probably would never have been raised.

(b) Kaczynski: His Right to Select Counsel of Choice Following Revocation of the Right to Proceed Pro Se to Trial

During a criminal proceeding, a defendant who engages in self-representation can have this right revoked.[1030] Regrettably, as dis-

---

1027. *See* Arrigo & Bardwell *supra* note 18, at 35–36. (noting the government could have avoided the problems resulting from Kaczynski's dubious plea arrangement). For example, whether Kaczynski's constitutional right to conduct his own defense was violated when his *Faretta* request was rejected. If Kaczynski could have implemented the *McKaskle* right, his trial might have addressed issues relative to the appeal, answered the questions surrounding Kaczynski's somewhat curious anti-technological beliefs and, more importantly, shed some light on Kaczynski's questionable mental health.

1028. *See Id.* at 524.

1029. Some Courts have more recently argued that "standby counsel is more akin to that of an observer, an attorney who attends the trial or other proceeding and who may offer advice, but who does not speak for the defendant or bear responsibility for his defense." *See* United States v. Taylor, 502 F.2d (5th Cir.), *cert. denied*, 502 U.S. 883, 313 (1991). This notwithstanding, the essential point we assert is that the potential buffer such legal assistance creates may have been significant in the Kaczynski verdict, particularly given the role of the CST proceeding in the case's outcome.

1030. *See* United States v. Romano, 849 F.2d 812 (3d Cir. 1988).

cussed in Ferguson, this did not occur there and, in light of the case developments in Kaczynski, (i.e., the defendant was not provided the opportunity to conduct his own legal action), we will never know if this right would have been revoked for this defendant. However, since the standards for competence-related matters are low, the benefit of allowing an accused who suffers from a questionable (and a debilitating) mental health condition to proceed *pro se* to trial, knowing that this right can be revoked, presents us with yet another legal policy remedy worth exploring. Indeed, taken together in-court counsel and the revocation of one's *pro se* status can offer options consistent with case law, curtailing problems stemming from problematic CST clinical judgements and judicial determinations. In short, revocation and the appointment of standby counsel can (similar to our suggestion in Ferguson) refocus on the issue of competence, given the defendant's questionable behavior (e.g., paranoid delusions), or can advance a defense strategy consistent with the conduct demonstrated (i.e., NGRI defense). However, neither of these scenarios may be consistent with the defendant's interests in the case.

As we mentioned in the context of legal policy remedies germane to the Colin Ferguson matter, the *Romano* Court held that a criminal defendant does not "irrevocably waive all right to select counsel of choice once he or she has decided to proceed *pro se* [to trial].... The denial of the opportunity to select counsel of choice [following the loss of *pro se* status] violates the defendant's rights under the Six Amendment."[1031] Thus, the issue of counsel of choice, following the loss of self-representation, is significant in cases where there is some question about the defendant's competence to stand trial. Although Theodore Kaczynski was not presented with this particular situation, standby counsel, in and of itself, may not have been sufficient to advance the administration of justice for him.

For example, assuming for the moment that Judge Burrell allowed Kaczynski to *pro se* to trial the case, the question of the defendant's mental impairment likely would have plagued this dispute. Similar to the courtroom problems surrounding Ferguson's psychiatric condition (i.e., his deranged conspiratorial theories became increasingly evident as the trial unfolded), it is probable that

---

1031. *See Id.* at 818–819.

Kaczynski's paranoid delusions concerning technology would have dominated his proceedings as well. Moreover, consistent with the Long Island Railroad gunman, it is reasonable to assume that the unabomber would have used his *pro se* status as an "instrument of self destruction,"[1032] especially given his unconventional, if not bizarre, views on industry and technology. Under these conditions and similar to Ferguson before him, instead of the Kaczynski trial being about a bonafide defense strategy, his delusions would have dominated the trial, ultimately to his own demise. Thus, the court in Kaczynski's case more than likely would have instructed standby counsel to assume responsibility for the defense.

However, following *Romano*, the accused still retains the right to choose counsel. Thus, in the unabomber matter, the defendant would have retained some control over the defense strategy by delegating his legal strategy to someone such as Tony Serra, a lawyer who demonstrated interest in the case and in whom Kaczynski felt some trust. Moreover, given the relative influence the unabomer would have retained and exercised in the legal dispute, federal prosecutors would not have been so quick to secure a conviction through the plea bargaining process, fearing a defendant proceeding *pro se* to trial in which psychiatric illness would manifest itself during the trial giving rise to a subsequent CST hearing and incompetency determination. Instead, confronted with the defendant's appointment of counsel of choice following a *pro se* revocation decision, the government would have aggressively put forth its case, attempting to secure a guilty verdict on the merits and strength of their argument. In other words, both the defense (i.e., Kaczynski) and the government would have gotten what they wanted, more than likely obviating suspicion and doubt concerning the dispute's outcome.

(c) Kaczynski and Hybrid Representation

Although it is not Constitutionally guaranteed hybrid representation is Constitutionally permissible, given the decision in *McKaskle*.[1033] We maintain that this ruling is suggestive for cases wherein questions persist about the accused's competence to stand

---

1032. *See* Faretta v. California, 422 U.S. 806, 840 (1975).
1033. *See* McKaskle v. Wiggins, 465 U.S. 168, 183 (1984).

trial. Although Kaczynski vehemently wanted to present his case to the jurors personally, his obvious mental impairment would have contributed to his own courtroom demise. Given the flawed predictive capability of diagnostic instruments assessing fitness to stand trial, and given the potential problems stemming from standby counsel (i.e., how much assistance can an in-court attorney really offer a *pro se* defendant?), a more meaningful solution may be hybrid representation. Had Kaczynski been allowed to invoke this legal option, he and his "co-counsel" might have been able to develop a defense consistent with the accused's views and the verdict might have been more consistent with what Kaczynski anticipated. Indeed, many of the problems in the unabomber matter could have been resolved had Judge Burrell permitted Kaczynski's request for new counsel and, at the least, allowed him to implement some form of hybrid representation. Specifically, we note that prior to Kaczynski submitting a motion to conduct his own legal action, he sought the aid of new counsel and, in particular, requested the *pro bono* services of Tony Serra. As Serra, stated:

> "I have always served the objective of the client. A person has the right to defend himself in the manner he chooses, even if it means death, as long as he appreciates the risk. Kaczynski appreciated and understood all the ramifications and wanted a trial based on an ideological defense."[1034]

Had Judge Burrell granted Kaczynski's request for new counsel, perhaps he would not have been inclined to pursue the outlet of self-representation, especially since the defense strategy of Tony Serra arguably would have been more consistent with what Kaczynski wanted. At the very least, the potential problems in allowing the unabomber to proceed *pro se* to trial would have been averted, given that Mr. Serra ostensibly supported Kaczynski's right to put forth his ideological views as a defense.

In response to Judge Burrell's ruling that Kaczynski could not acquire new counsel, the unabomber eventually requested that he be granted the right to represent himself in his own criminal matter. Although he was found competent to stand trial, the unabomber was not permitted to proceed *pro se* to trial. The subsequent plea

---

1034. *See* Finnegan *supra* note 953, at 56.

and verdict have raised troubling questions about the constitutionality of affording a defendant a right to conduct his own legal action. As we have argued here, the outcome in the Kaczynski case illustrates the pitfalls associated with inadequate CST evaluations and the problems associated with vague and ambiguous Supreme Court opinions (i.e., *Faretta* and *Godinez*). Had Kaczynski been authorized to participate in his own defense through hybrid representation, the government's suspicion about a possible CST hearing (resulting in a finding that the accused was not mentally fit to stand trial) could have been minimized. A plea arrangement and verdict, leaving the defendant unsatisfied, could have been avoided. A true adversarial trial, without substantial reliance on less than accurate forensic psycho-diagnostic evidence, could have occurred.

D. Summarizing Kaczynski

While clearly provisional and certainly speculative, the preceding chapter was designed to suggestively but meaningfully link CST psycholegal dilemmas with yet another high-profile case. In sum, the Kaczynski matter lends support to our position that criminal competence-to-stand trial, as both a clinical and legal matter, is seriously and egregiously flawed. Our comparative analysis makes painfully obvious the generalizability of our justice policy remedies, suggesting their utility in a myriad of other (non-controversial) criminal competency cases.

We contend that the Theodore Kaczynski matter remarkably demonstrates just how much the legal and clinical communities need to re-think the relationship between CST dynamics and the administration of justice. Precisely because competency determinations affect the criminal and/or civil adjudication process, future research in the area must carefully reconsider whether psychological fitness to stand trial, as currently assessed, is an adequate and effective indicator of competency for lower court judges. In addition, future investigators need to reexamine how *pro se* findings, where psychiatric impairment is at issue, can, nonetheless, result in meaningful and legitimate courtroom outcomes for all parties involved. In the final analysis, to defer these weighty and contentious matters, is to postpone and, therefore, to compromise prospects for justice.

Chapter 9

Conclusion

OVERVIEW

This book comprehensively examined criminal competency to stand trial. Focusing specifically on trial fitness, competence to waive counsel, and competence to conduct one's own legal action, we systematically explored an array of legal, psychological, and policy issues relevant to a critical assessment of this problematic and contentious inquiry. As a matter of practical significance, we thoroughly reviewed the case of Colin Ferguson and briefly considered the supplemental dispute of Theodore Kaczynski, mindful of where and how the relevant psycholegal CST matters discussed throughout this volume produced controversial, troubling and, ultimately, flawed outcomes.

In the wake of our detailed investigation, this chapter revisits and summarizes the essential points raised in the preceding chapters. This task is useful as it enables us to rethink the major issues impacting current-day decision making on competency to stand trial. In addition, however, this exercise allows us to appreciate more seamlessly the troubling disjunctures and possible reforms situated at the crossroads of law, psychology, and policy, especially as they relate to matters of trial fitness. We conclude our analysis by broadly commenting on the future role of psychiatrists/psychologists in the courts. Generally speaking, this cursory assessment forces us to come to terms with the significance of our overall thesis.

A. Revisiting the Chapters: A Brief Summary

In the Introduction, we explored the broad dynamics and problems associated with competency to stand trial, commenting on the limits of the law and the flaws of psychology. Indeed, this material provided the necessary framework within which one could best appreciate the complex and enduring relationship that exists among trial fitness, clinical assessment difficulties, paranoid and delusional mental health disorders, and the judicial decision making process. As we argued, these matters represented a deep-seated and largely unresolved controversy in law, psychology, and policy.

In chapter 1 we reviewed the history of the incompetency to stand trial doctrine, its conceptual confusion as found in the precedent case law, and the practical courtroom problems the doctrine poses for lawyers and judges. This chapter paid particular attention to the justifications for and purposes of the incompetency doctrine. We also explained how the legal issue of incompetency is often conflated (erroneously) with the legal issue of insanity.

To comprehend the practical problems affiliated with CST outcomes, in Chapter 2 we examined the development of the competency construct as founded on important legal doctrines and principles. In particular, this chapter explored the landmark United States Supreme Court decision on competency to stand trial (*Dusky v. United States*, 1960), and further examined the controlling Supreme Court decisions involving the right to waive counsel (*Faretta v. California*, 1975) and the mental competence required to waive this right (*Godinez v. Moran*, 1993). Moreover, this chapter reviewed the implications of these decisions, especially in relation to the competency construct and the problems they subsequently pose.

In chapter 3 we comprehensively reviewed the evolution of various instruments used to assess a defendant's competence to stand trial. The strengths and weaknesses of each instrument were enumerated. Specific and detailed attention was given to the most recent evaluation protocol; namely, the MacArthur Competence Assessment Tool-Criminal Adjudication (MacCAT-CA). The advantages and shortcomings of this instrument were also discussed. We acknowledged that leading accounts in the clinical forensic and assessment literature previously explored a number of points addressed in this chapter. However, we also asserted that while evaluation instruments appear sound in theory they are woefully deficient in practice. We argued that mental health experts who evaluate trial competence typically employ (highly) individualized assessments, frequently presenting the courts with competing results and, at times, less than objective ultimate issue opinions.

In chapter 4 we thoroughly reviewed paranoid and delusional mental health disorders. In particular, we examined the troubling intersection between the selected disorders (i.e., paranoid schizophrenia, delusional disorder, and paranoid personality disorder), competing clinical and legal goals in forensic settings, and other general problems in assessing trial competence when defendants evince paranoid and delusional symptomatology. As we indicated, a cataloguing of the general features and diagnostic criteria pertaining to these disorders demonstrated the subtle workings of symptoms associated with them and their respective impact on CST issues. In addition, this chapter identified the various limitations with the CST process; including, problems with legal standards in determining competence-related abilities and problems in current trial fitness assessment trends.

In chapter 5 we systematically investigated the pretrial competency hearing of Mr. Colin Ferguson, the Long Island Railroad gunman. Preliminarily, we explained the need for the case study analysis and presented background material on the defendant. We also commented on why relying on high profile cases is a useful endeavor when analyzing criminal justice-mental health policies. The substance of this chapter explored the events that led up to Ferguson's trial, including the crime, the CST pre-trial motion, and Ferguson's ancillary legal requests (i.e., to strike the insanity defense and to conduct his own legal action). We also described, based on the actual psychological report following Ferguson's arrest, the psychological background of the defendant.

Chapter 5 also provided considerable detail on the matter of Ferguson's pretrial competency hearing. Indeed, the substance of this chapter re-presented selected, though relevant, passages contained in the actual pretrial hearing transcripts. Indeed, by focusing specifically on the testimony provided by the expert for the defense and the experts for the prosecution, we canvassed the unabridged testimonial evidence concerning their clinical findings as articulated through both direct and cross examination. We concluded this chapter by presenting the closing arguments by both counsel for the defense and for the prosecution, and by documenting the Judge's ruling on the issue of Ferguson's competency and the defendant's ancillary requests regarding his defense strategy.

In chapter 6 we revisited the actual trial transcripts of the Ferguson case and the psychiatric report pertaining to it. We showed where and how the CST legal doctrine and the psychological fitness evaluation process produced a flawed competency to stand trial determination. To accomplish these objectives, we divided the chapter into two sections: a psychological analysis and a legal analysis. With respect to the former commentary, we reviewed the (highly) individualized CST examinations and documented the various clinical assessment problems that emerged, given psychiatry's role in the Ferguson case. With respect to the latter commentary, we discussed Judge Belfi's judicial opinion and rationale, and presented a number of examples from the trial documenting Ferguson's courtroom dilemmas when pursuing the path of self-representation. Overall, this chapter explained why Ferguson was able to conduct his own defense and described how this determination was an outgrowth of the questionable psycholegal decision that found him competent to stand trial.

In chapter 7 we examined several noteworthy ways by which to reform the psychological assessment process of trial fitness, and recommended a novel approach by which judges could (perhaps should) value and interpret the "expert" opinion of clinical forensic examiners. On this latter point, we emphasized how evaluators could (perhaps should) assume an information-oriented rather than an expert opinion-oriented perspective in CST matters. Further, this chapter identified a series of legal and constitutional policy remedies that provide guidance to judges and lawyers, respect the liberty rights of the accused (e.g., defendant's who waive counsel and pursue the path of self-representation), and help ensure fairness in the overall criminal trial process. To contextualize these reform strategies, we revisited the case of Colin Ferguson and demonstrated their ongoing and practical psycholegal utility.

In chapter 8 we supplemented our analysis of Colin Ferguson by reviewing the relevant criminal competency issues in the psycholegal case of Theodore Kaczynski (a.k.a. the unabomber). This chapter showed how problems identified in and solutions pertaining to Ferguson could be generalized to other (controversial) CST cases.

Similar to the Long Island Railroad gunman, Kaczynski not only exposed the shortcomings in routine CST assessment procedures (e.g., adhering to controlling legal standards and following current trends in CST assessment), but represented a competence-to-stand-trial case that exceeded expectation. In other words, as we argued, if psycholegal problems occur in well-publicized and controversial cases (e.g., Ferguson and Kaczynski), then the same problems would also be found, in some meaningful form, in less notorious cases. In addition, chapter 8 applied the proposed psychological and criminal justice policy remedies entertained in the Ferguson matter to the case of the unabomber. This strategy was significant as it helped substantiate our contention that the reforms were indeed generalizable beyond high-stakes disputes.

B. Sum and Substance: Blending of Chapters

The essential argument entertained in this book is that the competency to stand trial legal construct (*Dusky*), its progeny (*Godinez*), and the diagnostic instruments utilized to assess trial fitness abilities (e.g., MacCAT-CA), have failed, in large part, to assist lower court judges in rendering appropriate CST determinations. Moreover, the thesis we explored indicates that the psycholegal dynamics of CST proceedings are complicated further when defendants experience paranoid and delusional mental health symptomatology, and mental health professionals continue to conduct (highly) individualized evaluations. These legal limits and psychological flaws are transparent and appreciable, particularly when analyzing media-driven and politically-charged cases. Indeed, the Ferguson and Kaczynski matters profoundly reflect these troubling circumstances. Not only have some defendants wrongfully been found competent, resulting in psychologically-impaired and ineffective self-representation (i.e., Ferguson), other defendants have not proceeded to trial for fear that the competency to stand trial ruling would eventually undermine the government's otherwise evidence-filled case (i.e., Kaczynski).

As a delusional and paranoid defendant, Ferguson was found competent and proceeded *pro se* to trial. His subsequent court case produced a circus-like event where the defendant showcased his debilitating psychiatric disorder, causing additional trauma to the victims and their families, thereby undermining the administration of justice. As a delusional and paranoid defendant, Kaczynski was found competent to stand trial but, in a seemingly inexplicable decision, was denied his right to self-representation. His subsequent plea arrangement with the government cast a cloud of doubt and suspicion over the entire courtroom process, causing many members of the legal community to question seriously whether the unabomber ever really had his proverbial day in court.

Both cases underscore the problems stemming from troubling CST standards and the competency evaluation process in general. Taken together, these disputes not only demonstrate the limitations with the legal standards used to define competence-related abilities (*Dusky*, and *Godinez*) but show how CST evaluations are (highly) individualized and devoid of any type of structure. As a result, individualized clinical evaluation procedures pose sufficient validity and reliability problems and fail to assess a defendant's ability to make important trial decisions. When defendants are intelligent and articulate but, nonetheless, suffer from paranoid or delusional mental health concerns, current trends in measuring competence-related abilities offer little to no guidance with respect to the proper and appropriate clinical assessment of trial fitness. As such, the CST determinations rendered by judges are minimally instructive.

To remedy these matters, we proposed a series of criminal justice policy reforms, meaningfully and pragmatically demonstrating where and how clinical forensic evaluations and the legal standards for competency could be modified. As we explained, clearly the court's reliance on diagnostic judgements concerning trial fitness has not been productive. Indeed, trial judges must come to regard forensic psychological assessments as informational in nature rather than dispositive for the CST judicial finding.

In order to implement successfully this policy recommendation, several corresponding legal reforms were proposed. The right to standby counsel, the right to counsel of choice following *pro se* revocation, and the right to hybrid representation were three identified policy changes that could conceivably and considerably recast the manner in which the CST process occurred in cases where defendants experienced acute and chronic mental health disabilities. As we speculatively and provisionally documented, both the Ferguson and Kaczynski disputes substantiate the potential advantages these legal reforms offer for the effective administration of justice.

More fundamentally, however, we maintained that a direct resolution to the legal and assessment problems posed by the current competency to stand trial doctrine required that the Supreme Court recognize the narrow basis on which the *Godinez* case was decided. Accordingly, we respectfully asserted that the Court should overturn its decision. This recommendation is no small undertaking and will not occur without considerable force of will, political or otherwise. As such, we recommended that a collaborative effort involving both mental health and legal experts was necessary to establish and implement separate competency inquiries. Indeed, states should develop and adopt distinct legal guidelines and clinical tests on such matters as fitness to stand trial and competence to waive counsel and conduct one's own defense. The two ought not be collapsed and conflated.

Adopting separate and heightened competency formulations (i.e., on the matter of relinquishing counsel and on the matter of representing oneself) is not contrary to existing case law. As Justice Thomas observed in *Godinez*, "states are free to adopt competency standards that are more elaborate than the *Dusky* formulation...." Currently, however, most states use the *Dusky* standard without providing any more direction or guidance in particular instances. We argue that rather than investing precious time and energy in the development of assessment protocol consistent with *Dusky*, these efforts would be better served if re-directed toward establishing competency tests applicable within a given context. As we explained, for example, it does not follow that an adjudicated competent defendant on the matter of fitness to stand trial is, without question, similarly competent to proceed *pro se* to trial.

In one instrumental case from which our present-day incompetency doctrine was inspired, the court held "that no man shall be called upon to make his defence at a time when his mind is in that situation as not to appear capable of so doing; for, however guilty he may be, the inquiring into his guilt must be postponed...."[1035] Although more than two hundred years old, this case foresaw the very contentious problem our system of justice struggles with today

---

1035. *See* Frith's Case, 22 How. State Trials 307, 318 (1790).

in criminal trials around the country. Indeed, as we demonstrated, the *Dusky* decision makes constitutional the prosecution of mentally disordered citizens, and the *Faretta* and *Godinez* holdings provide a process by which such defendants can realize, unwittingly, their own courtroom demise. These circumstances are as problematic as they are misguided. In the final analysis, this state of affairs must be remedied. Accordingly, this book provided a legal, psychological, and policy basis by which to affect such profound, meaningful, and necessary change.

C. A Monumental Problem: Monetary Issues and Expert Services in the Courts

In wading through the thorny and murky psycholegal terrain of criminal competence to stand trial, other more insidious problems surfaced. Perhaps the product of individualized assessment practices or perhaps the consequence of actualized (mis)fortune, important questions concerning clinical objectivity and the role of mental health professionals in the courts have considerably informed this study. Although our central thesis entailed trial competence and ways to improve the ongoing abuses of it through forensic assessment and legal reforms, we would be derelict in our research duties if we did not at least comment on other, more inconspicuous, issues related to it.

Elsewhere, we argued that expert services are routinely used based on requests by the prosecution, defense, and the court, wherein fitness to stand trial findings function as a short-cut to achieve desired trial outcomes. For example, legal parties contractually employ forensic evaluators and diagnosticians to craft clinical opinions, and to corroborate or invalidate mental health views consistent with the litigator's theory of the case. As previously discussed, molding clinical findings to fit a perspective on a given legal dispute can be achieved in a variety of ways (e.g., maximizing or minimizing diagnostic conditions, couching findings in their most favorable light, and assigning pejorative affect to psychiatric labels).

The proverbial "battle of the experts" consumed much of the pretrial competency proceedings in the Colin Ferguson dispute; however, they offered limited utility on the matter of the defendant's trial fitness. Similarly, in the Kaczynski legal action, we saw clinical findings that were minimally instructive as the psychiatrist (Dr. Johnson) offered inconsistent statements that, nonetheless, resulted in a judicial determination of competence to stand trial. Regrettably, these circumstances only magnify a pervasive and insidious problem: forensic examiners, testifying in a court of law, often are no more than "hired hands" doing the bidding of the lawyers who employ them. Indeed, in far too many instances, clinical opinions are manufactured supporting the perspective of the litigator whom the expert serves. Although well beyond the scope of our investigation, this is a complex and enduring issue that goes to the core of psychological ethics and courtroom practices.[1036]

From our own observations and experiences, problems in competency are generally a product of self promotion and money. Admittedly, there are an array of circumstances in which expert clinical opinions are sought to address psycholegal matters beyond criminal competence. Moreover, other specialists are called on to testify in these cases (e.g., forensic pathologists, epidemiologists, law enforcement personnel), or to testify in non-psycholegal, though criminal, disputes. This notwithstanding, we draw attention to the troubling state of affairs in which forensic examiners testify on the matter of trial fitness, rendering inadequate clinical evaluations and flawed diagnostic opinions. We know what the problems are; however, the question is whether we are prepared to meaningfully and purposefully solve them. Along these lines, we contend that the pernicious and disquieting issues of self promotion and monetary gain, as we have tentatively described them here, are contributory factors impeding prospects for the proper administration of justice on the matter of criminal competence to stand trial.

In a fair, humane, and just society, much is demanded of those who present "data," indeed describe evidence, in a court of law. This logic obtains regardless of one's expertise. We submit that this same standard should apply in the case of mental health experts who assess trial fitness, tender diagnostic findings, and offer ulti-

---

1036. Recently, researchers critical of established psycholegal practices have called for considerable reform with respect to rethinking and reframing psychology's role in leal disputes, including the provision of expert testimony. *See, e.g.,* B. Arrigo, *The Critical Perspective in Psychological Jurisprudence: Theoretical Advances and Epistemological Assumptions.* 25 INT'L J. L. & PSYCHIATRY, 1-23 (2002).

mate clinical opinions on the legal issue of competence. Anything less compromises the entire adjudicatory process, abrogates the defendant's rights, and relegates the discipline of psychology to nothing more than pseudo-science. Thus, financial rewards ought not be *the* engine that drives the clinical practice of testifying in a court of law. Indeed, as mental health professionals serve the court, they must do so mindful of their responsibility to utilize the appropriate assessment tools that best evaluate the specific legal question under consideration. And where the law is less than clear on the standards by which to engage in such undertakings, then psychologists should enter the public policy forum and advocate vigorously for much needed change.

When faced with the prospect of deciding or significantly contributing to the fate of another person, it is impossible to do so without occasionally stumbling along the way. This is part of being human. However, in the context of criminal competence to stand, we know what must be done, we know what reforms are needed, and we know that change must occur now. The only question that remains is whether we are prepared to move to action, ensuring that justice is served. From our perspective, given all that is at stake, the legal, psychological, and policy communities can ill-afford to forestall or dismiss such decision making on the matter of criminal competence to stand trial. Indeed, to delay or disregard this call to action is to perpetuate the inadequacies of the present system, deferring or denying prospects for justice in the wake of our unfortunate and unnecessary stillness.

Index